We're Here Because You Were There

Immigration and the End of Empire

Ian Sanjay Patel

VERSO

London • New York

This paperback edition first published by Verso 2022
First published by Verso 2021
© Ian Sanjay Patel 2021, 2022

1 3 5 7 9 10 8 6 4 2

Verso
UK: 6 Meard Street, London W1F 0EG
US: 388 Atlantic Avenue, Brooklyn, NY 11217
versobooks.com

Verso is the imprint of New Left Books

ISBN-13: 978-1-83976-799-9
ISBN-13: 978-1-78873-768-5 (UK EBK)
ISBN-13: 978-1-83976-053-2 (US EBK)

British Library Cataloguing in Publication Data
A catalogue record for this book is available from the British Library.

Library of Congress Cataloging-in-Publication Data
A catalog record for this book is available from the Library of Congress
Library of Congress Control Number: 2020948731

Typeset in Minion Pro by MJ&N Gavan, Truro, Cornwall
Printed and bound by CPI Group (UK) Ltd, Croydon CR0 4YY

For Shantaben Patel (1923–2015)

Contents

At the time we were 'Black and Asian', we ticked the Black and Asian box on the medical forms, joined the Black and Asian family support groups and stuck to the Black and Asian section of the library: it was considered a question of solidarity.

Zadie Smith, *Swing Time*

Those natives were never meant to come here and live next door.

'Race relations' professional, London, 1972

Beneath every history, another history.

Hilary Mantel, *Wolf Hall*

Introduction

We are here because you were there. These were the pithy words of the writer Ambalavaner Sivanandan, born in the British colony of Ceylon (later renamed Sri Lanka), who migrated to Britain in 1953. His words addressed a British state that had denied an incontrovertible history about why so-called 'immigrants' were now in post-war Britain in greater numbers than ever before. *Here* meant Britain; *there* meant former British colonies. If poorly understood, there was a direct relationship, Sivanandan suggested, between the British empire and post-war migrations to Britain. Domestic British history had been separated from British imperial history, and from this false separation, confusion about and rejection of post-war immigrants had been allowed to spread.

If immigration did not exist, it would have to have been invented. No term better than 'immigrant' helped convert those post-war migrants into the insinuating ghosts of a colonial world supposedly separate from domestic British life. To this day Britain remains deeply equivocal, both socially and politically, about exactly what happened with respect to immigration, why it happened, and whether its happening was a welcome thing. This book animates the four corners of Sivanandan's aphorism, unearthing the *you*, the *we*, the *here* and the *there*, to reveal their overlapping, plural combinations of place, experience and encounter.

Overused, manipulated and exhausted, immigration somehow remains one of the most compelling words in the vocabulary of social and political life. We all know that immigration is complicated, controversial and important – and privately we each hold views on the subject that are more than likely firmly made up. Whether described in social, economic or ethical terms, immigration seems never to fail to command high emotion – to meet an apparent need for symbols and scapegoats, often signalling either progress or decline, depending on the observer.

Few words better stir a sense of national identity and destiny than immigration. The immigrant, by definition, does not belong to the nation-state in which she resides. The imagined idea of a nation-state – a people belonging to an ancestral territory under a state that protects both – finds its negative image in immigration. The claim that some do not belong only brings the belonging of those included in the nation-state into greater relief. One of the primary international prerogatives of the state is the ability and discretion to define who is a citizen (a national) and who is not. Yet British national identity has been less influenced by the nation-state than by the claims of its political traditions and the perceived uniqueness of its political institutions – above all the 'rule of law' that helped give purpose to the empire. The British national experience of immigration after 1945 was therefore caught between an indistinct nation-state and a conspicuous imperial past and present.

Immigration is also a byword for race, and for ideas about who is and who is not native to the nation – or, in Britain's case after 1945, native to the imperial heartland. In many ways, the primary domestic encounter of British political elites with questions of race occurred in the 1960s, when transformative immigration legislation was devised for the first time. Despite the presence of non-white people in Britain in smaller numbers for hundreds of years, post-war British politicians and officials saw the problem of 'coloured immigration' to be a new, unique, at times even eschatological threat.

The origins of the non-white people who migrated to Britain during the post-war period ranged from the Caribbean to Africa, South Asia and the Pacific. It is generally understood – perhaps more by intuition than concrete knowledge – that they held a form of British citizenship, or at least had the right to enter, live and work in Britain, despite the persistent referencing of them as immigrants. The so-called Windrush scandal that erupted into the media in 2018 centred on reports of people who had migrated as children from the Caribbean in the post-war period, and who were now facing deportation or had been deported. It was bewildering: surely they already had British citizenship? How could their claim to citizenship have been finessed away by legislation? It turned out to be fiendishly complicated – something to do with old nationality legislation in 1948, the ugly acronym CUKC (a 'citizen of the United Kingdom and Colonies'), and the key date of 1 January 1973, when the 1971 Immigration Act came into force. Confused? Perhaps that was the point.

In Britain, immigration has been conceived as a domestic problem, cloying and claustrophobic. To reckon with post-war immigration in Britain, one steps into a tightening circle, its air stifling, until one is – ultimately – in the same room as Conservative politician Enoch Powell, hearing his 'rivers of blood' speech on the first floor of a hotel in Birmingham in 1968. This book is about getting more historical oxygen to our understanding of post-war immigration in Britain. Following Sivanandan's words, this means more than anything else extending our horizons beyond domestic British history. From its origins in Britain's white-settler colonies to its post-war incarnations, immigration has been as much an international as a domestic problem for British political elites.

Only by retelling the story of immigration, not as a domestic national story confined to the British Isles but as a diverse international story connected to empire, can we begin to see it clearly. Going in search of post-war immigration leads us outwards into the colonial worlds Britain inhabited both before and after 1945. The international dimensions of post-war immigration tell us much about British political elites' own sense of Britain's fate in the world in the decades following the Second World War. Britain's politicians, senior civil servants and diplomats overseas – part of a generation that more than any other lived through a vast dilution of British imperial power – saw the big picture of immigration, however attenuated and decontextualised a version of it they presented to the domestic British public. Immigration was as much a concern to officials in diplomatic service and in the Foreign Office and Commonwealth Office (these merged in 1968) as it was to officials in the Home Office.

What happened to the British empire after 1945? And how was the fate of the empire connected to post-war migrations of peoples from its current or former territories? One common way of answering this question is as follows. Between 1945 and 1973, Britain began a painful transition from world imperial power to post-imperial power. Simultaneously, in these years it entered a period of domestic transition within its shores, moving from a relatively mono-ethnic and monocultural society towards a multicultural and multi-ethnic one. These were twin transitions, interacting in significant ways. In 1945 Britain still clung to colonial rule in India; by 1973 Britain's many colonial holdings were all but fully divested, and it was newly integrated into Europe, having in that year become a fully fledged member of the European Communities (the precursor of the European Union). In 1945 Britain's non-white population stood at 30,000. By 1973 this figure was over 1 million, and grew close to 5 million by 2001.[1] These post-war transitions are ongoing – not surprising, given their scale and stakes.

There is truth to this quick summary, although it makes the trajectory of Britain's post-war history of empire and migration appear inevitable and planned. In order to tell this story with more accuracy and understanding, some of our core intuitions about post-war immigration need to change. The first of these is that British imperialism ended with a clean break, decolonisation having been completed within twenty years of 1945. The second is that imperial citizenship ended within the same period. Both of these reasonable intuitions are misleading. The British empire never underwent an 'end of empire' moment. Rather, the empire was converted into the Commonwealth around the end of the Second World War, and entered a transitional period whose final end was consistently deferred. The Commonwealth was presented as the latest and most constitutionally advanced stage of the British empire. As the post-war world developed, however, British political elites enjoyed increasingly less control over it.

The post-war British empire – whose constitutional edifice was known as the Commonwealth – was a free association of independent states such as Australia, Canada and newly independent India, in addition to the territories that remained British crown colonies under direct imperial rule. An important part of Britain's effort to ensure the Commonwealth remained an imperial project was the British Nationality Act of 1948. This was a legal structure that aimed to ensure that the citizenships of Commonwealth states would be forever linked in the imperial heartland of Britain. Despite the fact that Australia, Canada and India, among others, were now sovereign entities, the Act was designed to ensure imperial continuity in the post-war world.

The Act created a single form of citizenship for 'the United Kingdom and Colonies'. This was an imperial version of what is currently called 'British citizenship', and should not be confused with the current legal term. At the same time, the citizenship created in 1948 was the primary and topmost form of British nationality, and was often referred to simply as 'British citizenship' by British politicians. After 1948, a non-white person born in colonial Kenya or Jamaica had enjoyed identical citizenship, on equal terms, to Winston Churchill.

The 1948 Act also constitutionally linked this imperial British citizenship to the citizenships of independent Commonwealth countries. Rights of entry and residence in Britain continued to follow an imperial scheme after 1948, and were extended to all British citizens and Commonwealth citizens. The old imperial idea of a 'British subject' was now given new life as that of the 'Commonwealth citizen', an underlying constitutional status of British nationality incorporating both British citizens and citizens of independent Commonwealth countries. As the Act declared, 'the expression "British subject" and the expression "Commonwealth citizen" shall have the same meaning'.[2]

Why would British politicians pursue such a form of British nationality in the post-war period, preserving British subjecthood, yet recognising independent Commonwealth states within a single constitutional structure? The imposition of unity, regularity and continuity over British nationality throughout the Commonwealth was a conscious attempt to keep Britain's post-war imperial ambitions intact. Yet this same effort also had the effect of granting British citizenship, and confirming the right of entry into Britain, to millions of non-white people in the post-war world. In other words, the constitutional unification of Britain with the empire and Commonwealth, and the post-war migrations to Britain that followed it, were intended and unintended consequences of a single post-war imperial project.

The 1948 Act enshrined rights of entry and residence in Britain to millions of non-white people throughout what we might call the 'Commonwealth empire'. Yet Britain's politicians in 1948 never expected large numbers of non-white British and Commonwealth citizens to exercise their right to migrate from one part of the Commonwealth empire to another. For them, the 1948 Act was chiefly an imperial device designed to maintain imperial unity throughout different territories. The need for imperial unity before 1948 had long exercised British political elites, who wanted to link the self-governing 'colonies of white settlement' (today's Australia, New Zealand and Canada) and colonies under direct imperial rule (such as India) within a single hierarchical imperial constitution.

Although it used the language of citizenship rather than subjecthood, the 1948 Act simply confirmed and re-codified the longstanding rights of British subjects. As A. V. Dicey, the venerable English constitutional scholar, proclaimed in 1885: 'every British subject, whatever be the place of his birth, or the race he belongs to … has, with the rarest possible exceptions, the same right to settle and trade in England which is possessed by a natural born Englishman.'[3] This fabled, ancient common-law right was sustained by the 1948 Act, but was now integrated within British 'citizenship' – a term deemed more appropriate for the post-war world than the existing idea of subjecthood.

When, in the 1950s, non-white British and Commonwealth citizens began to migrate to Britain in larger numbers, many British officials were shocked. Implicit in their shock was the idea that non-white peoples of the Commonwealth empire should passively enjoy their consular status overseas, but should not migrate to Britain in large numbers, nor actively attempt to participate in the British polity as citizens in large numbers – notwithstanding their legal right to do so. British politics, in other words, was not as inclusive as British nationality law.

The great, unspoken irony of post-war British immigration in the decades after 1945 was that the major incoming constituencies – from the Caribbean and South Asia, for example – were either British citizens or non-alien Commonwealth citizens with rights of entry and residence. The 1948 Act turned out to be an explosive piece of legislation. The numbers of non-white people around the world who had a right to migrate to Britain in the 1950s far outstripped the numbers of white British people already resident in Britain.

The story of post-war immigration is in fact a story largely about British citizens' attempt to enter Britain. A citizen who is also an immigrant at the moment of entry can be seen as a contradiction in terms. The immigrant, for better or for worse, is in a position of supplication before the state she wishes to enter; a citizen is not. A citizen or non-alien with a right of entry wishing to enter the state to which she belongs is free to do so. This might be a very crude description of the core of citizenship rights, but it captures something important. Yet, at some stage in post-war British history, non-white British citizens were reconceived and reclassified as immigrants – first politically, then in law.

The next stage of the story is even more counterintuitive. In the early 1960s, as decolonisation accelerated, the British government decided not to dismantle the imperial citizenship scheme of the 1948 British Nationality Act. Instead, it decided to split the classifications of British and Commonwealth citizenship into two tiers: one that conferred the right to enter Britain, and another that did not. In other words, Britain retained its structures of imperial citizenship, allowing it to keep its Commonwealth empire unified, and the right of return to white Britons overseas intact. Yet it also found ways to keep non-white British citizens and non-white Commonwealth citizens from entering Britain. This legal finessing began in 1962, initiating a stream of legislation that de-linked particular calibrations of British citizenship from the right to enter Britain, and ended Commonwealth citizens' automatic right of entry.

After the 1962 Commonwealth Immigrants Act, the right of entry into Britain referred in the first instance to 'a person born in the United Kingdom'.[4] Immigration legislation in 1962, 1968 and 1971 introduced various technical legal distinctions in order to uphold political definitions of 'connection' and 'belonging' to Britain. This upheld the existing constitutional structure of the Commonwealth empire, and at the same time prevented non-white British citizens and Commonwealth citizens from entering the country automatically without control. A maddening paradox was introduced: a person could be a British citizen even without dual citizenship of a Commonwealth state, yet somehow have no 'connection' or 'belonging' to Britain, and therefore no automatic right of entry. As the *Economist* put it in a 1968 article, 'The Cost of Whiteness', Britain had 'restricted the entry of many holders of British passports, simply and solely because they are brown'.[5]

After 1968, British citizens who 'belonged' to Britain in the eyes of British politicians and officials were those who enjoyed a legal right of entry primarily by way of a territorial connection to Britain, by birth or in virtue of their ancestry. British citizenship had been transformed. Gone was an inclusivity based on imperial largesse, and replacing it was an implicit racial exclusivity that dictated who belonged in Britain and who did not. Technically, the immigration laws of 1968 and 1971 employed a logic of distinction based on territory, not race. In practice, these technicalities served racist motivations, and constituted an indirect form of racial discrimination. The 1968 and 1971 immigration legislation appeared to recall Dicey's proposal in 1897 of a 'common citizenship for the English race'.[6]

Nevertheless, despite the effects of these immigration laws, the constitutional unification of an imperial Britain – combining the (now all but dissolved) empire with Commonwealth states – was retained throughout the 1970s. Britain wanted to have it both ways. It wanted a grand Commonwealth edifice, including imperial categories of citizenship and immigration laws that allowed white Britons overseas to return home should they wish, on the one hand, and restrictive immigration controls blocking non-white British citizens from entry to Britain on the other. It was this backhandedness that led to the paradox of British citizens who could not automatically enter Britain, and of newspaper descriptions of immigrants with British passports. To dismantle the 1948 British Nationality Act would have been to undermine the constitutional integrity of the imperial Commonwealth – a step too far for both Labour and Conservative governments.

Finally, in 1981, a new British Nationality Act was passed that for the very first time defined British citizenship by reference to the territories of the British Isles, rather than to the empire. After 1981, 'British citizenship' referred in the first instance to 'A person born in the United Kingdom' whose parent too was a British citizen.[7] Other types of British citizenship were now fundamentally distinct (signified by the words 'overseas' and 'dependant') from this primary 'British citizenship'. At this moment, British imperial citizenship was thus all but ended. British nationality law was finally in alignment with British immigration policies.

The handwringing over post-war immigration on the part of British political elites had been an effect of circumstances entirely of their own making. Non-white immigration was a consequence of the inclusivity of the 1948 Act, which Britain refused to dismantle until 1981, instead passing exclusivist immigration policies that rendered the Act's original inclusivity meaningless. Rather than blaming themselves, British officials and politicians were in the habit of blaming non-white 'immigrants'. It was the immigrants, after all, who did not 'belong' in Britain. The Commonwealth empire was a carefully theorised unity between white and non-white spaces under a progressive British idealism that believed itself uniquely gifted in world governance, including the governance of race. By attempting to exercise their British citizenship or Commonwealth citizenship by migrating to Britain in large numbers in the 1950s, immigrants were upsetting the balance of imperial geography and demographics. By the 1960s, non-white immigrants were the physical embodiment of a Commonwealth empire that Britain could no longer pretend to control.

Mirroring the anticolonialism of the United Nations, the Commonwealth was increasingly dominated by postcolonial states as decolonisation accelerated. They used the Commonwealth association not to celebrate Britain's imperial commitment to it, but to amplify their criticisms of colonialism, racism and international inequality, in an attempt to define the norms of a postcolonial world. British politicians and officials vied to be the makers of the post-war world, but appeared to be losing out to their counterparts in former colonies, who contributed to powerful new ideas of racial equality and international equality. British decline at the level of ideas began to merge with other forms of real and imagined British decline, both domestic and international.

At their most atavistic, some British officials and elites rehearsed old imperial fears that Britain's supposedly liberal approach to empire was complicit in global white decline. The global fate of the white racial 'stock' made their pitched battle against the influence of non-white immigrants domestically all the more urgent. Yet at the same time, in other ways, British officials believed that the Commonwealth empire was the only entity that could progressively solve the problem of race in the world. It is hard to overestimate the initial purchase of British idealism in the post-war world – the way in which it saw its brand of imperialism as a liberal and progressive force, by contrast to the unreconstructed racism of, say, apartheid South Africa.

The Commonwealth's great promise as a vehicle of post-war British imperial power ultimately became a damp squib. The late 1950s, 1960s and early 1970s were full of repudiations by British intellectuals of the Commonwealth's failure as a vehicle for British interests, particularly at the level of political economy. If British intellectuals had a love–hate relationship with the Commonwealth, their sentiments ran the full gamut. During the first post-war decades, British political elites could not give it up, since it was the only foundation for a British 'world role', as it was phrased in the language of the time. Keeping up a prized imperial vision of the Commonwealth included dealing with its negative side effects. These included international headaches such as dealing with key Commonwealth partners (frenemies *avant la lettre*) such as India. At the domestic level, this meant negotiating the imperial citizenship scheme associated with the Commonwealth – or, in other words, dealing with non-white British and Commonwealth citizens who wished to migrate to Britain.

Yet, throughout the 1960s, Britain proved unable fully to relinquish its vision of the Commonwealth as a highly evolved form of empire appropriate to the perceived British genius for governance. Britain was in decline; as an embattled island, it could not accommodate immigrants – yet, at the same time, it was at the helm of a great Commonwealth, and commanded a significant world role. At some point in the 1960s, the two themes began to blend together, before finally combusting.

Were immigrants a symbol of national decline or of imperial largesse, or of a Commonwealth that was itself a symbol of a declining empire? Immigration was presented as an outside force coming in. In truth, it was closer to a foil to Britain's contradictory self-images of prowess and decline, imperial inclusivity and domestic fragility, Commonwealth empire and embattled island-state. Immigration was really about Britain's relationship to change, to the outside world, and to itself.

In the post-war period, perceived crises related to immigration and perceived crises related to the end of empire were highly correlated (although not tied by direct causation). Immigration began to gain prominence in British political life as the 1950s wore on, as did the fate of the empire. There was a symbolic correlation between Ghana's independence in 1957 and the so-called race riots in Notting Hill in 1958. Prime minister Harold Macmillan's 'wind of change' moment, traditionally indicating decolonisation in British colonies in Africa, coincided with preparations for the 1962 Commonwealth Immigrants Act. The announcement of military retrenchment 'east of Suez' in 1968, traditionally seen as the final end of the British empire, coincided with the 1968 Commonwealth Immigrants Act and the 'Kenyan Asian Crisis', when South Asians from Kenya attempted to migrate to Britain. Britain's passing of the 1972 European Communities Act, formalising British entry into Europe, coincided with the 1971 Immigration Act and the 'Ugandan Asian Crisis' that followed the expulsion of South Asians from Uganda in 1972.

The loss of power internationally was coupled with an inflamed defensive racial hostility at home. The fragility of Britain's international claims to power was accompanied by a sense of domestic fragility. Britain was now less of an invading presence in the world, exerting its will on others; now it was itself the invaded space, prone to defensive reactions as a supposedly alien presence (the 'coloured immigrant') settled itself within Britain. Yet, at the same time, decline was simply the herald of imperial reinvention and renewal, as British officials adjusted to external changes, redefining the international in imperial terms.

Post-war British governments wanted to have their cake and eat it too. They wanted to be an empire at the level of the Commonwealth and citizenship, and yet also to frame Britain as a nation-state so far as immigration was concerned. On the one hand, post-war imperial citizenship was based in a British idealism that saw British history as a constant progression: the empire had evolved into an imperial Commonwealth, and imperial subjecthood had evolved into imperial citizenship. Yet, on the other hand, this idealism was interrupted by nativism. Imperial citizenship needed to be tempered by immigration laws that ultimately ensured automatic right of entry only to those whose ancestry was connected to the territories of the British Isles.

This was a political process that used law as its method. By effectively creating a problem – 'coloured immigration' – both Labour and Conservative governments were able to distract attention from their own imperial pretensions embodied in the Commonwealth, which persisted in the age of decolonisation. The tension between continuity and change – between Britain as an imperial power centred on the Commonwealth and a nation-state coterminous with the British Isles – was captured by the new fragility of citizenship rights of non-white British and Commonwealth citizens resident outside Britain.

How Did We Get Here? Citizenship and the International Rights of States

The novelist Salman Rushdie once remarked that the twentieth century was the 'century of the migrant'.[8] This, I think, is not quite right. But it might be called the century of belonging, in which states acted in powerfully destructive ways in order to define who did and who did not belong to the nation and the state.

The idea of subjecthood, on which the notion of a British subject rested, was rooted in Europe's feudal past. At its core was a direct personal bond between sovereign and subject based on the latter's fealty. In return, the subject received the protection of the sovereign.[9] Before 1948, colonial British subjects of the empire enjoyed protection from Britain itself (in theory, if not in practice). But citizenship has a different etymology, suggesting an individual's active participation in a polity – more than that, it suggests a rich array of rights and duties.

The 1948 British Nationality Act blended ideas of subjecthood and citizenship. Although subjecthood was not a pejorative term for British politicians, but in fact the topmost class of British nationality, they were aware that '"British subject" implies some form of subjection', as one MP put it in 1948, mindful of newly independent India, whose officials favoured a 'common citizenship' for the Commonwealth.[10] On the face of it, Britain was demonstrating its readiness to adopt apparently more egalitarian concepts, as if the use of the word 'citizenship' in 1948 was a concession to decades of imperial diplomacy (notably from Indian diplomats) arguing for the rights of colonial British subjects to be substantively upheld. As the Bengali novelist Nirad C. Chaudhuri wrote in 1951, in a dedication in his *An Autobiography of an Unknown Indian*:

> To the memory of the British Empire in India,
> Which conferred subjecthood upon us,
> But withheld citizenship.
> To which yet every one of us threw out the challenge:
> '*Civis Britannicus sum*'.[11]

Nonetheless, the emboldening language of citizenship after 1948, together with an international recognition of human rights in the 1940s, gave a false sense of security, at odds with the true motivations of the post-war British state and the realities of nationality and citizenship in the modern international system, including international law.

Citizenship is often recognised today as the gateway to all other human rights. Human rights are framed as universal, but you cannot universalise the person trying to claim them, who ultimately needs recognition as a particular individual within a particular jurisdiction. Yet the right to citizenship (or nationality, as it is termed in international law) is not guaranteed. Whether or not a person is granted nationality is a discretionary privilege of the state in question. The grant of nationality belongs to the 'reserved domain' of domestic jurisdiction, as the Permanent Court of International Justice put it in 1923.[12] The rights to freedom of movement (migration) and to nationality were upheld in the United Nations' Universal Declaration of Human Rights (Articles 13 and 15) in 1948. But the former right was confined to leaving one's own state, not entering another state, while the latter had to be balanced against the right of the state to control its borders, discriminate against non-citizens at the level of immigration, and to retain discretion over who were its citizens.

Although the Universal Declaration of Human Rights proclaimed: 'Everyone has the right to a nationality', and: 'No one shall be arbitrarily deprived of his nationality nor denied the right to change his nationality', it also omitted to say which state had the obligation to fulfil these rights. Ultimately, a sovereign state had the power – which it still retains – to define who are its nationals and who are not. The German Jewish philosopher Hannah Arendt, who herself lived as a stateless person between the ages of twenty-seven and forty-five, had written ominously in 1951 of 'the sovereign right of denationalisation' in her classic study, *The Origins of Totalitarianism*. Arendt would become associated with the importance of national citizenship for human rights. In the wake of war and the break-up of empires, the creation of new states and the redefinition of older states, the 'right to belong to some kind of organised community', as Arendt put it, meant nothing less than a 'place in the world'.[13] As the twentieth century progressed, people were being narrowly defined, whether as citizens, aliens, stateless persons, refugees or displaced persons.

Even if one were to be granted nationality, one's rights with respect to the polity were less than clear, since nationality was a status only recognised between states, and said nothing about an individual's active citizenship rights with respect to their affiliated state. The Victorian political philosopher John Stuart Mill suggested that the mutual acknowledgement of nationality was one of the 'sacred duties' of 'civilised nations'.[14] Nationality was an international status, not a binding set of claims between individual and state. In an extreme but revealing example, a German law passed in September 1934 declared that only persons of 'German or cognate blood' could enjoy political rights as 'citizens'; racial others were designated as 'nationals'.[15]

As counterintuitive as it might sound, one could also be a national of a country yet be deemed not to 'belong' to it. The 1955 *Nottebohm* case before the International Court of Justice saw nationality defined as 'a legal bond' based on 'a social fact of attachment, a genuine connection'.[16] This indicated a high threshold of belonging: one could have a nationality yet not truly have a genuine 'connection' to the state in question, which affected what a state could do on one's behalf.

The law and politics of nationality had an enormous influence on British post-war immigration. The apparent imperial inclusivity and largesse of the 1948 British Nationality Act concealed the fragility of individuals' claims on the British state at the level of nationality and citizenship. As a senior Conservative politician put it in 1954, Britain could take imperial 'pride in the fact that a man can say *civis Britannicus sum* whatever his colour may be and we take pride in the fact that he wants to come to the mother country'.[17] Yet, when the time came in subsequent years, Britain could also radically truncate citizenship rights for some without much legal difficulty. If not without incoherence, British officials and politicians picked up the thread of belonging and declared that, although certain non-white people overseas were British citizens, they did not belong to Britain in any meaningful social sense, and could be denied entry into Britain accordingly.

Nationality did not a citizen make. Strictly speaking, in international law, the possession of a passport was not a guaranteed means of establishing a nationality – since passport regimes were different between states, and passports were even occasionally granted to aliens for travel purposes. In Britain, the old idea of a passport was that it was a privilege, not a right. The 'hallmark' of it was that 'the person named was vouched for on behalf of Her Majesty', as *The Times* put it in 1967.[18] Passports could be forged or falsified, British immigration officials argued, especially if the person had been documented in a former British colony.

Passports were political as well as legal artefacts, and have long had a relationship to race. In early 1962, Nelson Mandela was attempting to travel around Africa as a representative of the ANC. He did not have a passport, but had been supplied a piece of paper by the government of Tanganyika (later Tanzania), under the authority of Tanganyika's prime minister, Julius Nyerere. En route to Accra, Mandela's plane stopped in Khartoum. He approached the Sudanese immigration official and handed him a makeshift document that read: 'This is Nelson Mandela, a citizen of the Republic of South Africa. He has permission to leave Tanganyika and return here.' Mandela was accepted warmly. But when his travel companion, Hymie Basner – a critic of apartheid and former South African parliamentarian who was now seeking political asylum in Ghana – handed the same immigration official an identical document, he looked at the piece of paper dubiously and exclaimed that it was not a formal travel document. Basner explained that he had been persecuted in his own country for criticising apartheid, but the immigration official remained perplexed: 'How can you not have a passport – you are a white man!'[19]

But international law relevant to nationality in this period was gradually becoming less skewed in favour of states. The rise of international human rights law – in particular the International Convention on the Elimination of All Forms of Racial Discrimination – gave Britain pause in its exclusivist immigration policies, though it could not prevent their passage. The legality of Britain's immigration legislation in the 1960s and 1970s was questionable, since it denied certain British citizens an irreducible minimum of nationality: the right to enter, work and live in one's own country.

In early 1968, the British cabinet met to discuss the 1968 Commonwealth Immigrants Act, designed to block the migration of South Asian British citizens travelling from Kenya. The attorney general gave his view to ministers in Harold Wilson's Labour government:

> [I]f we were to pass legislation depriving citizens of the United Kingdom and Colonies of the right to enter this country, our position in relation to the relevant international agreements and declarations would be difficult but not impossible. In the case of the Universal Declaration of Human Rights, the United Nations Convention on Racial Discrimination and the International Convention on Civil and Political Rights, we might justify our action on the grounds, among others, that the people concerned did not in any real sense belong to this country.[20]

The attorney general was confident that Britain could pass the 1968 Act yet escape serious censure. After all, Britain could appeal to itself as simply a nation-state doing what a nation-state does – exercising its prerogative to discriminate between those who belong to it and those who do not. More technically, in 1968 Britain had signed but not ratified (and thus was not yet bound by) both the International Convention on Racial Discrimination and the International Convention on Civil and Political Rights. The same applied to the Fourth Protocol to the European Convention on Human Rights, Article 3 of which declared: 'No one shall be deprived of the right to enter the territory of the state of which he is a national.' Despite provoking a minor constitutional crisis, the second Commonwealth Immigrants Act became law in 1968. To this day, Britain has not ratified the Fourth Protocol to the European Convention.

In this same period, however, international human rights law was strengthening, particularly at the level of racial discrimination. In 1973, the European Commission on Human Rights, a body of the European Court of Human Rights, declared that Britain's immigration legislation in 1968 was for certain numbers of those affected 'racially motivated and destined to harm a specific racial group'.[21] Britain had violated Article 3 of the European Convention on Human Rights, its racially discriminatory immigration law amounting to 'degrading treatment' of South Asian British citizens resident in East Africa. In its pursuit of citizenship-with-right-of-entry for some but citizenship-without-right-of-entry for others, Britain was prepared to jeopardise its self-image as a bastion of human rights and the rule of law.

The transformation of British citizenship into apparently race-based categories, in which many white British citizens resident abroad were free to enter Britain but many non-white British citizens resident abroad were not, caused outrage internationally. In the new diplomatic environment of the 1960s and 1970s, in which Britain was adjusting to international sentiment promoting racial equality, and to the claims of a bloc of new states that had previously been colonial territories, its behaviour towards its own non-white citizens caused disbelief and fury. British officials prized Britain's international reputational power very highly, but was this more precious than immigration laws designed to keep Britain white?

It is time to take another look at Britain's history of post-war immigration. This book takes up the domestic immigration story in order to reveal its fullest transnational dimensions. It breathes life into the domestic encounter between migrants, natives and nation in order to show the international networks and political ideas of empire, and subsequently decolonisation, in which immigration was forged. Covering a broad sweep of global twentieth-century history, this book reveals that immigration was born amid the transnational white solidarity of settler colonialism. This imperial experience was a key point of reference to those British politicians and officials who conceived 'coloured immigration' as a domestic problem whose salience grew in the 1950s.

The lives of British and Commonwealth citizens who chose to migrate to Britain in the post-war period were also affected by a historical near-sightedness deliberately cultivated in British political life. The onset of decolonisation put non-white British and Commonwealth citizens on a collision course with British political elites experiencing a rapid decline in imperial power. In the diplomatic world of decolonisation, formerly colonised states held colonial powers to account in a new international public sphere. Not simply immigration, but race, colonialism and international inequality themselves were contested at the international level. British officials experienced 'race' as being at the centre of transnational upheavals whose effects were disturbing the domestic balance. Immigration and citizenship remained critical questions for post-war Britain and the new postcolonial states.

Drawing on fresh material from Britain's national archives, this book shows that events akin to the 2018 Windrush scandal first occurred during this period, coinciding with the passage of immigration legislation in 1968 and 1971. In the late 1960s, it was the migration of South Asians from Kenya in particular that led all non-white British citizens resident overseas to have their citizenship radically redefined, leaving some of them stateless despite their still being described as British citizens in law. This book reveals the lived realities of non-white British citizens who found their automatic right to enter Britain taken away.

Chapter 1 describes the global dimensions of British immigration, which originally related to movements within the empire as opposed to simply post-war migrations into Britain. Chapters 2 and 3 describe Britain's post-war immigration and citizenship story, whose key years are 1948, 1962, 1968 and 1971. Chapter 4 traces Britain's apparent end-of-empire moments in the 1960s and early 1970s, placing them alongside diehard imperial visions of the Commonwealth. Chapters 5 and 6 discuss the new international diplomatic world of the late 1940s and beyond, in which the United Nations was a major player, and the critical importance of race. Chapters 7, 8 and 9 recount in more detail two episodes that make up a crucial period of post-war immigration in Britain: the Kenyan South Asian immigration crisis of 1968 and the Ugandan South Asian immigration crisis of 1972.

Like so many others, I have my own personal stake in this particular history. My paternal grandparents were born in colonial India, and my father in colonial Kenya. Like other families, they were referred to in the parlance of the time as 'coloured immigrants', arriving in London at various points in the 1960s and 1970s. My grandparents migrated from Gujarat to Mombasa to Nakuru under the auspices of the British empire – an inter-imperial migration. My father then migrated to London in 1966 as a teenager, and his parents followed him there in 1972. They lived in

Ilford, in north-east London; like many other South Asian women from East Africa, my grandmother immediately began work, in her case in a textile factory near Bow Church.

I have aimed in this book to look squarely at what ought not to have mattered in the history of my family, but did in fact matter a great deal: the British state. I wanted to know the answer to certain questions that led in turn to further questions. In what follows, I explore not simply the experiences of migrants, but the practices of the British state, its imperial power in the world (both real and imagined), and in particular its power over its own non-white citizens. In this endeavour, I have been careful not, as it were, to overstate the state – or to accept, as the historian John Darwin writes, 'the fallacy of believing that the decolonisation process was the intended consequence of the actions of British policy makers or colonial politicians'.[22]

I focus on three sets of lived experiences: those of non-white British and Commonwealth citizens; those of British officials and politicians; and those associated with new postcolonial states emerging from imperial rule. These generations experienced enormous change in the crucible of decolonisation in the 1950s, 1960s and early 1970s. In writing this history, figures such as the British treasury mandarin Alec Cairncross have struck me as far more remote than, say, the first president of Kenya, Jomo Kenyatta.

Speak, Historical Memory

The historical period most closely discussed in this book (1945–73) is remembered, among other things, as one of transition from the age of empires to an age of states based on sovereign equality. By the 1960s, it was no longer Britain's world; rather, Britain was in a new world where it had to exist alongside many sovereign equals, not to mention its senior in the post-war balance of power, the United States. The end of formal empires meant new possibilities and a scramble – both by former colonial powers and formerly colonised states – to define the terms of the new world amid new vocabularies of equality. British officials and elites knew that they had to adapt to a new world, and they attempted to negotiate the new environment of world politics in such a way as to protect their own imperial standing yet adhere to an apparent global shift in values. This negotiation was sometimes shrewd, sometimes inept, often hypocritical, and nearly always gymnastic.

It may be that much of what follows is unfamiliar to many readers. It is curious that many of the events this book discusses are not better known. I would suggest that the reasons for this are three-fold. First, British nationality law is notoriously difficult and byzantine, as anyone who has read Laurie Fransman's *British Nationality Law* will know. Second, the Commonwealth is now not generally seen as the serious policy initiative it was thought to represent until the early 1970s, when European integration and a low ebb in Commonwealth relations put paid to the more ambitious British imperial visions of the post-war world. Without understanding the salience of the Commonwealth, it is hard to make sense of why British policymakers refused to enact radical reform to the imperial scheme of British nationality that was only finally overhauled in 1981. Third, post-war immigration was intimately connected to the end of empire; historical confusion over the latter conditions our understanding of the former. Britain's transition to a post-imperial age has been subject to endless deferrals. Only by acknowledging the vagueness and ambiguities around the late end-of-empire moments of the 1960s and 1970s can we begin to make sense of immigration policies.

The changes in my family history have been rapid. My father was born in a British colony three years after India gained independence, before migrating to Britain a year after Winston Churchill's death in 1965. I was born in the 1980s, in the age of Margaret Thatcher and 'paki-bashing'; around the corner was Tony Blair's state multiculturalism. Yet there remained many continuities in this period, including a reluctance at the level of the British state to fully come to terms with imperial pasts and their relationship to British national identity. The European 'migration crisis' of 2015 indicated a new scale of need and urgency in relation to migration. With respect to British post-war migration, the Windrush scandal reveals that this particular history is never far away, and remains in thrall to the same historical abridgements, as Britain continues to redefine its relationship to old and new immigrants alike.

For many of us, the depth of feeling around these histories cannot be denied. The Jamaican cultural historian, Stuart Hall, in his posthumous memoir, *Familiar Stranger*, remarks that towards the end of his life he was 'fated to mix memory with desire – a combination that future historians will treat with due suspicion'.[23] Perhaps this is the inevitable longing that attends the lived experience of diaspora, in which the events and circumstances of the present and ancestral past begin to mix together, and memories and motives operating beyond conscious retrieval begin to inhabit one's sense of the historical world.[24]

Yet the project of historical retrieval could not be more urgent. The novelist Zadie Smith describes well the implications of Britain's national approach to its own history:

> It is very hard to live and to live well and in an undamaged way without having a history … And for diaspora people it's a more complicated journey back and certainly a painful one … I've been shocked in middle age to realise just how little black British people were taught in schools about where they came from … I've become so furious and amazed at it that I could spend two years studying the Chartists for example and never be told a single word about British slavery in Jamaica when half the class were the direct historical product of that experience … It's not an exaggeration to say … that a lot of [British] Jamaican kids did not know that they were not native to their island … And that is obscene, I think.[25]

On this view, British public institutions are well practised in either forgetting the empire or denying that parts of it ever existed. Signs of change are appearing, but currently the only statutory history module for students aged between eleven and fourteen in state schools in Britain is the Holocaust. As a 2019 survey of the British state-school history syllabus concludes: 'Notable historical developments, such as the colonisation of the Caribbean, Irish Home Rule and migration to Britain following the Second World War, are missing even from the non-statutory suggestions.'[26]

The history of migration and race in Britain after 1945 is not peripheral post-war British history, but one of its central dimensions: it is British history per se, not a specialist history for Britain's people of colour whose ancestors were colonised. Rozina Visram, the pioneering historian of South Asian life in Britain, describes the historical and social challenges that remain: 'We have to extend knowledge of our history here, which is part of Britain's history. It's not an immigrant history, it's not a ghetto history; it's our history but it's also part of Britain's history because we are part of this society.'[27]

PART I. *We're Here*

Immigration and Empire

1

Immigration and the White Man's World

The docking of the *Empire Windrush*, the passenger ship that surprised British officials by carrying at least 500 people from Jamaica to Britain in June 1948, should be resisted as a moment of origin. It is increasingly accepted by British institutions that Asian and African peoples have long had a presence in Britain, centuries before the famous *Windrush* docked at the port of Tilbury on England's eastern shoreline. If the arrival of the *Windrush* belonged to a new phase in British policymaking on immigration, its moment of arrival does not stand out in the wider history of migration to Britain.

To take one example from a longer history, an infant born in 1614 in the Bay of Bengal was brought to Britain by a chaplain attached to the East India Company. On 22 December 1616, this infant became the first recorded Indian to be baptised in Britain – at St Dionis Backchurch in the City of London – and was given the Christian name Peter. Little is known about his subsequent life, but it was intended that Peter would be instructed in Christianity and later repatriated to India to serve as a Christian missionary there.

Other parish registers provide tantalising clues of South Asian lives in Britain: '26 May 1769. Flora an East Indian (buried at Woolwich)'; and: '5 October 1730. John Mummud a Larskar Indian died at Ratclif (St Anne's Limehouse)'.[1] There is evidence that a very small number of black people were living in England in the sixteenth century. These included a man named 'Anthonye', mentioned in a will made out in 1570 in Barnstaple, Devon. Around the year 1598, the parish register of All Hallows (near Billingsgate, London) records two black women, Clare and Maria, among its residents.[2]

Despite the Naturalization Act of 1870, which gave the Home Secretary discretionary powers over immigration in the name of the 'public good', there was no statutory framework barring aliens from entering Britain until the twentieth century. The first piece of British legislation on immigration was the 1905 Aliens Act, designed to curb the impact of huge numbers of east European, mostly Jewish, migrants moving westwards from central and eastern Europe. Up to 150,000 of these east European Jewish migrants had entered Britain by 1914, settling largely in London's East End, with smaller communities in Leeds, Glasgow, Liverpool and Birmingham; they found work in shoe-, cabinet- and cigar-making, tailoring, market trading, and peddling (itinerant petty trading).[3]

But the origins of Britain's twentieth-century immigration laws were forged not in Britain itself, but thousands of miles away in the British empire. These first immigration laws appeared just before the advent of the contemporary passport regime, when states seized control of the legitimate means of movement, regulating the flow of people across borders as never before. The age of empires saw more freedom of movement than today's rigidly bordered world of nation-states. Forced migration also abounded. The nineteenth century is thought to have been the most intensive migratory phase in world history, with some 50 million Europeans, 50 million Chinese and 30 million Indians migrating globally over long distances.[4] Destinations for these migrants included the Americas, the Caribbean, Southeast Asia, Australasia and the Pacific nations. Huge numbers of people from Russia also migrated to Manchuria.

The pre-1900 British imperial world was implicated in this great age of migration, itself a part of the history of modern globalisation. The migration flows in this period – stretching into the first decades of the twentieth century – included white Britons leaving British shores (including white settlers) and colonised peoples moving, or being moved, between different imperial destinations (indentured labourers or those working in imperial trade, administration or military service).[5] Migration was broadly fuelled by difficult circumstances at home (in imperial China and colonial India as much as in Europe) and the promise of opportunities abroad (in the pursuit of commodities such as gold). After the abolition of slavery, first in Saint-Domingue (later Haiti) in 1793, and during the 1830s in Britain, and its subsequent decline in French, Dutch and Spanish colonies, the European colonies experienced labour shortages.

One type of migration within the British empire involved a system of indentured labour – a contract-labour model that originated in Europe and the Americas. It had begun in earnest after the British parliament revoked slavery in 1833, causing colonial planters to look to India for replacement labour. Put simply, indentured labour involved moving colonial labourers from one part of the empire to another in order to sustain plantation economies (mostly sugar) and infrastructural demands (such as the building of the imperial railway in British East Africa, running from Mombasa to Lake Victoria). Indentured labourers within the British imperial world migrated to locations including British Guiana, Trinidad, Jamaica, Mauritius, Ceylon, Malaya, Burma, East Africa, Natal and Fiji.[6] Thousands of Indians were also moved to Dutch and French colonies, principally Surinam and the island of Réunion.

One historian has calculated that throughout the nineteenth century almost 750,000 Chinese and 1.5 million Indians were formally indentured to European employers for use in their colonies.[7] Many Indian women migrated under the system of indenture, some accompanying their husbands and others impelled by social and economic circumstances, particularly to parts of the Caribbean, Fiji, Natal and Mauritius. A 1901 census of the British empire – capturing the movements of colonised people in Africa, the Pacific and India – recorded that some 1,467,275 people born in British territories overseas had now migrated to other parts of the empire.[8]

If you include additional forms of technically non-indentured labour, labourers from India alone moved to work in various plantation economies (not only sugar but also tea, coffee, rice and rubber) in their tens – and sometimes hundreds – of thousands. In addition to the so-called sugar colonies like Trinidad and Mauritius, there were rubber plantations in Southeast Asia and rice fields in Burma, while in Ceylon rice, tea and coffee were cultivated.[9] The overwhelming majority of indentured labourers in the age of empires were from India, but they included smaller numbers of Pacific Islanders, Javanese, Japanese, Europeans, Africans and Chinese. The horizons of indenture were vast, and saw Chinese labourers being moved to Peru, Cuba and Hawaii and Pacific Islanders being moved to Queensland.[10]

As a system that worked in parallel with the history of slavery (one historian went so far as to call it a 'new system of slavery'), indentured labour has an important place in the history of immigration and race. In many cases, an indentured or contracted labourer on a long-term (usually five-year) agreement for work on a plantation was referred to as a 'coolie' – a term probably adapted from the Telugu word *kuli*, meaning 'wages'. By the late nineteenth century, 'coolie' was used pejoratively by Europeans to refer collectively to Asian (Indian and Chinese) labourers. Ironically, the European agent who met the incoming 'coolies' at their imperial destination was termed a 'protector of immigrants'.[11]

There also emerged in this period a pattern of white British emigration – the creation of an Anglo-world of sorts – that had important consequences for the pre-1945 British empire and for Britain's post-war identity and policies on immigration. The extent of this emigration, fitfully encouraged and endorsed by British governments, was vast. Some 20 million people left British shores between 1815 and 1914, mostly to the United States, but also to Australia, New Zealand and southern Africa.[12] After the 1880s, fewer white Britons left for the United States, choosing instead to migrate to British white-settler colonies.[13] These outflows extended in equal proportions during the 1920s, when just over 1.8 million Britons chose to migrate. Between 1925 and 1929, some 576,146 emigrants left for 'empire destinations' – 35.3 per cent of this total leaving for Canada, and 28.8 per cent for Australia and New Zealand.[14]

The empire-wide census in 1901 recorded that 2,786,650 'Natives of the United Kingdom' were now living overseas in other parts of the British empire.[15] White British people migrated to the so-called 'colonies of white settlement' in today's Canada, Australia, New Zealand and South Africa, as well as to Southern Rhodesia and East Africa. Others in colonial service who had been born in Britain were resident for long periods in places like Gambia, Sierra Leone, Hong Kong, Malta, and of course India.

The British White-Settler World

The significant migration of people from Britain to various white-settler colonies reveals their nascent importance. In developments that at first glance may seem peripheral to British constitutional history, a crucial distinction within the British empire emerged in this period. The British empire was now formed of a constitutional amalgam of crown colonies, protectorates and white-settler colonies, plus India.

Despite their respective indigenous communities, British white-settler colonies (in today's Canada, Australia, New Zealand and South Africa) were often championed as 'other Englands' – as the Oxford historian J. A. Froude rather longingly called them.[16] A number of permanent white settlements gained from London a grant of 'responsible government' – effectively full self-government over their internal affairs, with Britain retaining control of their foreign policy – in the nineteenth century and beyond. These included Ontario (1839), Quebec (1839), Nova Scotia (1848), New Brunswick (1848), Prince Edward Island (1851), Victoria (1855), New South Wales (1855), Tasmania (1855), South Australia (1855), New Zealand (1856), Queensland (1859), Manitoba (1870), British Columbia (1871), Cape Colony (1872), West Australia (1890), Natal (1893), Saskatchewan (1905), Alberta (1905), the Transvaal (1906), Orange River Colony (1907), Newfoundland (1907) and Southern Rhodesia (1923). These self-governing white-settler colonies would go through a process of federation. The five Canadian provinces merged to form the Dominion of Canada in 1867 (others joined later); a similar federation occurred to produce the Commonwealth of Australia in 1900, the Dominion of New Zealand in 1907, and the Union of South Africa in 1909.[17]

It is in the legislative histories of these white-settler colonies that immigration as we know it today was born. The settler colonies tended to have an 'urgent want of labourers', as one early settler-colonial politician put it.[18] Needs in agriculture, mining and infrastructure in the fledgling countries could be met, in particular, by the labour of 'Asiatics' (a catch-all term for Japanese, Chinese and Indians). Yet, at the same time, white racial exclusivity in these settler colonies helped forge the first immigration laws. What might be seen as the very first modern immigration law was passed in the colony of Victoria, in today's southern Australia.

Gold had been discovered along the banks of the Bendigo Creek in the heart of the colony of Victoria. An 1853 census of the colony recorded 2,000 resident Chinese. Two years later, these goldfields had attracted a further 8,000 Chinese hoping to improve their circumstances; in March 1855 alone, four ships brought an additional 1,400 Chinese. The small group of Europeans in Victoria felt themselves to be overrun. In June 1855, Victoria's colonial government passed 'An Act to Make Provision for Certain Immigrants'. The Act defined an immigrant as 'any male adult native of China or its dependencies or of any islands in the Chinese seas or any person born of Chinese parents'. It also declared that a ship arriving in a port of Victoria could only bring one Chinese person for every ten tons of the ship's overall cargo. Moreover, the captain of a ship containing any immigrants would have to pay an entrance tax of £10. In the event, the law proved useless; ships began to dock instead further west, at Guichen Bay, and make their way to the goldfields overland. By mid 1857, there were between 30,000 and 40,000 Chinese migrants in the colony of Victoria.[19]

Similar acts restricting immigration ensued in the following years. Thousands of miles away, in British Columbia, the colony was inundated with people seeking gold amid the Caribou Mountains. British Columbia passed its own Chinese Regulation Act in 1884. As the Vancouver branch of the Dominion Trades and Labour Congress wrote to its colleagues a few years later, 'Chinese immigration is still the burning question of the day; and the more we see of them the more we are convinced of the great curse they are to this country. Incapable of improvement, they are nothing better than the filthy harbingers of disease. Morality, they have none.'[20]

The 1880s saw new immigration-restriction acts in Victoria, South Australia, Queensland, New South Wales, New Zealand and California. These Anglophone immigration laws were highly synchronised, often repeating phrasing verbatim. Race-based discrimination was not the only kind of discrimination at stake in these immigration laws; their criteria for entry also set in place medical, political, financial and moral thresholds.[21] Non-white immigrants were styled as an economic threat to standards of living, just as their perceived unfair business practices were a threat to commercial life.

The protection of Anglo-Saxon integrity in many of these colonies was a paramount motivation of the new immigration laws. As the settler-colonial politician Henry Parkes, born in Birmingham, England, declared to his white audience in Melbourne in 1890: 'The crimson thread of kinship runs through us all. Even the native-born Australians are Britons, as much as the men born within the cities of London and Glasgow ... we know that we represent a race for the purposes of settling new colonies, which never had its equal on the face of the earth.'[22]

Immigration was further discussed among representatives of Australia's various colonies at a conference at Sydney. In 1896, the colony of New

South Wales passed a more expansive piece of legislation, the Coloured Races Restriction and Regulation Act, designed to inhibit entry to '[a]ll persons belonging to any coloured race inhabiting the Continent of Asia or the Continent of Africa, or any island adjacent thereto, or any island in the Pacific Ocean or Indian Ocean'.[23] The colonies of South Australia and Tasmania passed similar legislation. This expanded type of immigration legislation was significant because it implicated British subjects who were 'coloured'. Brushing over the question of the rights of British subjects, the *Sydney Daily Telegraph* declared that the expanded immigration law was simply designed to free Australia from 'coloured aliens'. 'If we want a homogenous Australia', it declared, 'we must have a white Australia … It is not much use … to shut out Chinamen, and leave the door open to millions of Hindoos, Arabs, Burmese, Angolese, and other coloured races which swarm in British Asia.'[24]

Watching these new laws closely was the colony of Natal, in what is now South Africa. Natal was – wrote its colonial governor to London the following year – in danger of being 'flooded by undesirable immigrants from India'.[25] The colony of Natal had passed an Indian Immigration Act in 1891, which referred plurally to the presence of 'Indians', 'Asiatics', 'Arab traders' and 'Arabs' in Natal. Natal's white population made distinctions between 'coolies', or indentured Indians; 'free' Indians (those who had completed their indenture and remained in Natal); and 'passenger' Indians (those, usually with capital, who had migrated independently).[26]

These social and economic distinctions were often submerged by virulent racial theories on Asians, and especially on Africans, held by Natal's white settlers. The quintessential 'passenger Indian', Mohandas Gandhi, was to his chagrin referred to as a 'coolie lawyer'. It was in this period that Gandhi began his campaign to have the rights of Indian British subjects acknowledged, drawing on the rights and civilisational claims of the Indian merchant and diplomatic class at the expense of Africans and lower-caste indentured Indians.[27]

In Durban, Natal, a Colonial Patriotic Union formed in late 1896 to resist 'Asiatic' immigration. This Union declared early the following year that, just as the 'British Colonies of Australia and New Zealand' had 'passed laws having as their object the total exclusion of Asiatics', now Natal had to do the same. The *Natal Witness*, for its part, urged Natal's colonial government to 'follow the course resolved upon by

Australia'.[28] The Natal government obliged, and in correspondence with the Colonial Office in London confirmed that it was planning to pass a total ban on 'Asiatics'. Here was yet another British colony planning to pass an immigration law that conflated non-white British subjects with 'coloured' aliens, forcing the imperial parent government in London into action.

Constitutionally, colonies under 'responsible government' were empowered to make their own laws subject to imperial assent. Joseph Chamberlain, colonial secretary at this time, had to balance the settler colonies' claims to nationhood or national feeling against the unity of the empire. The empire, after all, was meant to be one people under one crown, not a series of discrete colonial nationalities. The rights of British subjects were a point of imperial pride. As Lord Palmerston (twice British prime minister) had declared in 1850, 'a British subject, in whatever land he may be, shall feel confident that the watchful eye and strong arm of England will protect him against injustice and wrong'.[29] In principle, any British subject had a right of entry not only into Britain, but into any other part of the empire.

For those imagining imperial futures, there was from this time onwards a tension between an idea of the British empire as a racially exclusive Anglo-Saxon endeavour, on the one hand, and as a plural yet hierarchical unification of white and non-white colonies under British ideals, on the other. More immediately, for Chamberlain, there was also the potential that these new immigration laws targeting 'coloured races' would disrupt the nascent alliance between Britain and an ascendant Japan, or upset the colonial government of India.[30] Explicitly racist immigration laws came at a significant political cost. Yet, at the same time, Chamberlain was loath to intervene in settler-colonial affairs 'without stringent necessity', as he put it to colleagues in February 1897 in the context of Natal's intentions. Chamberlain had to act, and wrote to Natal's colonial governor: 'I earnestly trust that the legislation be directed not against race or colour, but against impecunious or ignorant immigrants'.[31]

Natal's colonial government needed a law that could not be said to target Indians specifically, yet would bar them in practice. Borrowing a device from the United States Immigration Restriction Act of the year before, Natal's colonial politicians passed new immigration legislation in 1897, satisfied that it was non-discriminatory in its formulation. It would have a deep influence on immigration laws for decades to come. Natal's

'Act 17' of that year introduced a literacy test for new immigrants, along-side a financial threshold of £25. The device of a literary or education test was enough to allay the misgivings of the Colonial Office in London. In practice, the Natal literacy tests would involve an immigration officer sitting down a non-white aspiring immigrant upon arrival in Natal and asking him to trace out at dictation the Latin letters of any west European language; if he managed to do so, he was allowed in.[32]

Later that year, in June 1897, political leaders of the colonies of Canada, Cape Colony, Newfoundland, Natal, New South Wales, Victoria, Queens-land, Tasmania, South Australia, Western Australia and New Zealand travelled to London to mark Queen Victoria's diamond jubilee. Joseph Chamberlain seized the opportunity to hold a conference with these colonial leaders – the first of fifteen colonial and imperial conferences between 1887 and 1937. On the fifth day of the conference, the partici-pants discussed the problem of 'Alien Immigration'. Chamberlain skilfully appeased his audience of settler-colonial politicians: 'We quite sympa-thize with the determination of the white inhabitants of these colonies which are in comparatively close proximity to millions and hundreds of millions of Asiatics that there shall not be an influx of people alien in civilization, alien in religion, alien in customs.'

But Chamberlain then explained that their anti-Asiatic prejudices were, in the light of more pragmatic imperial considerations, a liability for a British imperialism that saw itself as liberal. He asked them to recall the 'traditions of the Empire, which make no distinction in favour of, or against, race or colour'.[33] Chamberlain was encouraged by Natal's appar-ent solution to the problem – supposedly more administrative than racial in its restrictiveness – and recommended Natal's example to all present. After some initial scepticism among the settler-colonial politicians, the London conference in 1897 led over the next three years to new immi-gration laws in Western Australia, New South Wales, Tasmania and New Zealand, all based on Natal's formula.

When, in 1901, Australia federated as the Commonwealth of Australia, immigration was the first order of business in its new federal parliament. Australia's first law in 1901 was an Immigration Restriction Act, based on the Natal model. It prohibited immigration on a range of grounds without reference to particular groups, including any person who 'when asked to do so by an officer, fails to write out a dictation and sign in the presence of the officer a passage of fifty words in length in an European language'.[34]

The trend lines towards indirect racial discrimination in immigration laws were now set. As one historian has put it, this was 'racial exclusion without naming race'.[35]

Australia's 1901 Act became the legal foundation of what would be referred to for decades to come as an official 'White Australia' policy. Such racial exclusivism disguised fears of white decline and the future of the settler-colonial empire. As William Hughes, the Australian prime minister, declared in a speech in Adelaide some years later: 'We have lifted up on our topmost minaret the badge of white Australia, but we are, as it were, a drop in a coloured ocean ringed around with a thousand million of the coloured races. How are we to be saved?'[36]

Racial exclusivism and nationalism in the colonies inevitably influenced ideas in Britain. The English constitutional scholar, A. V. Dicey, for example, proposed in 1897 a 'common citizenship for the English race'. Since Britain and the United States were destined to remain separate states, and Britain's self-governing colonies were seized by their own sovereign feelings, Dicey suggested that it made sense to smooth over differences by making 'every member of the English people a citizen of every country belonging to any branch of the English people'. The principle of English racial and national sameness furthered 'the permanence of peace' and 'moral unity' in the empire and in the world at the expense of French and German imperial power. The ability of the British empire to conceive of itself as a unifying 'community of interests' was 'the main service which the Anglo-Saxon race renders to civilisation'.[37]

The British Empire's Turn to Africa

Alongside the white-settler colonies in Australia, New Zealand, Canada and South Africa, a new British colony was taking shape at this time, in Kenya. In the late nineteenth century, two colonial powers competed in East Africa: Germany and Britain. Following the efforts of the British East Africa Company, Britain established Uganda as a protectorate in 1894, and a year later the larger protectorate of British East Africa. When the India-born British imperial soldier and captain, Frederick Lugard, travelled to East Africa in 1889 to explore its commercial opportunities, he subsequently waxed hopeful that 'British Central and British East Africa may be the embryo empires of an epoch already dawning'.[38]

This new section of the British empire, with its commercial agricultural capacity, would be sustained by white immigration as 'the teeming populations of Europe will turn to the fertile highlands of Africa', wrote Lugard. He also suggested that what would become Kenya could become a settlers' colony without the displacement or elimination of natives. There were 'large tracts of equally fertile country available for colonization' obtainable 'without dispossessing or in any way incommoding the natives'. Then Lugard suggested something unexpected. Acknowledging that Indians had been 'established probably for centuries on the coast of Africa', he advocated that 'Asiatic immigrants' actually be encouraged to settle in British East Africa as a source of labour:

> From the overcrowded provinces of India especially ... we could draw labourers, both artisans and coolies, while they might also afford a recruiting ground for soldiers and police ... [They are] unaffected by the climate, much cheaper than Europeans, and in closer touch with the daily life of the natives than it is possible for a white man to be ...[39]

It was true that merchants from the western coast of India had been trading along the East African coast since at least the sixteenth century. They were a part of a vast trade network focused on the Indian Ocean, encircling the littoral regions of South and Southeast Asia, eastern and southern Africa and the Persian Gulf. Following Lugard's advice – and by contrast with other white-settler colonies – British colonial administrators chose to sustain the Indian presence in East Africa and encourage further immigration.

It was the view of James Hayes Sadler, the first governor of British East Africa, that 'the protectorate has everything to gain from Indian settlement'. British colonial administrators not only tolerated Indian immigration into the colony, but romanticised it. As one colonial administrator suggested in 1901, 'East Africa is, and should be, from every point of view, the America of the Hindu.'[40] From this time, British, European and Indian settlement were all encouraged, the Europeans claiming ranching land in what became known as the 'white highlands' – fertile uplands in Kalenjin, Kikuyu and Maasi territories. One of the original ambitions of the British East Africa Company was to build a railway from the East African coast to Lake Victoria that would fully seize the trade opportunities presented by East Africa's hinterlands. In order to build this railway – an operation that involved digging vast trenches into the ground – some 40,000 Indians (mostly Sikhs and Muslims from Punjab) were transferred from India to East Africa between 1895 and 1908.[41]

What became Kenya Colony in 1920 was therefore not a white-settler colony per se, but a special 'multi-racial' domain in which the master distinctions between European, African and Indian were managed by imperial theories of race, governance and law. Very soon, however, this experiment in Indian immigration came under strain. In 1907, a thirty-three-year-old Winston Churchill (then under-secretary of state for the colonies) made a tour of Britain's new territories in East Africa. Visiting Nairobi, a town standing 'on a base of wooded hills', Churchill speculated about the possibility of racial discord between white settlers, Indians and Africans: 'There are five hundred and eighty whites, three thousand one hundred Indians, and ten thousand five hundred and fifty African natives … There are already in miniature all the elements of keen political and racial discord, all the materials for hot and acrimonious debate. The white man versus the black; the Indian versus both.'[42]

White settlers in Kenya had developed different ideas on Indian immigration from those of British colonial administrators. In order to soothe settler demands, an Immigration Restriction Ordinance was passed in 1906 targeting aspiring Indian immigrants. Half a dozen more pieces of immigration legislation would follow in the decades to come.

The Aliens Act of 1905: Britain's First Domestic Immigration Law

We can now briefly return to the first of Britain's statutory immigration laws, the 1905 Aliens Act, to acknowledge that it was inspired in part by the actions of Britain's white-settler colonies. Railing against the criminality and undesirability of 'pauper alien immigration' (namely, eastern European Jews) in the House of Commons, Hayes Fisher, a Conservative MP, demanded: 'Why should we not, in regard to this question, have similar powers to those possessed by the United States and almost every one of our Colonies?'[43]

A royal commission investigating immigration in the Anglo-Saxon world in 1902 and 1903 had provided details on immigration laws in the Australian colonies, New Zealand, Natal, Canada and Cape Colony, in particular. There was also the American example. 'It is impossible for

Englishmen not to feel a certain amount of envy at the energy and firm-ness', wrote the English writer W. H. Wilkins in *The Alien Invasion* (1892), upon hearing of the actions taken by the US government 'in excluding undesirable aliens'.[44]

Drawing on the existing vocabulary of 'prohibited' and 'undesirable' immigration, the 1905 Act introduced controls at British ports to be manned by immigration officers and 'medical inspectors'. Those migrants found to be below a given economic (or medical or criminal) thresh-old would be classified as 'undesirable immigrants' and refused entry. Some thirteen British ports – from London, Liverpool and Cardiff to Folkestone, Hull and Leith – subsequently introduced such controls.[45] Fear of the social 'evils' of immigrant penury from eastern Europe was often expressed luridly. Samuel Ridley, for example, the Conservative MP for Bethnal Green, described to the House of Commons a particularly memorable visit to an 'underground bakehouse' in his constituency:

> The place was in a filthy state. I turned out seven cats and four kittens from under the trough, as well as some dirty socks that smelt rather queerly. The floor was as black as coal; the baker, a Russian Jew, who gave an English name, was dressed in a woman's petticoat tied at the waist, and was kneading the dough on the black floor with his naked feet. The dough was adhering to his toes, and whilst we were there he scraped his toes with his filthy hands and mixed it with the other dough.[46]

However, the 1905 Act stopped short of controlling the entry of British subjects – as the white-settler colonies had done – mindful of the antiq-uity of the rights of British subjects and the gravity of such a precedent for the empire. In the same spirit of imperial beneficence, the 1905 Act (at Section 1(3d)) also acknowledged a principle of asylum and refugee status, albeit drawn very faintly. Any immigrant seeking entry in order to 'avoid prosecution or punishment on religious or political grounds … involving danger of imprisonment or danger to life or limb' was to be exempted from control.[47]

This exemption was tacitly aimed towards eastern European Jews, par-ticularly those fleeing Russia, a country whose antisemitism was notorious. Because the immigration controls under the 1905 Act only applied to those aliens travelling most cheaply (in steerage class), the majority of aliens escaped inspection. The subsequent Liberal government also made good on the asylum exception, and some 500 Jewish refugees fleeing fresh pogroms in Russia were granted entry in 1906. But this latitude in the administration of the 1905 Act was ended in 1914 by a further Aliens Restriction Act, using the framework of the 1905 Act to curtail alien entry severely – a restrictiveness that was carried forward into the inter-war period.[48]

Empire, Race and Immigration

Theories of white racial decline now circulated more energetically, often with reference to the sheer number of Asiatic peoples. In a 1903 speech, speaking in the American context, president Theodore Roosevelt himself warned against 'race suicide'. In the following years, a number of books published in Europe and the United States took up comparable sociological themes, including Madison Grant's *The Passing of the Great Race* (1916), Oswald Spengler's *The Decline of the West* (1922), John Walter Gregory's *The Menace of Colour* (1925), and Maurice Muret's *The Twilight of the White Races* (1926). The American historian and polemicist Lothrop Stoddard, who had gained his doctorate from Harvard, spoke of a global racial conflagration between white people and Asiatic immigrants in his 1920 book, *The Rising Tide of Colour*. 'The question of Asiatic immigration', wrote Stoddard, 'is incomparably the greatest external problem which faces the white world … three Asiatic countries – China, Japan, and India – together have a population of nearly 800,000,000. That is practically twice the population of Europe – the source of white immigration. And the vast majority of these 800,000,000 Asiatics are potential immigrants into white territories.'[49]

These early twentieth-century works of racial theory that took the threat of immigration as their jumping-off point set the tone for decades to come. A slippage between imperial decline and white decline was hard to resist for those white men dedicated to checking the flow of non-white immigration.

'A White Man's Country'

Britain's white-settler colonies were expressing their sense of nationhood, and their sovereignty as specifically white nations, by means of immigration laws. Neither the strong 'family' bonds of attachment between the white-settler colonies and Britain nor pride in the rights of British subjects could soften those colonies' experience of nationalism and racial exclusivism. As New Zealand prime minister Joseph Ward declared in 1907, New Zealand was 'a white man's country, and intends to remain a white man's country'.[50] Six years later, H. H. Stevens, a British Columbian MP, argued that anti-Asiatic immigration laws had been necessary 'if Canada was to remain a white man's country and develop properly'.[51]

What had the British empire become? It was now a clutch of crown colonies plus India, together with an assortment of self-governing white-settler colonies. Alongside the pressing realities of imperial rivalry and imperial defence, the task of maintaining this amalgamated empire as a single, unified entity dominated the minds of British intellectuals and political elites in the first decades of the twentieth century. To make matters even more confusing for the imperial parliament in London, Japan secured victory over Russia in a contest between the rival imperial powers in 1905, revealing to all Western onlookers that a non-white power could best a European one in the theatre of war. The claims of Asian powers (Japan, India and China) to the same civilisational and national standing as Western powers were becoming harder to refute.[52] 'Fifty years ago the Japanese were regarded as barbarians of a rather absurd type', declared the Liberal MP, Herbert Samuel, in the House of Commons in 1905, 'but today the whole world stands in admiration of their efficiency and bows in reverence before their heroism'.[53]

Theorising Empire

British imperial federationists, whose ideas had circulated for some decades, argued that only a proper theory of a 'greater Britain' could improve imperial governance, advance the culture of the 'British race' overseas, and meet the needs of imperial defence. But now the dream of imperial federation faced yet further challenges: a global colour bar over race and the intensifying demand for autonomy among the white-settler colonies. The whole direction of empire was changing.

In 1907, some self-governing white-settler colonies were granted a new constitutional status as 'dominions'. This acknowledged that not all British colonies were alike; the white colonies were special. This was a grand way of acknowledging both the white-settler colonies' allegiance to the crown and their superior status to that of non-white colonies such as India.[54] Those colonies deemed dominions were Canada, Australia, New Zealand, Newfoundland, Cape Colony, Natal and Transvaal. The Union of South Africa, now a single dominion, was created in 1910. The Irish Free State, something of an anomaly in this history, became the sixth dominion in 1922.

British nationality was finally formalised in the British Nationality and Status of Aliens Act of 1914. The 1914 Act reaffirmed the uniformity of British subjecthood, defining a British subject as '[a]ny person born within His Majesty's dominions and allegiance'.[55] Even a person who was not 'natural born' but became a British subject through naturalisation enjoyed the same 'rights, powers, and privileges' (Article 3(1)) as a natural-born British subject. However, Article 26(1) of the Act contained an important hedge – an exemption that indirectly laid the ground for the future trend of immigration policy in post-war Britain. It stated that the laws of self-governing legislatures in the empire were legitimate in 'treating differently different classes of British subjects'. All British subjects were equal, but some were clearly more equal than others. As the colonial secretary reminded the House of Commons, Article 26(1) was a diplomatic concession to the effect that nothing from the imperial parliament in London could 'affect the validity and effectiveness of local laws regulating immigration'.[56]

This severely undermined the pretensions of British imperial citizenship – namely, the supposed equal status of all British subjects, and by extension a principle of free movement within any part of the empire. As a pre-war study of British nationality law put it, 'the simple nomenclature "British subject" affords, within the Empire, no clue as to his rights'.[57] The empire remained constitutionally unified under a common British nationality, but only at the expense of imperial control over local immigration laws.

Canada, South Africa, New Zealand and Australia continued to pass dozens of immigration laws – including Canada's Immigration Act of 1910 and New Zealand's Immigration Restriction Amendment Act of 1920 – whose indirect racial criteria came increasingly into conflict with the strengthening principle of non-discrimination in the middle decades of the twentieth century. The inequity of white-settler immigration laws was symbolised most powerfully at this time by the so-called

Komagata Maru incident. The *Komagata Maru* was a chartered passenger ship that carried close to 400 British subjects (mostly Sikhs) from India to Canada in 1914. It was denied entry to every port on the British Columbian coastline, and, after remaining anchored off Vancouver for over two months, was forced to return to India.[58]

The end of the First World War introduced still more rapid change. India's own claims to nationhood were, if not fully accepted, acknowledged on the basis of its enormous contribution to the war effort. In 1917, the Montagu Declaration acknowledged that the purpose of British rule in India was now to steward it towards 'responsible government'. India's claims to civilisational parity with the West had succeeded. Had something irrevocable happened to the British empire? The master divide between white-settler colonies as self-governing and non-white colonies was no more; a non-white colony within the empire too could be vouchsafed responsible government, if not self-government.[59]

These developments spurred the British intellectual, Alfred Zimmern, in a series of lectures in 1925, to proclaim a 'Third British Empire'. 'Does the Empire, in any real sense, still exist?' he asked his audience at Columbia University, New York. 'And, if so, what are the ties that bind its members together?' He answered that the British empire had recently transformed into a 'multi-national association'. The population of the empire was 'about 440 million' of whom 'some 380 millions are non-white'; then there were the 'overseas English, Scottish, Welsh' and 'Ulstermen'. But the white-settler colonies could not claim to be exclusively Anglo-Saxon, since there were 'Dutch, Germans, and Huguenots' in South Africa and 'French-Canadians, Slavs, and other Continental immigrants' in Canada.[60] The empire was now to be celebrated as a multinational and multiracial partnership based on the special British facility for building political institutions and values held in common.

This theme had already been taken up by Zimmern's contemporary, Lionel Curtis – a British official and intellectual, and founder of the London research institution, Chatham House. Curtis was determined to solve the problem of imperial governance and bring federated unity to the empire. 'England contains a population of 34,000,000', he wrote in 1916, 'but it is an indisputable fact that upwards of 433,000,000 souls, drawn from all races and civilisations and scattered through every continent across the world, have been brought within the range of its constitution'.[61] For Curtis, the only means of realising a federal unity within the empire under an Anglo-Saxon constitution was to conceptualise carefully and distinguish between its peoples. Curtis identified three categories of peoples within the empire that corresponded to three tiers of political development: white Europeans occupied the top tier, Indians the middle tier, and Africans the bottom tier. Wherever they might live in the 'British Commonwealth', those of the Anglo-Saxon race would superintend other races in their constitutional development.

Like Zimmern and others, Curtis preferred not to call the British empire an 'empire' but a 'Commonwealth of Nations' or 'British Commonwealth'. Comparable ideas shared between them and their colleagues of an 'organic union' of the empire and a 'world commonwealth' were nothing less, for this set of imperial philosopher-kings, than a blueprint for world government, or ultimately a 'world state' under British auspices.[62] Curtis's book, *The Commonwealth of Nations*, was decisive in popularising the idea of the Commonwealth as the evolutionary successor to the British empire, and from around the end of the First World War the term 'empire' itself began to be replaced. Whether this was in direct response to Curtis's thought or a function of the growing diplomatic importance of the white-settler colonies, British political elites began to refer not simply to the 'empire', but to the 'British Commonwealth of Nations' or the 'autonomous nations of an imperial Commonwealth'.[63] The refashioning of empire in this way – a kind of 'post-imperial imperialism', as one historian terms it – was crucial to the development of empire and to Britain's engagement with 'race' after 1945.[64]

Lionel Curtis's mentor, the senior Liberal politician and colonial administrator, Alfred Milner, was less interested in such multicultural theories and more concerned to emphasise his belief that the white-settler colonies had transformed the empire into an Anglo-Saxon world. *The Times* published Milner's short manifesto on the imperial Anglo-Saxon world posthumously in 1925, the year of his death:

> I am a British (indeed primarily an English) Nationalist. If I am also an Imperialist, it is because the destiny of the English race … has been to strike fresh roots in distant parts of the world. My patriotism knows no geographical but only racial limits. I am an Imperialist and not a Little Englander, because I am a British Race Patriot. It seems unnatural to me … to lose interest in an attachment to my fellow-countrymen because they settle across the sea. It is not the soil of England, dear as

it is to me, which is essential to arouse my patriotism, but the speech, the tradition, the spiritual heritage, the principles, the aspirations of the British race. They do not cease to be mine because they are transplanted. My horizon must widen, that is all. I feel myself a citizen of the Empire. I feel that Canada is my country, Australia my country, New Zealand my country, South Africa my country, just as much as Surrey or Yorkshire.[65]

Ensuring the sustainability of British emigration to these Anglo-Saxon worlds overseas was the focus of the Empire Settlement Act of 1922. The British government committed to financially aided migration in the form of 'assisted passage' schemes – sharing with white-settler colonies the cost of ship passage fares. Between 1922 and 1933 alone, Britain contributed £6 million to such schemes. Some 500,000 white British people received assistance in emigrating to 'white' destinations – chiefly Canada, Australia and New Zealand – between 1921 and 1929.[66]

The World After 1919

The idealism of British imperialists notwithstanding, the world was changing rapidly in the years following the First World War. Japan took part in the Paris Peace Conference in 1919 as one of the five great powers, and the only non-European great power. Significantly, India was also included as a non-sovereign member of the newly created League of Nations (the outcome of the 1919 conference). Mindful of the history of anti-Japanese immigration laws in the British white-settler colonies and the United States, Japanese delegates at the 1919 Paris Peace Conference proposed a principle of racial equality for inclusion in the Covenant of the League of Nations. The Japanese proposal suggested that, as an extension of the 'equality of nations', all members of the League should 'agree to accord, as soon as possible', to 'all alien nationals' of states who were members of the League, 'equal and just treatment in every respect, making no distinction, either in law or fact, on account of their race or nationality'.[67]

One of the British delegates, foreign secretary Arthur Balfour, recorded privately that he felt the Japanese proposal represented less a universal principle of racial equality than something designed to secure 'a formula on the subject of Immigration which would satisfy the Japanese'. Given that the 'English-speaking communities' would never tolerate significant Japanese immigration, the proposal was presumably, Balfour wrote, an act of blackmail or sabotage attached to Japanese inclusion in the League of Nations. Despite the Japanese delegates' subsequent claims that the proposal was not about immigration per se, its inclusion in the Covenant of the League of Nations was rejected by the unified opposition of the United States, Britain and Australia.[68]

Nonetheless, the Japanese effort did provoke the Foreign Office to produce, in 1921, a lengthy internal report on 'Racial Discrimination and Immigration'. The international debate on racial equality, it reasoned, turned on the claims made by Japan, China and India, which 'demand the right of free immigration and freedom from discrimination disabilities for their nationals' in the United States, Canada, Australia, New Zealand and South Africa. Its perception of the future of this conflict was in stark contrast to the idealism of Alfred Zimmern and Lionel Curtis. 'The white and the coloured races', wrote Frank Ashton-Gwatkin, the author of the Foreign Office report, 'cannot and will not amalgamate. One or the other must be the ruling caste'.[69]

In Kenya, meanwhile, Britain's experiment in creating a multiracial colony built on Indian and European immigration was souring. In August 1921, white settlers in Kenya threatened nothing less than armed revolution – that is, they threatened to secede from the British empire – unless the colonial government abandoned the idea of a common franchise that included South Asians alongside whites.

An association of white British settler women, the Kenya Women's Committee, circulated a pamphlet declaring that 'unrestricted immigration would mean Asiatic supremacy, as India with her 320,000,000 could at any moment flood the colony'. Britain's Colonial Office balked at the idea of settler violence and turned towards further anti-Indian immigration legislation. British colonial administrators presented these anti-Indian immigration policies as protecting the interests of the African population from Indian avarice. Racial discrimination also operated at the administrative level, South Asians being made to compete unsuccessfully with white settlers for entry and employment passes and residence certificates within Kenya Colony.[70]

In Britain itself, too – specifically, in Cardiff's docklands area, where Britain's shipping industry had transformed the city into a multi-ethnic area – there was a rising white hostility. Supposedly inhibiting local white employment were 'coloured seamen', as they were known – replacing older epithets like 'lascar', 'kru', and 'seedee' – who included not only South Asians, West Africans and Chinese, but various peoples associated with Aden Protectorate and Somaliland. The Special Restriction (Coloured Alien Seamen) Order of 1925 was unusual in specifying 'colour', and stands as one of the more indisputable pieces of race-based immigration legislation. It blurred the line between non-white British subjects and non-white aliens, introducing a range of administrative checks on Cardiff's non-white community (Cardiff police required registration of 'coloureds' and proof of identity).[71]

In London, the Imperial Conferences of 1918 and 1921 only strengthened acceptance of the idea that each white-settler colony should 'enjoy complete control of the composition of its own population by means of restriction on immigration from any other communities'.[72] This was despite the brilliant diplomatic efforts of the Indian delegate, V. S. Srinivasa Sastri, whose arguments in favour of the rights of Indian British subjects throughout the empire had to be confined to those already resident in colonies.

The end of the war had also seen the rise of the modern passport regime, with which came indirect racial discrimination both at and inside borders. Even an international luminary such as the Bengali intellectual Rabindranath Tagore found himself mistreated by immigration officials when trying to pass from Canada into the United States in 1929; he was so appalled that he cancelled his planned lecture tour (he had recently won the Nobel Prize for literature) and returned to India.[73] Under the 1931 Statute of Westminster, Canada, Australia, New Zealand and South Africa were given complete legal autonomy: they were made sovereign states, although constitutionally the British monarch remained their head of state and was represented by a locally stationed British governor-general.

British elites chose to believe that the empire was evolving, not ending, despite the reality that Britain was transferring sovereign power to its former colonies, and that India was growing ever stronger in its commitment to becoming a republic. Yet, reading the 1931 Statute of Westminster, one sees that, rather than articulating a concession of British power, it describes simply a new constitutional view of the composition of a section of the empire. Canada, Australia, New Zealand and South Africa (as well as Newfoundland and the Irish Free State) are described as part of the 'free association of the members of the British Commonwealth of Nations', whose unity was sealed 'by a common allegiance to the Crown'.[74]

In 1931, Mohandas Gandhi was in London to discuss with British politicians the scope of reforms to British rule in India. British politicians at the time were set on offering India, in lieu of full independence, 'dominion status' – that is, the same Commonwealth-based constitutional status as Canada, Australia, New Zealand and South Africa. This was a clever manoeuvre, in the sense that it represented an attempt by Britain to use a device designed to serve imperial unity in order to contain anticolonial nationalism in India.[75] In London, Gandhi told an audience that, for him, Commonwealth membership (India becoming a dominion) referred to 'a status common to members of the same family – Australia, Canada, South Africa, New Zealand etc. These are daughter states in a sense that India is not. The bulk of the population of these countries is English speaking and their status implies some kind of relationship with Britain.'[76]

Without mentioning race as such, Gandhi's point was clear: India was not a part of the Anglo-Saxon family of states. Nevertheless, in a point sometimes overlooked in post-war histories, both India and Pakistan (and later Ceylon) gained independence in 1947 as British dominions, not as sovereign republics. Despite the declaration of India's Constituent Assembly in early 1947 that it was destined to become an independent sovereign republic, the Indian National Congress nevertheless accepted that India would become a dominion, with the right to secede from this status, in order to ensure a smooth transfer of power and bring forward a British handover date.[77] India and Pakistan remained British dominions with allegiance to the British crown until 1949 (and Ceylon until 1972).

This was a pivotal moment for Britain – but for reasons that went beyond the obviously momentous nature of India's determination to become a republic. Rather than lose India altogether, Britain was prepared to upset the racial scheme of the Commonwealth empire by making India a dominion – a status previously reserved for and symbolic of a white, Anglo-Saxon constellation of states based on the providence of global white immigration. From 1947 onwards, the Commonwealth empire was never simply a white man's club. In particular, India's entrée to the Commonwealth as a republic in 1950 marked a watershed, and the 'multiracialism' of the Commonwealth was from this moment to be pulled in two directions: on one hand, a euphemistic multiracialism that was racially hierarchical and in the service of British interests, and, on the other, a broadly egalitarian multiracialism spurred by (Asian and African) efforts towards anticolonialism and racial equality.

Why was India so important that Britain was prepared to adapt the implicit racial hierarchy of the Commonwealth empire? Beyond the unending need for imperial unity, India had long been at the heart of imperial defence, indispensable in times of colonial emergency and war. Defence officials noted in 1946 that India presented 'an almost inexhaustible supply of manpower' and might be drawn upon for 'almost as many soldiers as the Commonwealth could maintain'.[78] Britain would need India in case the Commonwealth became engaged in a war, especially in places like the Middle East and Persian Gulf, where Britain wanted to maintain an imperial footing. It was assumed that the foreign and defence policies of the white Commonwealth states would not run against British interests; but their support alone was not enough. Britain needed India to remain in the Commonwealth.

British officials knew all too well that Indian prime minister Jawaharlal Nehru was set on India's becoming a republic, and that its post-1947 allegiance to the British crown could not last. Having previously doubted that the Commonwealth could ever be egalitarian given the persistence of British imperialism, Nehru changed his stance after the Second World War, having been influenced by one of his senior diplomats and civil servants, Girija Shankar Bajpai. Nehru made a set of demands to the British for Indian membership in the Commonwealth, culminating in negotiations in London in 1949. Not the least of his demands was India's inclusion as a republic without allegiance to the crown.[79] 'I have loved much that was England', Nehru wrote in 1940, but any bond between England and India 'can only exist in freedom'.[80] Both India and Pakistan had a range of reasons for wishing to maintain Commonwealth membership. For Nehru, these included opportunities in trade and defence, as well as potential international partnerships in science, technology and education.

British government departments (the Foreign, Colonial and Commonwealth Relations offices) intensely debated India's place as a republic in the Commonwealth – a deep symbolic change whereby Commonwealth membership might not be dependent on allegiance to the British monarch. The sentiment of officials was that an Indian presence was essential to maintain the Commonwealth in 'the eyes of the world, and particularly of potential aggressors'. Britain needed India as much as India needed the Commonwealth; yet a decision to keep India in as a republic might be presented as 'a further tribute to the Anglo-Saxon genius for compromise'.[81]

As Labour politician Patrick Gordon Walker remarked in his diary following a meeting of the cabinet's Commonwealth affairs committee in January 1949: 'The Crown link is out. Let's fit in India as a Republic.'[82] Nehru was reassured that 'British' would be dropped from the title of the Commonwealth.[83] In the 1949 Declaration of London, Britain finally jettisoned the formerly key element of 'common allegiance' to the crown as a condition of Commonwealth membership. On 26 January 1950, India became a republic but also remained in the Commonwealth, rupturing the latter's equivalence with the British empire.

Nehru had fundamentally changed British constitutional history; or perhaps British history was now following Indian history. It was unclear what the new Commonwealth – now including India and Pakistan, and no longer an exclusive white man's club – might mean. Former Indian diplomat Krishnan Srinivasan has written wryly that the British were 'deliberately vague' about definitions of the Commonwealth after India assumed membership on equal terms. This ambiguity turned on whether the Commonwealth was properly seen as a continuation of empire, or simply a free association of sovereign states.[84]

The Commonwealth now officially lost its 'British' prefix. It was a free association comprising the British empire, Australia, Canada, Ceylon, India, New Zealand, Pakistan and South Africa (Ireland withdrew in 1948, Newfoundland joined Canada, and republican Burma declined to join). Of these, India divested itself of dominion status first, and the very term 'dominion' soon fell into abeyance, while a new term, 'Commonwealth realm', came into use.[85]

Loss was nothing new to the British empire. Long ago America had been lost. The white-settler colonies, too, had long since been promoted as the co-heirs of empire as a salve to their desire for nationhood. And now colonial South Asia was split into four new states (India, Pakistan, Ceylon and Burma). But new post-war imperial enterprises were now beginning: a new phase in the development of trade, investment and raw materials in Africa and other so-called tropical colonies. Part of what sustained Britain's post-war empire into the 1950s was the perceived significance of a British world overseas; but the identity of Australia, Canada, and South

Africa as British white-settler colonies had clearly receded, their own status as both nations and states now being undeniable.

Tellingly, Commonwealth countries like Australia and Canada signed the United Nations Charter in 1945 as individual states, without reference to a Commonwealth bloc.[86] But the African colonies inhabited by British white settlers remained. One of the acts of national forgetting that has taken place in Britain over the past thirty years relates to the British white-settler experience in Africa that persisted well past 1945 in places like Kenya, and of course Southern Rhodesia (later Zimbabwe). Rhodesia eventually became a rogue white-settler state, declaring unilateral independence from Britain in 1965; settler-colonial life and white-minority rule continued there until as late as 1979.

Settler Colonialism After 1945

The importance of post-war British settler colonialism was evident in the popularity in Britain of the author and journalist Elspeth Huxley, the daughter of white British settlers in Kenya and a chronicler of the pioneer European settler experience there. Huxley spoke of the British in Africa as 'the fourth and last empire'. Britain's imperial success in Africa was urgent: 'she must win it quickly from the swamps and forest and highveld of the last continent to be pioneered', wrote Huxley in her unmistakable turn of phrase.[87]

In 1912 her parents had invested capital in coffee plantations in the newly created British East Africa protectorate. As a young woman, she was commissioned to write a biography of Lord Delamere, a settler–farmer who became a leader of the settler community. This two-volume work appeared in the 1930s as *White Man's Country: Lord Delamere and the Making of Kenya*. In it she paid what she felt was her due to Delamere:

> He would be the first to show that in East Africa England had possessed herself of a miniature new dominion, a little New Zealand tucked away between deserts and tropics and lakes, where yet another cutting from the British parent stock could be planted and would grow and flourish. This was the ultimate ideal – this and nothing else. He wanted to prove to the world that East Africa was a white man's country. He wanted it to become a true British colony in the sense that Australia and Natal

had been colonies – places where people settled for good and tried to build a replica of England that would endure so long as the British race itself persisted.[88]

Huxley was utterly romanced by colonial Kenya – a landscape she saw as veld, forest and bush, whose skies were crimson and purple, its lakes splashed pink by flamingo wings, and the trees a brilliant flame-red. Huxley continued to write prolifically about East Africa and the exigencies of settler farming and agriculture for major British and American newspapers. She gave talks on the BBC, joined the BBC's General Advisory Council, and appeared on radio. In the late 1950s she was called upon to advise the government in matters of East African colonial administration.

Elspeth Huxley was writing about Kenya during the so-called Mau Mau Emergency (1952–60). Historians have puzzled over the fact that the domestic British public did not know of the full horror of the British counterinsurgency atrocities there until March 1959, when information from the Hola detention camp provoked an outcry. A Quaker named Eileen Fletcher – who had gone to work for the colonial state in Kenya as a rehabilitation officer in 1954 – wrote a pamphlet, *The Truth about Kenya*, in 1956 based on these experiences. Her tone was combative – 'Colonial powers must remember that the so-called "Backward Races" have Human Rights!' – while her calls for a 'full judicial inquiry' were enough for her accusations to receive mention in parliamentary debate, on 31 October 1956.[89]

One of the reasons why British people remained distracted from the realities of counterinsurgency in Kenya was the public-relations campaigning of white-settler organisations like the European Elected Members Organisation and the Kenya Association. The latter was set on attracting more settlers, and distributed pamphlets in the metropole, one of which was entitled, 'Kenya: Britain's Fairest Colony'. Kenya was also a successful British tourist destination throughout the 1950s.[90] In the British public media, any coverage of potential colonial crimes was offset by reporting on the embattled domestic lives of white settlers.

The fate of white settlers in Africa had long enjoyed cultural purchase. Sensational media reporting had spiked in 1953, following an attack on a settler family living on a farm in Kenya. Roger Ruck, his wife Esmé, and their young son Michael were discovered dead in their farmhouse on the so-called white highlands. The murders were extremely violent – the wounds presumed to be the result of *panga* blades – and photographs of the bodies were disseminated among the settler community. The *London Illustrated News* carried the following headline about the attack: "'A Vile, Brutal Wickedness": The Murder of the Ruck Family by Mau Mau Terrorists in Kenya, A Shocking Crime Redeemed Only by the Heroism of an African Houseboy'.[91]

The settler organisations wanted the anticolonial resistance in Kenya to be seen in terms of a civilised white society made vulnerable by native terrorism. The settler community was not insignificant. By 1948 there were some 29,660 white Europeans living in colonial Kenya, while South Asian communities in Kenya, despite previous immigration legislation, now numbered closer to 100,000 people (both of these figures would increase considerably over the next ten years).[92] White settlers continued to turn the screw on South Asians as well as Africans. Colonel Ewart Grogan, the buccaneer British explorer and a doyen of Kenyan settlers, declared in the mid 1950s a sentiment that went back to the early part of the century: 'South Africa has shut the back door to Asiatics in Durban, now East Africa must shut the door at Mombasa.'[93]

What does Kenya in the 1950s tell us about post-war Britain? Kenya was a colony throughout the 1950s, before finally gaining independence in 1963. Its imperial and settler-colonial identities having been forged by immigration of both whites and Indians, Kenya Colony revealed the convergence of settler interests and wider British imperial interests in Africa after 1945. It also proved itself a challenging test-case of imperial claims to the benevolence of racial management. Britain's Colonial Office referred to Kenya euphemistically as a 'plural society'. The master-distinctions between African natives, 'Asians' and white settlers were absolute. The imperial task was to manage the perceived differences between races living together in a single colony.

The Colonial Office saw itself as particularly well placed to execute this task. Presented as being far removed from the racism of, say, South Africa, British policies claimed to uphold a liberal sensibility of 'multi-racialism' – the imperial precursor of future ideas of state-led multiculturalism. Kenya Colony's mixture of South Asians, Europeans and Africans was a symptom of empire; yet this multiracial situation now became the rationale for the continuation of empire in places like Kenya. As Elspeth Huxley put it, African societies were 'too immature, backward and unstable' to risk having the ballast provided by British colonial rule removed.[94]

The Anglo-Saxon World After 1945

The immediate post-war period in Britain did not see the end of empire; nor did the Second World War mark the end of British emigration to the traditional settler colonies. The Empire Settlement Act – the state-sponsored cooperative scheme to assist those white Britons who wished to become migrants – was renewed in 1952, 1957 and 1962. Between 1946 and 1957, over 125,500 people of so-called 'British stock' migrated to South Africa. Over 82,000 people migrated from Britain to Southern Rhodesia between 1946 and 1960; over 582,700 people went to Canada during the same period; over 151,700 people went to New Zealand; and over 566,400 people to Australia. Of the white British immigrants to Australia, over 380,400 received financial assistance (amounting to £3.8 million) from the British state – making their passage either free or considerably cheaper.[95]

The maintenance of an Anglo-Saxon world based on white migration was not a unilateral effort by the British state. Upon becoming Australia's new prime minister in 1949, Robert Menzies declared, in a national Australia Day address, that Australians were not simply 'citizens of Australia'; they belonged to the British-led Commonwealth, describing it as 'our ancient family association, unique in history, the love of which is bone of our bone, flesh of our flesh'.[96] In 1959, Australia's immigration minister, Alexander Downer, declared to the Commonwealth Club that sustenance of the Commonwealth depended on 'a deliberate policy of dispersal of population from the Mother Country to her proven friends, Australia and New Zealand'.[97] After more independent non-white states joined the Commonwealth in the late 1950s, prime minister Robert Menzies became deeply distressed. 'If only we could shed these new, immature and utterly alien excrescences on our hitherto homogenous family', he wrote desperately in 1961 to a senior British official.[98]

If non-white immigration into Britain was a 'problem', white immigration abroad was still being actively supported by the British state throughout the 1960s. The Empire Settlement Act was renewed yet again in 1967, for a further five years, under the updated title of the Commonwealth Settlement Act. Speaking in the House of Lords in 1967, Labour politician Frank Beswick remarked upon an unbroken legislative thread running across many decades. The Commonwealth Settlement Act pledged an overall maximum expenditure each year of £1.5 million on 'migration schemes', of which a maximum of £150,000 was dedicated to the assisted passage scheme:

> I still believe that all of us here would wish well to those who, for their own good individual reasons, decide to start a new life among others largely of British stock and who speak the English language in other parts of the world. In the period 1946 to 1965, 1,802,000 people have migrated from the United Kingdom to Canada, Australia and New Zealand – about one-third of all the immigrants to those countries. Over a more recent period, from 1962 to 1965, of the 860,000 people who have emigrated from Britain nearly two-thirds have made their way to Australia, Canada and New Zealand.[99]

The Commonwealth Settlement Act finally expired in 1972, a year before British entry into Europe. By 1972, the total number of white British immigrants who had settled in Australia under financially aided post-war migration schemes totalled 1,011,985.[100]

Faith in an Anglo-Saxon world created by British imperialism was reconfirmed by various British high commissioners in late 1966. They were asked by the Commonwealth Office to give their thoughts on the subject of 'the Commonwealth as a British interest', as part of a major review of Commonwealth policy. The British high commissioner in Canberra, T. D. O'Leary, gave a very positive response:

> The British connection is basic to Australia (about 85% of Australians derive originally from the British Isles; while almost one Australian in ten has migrated to Australia from Britain since the Second World War). Australia is completely impregnated with Britishry – Australia's way of life, law, language, institutions, the atmosphere of its society, in fact almost everything Australian has reflections and overtones of Britain.[101]

'Anglo-centricity', as British officials termed it in the late 1960s, was a perpetual presence in the world. The Commonwealth, with its various peoples, states and societies, would always remain an Anglo-Saxon vehicle in the world: 'We speak the same language and understand each other – all the more so because we have largely common systems in administration, the law, the armed forces, education, British merchanting and banking traditions and interests. Oxbridge, Sandhurst, Shakespeare, the authorised version of the Bible are all genuine links.'[102]

The British Empire Is Dead – Long Live British Imperialism!

British governments and officials were wedded to the Commonwealth empire as a British-led source of Anglo-Saxon civilisation well into the 1960s. For example, in the summer of 1968, British officials had a chance to put 'Anglo-centricity' into action with the diplomatic visit of Hitendra Desai, chief minister of Gujarat State, India, to London as an official guest of the Commonwealth Office. Officials judged Desai an influential member of the Congress leadership headed for a cabinet post in Delhi, and therefore in a position to promote British commercial and political interests.[103]

Desai's visit included lunch with MPs at Westminster and meetings with the Board of Trade and Ministry for Overseas Development. Yet officials seemed to have little idea of who Desai was, or of any of the nationalistic and religious trends within the Indian state. Desai was taken to the offices of the Royal Commonwealth Society, where he was informed that, although it used to be named the Royal Empire Society, it now boasted a membership drawn from the Commonwealth, which included 'people of all creeds, ages and colour'. Meanwhile, he was told about the Commonwealth Parliamentary Association, formed in 1911, which aimed to 'promote understanding and co-operation between Commonwealth parliaments'. The venerable political institution, Chatham House, sought to encourage branches throughout the Commonwealth for 'the scientific study of international politics', Desai was told.

At a quarter past three on Friday, 28 June 1968, Desai was met by a Miss V. Evans-Walker of the Central Office of Information, who accompanied him on a drive to Stratford-upon-Avon, made famous by Shakespeare and the 'ever-widening appreciation of his genius', as Desai was told. After an evening performance of *Dr Faustus* by Christopher Marlow at the Royal Shakespeare Company, Desai was conveyed to Oxford, where the following evening he enjoyed a *son et lumière* display at Christ Church College. Desai was from here taken to Newcastle and Edinburgh, and then back again to London, where, before his departure, he would see Bush House, headquarters of the recently renamed BBC World Service.

Desai was told that this branch of the BBC was 'intended to provide a link of information' between 'the people of Britain and those in other parts of the world', in order to 'reflect British opinion and the British way of life'.[104] It is unclear what effect, if any, these considered efforts had on Desai.

Net losses in British migration flows – that is, more people leaving Britain (emigrating) than coming in (immigrating) – were a consistent feature of the decades of the twentieth century up to 1983. Among British nationals, however, this net loss has continued. Between 1966 and 2005, the average net loss amounts to some 67,500 British nationals per year; this means that every year, the pace at which people with British national- ity have left Britain has outstripped those with British nationality coming into Britain by almost 70,000. A 2005 study concluded: 'there are more Britons living abroad than there are foreigners living in the UK'.[105] If we choose to include those around the world who identify as British in terms of their ancestry, the figures only rise. The 2005 study identified a clear imperial pattern in the places of residence of British immigrants, citing the following countries in descending order: Australia, Canada, Ireland, New Zealand, South Africa, Cyprus, Pakistan, Singapore, India, Kenya, Nigeria, Malawi, Ghana, Uganda. The only global diasporas that can match this geographical diversity are probably the Chinese and Indian diasporas.

Changes in the British empire were intimately connected to the evo- lution of imperial migration. Anglo-Saxon immigration had made it a 'British Commonwealth of Nations', and the presence of immigrant South Asians in certain colonies had made it an empire that included 'plural societies', stimulating British imperial theories of how to manage what were seen as fundamental racial or developmental differences. Having considered this story, we can turn now to the history of post-war immi- gration in Britain itself.

2

Beyond Windrush: A Short History of Post-War Immigration (1945–1962)

Britain is famous, or infamous, for not having a written constitution. Instead it has constitutional conventions. Walter Bagehot wrote in 1867 that the 'English constitution' was divided into two parts: the dignified and the efficient. At the pinnacle of the dignified part was the British monarch, and at the core of the efficient part was parliament. The synergy of these equal parts made for a successful constitution, but their roles were different. The dignified part was to inspire awe and devotion in the population; the efficient part was to do the work of enacting the rules of government.[1]

Queen Elizabeth II assumed the throne at the age of twenty-five, in 1953. The news of her father's death – and her approaching coronation – came during a visit to a game reserve on Kenya's Central Highlands. Ushering in the first British monarch to be styled 'Head of the Commonwealth' – notwithstanding the membership of republican India – Elizabeth II's coronation in June 1953 was a fulsome pageant of colonial life. On television and radio, the BBC aired a calypso song by the Trinidadian singer Young Tiger, whose real name was George Browne. African-Caribbean calypso had been popular in London for several decades. Browne had composed the song specifically for the coronation, hoping to sell copies as a souvenir item on the day.[2] His lyrics deftly anticipated the scale and emotion of the celebration:

> Troops from Dominions and Colonies,
> Australia, New Zealand, and West Indies,
> India, Ceylon, West Africa
> Newfoundland, Gibraltar, and Canada.
> They were there
> At the Coronation,
> I was there
> At the Coronation.

In her first Christmas message, broadcast from Auckland, New Zealand, in 1953, the Queen described the Commonwealth as 'an equal partnership of nations and races'. She had just completed a tour that included visits to Jamaica, Tonga and Fiji, and would later visit Australia and Ceylon. This tour had provided an opportunity to see at first hand the 'peoples and countries of the Commonwealth and empire'. The Commonwealth was 'a worldwide fellowship of nations of a type never seen before'. Bearing 'no resemblance to the empires of the past', the Commonwealth was 'an entirely new conception' that was 'moving steadily towards greater harmony between its many creeds, colours and races'. Despite any imperfections, it was 'the most effective and progressive association of peoples which history has yet seen'. Referring to the independent Commonwealth states, she described Britain as 'an equal partner with many other proud and independent nations'. Referring to Britain's colonies, she reassured listeners that Britain was 'leading yet other still backward territories forward to the same goal'. The crown, the seal of both Commonwealth and empire, was not a mere cypher, but 'a personal and living bond between you and me'.[3]

This royal message was one of imperial intimacy and faithfulness. In a modified vision, both Labour and Conservative post-war governments presented the Commonwealth as a fellowship of peace. The Commonwealth's status as a 'third force' in the Cold War was, prime minister Clement Attlee declared, 'recognised as such by foreign countries, in particular by the United States and Soviet Union'.[4] The Labour Party's *European Unity* manifesto in 1950 asserted:

> Britain is not just a small crowded island off the Western coast of Continental Europe. She is the nerve centre of a world-wide Commonwealth which extends into every continent. In every respect except distance

we in Britain are closer to our kinsmen in Australia and New Zealand
on the far side of the world, than we are to Europe.[5]

This was a bipartisan sentiment. The 1955 Conservative government
boasted in its manifesto that the 'British Commonwealth and Empire is
the greatest force for peace and progress in the world today'. It represented
nothing less than 'the most fascinating and successful experiment in government and in international relations ever known'.[6] But away from these
idealistic visions of the Commonwealth empire, a not unrelated event at
the level of British citizenship would – unbeknownst to the Queen or to
British politicians – transform British society in very real ways.

This momentous event was the passing of the British Nationality Act
in 1948. Without it, post-war immigration to Britain would never have
occurred in the same way or in such numbers. The *New York Times* –
under the headline, 'British Empire Gets New Nationality Act' – declared
that a 'sweeping legislative measure' had formalised British citizenship
into several categories, many of which would enjoy 'equal rights and
privileges in the United Kingdom'.[7]

The 1948 Act converted the status of all those who had previously been
British subjects into the new status of 'citizen of the United Kingdom and
Colonies', often referred to by politicians simply as 'British citizenship'.
British citizens after 1948 – 'citizens of the United Kingdom and Colonies' – acquired their status principally through birth either in Britain
itself or in a British colony. A person born in Britain and a person born in
a British colony had an identical citizenship, and the same right to move
to and live in Britain, including political rights such as the right to vote,
and the right to hold public office or work in the public sector.

The 1948 Act also recognised a citizen of a newly independent Commonwealth country as a British subject (British subjecthood being
retained within the new scheme). At the time, the independent Commonwealth countries were Canada, Australia, New Zealand, the Union
of South Africa, Newfoundland (soon to incorporate with Canada),
India, Pakistan and Ceylon, as well as the sui generis Southern Rhodesia (a colony, but under self-government). 'Commonwealth citizen' was
declared in the 1948 Act to be a synonym for 'British subject'.

Confusingly – but helpfully for the purposes of imperial unity – the
new concept of 'Commonwealth citizen' was also a constitutional term
referring simultaneously to both British citizens (citizens of the United

Kingdom and Colonies) and citizens of the newly independent Commonwealth countries. In this sense, the 1948 Act took the idea of the Commonwealth and used it as the underlying foundation of British nationality, despite the fact that independent Commonwealth states had their own independent legislatures. Citizens of independent Commonwealth countries held a type of British nationality in the sense they were not aliens under British nationality law, and carried near-equal rights to those of British citizens to enter and reside in Britain.

If, for example, you were an Indian or Canadian citizen, your status in the eyes of British law was nonetheless as a non-alien Commonwealth citizen within British nationality in a wider imperial sense. Equally, a British citizen, a 'citizen of the United Kingdom and Colonies', was in a wider imperial sense a 'Commonwealth citizen' attached to the Commonwealth empire. This conceptual recognition of Commonwealth citizenship occurred despite the fact that the British parliament could not legislate in independent Commonwealth states. Each independent member-state in the Commonwealth had (or would soon have) its own respective citizenship laws, and was itself free to choose to recognise Commonwealth citizens (or British subjects, if you prefer) only as subsidiary to its own citizenship. The 1948 Act, in other words, applied directly only to Britain and its colonies still under direct imperial rule, despite its claim of an even broader imperial scheme. The various citizenship regimes of independent Commonwealth states were supposed to be linked and reciprocal, but Britain would have no way of enforcing this principle.[8]

Although discrete, the two primary statuses invoked in the 1948 Act – citizenship of the United Kingdom and Colonies, and citizenship of an independent Commonwealth country – were interactive: a holder of the latter could register to achieve the former after a twelve-month period of residency in Britain. Only British Protected Persons – those born in protectorates or protected states, or other nominally foreign territories administered under British 'protection' – did not have full rights of entry into Britain. In this sense, the continuing existence of the status of British Protected Person gave the lie to the 1948 Act's inclusive conception of citizenship. A very large number of people within the British empire, living in territories that had not been designated as 'colonies' under direct rule from London but as 'protectorates', were excluded from the new citizenship framework. Although they were governed within the Commonwealth empire, they were never 'Commonwealth citizens'.

This may all seem very complex – it is. But, most importantly for the story of post-war immigration in Britain, the 1948 Act confirmed inclusive rights of entry into Britain to people in British colonies and independent Commonwealth states (and also Irish citizens, who had a separate status within British nationality having left the Commonwealth). The radically lesser status of British Protected Person was ironically acknowledged by Nigerian novelist Chinua Achebe in the title of his memoir, *Education of a British-Protected Child*.

British nationality law was also – as it would continue to be until 1981 – an obvious instance of gender discrimination: nationality was passed through the father, but not through the matrilineal line. But the 1948 Act did remedy the egregious gender discrimination whereby, before 1948, a woman's nationality was tied directly to that of her husband, and a woman who married an alien lost her British nationality.

The 1948 Act was unusual in that it went against the trend of the post-1945 world towards national citizenship models in which membership was defined in more bounded ways (ethnicity, territory) around an imagined nation-state. Britain was in fact retaining old ideas of subject-hood and allegiance, in other words, but presenting them as citizenship. This was a trend towards non-alienage, when states more generally, including Commonwealth member-states, were moving towards alien-age: defining non-nationals in law. Britain was waiving its sovereign prerogative to consider peoples in independent Commonwealth states as aliens. Huge numbers of non-white peoples were in 1948 reconfirmed in statute as non-aliens in British nationality law, and were in principle free from any controls on their movement into Britain.[9]

One historian estimates that the 1948 Act granted no less than 600 million persons across the globe full rights to move to and live in Britain – roughly nine times today's British population.[10] The 1948 Act was explosive – one of the more astonishing pieces of legislation ever passed by a British parliament. It gave identical citizenship and entry rights into Britain both to white Anglo-Saxons born in England and those born in one of forty-seven territories designated as 'colonies' around the world. Whatever your race – whether you were born in Sarawak or Penang, British Honduras or British Guiana, Ashanti or Aden Colony, Hong Kong or Montserrat, Gold Coast Colony or Gambia Colony, St Lucia or Basutoland – you now had the same citizenship rights as white people born in England under a single citizenship. Each person born in these territories was to become a 'citizen of the United Kingdom and Colonies'.[11]

But politicians in Clement Attlee's Labour government had little sense of the 1948 Act's implications for immigration. Britain's politicians saw the Act simply as the latest exercise in constitutional practice, avoiding imperial dissonance and regularising the Commonwealth empire. It also allowed for a flexing of the muscles of imperial paternalism. James Chuter Ede, Attlee's home secretary who presided over the adoption of the Act, tentatively assured the House of Commons as to its good sense:

> Some people feel it would be a bad thing to give the coloured races of the Empire the idea that, in some way or other, they are the equals of people in this country. The government do not subscribe to that view … We recognise the right of the colonial peoples to be regarded as men and brothers of the people in this country.[12]

But the more he spoke, the more Ede's paternalistic language looked to the past rather than the future. He referred not to future possibilities of immigration into Britain, but to John Bunyan's seventeenth-century protestant epic *The Pilgrim's Progress*, which had argued that the only true citizenship lay in heaven, and to classical ideas of imperial Roman citizenship. The three references to immigration during the debate all imply that it was more a concern for the white-settler Commonwealth states than something meaningful for Britain.

Ede also made clear that, although the Act renamed a British subject a 'citizen', this was not meant to suggest 'a person belonging to Great Britain'. Rather, a non-white citizen, their rights notwithstanding, was to be seen simply as a person who 'owes allegiance to the King' in continuity with the traditional definition of subjecthood before 1948. The new language of the Act was simply a concessionary change in nomenclature, a salve to India, Pakistan and Ceylon, now 'dominions' in the Commonwealth empire: 'the word "subject" unfortunately has the significance of being a member of a subject race', Ede explained.[13]

John Grigg, an aristocrat, contrarian and Liberal MP whose father had been a colonial governor in Kenya, asked his Labour colleagues for clarification as to whether people in the colonies were subjects or citizens under the new Act – reflecting an ongoing confusion about the terms that persists to this day. 'They are British subjects and British citizens', came the reply. William Jowitt, the lord chancellor – acknowledging an apparent contradiction between past and present – suggested that the Act's all-pervading character was, 'if you like, rather mystical', but remarked: 'none of us, I suggest, is any the worse for a little mysticism in our life'.[14]

Grigg, known for his candour, declared that the Act's concept of citizenship was 'in many ways a sham, because the Dominions immigration laws, whatever we may say, will assuredly continue to differentiate in practice between different types of the United Kingdom citizens, however much we may assert that they are, whatever their origin, on a par'. A more honest way of conceiving post-war citizenship, Grigg suggested, was to create a 'national citizenship' based on 'blood and soil' for 'the people of this Island'. But this would not occur until 1981. The politician and novelist John Buchan noted wryly that it was now 'possible for a Dyak head-hunter from Sarawak to land in this country and become chairman of the National Coal Board'.[15]

What had triggered the 1948 Act? Almost immediately after the end of the Second World War, Canada had notified Britain that it planned to pass a law defining Canadian citizenship – this was a *fait accompli*, not a request for permission. From the perspective of the Canadian government, this would promote national unity in Canada by further helping to define Canadian nationhood, and would provide other benefits like immediate control of its passport regime. Canada's action summoned the spectre of imperial dissolution, and in 1948 Britain had yet again tried to impose unity by way of a system of imperial citizenship.

One point bears repeating a final time: in no way was the 1948 Act a move towards a post-imperial Britain. It was the latest iteration of what Winston Churchill, as home secretary, had summarised in 1911: 'Imperial nationality should be worldwide and uniform, each Dominion being free to grant local nationality'.[16] But how meaningful was this unity when, after all, independent Commonwealth states were free to pass their own citizenship laws unilaterally? The 1948 Act meant that unity was at least retained at the level of nomenclature. The term 'Commonwealth citizen', a synonym for British subject, had been wrapped around the discrete citizenships of the Commonwealth, preserving an imperial reach. All peoples in the Commonwealth empire 'have in common the privileges of British nationality', as a senior British civil servant argued in 1961 – failing to recognise the lesser position of British Protected Persons.[17]

Post-War 'Coloured Immigration'

The Second World War saw not only large numbers of South Asians, African-Caribbean people and West Africans serve in the British army, navy and air force, but also the direct recruitment of colonial labour into Britain to serve in munitions factories, as well as other areas of defence. This included an estimated 1,200 labourers from British Honduras (later Belize) who were sent to various parts of Scotland to fell much-needed timber. After this forestry unit was disbanded in 1943, some labourers rejected the terms of repatriation (nearly always encouraged for non-white personnel who had served the war effort) and chose to remain in Britain. One of these British Honduras labourers was Sam Martinez, who died in Edinburgh in 2016 at the age of 106. In an interview about his migration before his death, he remarked: 'The war started and we, being Britishers, were asked to come to do forestry work'.[18]

Many of those on the SS *Almanzora* and the more famous *Empire Windrush*, which sailed from Jamaica in 1947 and 1948 respectively, had either served with British forces or worked in munitions factories.[19] Clement Attlee's Labour government was taken by surprise by these arrivals of migrants. Before the *Windrush* migrants had even touched shore at Tilbury Docks on 22 June 1948, colonial secretary Arthur Creech Jones provided a memorandum to the cabinet warning of their arrival. 'It will be appreciated', wrote Creech Jones, 'that the men concerned are all British subjects.' The colonial government of Jamaica thus had 'no legal power to prevent their departure', and the British government had 'no legal power to prevent their landing'. Acknowledging that an estimated 'two-thirds are ex-servicemen', Creech Jones explained that they appeared to have 'saved up enough money to pay for their own passages to England, on the chance of finding employment'. This was disappointing, since 'every possible step has been taken by the Colonial Office and by the Jamaica Government to discourage these influxes'.[20]

Despite this unambiguous political rejection of the *Windrush* migrants, future migrants were able to exercise equivalent rights of entry and residence codified in the 1948 British Nationality Act. The *Windrush* also held a small number of stowaways, some of whom, one *Windrush* passenger later claimed, 'jumped from the ship into the water and started swimming ashore' as the boat neared Tilbury at the mouth of the river Thames.[21]

It is one of the more commonly disseminated half-truths that post-war immigration into Britain was driven by a state-led desire to offset labour shortages. Although Britain did contemplate recruiting labour from the Caribbean after the war, direct recruitment from the Caribbean was on a small scale and focused on Barbados. Large-scale recruitment was rejected in favour of selecting Europeans (both men and women) to fill sectoral labour shortages. Despite Britain's crushing need for skilled and semi-skilled labour after the war – a shortage estimated at between 600,000 and 1.3 million workers by British officials in 1946 – Attlee's government rejected the recruitment of British citizens from among African-Caribbean communities for work and permanent residence in Britain, despite the small existing African-Caribbean community in Britain that had just contributed to the war effort.[22]

Instead, various labour schemes were set up over a ten-year period to recruit European aliens for work in areas such as agriculture, mining, construction, health services and institutional domestic service. In the first instance, in 1947, these European aliens were some 130,000 former members of the Polish armed forces (some of whom had been prisoners-of-war in the Soviet Union) to whom British nationality was extended. In addition, various European populations displaced by the Second World War were combed for worthy economic migrants – so-called 'European volunteer workers' – by the British government, and recruited by way of discrete labour schemes. These included Bulgarians, Estonians, Latvians, Lithuanians, Poles, Romanians, Ukrainians, Czechoslovakians and a number of Sudeten women. Also recruited were German, Italian and Ukrainian prisoners-of-war, and single women from Italy, Austria and Germany.

Labour recruitment schemes were tied to particular industries and jobs, including everything from coalmining, clay-pit labour, steelwork, railway construction and stone quarrying to nursing, textile work and domestic service. The traditional estimate of the total number of European aliens given settlement and nationality in Britain on the basis of their economic utility in the first post-war years is 215,000 (a more recent estimate puts this total figure at 345,000). Astonishingly, European Jews were excluded from each of these recruitment schemes on the basis that their inclusion would arouse public opposition. Only 80,000 European Jews were permitted entry into Britain (not necessarily permanent settlement) between 1933 and 1939, of whom some 40,000 settled after 1940.[23]

There is also the question of the extent to which these Europeans were intended to replenish British racial 'stock'. During a parliamentary debate on plans to take in numbers of European 'displaced persons' into Britain in 1947, Martin Lindsey, a Conservative MP who had served in colonial Nigeria with the Royal Scots Fusiliers, picked up the old theme of racial decline. The war had left Britain with a falling birth rate and 'no fewer than 200,000 numerically surplus women'. Given this context, there were, Lindsey declared, 'the strongest possible ethnographical reasons for having an infusion of vigorous new blood from overseas at the present time'. Compounding the problem was the sustained loss of young white men to white-settler Commonwealth countries:

> In addition men are going overseas every day to emigrate to the sunny lands they visited in the course of the war. It would, of course, be a most terrible thing if we ever had to do anything to discourage emigration to our own Empire, but I do not believe we can afford the loss of this vigorous young blood of our nation unless we replace it by something comparable.[24]

In other words, European workers – explicitly identified as 'ideal emigrants' and a 'white population' by other members of parliament – might be used to replace those white British men leaving for imperial destinations. As non-white immigration of largely British citizens increased in the 1950s, state-sponsored emigration schemes were sometimes compared against increases in 'coloured immigration' – a balance sheet, as it were, of white and non-white people flowing in and out of Britain. In 1948 George Isaacs, Attlee's minister of labour, acknowledged the contribution of the European aliens-turned-nationals, assuring the House of Commons that their residence in Britain was 'of a permanent character'. 'These people come here, working their passage to British citizenship', declared Isaacs.[25]

Myths of Arrival

Despite the state-sponsored schemes to secure European workers, the labour shortage remained. But successive British governments did not attempt large-scale recruitment of non-white labour from the colonies or Commonwealth. British officials perceived colonial labour to be unskilled by definition, and accordingly non-white workers (particularly African-Caribbean people from the West Indies) were earmarked during the 1950s for employment in public transport, health-service delivery, the textile industry and metal manufacturing. Needless to say, this perception ignored the fact that a large percentage of migrants from the Caribbean were skilled.[26] With full right of entry as British or Commonwealth citizens, non-white migrants, particularly British citizens from the Caribbean, began to pass freely into the country, while British officials struggled to compile accurate figures on their entry.

The migrant's moment of arrival into Britain is often mythologised as an experience of shock. We are urged to recall the migrant's long journey from a warm place by ship to England, where she meets for the first time a cold northern wind and English flora such as holly, blackthorn and box. And thence she travels across English soil to London, and an inevitable memory of a great Victorian London lit in the soft orange of gaslights. Such mythologies of arrival should be resisted, diminishing as they do the centuries of non-white migrant settlement before 1945, albeit in small numbers. Moreover, Britain's civilisational claims were hardly unknown to its post-war non-white migrants.

Students from British colonies and Commonwealth states (mostly men) migrated to Britain in order to study at prized institutions of higher education; over 10,000 such students had arrived by the mid 1950s.[27] Adil Jussawalla, born in British-ruled India and a migrant to Britain in 1957, recalled being a fully Anglicised subject growing up in Bombay. His eventual migration to Britain was simply a 'logical end' to a colonial education that had laid 'greater stress on Lancashire cotton-industries, the Elizabethans, the Corn Laws, than on anything the Indian peoples had achieved in the past, or were likely to do in the future', he wrote. Sillaty Dabo, born in Sierra Leone Colony and Protectorate, migrated to England to pursue postgraduate work at Oxford, having studied at the Sorbonne in the 1950s. He recalled his introduction to the peculiarities of English racism:

It is not uncommon to meet children walking with their parents on the street, and who, on seeing an African, point to him or her saying, 'Mum (or Daddy) look at that Blackman', or, very rarely 'N——r' [*author's elision*]. Quite often the parent feels embarrassed, draws the child away with such statements as 'Don't be rude to the gentlemen (or lady)'.[28]

The enigma of arrival was a racial reawakening for some white British people, not for the migrants who had travelled from colonised places. Another such migrant was Chikwenda Nwariaku, who was born in colonial Nigeria in 1929 and travelled to England to study civil engineering in the north of England. Nwariaku had grown up drinking Ovaltine and eating Quaker Oats, and at school had been taught by 'Englishmen, Scots, and Irishmen'. His early experiences in England left him wondering at the meaning of a white bus conductor in Newcastle who desired 'confirmation that the black hair was really soft and woolly'. Was this man treating a 'grown-up like a child because he was dark and therefore must be mentally young'? Patricia Madoo, born in Trinidad in 1940, migrated to England to study history at Oxford. She gave a telling summary of the 1950s racial imagination: '[T]he Indian is a strange, rather frightening creature … The African is alien and exotic, very much nearer the primitive than he is.' Ironically, Madoo claimed, 'light-coloured' West Indians were likely to share exactly the same prejudices as whites – although based on class, not on 'antipathy to blackness'.[29]

One particularly confident upper-middle-class migrant was the poet Dom Moraes. Born in 1938 in Bombay to a Goan Christian family, Moraes had left India for England by ship at the age of sixteen, and during the journey had read books 'designed to inform me about England'. These were books of pastoral verse in which he learned about 'badgers, flowers, and village life'.[30] Upon landing at Tilbury Docks he noticed the 'scrubby flat coast of Essex', and on the train to London's St Pancras station, Moraes saw 'vista upon vista of ugly prefabricated houses, laundry flapping sadly in the backyards'. Noticing 'pale and scruffy' people in these houses, he describes feeling 'a slight shock, I hadn't realised there were poor people in England'. On his very first evening in London, he claims to have dined at the Ritz with an Indian journalist and kissed an English woman. At Oxford, Moraes was soon befriended by fellow poets W. H. Auden and Stephen Spender. He claimed that, during a meeting with the novelist Raymond Chandler in London, Chandler had burst out 'Nehru's a fool … He's selling out to the Communists everywhere.'[31]

Claudia Jones migrated to Britain in very different circumstances. Born in 1915 in Port-of-Spain, in the colony of Trinidad and Tobago, Jones had originally migrated to New York City in 1924. After she had become politically active, her application for US citizenship was refused and she was deported in 1955, electing to travel to Britain as opposed to returning to colonial Trinidad. Aboard the *Queen Elizabeth* passenger ship, Jones wrote a diary entry to mark her passage on 'the high seas for England'. Having lived in Harlem, Jones took note of the ship's odd cuisine: 'We went to dinner at seven to eat English lamb roast, mint juice or sauce, iced pineapple, salad and a fat baked potato'. What would England be like?, she wondered. 'Tomorrow – the first morning of my exile for my independent political ideas – we will see its beauty at dawn', wrote Jones.

Jones was one of the most outspoken political activists of her generation, declaring in an interview with the *Caribbean News* in London the following year: 'I was deported from the USA because as a Negro woman Communist of West Indian descent, I was a thorn in their side in my opposition to Jim Crow racist discrimination.' She condemned the American law under which she had been deported (the 1952 McCarran-Walter Immigration Act) as encouraging 'immigration of fascist scum from Europe' into the United States at the expense of 'West Indian immigration'. Settling in London, Jones launched the *West Indian Gazette* in 1958, later renamed the *West Indian Gazette and Afro-Asian Caribbean News*. Based in an office above a record shop in Brixton, south London, the publication garnered a circulation of some 15,000, and supported important local community ventures – most significantly a Caribbean carnival.[32] Jones would become an important voice on the significance of what she termed the 'Caribbean community' in Britain.

Many migrants recorded their arrivals in terms of an encounter with the British class system, noting the ways in which lower class status could inhibit the privileges of whiteness. Syed Ali Baquer, born in India in 1937, recalled one such encounter:

> My next job was as a porter at the local teaching hospital. I worked there for nearly twelve months in various departments and had the opportunity of studying the hierarchy of hospital administration. Porters were not treated as Whites or Blacks. They were just porters. Any attempt to cross intangible frontiers was disapproved … Most of us willingly put up with the work, the coloured ones especially avoiding conflict by making fewer demands.[33]

Another anonymous migrant from the West Indies described this race–class dynamic in yet more immediate terms:

> After a tiring two weeks at sea and a five-hour train ride in from Plymouth one awakes to the scurryings of white porters who not only seem eager to carry one's bags – but are extremely deferential. Little do the porters know what an impact they make on coloured immigrants. The average non-student immigrant will perhaps not have been addressed as 'Sir' very often in his life. And he will most certainly not have seen so many white men doing this type of work before.[34]

The fuller dimensions of this race–class encounter, and of the social and economic background of such migrants, are beyond the scope of this book; but we can acknowledge the progressively more virulent response of sections of the white British population to the presence of African-Caribbean students and workers during the 1950s.

By the mid 1950s, the phrase 'coloured immigration' had taken hold among British political elites as a synonym for social unrest and a matter demanding legislative action. The new prime minister, Winston Churchill (now eighty years old and in office for a second time), was privately warned by a Conservative colleague in 1954 of 'an explosion in Brixton' if the 'arrival of immigrants from the West Indies' was allowed to continue. In reply, Churchill is said to have remarked gravely, 'I think it is the most important subject facing this country.'[35]

That same year, Churchill privately expressed to colleagues his continued misgivings about 'coloured immigration', having read in the *Daily Telegraph* that the Jamaican minister of labour had told local journalists that his government would make no efforts to restrict migration from Jamaica, since employment was easier to find in Britain.[36] Churchill's concern, and the various indecisive cabinet debates on 'coloured immigration' in the mid 1950s, seem disproportionate given that the non-white population of Britain stood at less than 100,000 by the end of 1955.

As the 1950s wore on, declarations that immigration now represented a national social crisis began to increase. In the House of Commons, John Hynd, a Labour MP born in Perth, Scotland, spoke of 'these coloured colonial immigrants pouring into the country every year', who came without 'any prospects of work, of housing accommodation or anything else'. In his view, the whole of the Caribbean, Africa and Pakistan, among other places, were wellsprings of socially deleterious immigrants intent on entering Britain. 'I have met some stupid Jamaicans', Hynd remarked, by way of explanation of his position. Henry Hopkinson, the then minister of state at the Colonial Office, disagreed, offering a classic statement of imperial largesse:

> As the law stands, any British subject from the Colonies is free to enter this country at any time as long as he can produce satisfactory evidence of his British status. That is not something we want to tamper with lightly. In a world in which restrictions on personal movement and immigration have increased we still take pride in the fact that a man can say *Civis Britannicus sum* whatever his colour may be, and we take pride in the fact that he wants and can come to the Mother country.[37]

Two years before, Eton-educated Hopkinson had been in central Africa promoting federation as a means to sustain white-minority rule in Southern Rhodesia, Northern Rhodesia and Nyasaland. He had caused a stir a few months previously by stating publicly that Cyprus should never expect to gain freedom from British rule (which it did in 1960). In later years, Hopkinson would oppose decolonisation in both the British and Portuguese empires.

British Nationality: Imperial Blessing or Domestic Curse?

The British Nationality Act of 1948 had created an insuperable problem for British politicians: 'coloured immigrants' were often fully fledged citizens or Commonwealth citizens, many of whom were willing and able to migrate to Britain despite the huge costs involved. In a September 1955 cabinet memorandum, Commonwealth relations secretary Alec Douglas-Home identified a problem with any future law attempting to block these non-white migrants from entry into Britain. 'On the one hand it would presumably be impossible to legislate for a "colour bar" and any legislation would have to be non-discriminatory in form', he wrote to cabinet colleagues. 'On the other hand', he continued, 'we do not wish to keep out immigrants of good type from the "old" dominions'.[38]

Nevertheless, Britain was edging closer to introducing legislation designed to block non-white migration of British and Commonwealth citizens. The irony was not lost on the preceding Commonwealth relations secretary, Philip Cunliffe-Lister, who wrote to colleagues that Britain was being pushed towards 'the more or less open discrimination practised in the "old" [white] Commonwealth countries'.[39] Britain was now being projected as a fragile, embattled domestic space – not unlike the old white-settler colonies of New South Wales, British Columbia and Natal, and the current African colonies with white-settler populations such as Kenya and Southern Rhodesia, that had garnered Conservative Party sympathy.

In the event, British politicians in the 1950s stopped short of passing immigration legislation, and instead pursued administrative means of preventing further migrations. Until the late 1950s, the Commonwealth Relations Office had successfully limited the numbers of South Asian migrants to Britain by asking the governments of India and Pakistan to withhold the issuing of passports to South Asians wishing to migrate to Britain by means of a range of financial and educational restrictions. This was a covert means of outsourcing the control of South Asian migration to the governments of India and Pakistan. The Indian state had long seen emigration as a privilege, not a right, and agreed to cooperate.[40] The Commonwealth Relations Office pursued similar administrative devices for checking migration from West Africa by collaborating with the colonial governments of Nigeria and the Gold Coast.[41] Colonial governments in the Caribbean, however – exercising the measure of self-government they enjoyed – did not cooperate in this administrative scheme to block non-white British citizens from migrating to Britain. The largest numbers of non-white migrants in the 1950s were African-Caribbean people from the West Indies.

One of the most interesting early studies of immigrant life – or, more precisely, of the lives of non-white British and Commonwealth citizens – was by a Gujarati anthropologist named Rashmi Desai. In his book *Indian Immigrants in Britain*, Desai gave a portrait of what he described as a 'typical immigrant household', based on an actual household he had come to know in 1956. A large terraced house just outside a 'working-class district' of Birmingham was owned by two Gujaratis – an uncle and nephew. Their tenants included a 'West Indian with his common law wife, an Irish woman', the Irish woman's sister, and a Punjabi. Each of them, including the Gujaratis, worked as bus conductors, and had originally met as co-workers. There were in all twelve adults and one child living in the house. The Punjabi used a gas ring in his own room for cooking. The houses on their street were owned by Irish, Indian and African-Caribbean people, and a 'Jewish landlady who took Asian (but not African) students as lodgers'. The nephew soon returned to India to get married. Eventually others moved on and were replaced by new African-Caribbean and Gujarati occupants, who also worked in public transport.[42]

The 'typical immigrant' at this time was portrayed as a young, single man from the Caribbean. This was a simplification of the diversity (whether in terms of religion, gender or class) to be found in Britain's non-white population, most of whom were British citizens. Representative areas of work for new migrants in Britain included car and metal factories in the West Midlands (Birmingham and Wolverhampton), textile mills in West Yorkshire (Bradford) and factory and service-sector employment in London. Many African-Caribbean women worked as nurses or in other areas of hospital delivery in the National Health Service.

As Claudia Jones wrote in the early 1960s, in one of the first accounts of African-Caribbean life in Britain by a member of the community, West Indians had been sought out by post-war Britain for their 'cheap labour', and the 'West Indian contribution' to the British economy was 'undoubted'. West Indians had become part of the economic life of the country in crucial ways, as 'building workers, carpenters, as nurses, doctors and hospital staffs, in factories, on the transportation system and railway depots and stations', wrote Jones.[43] Women from the Caribbean also migrated independently or with family members to study or work in their own right. Unaffected by future immigration laws, the right to bring dependants – the right to family reunification, in other words – led many more non-white women who were British or Commonwealth citizens to migrate to Britain.

Ten years after the passage of the 1948 Act, the city of Nottingham and west London's Notting Hill saw episodes of racist violence during the months of August and September. On 1 September 1958, a West African student named Seymour Manning was visiting London from his home in Derby. Emerging from the London Underground at Latimer Road station in Notting Hill in the mid-afternoon, Manning was on his way to visit a friend who lived nearby when he was chased by 'marauding white gangs', as the *New York Times* would report. Following violence the previous weekend, a large group of young white men had gathered by the railway arches near Latimer Road station, some of whom were armed with sticks, knives and iron bars (the police later confiscated a butcher's cleaver, a bicycle chain and an open razor).

The fact that Manning was West African and not from Notting Hill's resident African-Caribbean community was lost on a section of the group of white men, who chased the twenty-six-year-old Manning down Bramley Road. Eyewitnesses overheard shouts of 'lynch him' and 'down with the n——rs [*author's elision*]', as Manning was briefly physically assaulted before taking refuge in a grocery shop whose owner – a woman named Pat Howcroft – gave him shelter. One of the young men chasing Manning later confided to a journalist from the *Manchester Guardian*: 'We'd have tore 'im apart if it hadn't been for the police'.

Meanwhile, as Manning waited in safety, the larger group of white men descended on Bramley Road and its surrounding streets later that evening, together with 'teddy boys' from local pubs. According to conflicting reports, between 200 and 1,000 'white and coloured people' subsequently clashed together and with police, amid the throwing of broken bottles and a chorus of racist slurs. This was a Monday evening, the violence having started on the previous Friday evening and peaking on Sunday evening. The violence continued on Tuesday, when 'rioters stormed through the neighbourhood's shabby streets attacking Negros and destroying their property', as the *New York Times* put it.[44]

These so-called race riots led to a flurry of media attention. The *Economist* reported that the new view of the British civil service was that 'the liberal line – uncontrolled immigration – can be held for a few more years, but not indefinitely'.[45] In a comment that would become a consistent refrain throughout the 1960s, the Commonwealth Migrants Committee stressed to the cabinet in May 1961 that anti-immigration legislation was necessary 'if we were not to have a colour problem in this country on a similar scale to that in the USA'.[46]

In reality, the violence in 1958 was not new, and might be seen alongside racist violence in Cardiff in 1916 against 'coloured seamen', and anti-'Asiatic' riots in Vancouver in September 1907. Adil Jussawalla wrote of his frustration that, despite the non-white population in Britain being at 'a ludicrous one per cent', racial discrimination was 'open, violent and bloody'. The events in Notting Hill in 1958 were merely 'a symptom of unrecorded currents of violence running through Britain's bigger cities', he wrote.[47] Until white British people went through some kind of 'collective emotional crisis', reflected Jussawalla, their resentment would remain unchecked.

By the end of the 1950s, one study estimated that the total number of non-white people living in Britain was 210,000, including 115,000 West Indians, 25,000 West Africans, 55,000 Indians and Pakistanis, and 15,000 from other territories. Around 70,000 Cypriots also migrated to Britain during this period.[48] From 1958 onwards, the numbers of South Asians migrating to Britain began to rise exponentially. The British and Indian governments were confused by this rise in South Asian migration, since it far outstripped the official numbers of passports endorsed in India and Pakistan for travel to Britain. The internal correspondence of the Home Office began to document its powerlessness over an illicit trade in forged passports. The *Sunday Telegraph*, reporting the trade in forged documents in India and Pakistan, lamented that the passport photographs of bearded Sikh men all looked alike.[49]

British politicians began to draw distinctions between migrants from the Caribbean and those from South Asia by using a prism of employment. The new South Asian arrivals were 'not as readily employable as West Indians', wrote future prime minister Alec Douglas-Home to officials in the diplomatic service. African-Caribbean migrants, Douglas-Home continued, were 'English-speaking, literate, Christian, able-bodied and reasonably capable', whereas South Asians – mostly from Mirpur in Azad Kashmir, Attock and Jhelum in West Pakistan, Sylhet in East Pakistan, and Punjab in India – were 'handicapped by their inability to speak English, by illiteracy and by poor physique, which makes it impossible for them to take normal labouring jobs'.[50] Social fears about the influence of South Asians would only increase in the 1960s, when wives and children travelled to Britain under the right of family dependants to join the young men who had migrated between 1959 and 1962. As the *Economist* noted in 1968, the 'religious-sartorial peculiarities of Sikhs', who fought to wear the turban during employment, had received significant attention.[51]

In an internal report on Pakistanis in Britain, a government researcher named Kath Kazer recorded that Pakistanis were not only in London – where in 'the East End, East Pakistanis have replaced the Jews in the clothing trade' – but had spread across Birmingham and the Midlands, Manchester, Leeds, Newcastle, Glasgow and the 'West Yorkshire conurbation'. They held jobs in textiles, transport, manufacturing industries and in foundries casting metals, particularly in the mills and factories of Bradford, Sheffield and Leeds. Pakistani political organisations were a source of concern. Although some organisations were 'chiefly for welfare and self-help purposes' and were reliably 'moderate', others were decidedly 'subversive', wrote Kazer. The Kashmir Plebiscite Front had been created in the early 1950s, and was 'supported by Kashmiris mainly in South Shields and the North East'. The British branch of the All-Pakistan Women's Association, founded by the economist and First Lady of Pakistan, Ra'ana Liaquat Ali Khan, was, like other 'cultural and social' organisations, being used as a source for 'reservoirs of potential support by left-wing Pakistanis', warned Kazer.[52]

Dom Moraes, the upper-middle-class, Bombay-born Goan Christian who had settled in Britain, wrote with piquant social and class awareness about the rise in South Asian arrivals. Although a 'small Asian professional class' of doctors, lawyers and accountants had established itself in Britain, the 'bulk of immigrants from Asia are poor', he wrote in the 1960s. His description of Bradford has the same haunted urgency found in the writings of many white British commentators arguing against non-white immigration:

Bradford in Yorkshire is perhaps the least attractive town in England. Its ghoulish brick terraces, cowled with smoke, brood on a hillside. The centre of the town, around the Railway Station, is bleakly neat, but the terraces sprawl away around it, and there the immigrants live. Lumb Lane, a cold snake of a street, is speckled with Pakistani shops. The posters on the chipped walls advertise Urdu films, and there is scarcely a white face to be seen. Pakistanis in ragged overcoats hunch their way down to the factories. Bradford's main product is wool, and a lot of the Pakistanis work as unskilled labour, doing menial tasks. Many, for instance, are employed to wash raw wool, an occupation described to me by an English worker as a job no white man would do.[53]

By the end of the 1950s, non-white British and Commonwealth citizens now settled in Britain began to record the intricate hostilities they faced. Adil Jussawalla summarised the lived realties facing some of the largest constituencies of non-white people in Britain – namely, African-Caribbean people, West Africans and South Asians:

If he is Indian or Pakistani, he is part of that coloured tribe that lives squalidly twelve to a room, because there is no better place for him, and most of the better rooms he applies for are mysteriously taken. If he is a West Indian or an African he will have to put up with a murderous sex-envy, scandals concerning his private life and obscene myths concerning his background.[54]

Another student from a former British colony was Susunaga Weeraperuma, born in Ceylon, who arrived by ship in Southampton in 1960, and soon began studying law at Lincoln's Inn in London. Part of life as a non-white migrant to Britain was a daily rehearsal of slurs. As he wrote in the early 1960s: 'Another glaring example of prejudice occurred when I accidentally trampled the foot of an elderly woman in a London street. My instantaneous apology was ignored and she screamed frantically, "Coloured Indian bastard!"'[55]

As migrant arrivals were reconceived as permanent migrant settlement in Britain, ideas about what Britain had become began to crystallise around 'race relations'. These ideas interacted with Britain's international place in the world and the fate of the empire.[56] Especially after the so-called race riots of 1958, British politicians were primed to take drastic action to stem any further immigration of non-white British or Commonwealth citizens.

3

A Hostile Isle: Post-War Immigration in Britain (1962–1981)

At the beginning of the 1960s the number of non-white British and Commonwealth citizens newly arriving into Britain was rising quickly. Government figures record that in June 1960 the non-white population in Britain (defined in terms of African-Caribbean people from the West Indies, West Africans and South Asians) stood at roughly 250,000 people. In 1961 the number of arrivals exponentially increased, and over the next two years Britain's non-white population would double to some 500,000 people, helped along by migrants spurred to beat the deadline of the Commonwealth Immigrants Act of 1962 coming into effect.[1] Just over half of these 500,000 people were African-Caribbean, subject to pernicious social and institutional prejudice despite being prized for certain kinds of labour.

It should be recognized that the 1963 figure was still below 1 per cent of the overall population of Britain. The presence of non-white British and Commonwealth citizens resident in Britain in relatively large numbers was nevertheless no longer an unfamiliar spectacle, but a new social reality. As the writer and former adviser on colonial administration, Elspeth Huxley, wrote in her ironical social investigation of immigrant life in Britain in the early 1960s, *Back Street New Worlds*, it was not unusual to meet 'a Jamaican bus conductor, a Pakistani factory hand, an Indian shopkeeper, a Cypriot café owner, a Polish toolmaker, a Nigerian nurse, or a Lithuanian wardmaid'.

Huxley reflected a consensus within the Conservative Party when she cast doubt on Britain's 'long tradition of free entry', asking: 'how many immigrants (black, brown, white or yellow) can we in these islands, however much we may need their labour, provide with jobs, houses or rooms, transport, places in schools for their children, and hospital beds?'[2] Now that the major phase of post-war reconstruction was over, it no longer made social or political sense to maintain the traditional rights of entry and residence of British subjects, despite their being recast as 'Commonwealth citizens' in 1948. British officials narrated the end of the centuries-old right of entry to British subjects (now British or Commonwealth citizens) at the beginning of the 1960s in the becalming prose of British officialese. 'By 1962', a government pamphlet prepared for visiting dignitaries declared, 'it had become clear that, given their understandable tendency to live near other people from their home country [non-white immigration] was leading to the formation of concentrated immigrant communities and was producing serious problems of assimilation in certain areas'.[3]

It was on 10 October 1961 that British cabinet ministers made the decision to introduce the first major piece of post-war immigration legislation – what would become the 1962 Commonwealth Immigrants Act – following the conclusion of the government's Commonwealth Migrants Committee that 'too many coloured persons were settling here'. A new immigration law was not ideal, because it would intervene in the constitutional arrangements of the Commonwealth. Any legislation would inevitably affect white Commonwealth citizens in Commonwealth states like Australia and New Zealand, and would inevitably damage political relations with these states. But ultimately the incentives to restrict non-white migration proved too strong for British officials, and the implications for the Commonwealth were less compelling than usual given that Britain was at this same moment making an overture towards Europe, having applied for membership of the European Economic Community in 1961.[4]

The person charged with enacting the first piece of immigration legislation in post-war Britain was Richard (known as 'Rab') Butler, home secretary in Harold Macmillan's Conservative government. Butler was the son of a senior colonial administrator, and had been born in colonial Punjab. His father had been governor of India's Central Provinces, where he faced anticolonial resistance in the 1920s. In 1961, Butler set out to the

House of Commons the impending legislation, using a line of reasoning that would come to redefine British citizenship: 'The objective here is to except from control – and, therefore, to guarantee their continued unrestricted entry into their own country – persons who in common parlance belong to the United Kingdom.'[5]

Butler could speak in this way because all of the political preconditions for such a change were now well established. The inclusivity of the 1948 British Nationality Act had backfired. In the 1950s, non-white migrants – be they citizens of the United Kingdom and Colonies from Jamaica or citizens of Commonwealth states like India and Pakistan – had decided to exercise their rights of entry and residence in large numbers. In terms of its broad effect rather than its specific provisions, the new law had to prevent non-white migration while at the same time preserving the structure of British nationality set out in 1948, acknowledging that migrants with British ancestry from the 'old' Commonwealth (places like Australia) 'belonged' to and in Britain.

The new legislation would not be easy to pass. Butler was suggesting that it had to protect those who 'belonged' and block those who did not 'belong', but without changing the fundamental architecture of the 1948 Act. It would inevitably interfere with the unity of rights traditionally given to British subjects (known as 'Commonwealth citizens' since 1948), and in this sense it presented a radical break with the past. There was also the unity of the Commonwealth to consider. As a cabinet memorandum had explained the conundrum as early as 1955, 'we do not wish to keep out immigrants of good type from the "old" Dominions', yet at the same time it would be 'politically impossible to legislate for a 'colour bar'. Any new immigration law could not be racially explicit, but would need to be ingeniously constructed so as not to draw attention to any division of the Commonwealth by race. 'It would probably be quite easy to discriminate in favour of white members of "old" Commonwealth countries', the 1955 memorandum suggested, but 'what is to be the position about immigrants from the Asian Members of the Commonwealth?'[6]

In 1962, Butler presented the government's solution to this puzzle in the form of a Commonwealth Immigrants Act. It might have been more accurately called a British Subjects Act or a Commonwealth Citizenship Act (the latter referring to the broader sense of 'Commonwealth citizen'), since it affected many with British status, including British citizens born in remaining colonies. But the Commonwealth Immigrants Act of 1962 was presented as affecting principally citizens of Commonwealth states, including those in Jamaica and Trinidad and Tobago who transferred from British to local citizenship upon those countries' independence in 1962.[7] The 1962 Act declared that the only persons with an unfettered right of entry to Britain were those 'born in the United Kingdom' or 'a person who holds a United Kingdom passport' in addition to being a British citizen (a citizen of the United Kingdom and Colonies). For the first time, the right of entry to Britain was being associated with birth in the United Kingdom itself, no longer in tandem with birth in certain overseas British territories.[8]

Drawing on a device used in Australian immigration legislation, the 1962 Act was cleverly designed to use the issuance of passports as a means to control the migration of non-white Commonwealth and British citizens.[9] This was an example of a legal-administrative device that meant that the new immigration law avoided mentioning race explicitly, recalling the so-called Natal Act of 1897, which had introduced a European literacy test. It did not matter if you were a British subject in the primary sense of a British citizen (a citizen of the United Kingdom and Colonies) or if you had gained that status as a citizen of an independent Commonwealth state. If your passport had been produced under the delegated authority of a colony or a Commonwealth state, you now had a different immigration status from those whose passports had been issued under the sovereign authority of Britain. A 'United Kingdom passport' meant a passport produced by a British embassy or high commission, or from within Britain itself, not by a colonial authority or the authority of an independent Commonwealth state.

An African born in Kenya Colony would now be subject to immigration control, but a person born in the British Isles and resident overseas with access to a British embassy would not be subject to such control. On the face of it, a person with ancestral ties to the British Isles born in Australia was subject to the same control as somebody with South Asian ancestry born in India. Yet the wider architecture and enforcement mechanisms attendant on the 1962 Act gave wide discretionary powers to British immigration officials to refuse or admit entry. In practice, white people from the traditional white-settler Commonwealth (Australia, New Zealand, Canada) would generally be allowed in. Entry into Britain for those under immigration control would now involve a voucher or quota system. However, Butler reassured colleagues in a memorandum to his department that, in practice, the 1962 Act would work along racial lines. Although the Act 'purports to relate solely to employment', he wrote, 'its aim is primarily social and its restrictive effect is intended to, and would in fact, operate on coloured people almost exclusively'.[10]

Following the 1962 Act, immigration law rather than nationality law was more determinative of who 'belonged' in Britain and who did not. The 1962 Act was an attempt to ensure minimum interference with the British Nationality Act of 1948 – a shorthand for imperial relations – while also maximising limitations on the entry of non-white British and Commonwealth citizens hoping to migrate to Britain. The traditional imperial inclusiveness of British subjecthood, now expressed as Commonwealth citizenship, was over.[11] Writing in 1964, Trinidad-born Claudia Jones described the 1962 Act as a 'colour-bar' that imposed 'second-class citizenship' on non-white British or Commonwealth citizens born outside Britain. Britain's colour-bar immigration law was pushing against recent trends in world politics, argued Jones, having been passed 'at a time when apartheid and racialism is under attack throughout the world'.[12]

We can also acknowledge that the 1958 British Nationality Act, the 1962 South Africa Act, the 1964 British Nationality Act and the 'Southern Rhodesia (British Nationality Act 1948) Order' in 1965 were similar efforts designed to privilege white settlers overseas with a route to citizenship of the United Kingdom and Colonies that was free from immigration control. There were, for example, many British white settlers in Southern Rhodesia (later Zimbabwe), and officials in the Commonwealth Office were of the opinion that 'we should not go so far as to introduce a visa system or other restrictions' on the entry of British citizens resident in Rhodesia. The white Rhodesians attempting to enter Britain had, after all, 'a real connection with this country'.[13]

Despite the immigration law of 1962, citizens of Commonwealth states were still able to enter Britain, albeit in vastly restricted numbers. Nor had the 1962 Act attempted to restrict in statute the right of spouses and children under sixteen to join their immediate relatives in Britain. In practice, after 1962 the right of family reunification also extended to fiancées and elderly parents. Despite a tiered voucher system based on employment criteria, one historian estimates that between 30,000 and 50,000 African-Caribbean or South Asian people entered Britain per year between 1963 and 1989 (with the two exceptions of 1972 and 1984).[14] In other words, despite the clear political intention to restrict numbers, and the end of the automatic right of entry for Commonwealth citizens (in the sense of British subjecthood), the legal architecture of the 1962 Act did not stop non-white migration to Britain. This was one context of the explosive racial politics of the 1960s and beyond.

Towards Entry Based on Ancestry

In 1965, the year among other things of the International Convention on Racial Discrimination and the independence of Singapore and the Gambia, Godfrey Elton turned seventy-three. Born in Buckinghamshire, Elton had long been an independent peer in the House of Lords, a platform he used often. In 1946 he had published a breathless solution to the decline of the British empire in the form of a book titled *Imperial Commonwealth*, presenting the Commonwealth as the natural post-war vehicle for British imperial trusteeship of the world's peoples. A confident piece of work in the canon of imperial hagiography, it describes British efforts in the Boer war as 'singularly humane'.[15] An American reviewer counted six factual errors, and concluded that it was 'painfully evident that Lord Elton is not familiar with the work done during the last twenty-five years on the history of the British Empire'.[16]

In 1965 Elton published a new book, *The Unarmed Invasion: A Survey of Afro-Asian Immigration*, which claimed among other things that the United Nations was 'largely responsible' for dulling the British people to the dangers of racial 'miscegenation'.[17] His argument was simple: the 1962 Commonwealth Immigrants Act had not gone far enough, immigration was subject to new spikes to which the government appeared oblivious, and Britain was moving headlong towards 'the gravest social crisis since the industrial revolution'. Non-white immigrants numbered 'perhaps half a million'. Brixton and Southall were fast becoming 'miniature potential Harlems'.[18] Elton had perhaps been spurred on by a notorious sequence of articles in *The Times* earlier in 1965 on Britain's 'dark million', which had injected a shot of Conradian peril into the public discourse on non-white immigration in Britain. Sociologist Ruth Glass, a German Jew who had left Germany in 1932, wrote to *The Times* to record her misgivings, pointing out that there was 'not one coloured minority in Britain; there are several heterogenous groups, living among other heterogeneous groups in a plural society'.[19]

Towards the end of the 1960s, further legislation on immigration was now being considered. As the assistant under-secretary at the Commonwealth Office, Roland Hunt, wrote to colleagues in 1967, 'thought is now being given to ways and means of cutting down "coloured" immigration without affecting immigration from the old Commonwealth'.[20] The employment voucher system that regulated the inflow of citizens of Commonwealth states also needed to be revised so that only the most desirable non-white people could be allowed to enter. Immigration into Britain had long been linked to the perceived hierarchical value of a person according to profession – 'the value of a computer systems analyst as compared with a nurse or physiotherapist', as one British official put it.[21]

Analysis by the minister of labour in October 1967 revealed that the estimated waiting time for a citizen of a Commonwealth state who had newly applied for a category-A employment voucher (affording entry into Britain) was 212 weeks for Pakistan, 127 weeks for India, and 87 weeks for other Commonwealth countries.[22] Two-thirds of all category-A employment voucher applications were for jobs in the service industries. Pakistanis and Indians, recorded British officials in the Commonwealth Office, were hoping to take up jobs 'mainly in restaurants and retail food shops', while West Indians from various places in the Caribbean (largely Barbados in practice) were hoping to respond mostly to the 'organised recruitment' of the London Transport Board and the manufacturer J. Lyons & Co.[23]

This voucher stream, it was proposed, should be revised in order that 'vouchers should be issued only for jobs of economic value to the country, mainly manufacturing'. This was part of a wholesale effort to reassess immigration in 1967. If 'coloured immigration' was to be a reality in Britain, at the very least it would meet 'the manpower needs of this country'.[24] If, the Ministry of Labour anticipated, Britain was accused of '"creaming off" skilled manpower' from former colonial territories, it could at least point to reduced waiting times for employment vouchers.

Immigration Crisis: 1967 and Beyond

British officials had put in place a voucher system and existing immigration legislation that it was keen to refine further. There was one sizeable group of non-white British citizens that had slipped through the net of these restrictions. As a consequence of Kenyan independence, there were over 100,000 South Asians resident in Kenya who had either not applied for or not been granted Kenyan citizenship, meaning that they retained their status as British citizens (a minority were British Protected Persons).

Following Kenyan independence in 1963, the passports of Kenyan South Asian British citizens were issued under British sovereign authority by the British High Commission in Nairobi – instead of the authority of Kenya's former colonial government, as had previously been the case. They were therefore not subject to the immigration controls established by the 1962 Act, and their automatic right of entry remained intact. The British government was well aware of this exception, but regarded it as a necessary outcome of enacting control through the device of passport issuance and of appeasing Kenyan white-settlers. The Kenyan Independence Act of 1963 meant that Kenyan South Asian British citizens were, as *The Times* put it, 'offered a choice – Kenyan or British citizenship', under a promise designed for white-settlers that no British citizens resident in Kenya would be subject to immigration control.[25] It appears that the British were hoping that Kenyan South Asians would choose not to migrate to Britain – a hope that soon proved unrealistic.[26]

These circumstances led to what became known as the 'Kenyan Asian Crisis', and the passage of a second Commonwealth Immigrants Act in 1968.[27] In February 1968, an editorial in *The Times* attempted to summarise the situation, explaining who the South Asians in Kenya were and why, in its view, they were facing majoritarian policies in Kenya that undermined their status as residents and workers, causing them to migrate to Britain – the British government powerless to stop them. South Asians in Kenya, the editorial explained, 'have always been resented throughout East Africa', their status as a minority having been 'one of the delicate matters in the negotiations leading to independence'. During the negotiations for Kenyan independence, the British government had ensured that South Asians resident in Kenya could retain British citizenship along with white settlers.[28]

'That so many Kenyan Asians are now claiming their legal right of entry to Britain is embarrassing', the editorial continued, since British governments had counted against such an outcome. Acknowledging that 'any large influx of coloured immigrants' raised a danger of 'a depressed coloured proletariat, where the problems of race and of poverty are synonymous', the editorial acknowledged a need for legislation blocking the

Kenyan South Asians, but asserted that it would be impossible to pass such legislation without transparent racial discrimination.[29] As a subsequent article in *The Times* put it: 'Politically, one of the difficulties in framing any kind of controls over the rate of entry of Asians with British passports is that they would have to be flagrantly based on race distinctions, since there are children of British-born parents in East Africa whose passports are identical.'[30]

Like other national newspapers, *The Times* continued to cover the story, and a consensus took hold among politicians and journalists alike that the 'Kenyan Asians' represented a full-blown immigration crisis. Compared to the numbers involved in the more recent 2015 European 'migration crisis', the figures appear very low. Between October 1967 and March 1968, approximately 33,000 Kenyan South Asian British citizens left Kenya for Britain – around 18 per cent of the community.[31]

The first serious indication of the emergence of new immigration legislation specifically designed to stem the unrestricted arrival of Kenyan South Asian British citizens was an apparent slip during a public statement in Birmingham by the Labour home secretary, Roy Jenkins. Jenkins stated that 'if 100,000 Asians tried to enter this country in the next two years he would have to revise existing legislation', in the *Observer*'s paraphrase of 24 September 1967.[32] At this time, according to opinion polling, around 70 per cent of the British public wanted further immigration controls.[33]

Soon afterwards, future prime minister James Callaghan replaced Jenkins as home secretary. Callaghan was determined to solve the immigration crisis, shocking the House of Commons with his belief that there were 'at least' 200,000 East African South Asian British citizens 'mostly in Kenya' with passports conferring an unrestricted right to move to Britain.[34] Britain's political elite were at this time consumed by a parallel crisis of race. The terms 'racial', 'racialism' and 'racialist' appeared no less than 113 times during the House of Commons debate on the new anti-immigration legislation in early 1968.[35] As Violet Bonham Carter, daughter of former prime minister Henry Asquith, put it in the House of Lords debate, 'a belonger usually has a white face'.[36]

The blocking of certain non-white British citizens from access to Britain was already one of the functions of the 1962 Act – but the new immigration law would explicitly be targeted against British citizens. As Callaghan admitted in a cabinet memorandum on 12 February 1968: 'If we take away their right of entry to the United Kingdom, it may well be argued that, while we are not leaving them Stateless, we are leaving them with no more than the husk of citizenship.'[37]

Nevertheless, in a subsequent Cabinet meeting, on 22 February, Callaghan reiterated the necessity of passing legislation. Kenyan South Asian British citizens 'were now arriving at a rate of from 200 to 300 a day'. If this rate of entry were to continue, the pressures on the social services (particularly housing and education) would be unbearable:

> Consultations with the Government of Kenya had shown that they were not willing to take any action publicly to reassure Asians who were not citizens of Kenya about their future ... We should therefore legislate so as to deprive citizens of the United Kingdom and Colonies who did not belong to this country, not of their citizenship but of the automatic right to enter this country, and at the same time fix a rate of entry for them that was reasonable in relation to the problem itself, to our own social and economic difficulties.[38]

The Labour government ultimately passed the 1968 Commonwealth Immigrants Act as emergency legislation at the end of February 1968, managing to whip it through all of its parliamentary stages in three days. The 1968 Act amended existing legislation to create, for the first time, ancestral distinctions within British citizenship affecting the automatic right of entry. Only those British citizens who themselves had been born, adopted, registered or naturalised in Britain – or who had at least one parent or grandparent who had been – were free from immigration control and had the right to move to Britain unrestricted.[39] Kenyan South Asians remained British citizens, but were deprived of the irreducible minimum of what constitutes a nationality – namely, the right to enter, live and work in one's own country. Their access to Britain was now subject to an ad hoc entry voucher system (initially 1,500 entry vouchers per year for a community of British citizens upwards of 100,000).

The entry of Kenyan South Asian British citizens, in other words, though not curtailed completely, was radically restricted. Over several years, many so-called 'heads of households' (both men and women) were able to access entry vouchers and enter Britain. Because of the right of family reunification, the overall numbers of East African South Asian

British citizens settling in Britain over the next few years were higher than expected given the restrictiveness of the 1968 Act. In April 1974, in a report to the attorney general, the Home Office recorded that Britain had 'admitted for settlement over 100,000' British citizens from various countries across East Africa.[40]

Nonetheless, in early 1968 the situation for many East African South Asian British citizens was a dire one.[41] In the wake of the 1968 Commonwealth Immigrants Act, the International Commission of Jurists declared that there was 'no doubt' that Britain's 'reputation as a bastion of civil liberties has been seriously shaken'.[42] An editorial in *The Times* on 27 February 1968 described the Act as 'probably the most shameful measure that Labour members have ever been asked by their whips to support'.[43] East African South Asian British citizens would remain a constant source of anxiety for British officials well into the 1970s.[44]

The 1970s: One Law to Rule Them All

In the general election of 1970, Edward Heath won a surprise victory. This Conservative victory had been partly secured by an electoral promise to reform immigration law – a promise made largely in order to appease the fanatical anti-immigration campaigning of former Conservative minister Enoch Powell. As the Conservative manifesto had put it, in the original blueprint of the idea of the 'hostile environment':

> We will establish a new single system of control over all immigration from overseas. The Home Secretary of the day will have complete control, subject to the machinery for appeal, over the entry of individuals into Britain. We believe it right to allow an existing Commonwealth immigrant who is already here to bring his wife and young children to join him in this country. But for the future, work permits will not carry the right of permanent settlement for the holder or his dependants.[45]

Echoing the earlier Conservative government of the late 1950s, the new government was particularly concerned with forms of illegal immigration based on the falsification of documents. Immigration from East Pakistan (the new state of Bangladesh was created the following year) was identified as a particular problem in the early 1970s. Local entry-certificate officers whose duty was to regulate migration to Britain, including the migration of dependants, through the system of employment vouchers, were allegedly being duped. Given that British immigration control turned on administrative checks, drawing on a person's identity and travel documents, East Pakistan presented the problem of 'an unordered, rural and oriental society whose records of births, marriages and deaths are not kept as in Britain', wrote the British High Commission in Dacca to London.[46] A subsequent internal report by the Foreign and Commonwealth Office (FCO) recorded that there were 'at least 100,000 people of Bangalee origin mainly from Sylhet' in Britain, most of whom were 'unskilled and semi-skilled workers' or 'free-lance caterers'.[47] These people had settled in major industrial areas. 'Most of the curry restaurants in Britain', the report went on, 'are now run by Bangalees from Sylhet'.

The political activity of Pakistani communities in Britain was also a concern to British officials. The Pakistan Workers Union, founded in 1968, was declared to be 'a left-wing communist organisation' aligned with other 'extremist organisations', whose Birmingham branch had developed out of the Black People's Alliance. One official blamed Pakistanis' 'lack of integration' for the various incidents of 'Paki-bashing' carried out in 1970 by white 'skinheads'. An activist named Mohammed Abdul Hye had subsequently suggested judo and karate classes for 'Pakistani self-defence' to his followers in east London. In 1971 there was 'considerable agitation' among 'Pakistani immigrants' in Britain, a government researcher claimed that year, over 'a pornographic book' that was 'said to insult the Prophet'. This was an anthology of erotica, *The Turkish Art of Love*, recently reissued by a British publisher. In response, a Manchester resident, Ehsan-ul-Haq Alvi, had founded the Defence of Islam Committee in January 1971, running the organisation out of the Mosque and Islamic Cultural Centre on Eileen Grove in Rusholme, Manchester.[48]

It was in this febrile context that the 1971 Immigration Act was passed. Building on previous legislation, the 1971 Act introduced the term 'patrial' – based on ancestral territorial connection to Britain – and tied this to the 'right of abode', a new phrase in immigration policy, meaning the right to enter and live in Britain. The 'word "patrial" is used of persons having the right of abode in the United Kingdom', the 1971 Act declared in Section 2(6). Sharing the same etymology as *patriot*, the term 'patrial' was used to describe any British citizen who had been – or one of whose parents or grandparents had been – born, adopted, registered or naturalised in Britain. A citizen of a Commonwealth state with a parent born in Britain was also considered a patrial. British citizens 'ordinarily resident' in Britain for five years or more – therefore not subject to existing immigration control – were also considered patrials. Gender discrimination (in immigration law, not nationality law) was gone: patriality also passed through the matrilineal line. But the racial discrimination embodied in the term was unmistakable, if indirect.[49]

The concept of patriality was transparently designed to favour those with ancestral ties to Britain while denying the right of entry, now termed the right of abode, to non-white British and Commonwealth citizens without parents who enjoyed territorial ties to Britain itself.[50] The Labour MP Charles Royle expressed his dismay at the new scheme in the House of Commons: 'There is the introduction of this word "patrial". I had never heard of this word ... and even the Home Secretary himself said that he was not quite sure how to pronounce it. If the introduction of this word and the principle behind it is not discrimination, what on earth is discrimination?'[51]

The *Economist*, meanwhile, called it 'a nasty bit of tribal jargon'.[52] In principle, all non-white British and Commonwealth citizens already 'settled' in Britain by 1 January 1973 enjoyed a right to remain identical to that of white patrials. This date served as a line drawn in the sand, and would be resurrected in public debate during the Windrush scandal that erupted in 2018. Only those migrants already 'ordinarily resident' in Britain before the 1971 Act had come into force on 1 January 1973 would have settled status, and therefore 'indefinite leave to remain'.[53]

The 1971 Act declared that any citizen of a Commonwealth state with a parent born in Britain qualified as a patrial. But this open door to second-generation white British people born overseas did not satisfy the political spirit of the 1971 Act or its predecessors, or indeed the broadest objective of the concept of patriality: to ensure maximum immigration concessions to British 'kith and kin' abroad. The Conservative home secretary Robert Carr told officials in various government departments that it was essential, for various political reasons, that 'our family ties with people in Australia, New Zealand and Canada should be given special recognition'.[54] The subsequent immigration rules appended to the 1971 Act adjusted it to expand the entry rights of white British 'kith and kin' in Commonwealth states. 'Commonwealth citizens with a grandparent born here', Carr declared to the House of Commons, while not patrials, would 'not have to obtain a work permit or be subject once here to any form of supervision' should they wish to migrate to Britain.[55]

This addendum to the 1971 Act granted rights of entry and residence to citizens of Commonwealth states who were ancestrally tied to the British Isles going back two generations. If you were a citizen of a Commonwealth state with a grandparent born in Britain itself, you could attempt to move to and live in Britain; at the same time, a British citizen born outside Britain without such a tie was subject to immigration control.[56] Enoch Powell, whose influence was at its height, was concerned that the new idea of patriality would allow 'Anglo-Indians' – those of dual white British and Indian descent in India – to enter Britain. But the British High Commission in Delhi wrote reassuringly to London to say that, though the 'Anglo-Indian community is 140,000', most of them 'will certainly not be able to claim patrial status since most Anglo-Indian families have been resident in India for four generations'.[57]

Although patriality was the most bald-faced attempt yet to make British citizenship a two-tier system based indirectly on race and attachment to the soil of Britain itself, further compromising the imperial constitution of the Commonwealth empire, it is important to realise that it was still not an openly racist concept. Part of the long history of indirect racism using non-racial laws, the idea of patriality adumbrated in the 1971 Act was ultimately based on the location of birth of a person or their recent ancestor, as opposed to outright racial designations. After all, in principle you could be non-white and still be a patrial. Racial discrimination was nonetheless routine in the application of the law. The legal scholar T. C. Hartley pointed out in the 1970s that the wording of the 1971 Act qualified the unfettered right of patrials to the right of abode in Britain by providing that the concept of patriality was not absolute, but must be proved. In practice, immigration officers thus enjoyed considerable discretion in judging whether a person had proved their patriality. He gave an example of a non-white 'patrial' who was denied entry by an immigration officer.[58]

The 1971 Act represents the ultimate source of today's 'hostile environment' for immigrants. It introduced police registration for citizens of Commonwealth states who had been issued a work permit (to cease only after four years' employment), as well as for Commonwealth students, 'au pair girls' and visitors in such cases where 'the immigration officer thinks the requirement desirable'. Under the new law, the home secretary enjoyed a number of new powers, and could 'make a deportation order against anyone who is subject to immigration control' or anyone 'who is convicted on an offence punishable with imprisonment' – and, most expansively, anyone in relation to whom 'the Home Secretary deems it conducive to the public good to make a deportation order'.[59]

The rights of appeal established by the 1969 Immigration Appeals Act would not apply where the home secretary had deported a person on the basis of 'national security' or a declaration that their presence was 'not conducive to the public good'. Equally, the home secretary could deny entry to a person by way of the same reference to the 'public good'.[60] Under the 1971 Act, an employment voucher no longer conferred an automatic right to settle; it now only conferred a right of entry and residence tied to an employment contract for an initial period of one year, any extensions being at the discretion of the Home Office. Those deemed to have entered illegally could be detained for long periods – 'virtually indefinite', in the words of one immigration lawyer – without a hearing and without being informed of the evidence against them.[61]

The 1971 Act came into force on 1 January 1973, replacing the Commonwealth Immigrants Acts of 1962 and 1968. Prime minister Edward Heath passed the Treaty of Accession and the European Communities Act in 1972; effective on 1 January 1973, Britain became a member of the European Economic Community (a subset of the so-called European Communities – today's European Union). Britain's laws were now integrated with Europe's. In other words, fortuitously, on the same day that the 1971 Immigration Act came into effect, 1 January 1973, Britain entered Europe. Britain's imperial pretensions had not been fully shed, but immigration and the financial promise of the European Economic Community had caused the British government to splinter away from the Commonwealth while embracing European regional integration. Britain's entry into the European Economic Community meant that all citizens of its member-states were given unrestricted rights of entry, residence and permanent settlement in Britain. This gave millions of former European aliens the right of free movement to Britain when most non-white British citizens resident outside Britain were subject to immigration control.[62]

After the 1971 Act, immigration was reconceived in terms of a problem of dependants – despite the fact that numbers of dependants joining from the non-white so-called 'New Commonwealth' had fallen 'steeply', as one British official in the Foreign and Commonwealth Office noted.[63] Still, in

1971 there were '18,755 married men from India unaccompanied and 35,845 from Pakistan and Bangladesh' – all of whom were entitled to family reunification.[64] The immediate family dependants of citizens of Commonwealth states already settled in Britain on 1 January 1973 were not 'any less free to come into [Britain] than if the Act had not been passed', the same official remarked.[65] The FCO contemplated an attempt to 'whittle away the right of entry' of dependants, but stopped short of doing so. After all, the values of family cohesion had always carried enormous political capital. Instead, the immigration rules attendant on primary legislation were adjusted at various points in the 1970s and 1980s to make the conditions for entry of migrants' dependants significantly more strict.[66]

Despite the immigration laws and administrative discretion that they provided in the years 1962–71, successive British governments remained – within the terms of their own experience and perspective – unmanned and outgunned by the spectre of 'coloured immigration', especially with respect to the issue of dependants. As one official within the Foreign and Commonwealth Office wrote forlornly about the flow of dependants from newly created Bangladesh: 'The full total of potential immigrants under existing laws is unknown and unknowable, but could be of a very high order. No prospect of diminution.'[67]

Immigration Control or Human Rights?

In their reaction to 'coloured immigration', British governments jeopardised the country's prized self-image as the benefactor of imperial citizenship to a Commonwealth empire. The Commonwealth as an imperial project had faltered and progressively waned roughly in line with the tiering of citizenship rights along racial lines in 1962, 1968 and 1971. But post-war immigration policies also compromised Britain's indelible self-image as a source of human rights and the rule of law.

Wanting to have it both ways, Britain saw itself in the vanguard of the development of human rights at the same time as it pursued immigration laws and its own imperial interests in the Commonwealth empire. 'In the field of human rights', concluded cabinet ministers in Harold Wilson's Labour government in April 1967, 'and in other legal fields we had contributed much to European development ... we could easily assume a leading, and even dominant, role.'[68] There was important reputational power to be gained by such a role at the European level. The United Nations General Assembly would designate 1968 as the International Year of Human Rights, and an international treaty banning racial discrimination would come into operation in 1969. But the dubious legality of the 1968 Commonwealth Immigrants Act showed Britain to be on the wrong side of the strengthening of the international human rights regime.

The European Convention on Human Rights in principle extended rights to Britain's colonial citizens overseas. As we have seen, South Asian British citizens resident in East Africa had been barred from entry into Britain, many of whom were now living illegally in Kenya as non-citizens. The queue to receive an entry voucher for Britain was several years long. Without a British judicial remedy to call on, some 243 East African South Asian British citizens began to complain, from February 1970 onwards, to the European Commission on Human Rights (a subsidiary body of the European Court of Human Rights), using their right of individual petition. Of these applications, the Commission judged thirty-one to be admissible.[69]

As Cedric Thornberry reported in *The Guardian* in October 1970, '31 Kenyan and Ugandan Asians, all holders of British passports, will ask the European Human Rights Commission [in Strasbourg] to accept their claim that Britain is in breach of several articles conferring and protecting basic human rights'. The thirty-one people were currently 'either stranded' in a European country or had been '"conditionally" allowed to land in Britain', their 'unconditional right to entry having been taken away', wrote Thornberry.[70] Having delayed the process while it sought a friendly settlement with the British government, the European Commission on Human Rights gave its final ruling on 14 December 1973 (known as *East African Asians v United Kingdom*).

With respect to twenty-five of the applicants, it concluded that Britain had in 1968 'discriminated against the applicants on the grounds of their colour or race', the legislation in question being 'racially motivated and destined to harm a specific racial group'. This group consisted of two young women; the rest were young single men. The group included eleven teenagers, two of whom were aged just fifteen. A 'special importance', the Commission's ruling went on, 'should be attached to discrimination based on race'. Legislation that worked 'publicly to single out a group of persons for differential treatment on the basis of race' could be said to constitute 'a special form of affront to human dignity' and 'degrading treatment'.[71] The European Commission on Human Rights had found the 1968 Commonwealth Immigrants Act to be in violation of Article 3 of the European Convention on Human Rights ('No one shall be subjected to torture or to inhuman or degrading treatment or punishment').

Years later, the British human rights lawyer and co-counsel for the group, Anthony Lester, remembered how he came to present the case as a potential violation of Article 3. Having failed to connect the argument to the more obvious Article 14 (enshrining non-discrimination), Lester had gone to see his former law professor at Yale, Charles Black, who 'persuaded us', Lester remembered, 'to argue before the Commission that racial discrimination is inherently degrading and hence contrary to the prohibition against degrading treatment in article 3'.[72] Lester persuaded Black – best known for contributing to the brief for the landmark American civil rights case, *Brown vs Board of Education* – to travel with him to make the case in Brussels to the Commission. The Commission accepted the argument, and this was the first time in the case law of the European Court that racial discrimination was interpreted as an Article 3 violation.

Charles Black's involvement presents an interesting connection between the American Civil Rights movement and South Asians from East Africa. However, *East African Asians v United Kingdom* was far from an outright victory for racial justice and equality. The report of the European Commission on Human Rights remained secret for some twenty years; nor was it able to restore the citizenship rights of the applicants. The Commission did not escalate the case to the European Court of Human Rights proper, but instead transferred it to the European Committee of Ministers – a political body that effectively sided with the British government, failing to reach a majority view on the question of Britain's violation of Article 3. Nor did the Commission find in favour of those applicants who were British Protected Persons, who had never enjoyed British subjecthood. Privately the British government was confident that ministers on the Committee were 'sympathetic' to Britain, and in the crucial years of the case (1970–74) it made marginal increases to the overall quota of entry vouchers for East African South Asian British citizens in order to distract from the underlying violation of the 1968 Act.[73]

Ending Imperial Citizenship

Successive post-war British governments passed increasingly exclusivist immigration laws from 1962, culminating in the Immigration Act of 1971. If this was the last major piece of legislation in the 1970s, administrative practices relating to immigration would only become more severe. In the most egregious example, doctors working at the behest of immigration officers – themselves recruited to the British government's war on dependants' right to join family members already settled in Britain – conducted invasive virginity tests on South Asian women attempting to join their fiancés in Britain. Believing young, mostly working-class South Asian women to have falsified their engagement, immigration officials had made virginity tests 'a routine part of the entry certificate procedure', the *Times of India* reported in 1979.[74]

In another telling episode, when white-minority-ruled Rhodesia finally became independent Zimbabwe in 1979, many people of ancestrally white British descent were able to return to Britain without much notice. When quizzed on the exact number, a minister at the Foreign and Commonwealth Office told the House of Commons in 1980 that there were 'approximately 125,000 people' in 'Rhodesia-Zimbabwe' who 'have a right of abode in this country'.[75]

Towards the end of the 1970s there was bipartisan political agreement that British nationality law was sorely in need of redefinition. *Who Do We Think We Are?* asked a pamphlet published in 1980 by the Conservative Study Group. 'British nationality law no longer makes sense', it declared, since it 'ignores the course of our history since 1948, confuses the problems of immigration and nationality and misleads any inquiry into who are the citizens of this country'.[76]

In 1981, a new British Nationality Act finally established a 'British citizenship' for the very first time, at last replacing the imperial architecture of the 1948 British Nationality Act. At the level of citizenship, in other words, decolonisation in Britain did not begin until 1981. The 1981 Act used the phrases 'British citizenship' and 'British citizen' for the first time in British nationality law. The traditional idea of a 'British subject' was now finally put to rest. A British citizen was a person who carried the 'right of abode' – a patrial in the sense of the 1971 Act. In this sense, nationality and immigration were now intimately tied together. Under the 1981 Act, a person was considered a British citizen only if at least one parent was a British citizen, or was 'settled' in Britain.

Despite the greater focus of the 1981 Act on the geography of the British Isles as a determinant of nationality, the definition of British nationality did not fully divest itself of imperial associations. There were still citizenship statuses – such as British Dependent Territories citizens and British Overseas citizens – that remained imperial, and did not carry the right of abode in Britain. In 1983, when the 1981 Act came into effect, South Asian British citizens in East Africa who by the 1980s had not been able, or did not wish, to gain entry to Britain (thus remaining in, say, Kenya without Kenyan citizenship) went from being citizens of the United Kingdom and Colonies to becoming British Overseas citizens.

Finally, in 2002, a year of reform, Britain conferred British citizenship (and therefore the right of abode in Britain) on virtually all British Dependent Territories citizens in the 2002 British Overseas Territories Act. Meanwhile, the Nationality, Immigration and Asylum Act, passed in the same year, finally provided British Overseas citizens with no other citizenship or nationality (for example, certain South Asians in East Africa) with a route to register as British citizens. This came after the final termination of the ad hoc entry voucher system set up for East African South Asians in 1968 (there were still around 500 applications for such vouchers each year).[77]

This effort in 2002 was the design of Labour home secretary David Blunkett, who told the House of Commons that it was a matter of 'righting an historical wrong, in terms of what happened back in the late 1960s'.[78] Home Office officials privately tried to convince Blunkett to abandon elements of the 2002 Act, citing their concerns that large numbers might choose to migrate to Britain. This revealed a remarkable post-war continuity within British officialdom, for which immigration was a corollary of British social decline, if not ruination, through the arrival of large numbers of non-white people. 'Nationality policy has been driven mainly by the immigration implications' – wrote officials to Blunkett in 2002 – a policy which 'has, of course, been determined largely by numbers'.[79] Following Britain's decision in 2016 to leave the European Union, the debate on Britishness, immigration and Britain's place in the world has been revived yet again. The only way to gain some sense of the long-term trajectory of Britain's approach to these issues since 1945 is to retrace its post-war imperial story more fully.

PART II. *You Were There*

International Voices

4

The Persistence of Empire

A too-often repeated narrative of the end of the British empire, serving almost like a national superstition, can be summarised as follows. The dissolution of direct imperial rule – decolonisation – occurred promptly after 1945, and was more or less controlled and consensual. Direct imperial rule was relinquished more in benevolence than in struggle, British authority having assured political stability, moderation and the institutions of Westminster in a postcolonial regime now fit to stand on its own two feet. On the whole, the end of empire occurred without British elites paying much attention.

Historians have established, however, that decolonisation was from a British perspective uncontrollable, unwanted and unexpected. Direct imperial rule was dissolved largely in two currents of anticolonial nationalism – in Asia in the 1940s and in Africa in the early 1960s.[1] The Commonwealth was already in place as a new imperialism, and helped to rationalise decolonisation within the Commonwealth as the constitutional evolutionary successor to direct imperial rule. Formal decolonisation of the British empire in Asia, Africa and the Pacific spanned a longer period than is generally recognised (from 1947 to 1980, when Zimbabwe gained independence). Anticolonial resistance, in diverse forms that went beyond nationalism, was the primary generator of change. In 1948, for example, as the British Nationality Act consecrated the post-war empire, strikes and riots in the Gold Coast (later

Ghana) signalled to the Colonial Office that it could not ignore the years of trade union mobilisation there.[2]

An additional difficulty with some popular accounts of decolonisation is that they present it as a simple reversal of colonialism. Although coined in the nineteenth century, the term 'decolonisation' rarely appeared until 1960, after which point its usage exponentially increased. Decolonisation refers to the transfer of power to formerly colonised territories that became new sovereign states upon that transfer. But this simple definition obscures the complexities and conflicts in the story of the end of the age of European empires – doing justice neither to the diversity and depth of anticolonial resistance and thought, nor to the determination of British elites to make the empire live on in formal and informal ways. In this sense, the term decolonisation is amorphous and misleading. Although it registers the incalculable importance of formal sovereign equality between states, it captures neither the struggle by formerly colonised peoples to make that formal sovereign equality meaningful and substantive, nor the ways in which that struggle changed the world.[3]

This chapter records the determination of British political elites to sustain the empire in the post-war world well into the 1970s and beyond, inventively reframing the notion of empire itself as British imperial power was taken away. Most former British colonies chose to remain within the Commonwealth as republics after gaining independence. Burma and South Yemen were the exceptions. Only Ireland, South Africa and Pakistan withdrew from the Commonwealth, each for very different reasons, in the first post-war decades. It was this apparent consistency that allowed British imperial idealism to endure.

A received view of the end of empire as orderly and swift helped to rationalise British immigration policies. If Britain was making a planned transition from an empire to a nation-centred state around the British Isles – ostensibly completed in 1973 when Britain joined Europe – it would become easier to justify the revocation of citizenship rights for those with British nationality overseas. But did such a transition in fact ever take place? As historian John Darwin has bluntly remarked: 'Decolonization was the continuation of empire by other means.'[4]

The acceptance of a tidy period of decolonisation has led to surprisingly loose references to 'declining empire', 'end of empire', and the 'post-imperial' in the historiography of twentieth-century Britain.

These movable usages suggest an ineffective attempt to locate an elusive moment in time when Britain became post-imperial. The end of empire is the black box of recent British history – if only the mechanics of this particular device could be understood, the rest of recent British history could suddenly also be deciphered. Deciphering it reveals answers about unfinished puzzles within post-war immigration, about the agency of formerly colonised peoples and states in the Global South, and about the shape of British imperialism in the post-war world.

Historians have struggled to make sense of the fact that a huge loss of colonial power was not the same thing as an end to imperialism. Even the word 'imperialism' has been rejected by some historians of the British empire. Keith Hancock, born in 1898 in the colony of Victoria and recently styled as the greatest historian of the British empire, dismissed the term imperialism out of hand, calling it, with a characteristic barbed irony, 'a pseudo-concept which sets out to make everything clear and ends by making everything muddled; it is a word for the illiterates of social science'.[5] Hancock's understanding of empire was that it was complex, 'an untidy patchwork of naval bases, coaling-stations, trading companies, Protectorates, Crown colonies and self-governing Dominions rapidly advancing to equality with Great Britain both in law and in fact'.[6]

The idea that the empire was 'advancing to equality' at first glance circumvents imperialism entirely; but in fact this captures British imperialism well in its putative liberality and idealism. As we have seen, the British empire had long shielded itself from censure by means of its progressive self-image. This applied equally to post-war imperialism. In an attempt to seize control of events, British political elites were in a constant process of reconceiving the end of direct imperial rule as a purposeful decision designed to develop the empire towards new forms of equality under British stewardship. This was a form of what might be termed post-imperial imperialism that actively tried to author the post-war world as a British initiative, adjusting itself accordingly when the post-war world proved itself, as it often did, beyond its material or political reach. As we shall see in the chapters in this section, British post-war imperialism manifestly failed to capture and contain the new international public sphere after 1945, whose ideas of racial and postcolonial equality put paid to British imperial paternalism.

Empire After 1945

Most historical accounts of Britain after the Second World War emphasise its deep vulnerability. The post-war government was besieged by
the economic costs of domestic policy (and the new commitments of
welfarism), by war debt to the United States, by a balance-of-payments
deficit, and by the exigencies of foreign policy (imperial defence and
Cold War imperatives). The civil servant and economist Alec Cairncross
recalled this moment decades later with a still perceptible sense of shock.
Not only did those in government find themselves in 'a world completely
out of balance', Britain had 'ended the war with the largest external debt
in history' and a deficit in 1944 running at a cool £2,500 million. Despite
facing what economist John Maynard Keynes called a post-war 'financial Dunkirk', Britain had 'economic and military obligations' around
the world, wrote Cairncross, and was determined to keep up its military
presence in Greece, Palestine, Germany, Egypt, Iraq, Malaysia, Malta
and India.[7]

The first post-war British winters were unusually cold, fuel was limited,
and even staples like bread and potatoes were rationed. This was the
context in which British politicians felt the 'loss' of India in 1947. George
Orwell had written in his pre-war book *The Road to Wigan Pier* that, sans
empire, Britain would be reduced to 'a cold and unimportant little island'.[8]
Certainly there were British people who might have accepted this sentiment in the late 1940s. A young Enoch Powell had served as an officer
in the British army in Delhi from 1943 to 1946, and in his own words
had fallen 'hopelessly and helplessly in love with India'. On his return to
England he immediately joined the Conservative Party and resolved to
become viceroy of India, studying Urdu at the School of Oriental and
African Studies in London to further his chances. He took the news
of India's independence on 15 August 1947 badly, walking the streets of
London all night. 'One's whole world', he wrote, 'had been altered'.[9] Keith
Hancock, for his part, acknowledged the implications of India's inde-
pendence for Britain's military position in the world: 'She no longer has
Indian divisions at her disposal to send to South East Asia or the Aden
Protectorate or East Africa or the fringes of the Mediterranean.'[10]

But it is important to realise that Britain's political elite was more
sanguine. In 1948, Labour prime minister Clement Attlee declared
that Britain was 'not solely a European power but a member of a great

Commonwealth and Empire'. Churchill made a speech that same year in which he rhetorically conjured Britain's role in the world in terms of 'three circles' – one circle was a newly united western Europe, the other was the traditional white-settler Anglo world (the white dominions, Canada and the United States), and the third was the imperial 'British Commonwealth'. Britain's felicity, said Churchill, lay in its overlapping position within each. Despite the 'ascendancy of the United States in world affairs', recalled Alec Cairncross, Britain's political elite 'accepted without question that Britain was still a world power and should have a world presence'.[11]

Economic wounds led to a narrative of British decline that has distracted attention from the economic importance of the Commonwealth empire until at least the late 1950s. After a monetary crisis in the late 1940s, Britain turned in the first years of the 1950s to the 'sterling area' – made up of British crown colonies, Commonwealth states excluding Canada, and a smaller number of non-Commonwealth states – whose currencies were pegged to sterling and whose foreign exchange balances were held in sterling. In the first post-war years, Britain sought to exploit imperial protectionism with respect to extractive industries in the colonies. Commodities – things like cocoa, sugar, tea, palm oil, timber, rubber, nickel, copper and tin, from places like the Gold Coast, Nigeria, Malaya and Rhodesia – were deemed vital to Britain's need to reconstruct domestically and repay the United States.[12]

The so-called Malayan Emergency that began in 1948 can be seen in the context of rubber and tin exports that produced precious dollar earnings for Britain. Britain was also ensconced economically with the white-settler Commonwealth states; between 1950 and 1954, 65 per cent of British capital exports went to Commonwealth states and colonial dependencies, and between 1955 and 1959, 45 per cent of British imports came from them.[13] The pursuit of commodities (including oil), defence priorities, a new strategic vision dictated by the Cold War and a new British imperial vision more generally, combined to sustain British interests in the Persian Gulf, West Asia (the Middle East), Southeast Asia and Africa. The Indian Ocean remained a 'British lake'.[14] The post-war Labour government cultivated 'development' as the new catchword of a supposedly progressive imperialism – alongside 'modernisation' and 'partnership'. Even Keith Hancock acknowledged, as early as 1950, that the supposed difference in treating a territory in colonial terms and calling it 'underdeveloped' was marginal. There was an 'informal empire', and an 'invisible empire' to use Hancock's phrase, in addition to Britain's remaining crown colonies.[15]

The 1945 Colonial Development and Welfare Act of Clement Attlee's Labour government signalled a fresh turn to sub-Saharan Africa, where imperial gains including benefits to British white settlers in places like Kenya were presented in the guise of development. In 1947, Labour set up the Colonial Development Corporation (later renamed the Commonwealth Development Corporation), focused less on welfare and more on producing a return on investment in the colonies. As early as the 1970s, historians termed this a 'second colonial occupation'.

Joining the existing ranks of white settlers in Africa, this second colonial occupation in practice meant more white immigration, in which various experts, technical and professional staff, so-called development officers, doctors, teachers and engineers migrated to help 'develop' Africa.[16] Indeed, the idea of 'colonial development' had its origins in the 1920s as part of a mandate to expand the opportunities of white settlers in Kenya. Celebrating advances in colonial development in 1953, colonial secretary Alan Lennox-Boyd acknowledged 'the many people of our own race who have made their homes in the Colonial Territories'. By helping white settlers – some of whom had 'lived in Colonial Territories for two or three generations or even longer' – development would in turn help the 'other races' in Africa.[17]

Meanwhile, the post-war British military presence ran along defined maritime corridors, linking a constellation of bases including those in Singapore and Aden. Britain tried to exploit its ties with the former white-settler colonies (South Africa, Australia and New Zealand) in the area of imperial defence. Britain, Australia and New Zealand were part of a cooperative imperial defence strategy not only in Southeast Asia (the British Commonwealth Far East Strategic Reserve), but also briefly in the Middle East. Australia, a key economic partner to Britain at this time, even provided facilities for nuclear testing.[18] Announcing this joint Australian–British venture to develop a nuclear weapon in 1943, Australia's prime minster John Curtin declared it to be the start of a 'fourth' British empire. Such declarations were not uncommon for a brief period after 1945. In the context of the evolving Commonwealth empire, for example, the *Sunday Times* declared in 1947 the commencement of a 'Fourth British Empire of independent peoples freely associated'.[19]

One of the more incisive criticisms of Britain's new development-based imperialism in Africa was made by the Trinidad-born Pan-Africanist and socialist, George Padmore, who migrated to London in 1934. In 1949, the same year in which he wrote to W. E. B. Du Bois that Pan-Africanism had to remain separate from 'either the Anglo-Saxon or Russian power blocs', Padmore released a book titled *Africa: Britain's Third Empire*. Here he gave a unique summary of Britain's post-war empire:

[T]wo factors are generally responsible for this post-war interest in the African El Dorado. The first is the decline of British Imperial power in the East. For centuries Asia, the largest, richest and most densely populated of the continents, was Britain's chief milch-cow ... India and Burma have broken the fetters of Imperialism, Ceylon has attained qualified Dominion status, and Malaya is straining at the leash ... The second factor is Britain's own desperate economic situation at home, due to her exertions in fighting for self-preservation. Both these factors combined have adversely affected Britain's status as a great World Power ... To redress her unfavourable position at home and abroad, Africa is being called upon to provide the maximum of foodstuffs of all kinds and other essential raw materials for peace and war.[20]

The Nigerian publication the *West African Pilot* recorded that at Padmore's funeral in September 1959 at Golders Green Crematorium in London, 'all coloured communities' in Britain had 'turned out boldly to show the world how great George Padmore was to the liberation movements'. In attendance were officials from Ghana, Sudan, Nigeria, Haiti and Liberia, while Patrice Lumumba and Jomo Kenyatta, the Congolese and Kenyan leaders respectively, were invited to a separate burial service in Ghana.[21]

Decline, Crisis and Imperial Rebirth

The received story of the end of empire gathers pace at the end of the 1950s. In the wake of prime minister Harold Macmillan's famous acknowledgement in 1960 of the 'wind of change' making itself felt in Africa, so the story goes, decolonisation was finally achieved.[22] Britain turned away from the Commonwealth empire for both political and economic reasons, divesting from the idea of an Anglo-Saxon world across the globe. The final 'end of empire' moment occurred in 1968, in the form of military retrenchment 'east of Suez', before Britain finally integrated with Europe in 1973. For the rest of this chapter, I will reassess this received sequence of events. Many of its elements are undeniable – and by 1964 the colonial empire was largely gone. But British political elites, as we shall see, did not experience an 'end' of empire so much as a 'decline' and a series of interrelated imperial crises. These were experiences that led at every turn to imperial reimagining and readjustment.

In 1956 – the year of the Suez Crisis – Doris Lessing wrote in her novel *The Four-Gated City* of 'an idea of change, breaking up, clearing away, movement'.[23] The following year – a full three years before the 'wind of change' ostensibly heralded decolonisation – the Gold Coast (as Ghana) and the Federation of Malaya (later Malaysia) gained independence. That same year, 1957, Macmillan commissioned a multi-departmental 'profit and loss' or cost–benefit reappraisal of the empire. Although this clearly indicated a commitment to the type of change resisted by Winston Churchill earlier in the decade, its outcomes could hardly be called post-imperial. The report of the Official Committee on Colonial Policy to cabinet in September 1957 advised that Britain should be economically indifferent to the end of direct imperial rule, since British interests could be sustained in other ways:

> Although damage could certainly be done by the premature grant of independence, the economic dangers to the United Kingdom of deferring the grant of independence for her own selfish interests after the country is politically and economically ripe for independence would be far greater than any dangers resulting from an act of independence negotiated in an atmosphere of goodwill … Meanwhile, during the period when we can still exercise control in any territory, it is most important to take every step open to us to ensure, as far as we can, that British standards and methods of business and administration permeate the whole life of the territory.[24]

The idea that the end of direct imperial rule was the same as an end to British imperialism showed, perhaps, both a lack of understanding of burgeoning economic structures of development and a lack of imagination. The Foreign Office and the Commonwealth Relations Office were

to be given greater financing after 1957 for technical and military assistance overseas, and to support efforts that strengthened the culture of the
Commonwealth empire.[25] In 1959, a matter of months before Macmillan's
'wind of change' speech, British colonial officials deemed East Africa constitutionally unripe for independence, projecting Tanganyika's eventual
independence in the year 1970, independence for Uganda in 1971, and
independence for Kenya in 1975.[26] The actual dates, respectively, would
turn out to be 1961, 1962 and 1963.

The tenacity of empire as development, and the lure of 'great power'
status, in Labour and Conservative post-war governments alike, is often
obscured by the rapidity of the succeeding dates of independence from
colonial rule in the 1960s and beyond. These dates included Somaliland
(1960), Cyprus (1960), Nigeria (1960), Sierra Leone (1961), Tanganyika (later Tanzania, 1961), Jamaica (1962), Trinidad and Tobago (1962),
Uganda (1962), North Borneo (1963), Singapore (1963), Sarawak
(1963), Zanzibar (1963), Kenya (1963), Nyasaland (as Malawi, 1964),
Malta (1964), Northern Rhodesia (as Zambia, 1964), the Gambia (1965),
British Guiana (as Guyana, 1966), Bechuanaland (as Botswana, 1966),
Basutoland (as Lesotho, 1966), Barbados (1966), South Arabia (1967),
Mauritius (1968), Tonga (1970), Fiji (1970) and the Bahamas (1973).[27]
The direct phase of empire had ended largely by the mid 1960s, but the
struggle to shape the contours and interests of the postcolonial world
remained.

Prophets of Decline

In the 1960s the British writer and sometime advisor on colonial administration, Margery Perham, was styled – perhaps more by herself than
by others – a British conscience of the 'end of empire'.[28] She is a good
person to begin with in our sojourn among lived experiences of the end
of empire. Perham had begun her professional life in 1917 as a history
lecturer at the University of Sheffield, where she was the only woman on
the history faculty. Her decision during a period of sick-leave in 1921 to
visit Somaliland, where her brother-in-law had been posted as a district
commissioner, propelled her into a life of imperial travel, and increasing
expertise and influence in colonial administration in Africa, particularly
the educational and constitutional elements of 'native administration'.

In 1961 she became the first woman to deliver the prestigious annual Reith lectures, which she titled *The Colonial Reckoning*. Prudence Smith, the BBC producer who invited her to give the lectures, remembered years later that for her Perham was 'that rare and precious thing, a cautious, respectable radical'.[29] 'Radical' here meant that Perham acknowledged African nationalism – she was one of the few to attribute some legitimacy, however elemental, to Mau Mau nationalist resistance in Kenya. Both privately and publicly, however, she expressed vacillations and misgivings about the constitutional readiness of African territories for independence. This dialogical engagement with British imperial tutelage and African nationalism was captured in her correspondence with the Kenyan political leader, Tom Mboya, which she hoped would one day be published as a book.[30]

Her radio broadcasts in 1961 explored the new world of decolonisation, leaving the listener with an understanding of a new agency in the world, but also with an assurance that British liberal imperialism remained the arbiter best placed to measure its significance. 'The wheel has indeed come full circle', she told BBC listeners. 'The Western world must pay to the uttermost for its period of world domination and colonial power'.[31] If Britain was losing British Africa, this was because 'the new nationalists felt that colonialism was so oppressive that it could not be ended too quickly'.[32]

The new African leaders 'will use the materials of the West, but they will use them their own way and will add more, much more, of their own creation. Above all they alone can provide the dynamo of nationalism, which will make the model work'.[33] The 'present mood' of African nationalists 'is to give up being grateful, or humble, or afraid, or ashamed, or even impressed. They have had so much of all that. They are determined to be something quite new, Africans!'[34] The onset of decolonisation was unstoppable.

Yet Perham ended her final broadcast with a peroration designed to provoke doubt, fear and suspense as to what the end of empire might mean, and the ways in which it might live on implicitly. 'There is no certainty', she declared, 'that they will succeed. The lamps of Africa may go out even before they are fully alight, as some of the lamps of Europe have gone out.' When the British had attempted to discuss the finer points of Westminster-model politics with African nationalists – parliamentary democracy, universal suffrage, human rights and civil liberties – they had answered 'from the blood and not from the brain'.

The reference to blood here referred listeners back to her earlier reference to the Congo, which had undergone 'the welter of fragmentation and murderous bloodshed'.[35] The whole success of the experiment of African freedom 'will depend very much upon the degree of understanding and help which we in the West give to Africa'. The question of what would become of 'Britain's own relations with our former subjects' represented one of opportunity, not loss. Certain links would remain – 'the Queen, if not the Crown, the English language, the great gift of our law and procedure, the ideal, at least, of our democracy' – and Britain might send out 'young doctors, lawyers, scientists, above all teachers of every kind, to go out for at least two or three years to serve the great needs of Africa'. This was a political, social, and even moral necessity in Britain's 'adjustment from power to service'.[36]

Not all the assessments of the apparent end of empire were as subtle as Perham's. Historian Max Beloff, the son of a Russian Jewish immigrant who had arrived in Britain in 1903, wrote a two-volume study dedicated to the question of the end of the British empire in an earnestly contrarian vein. Beloff declared that Britain's 'imperial sunset' had truly begun when Britain decided to try to join Europe at the beginning of the 1960s. The end-of-empire moment could be pinpointed, Beloff argued, to 31 July 1961, when Harold Macmillan announced to the House of Commons, in Beloff's words, 'the intention of his government to make a formal application under article 237 of the treaty of Rome for membership of the European Economic Community'.[37] Beloff marvelled that Winston Churchill, having witnessed Queen Victoria's diamond jubilee as a young solider in India in 1897, 'was to survive to vote … on 3 August 1961 in favour of the motion approving Britain's application to join the EEC'. Making Churchill stand bizarrely for a fitful abdication of imperial responsibilities in favour of 'the European cause', Beloff concluded that 'decline and fall of the British Empire had been consummated within a single active lifetime'.[38]

Beloff was not alone in setting up Britain's attempt in 1961 to join the EEC in terms of a political choice between the pragmatic gains of Europe and British imperial claims on the world. The latter stood for Britain's claims to a 'world role' – an adjacent idea to the Commonwealth empire.

To abdicate that role in pursuit of entry to Europe – so the logic went, at its most basic – would be finally to close off British post-war imperial ambitions. Of course, Britain's attempt to join the EEC in 1961 was vetoed by French president Charles de Gaulle, who famously said *non*.

Nonetheless, despite the apparent willingness of Harold Macmillan's Conservative government to surrender to formal decolonisation in Africa and invite the economic opportunities of integration in Europe, key politicians did not accept the thesis that Britain's imperial life was at an end. As the foreign secretary, Alec Douglas-Home, put it in 1963, in a cabinet memorandum to the defence committee, the current presentation of Britain's imperial fate invoked a false binary between Europe and the world. 'We have rejected the idea that we should "choose between Europe and a world role"', Douglas-Home wrote. 'We have worldwide interests', he went on, 'and must therefore have available a worldwide presence to protect them'.[39] There was no necessary contradiction between British membership of the EEC and its flagship role in the Commonwealth. This was of course a contentious point, but arguments in support were available. As British economist Eric Roll argued in 1961, Britain would have much to offer its Commonwealth partners from within the EEC – namely, 'a faster rate of economic growth, with wider trading possibilities, with a stronger voice in Europe'.[40]

Paradoxically, the very justification for a sustained British imperial presence in the world was the experience of direct imperial rule that it was being forced to relinquish. The idiom used to express the supposed choice of ending the empire was more often than not phlegmatic, superior and dignified. As Commonwealth relations secretary, Duncan Sandys, said in a speech to the Conservative Commonwealth Council in 1962: '[T]he British race will, to the end of time, remain profoundly proud of the glorious achievements of the old British Empire'.[41] He was 'equally proud', he continued – here whitewashing anticolonial resistance and British counterinsurgency with a bogus story of progress – 'of having converted it peacefully and amicably in the new independent Commonwealth – a development without parallel in history'. This particular version of the myth of decolonisation was that it was a Whiggish affair, orderly and swift.

With imperial loss also came pique. In 1962, Dean Acheson, a former US secretary of state, made an oft-quoted comment about Britain. Acheson's involvement in Bretton Woods, the Truman Doctrine and the

Cold War gave him a sensibility closely associated with post-war global power:

> Great Britain has lost an empire and has not yet found a role. The attempt to play a separate power role – that is, a role apart from Europe, a role based on a 'special relationship' with the United States, a role based on being head of a 'commonwealth' which has no political structure, or unity, or strength – this role is about played out.

In response, an editorial in the *Spectator* protested with some hurt that Britain was in a 'transitional period'. Today, political 'transition' is a liberal democratic badge pinned on states in the Global South after a period of conflict or authoritarian rule. The *Spectator* here acknowledged Britain's own attempted transition from empire to a more nation-centred power focused on the British Isles as the determining motivation of post-war British politics. Britain was, the *Spectator* editorial team reassured itself, 'facing facts of our position in the world which had not made their full emotional impact before'. Since 1945, Britain had been 'engaged in a planned withdrawal from imperial commitments, replacing them by a Commonwealth association resting on intangible qualities of good will rather than on any more material bonds of power or even common interest'. And yet its defensive response to Acheson's comments revealed an unwillingness to let go: 'Why should we be so super-sensitive to facts which are not in dispute?'[42]

In the British public sphere, social and economic treatments of British life were at odds with the more sanguine imperial view of certain policymakers. The idea of British 'decline' – economic and social, as well as imperial – was hard to resist as a master narrative of post-war Britain. British declinism – the haunting alter ego of Whiggism – inspired both social critique and diagnoses of economic malaise. The early 1960s duly saw a round of declinist literature by economic and political commentators, including Anthony Hartley's *A State of England* (1963), Norman MacRae's *Sunshades in October* (1963), Anthony Sampson's *Anatomy of Britain* (1962) and Michael Shanks's *The Stagnant Society: A Warning* (1961).

For Sampson, it was inevitable that the 1960s presented Britain with its first real loss of purpose against a background of imperial divestment. Finally, Sampson wrote, 'those acres of red on the map [were] dwindling, the mission of war dissolving, and the whole imperial mythology of battleships, governors and generals gone forever'. 'Of all the stages in a great country's history', Sampson concluded, 'the aftermath of Empire must be the hardest'.[43]

The Hungarian intellectual Arthur Koestler plumbed still deeper as editor of a book of essays titled *Suicide of a Nation? Enquiry into the State of Britain* (1963). Koestler pronounced that deeply hidden 'psychological attitudes' were, in truth, 'at the root of the economic evils'. It was not 'the loss of empire' or 'the huge sums we must spend on armaments' that accounted for British decline, but a psychic condition. 'We are at the moment dying by the mind', concluded Koestler.[44] Meanwhile, the Marxist writer Perry Anderson expounded at length on the 'origins of the present crisis' in the *New Left Review* in 1964, judging that 'the character and ethos of the ruling bloc' had corroded under a pre-war imperialism 'so suffused with chauvinism and so glutted with rank' that it reverberated into the present day.[45]

Assessing this period, cultural historian Paul Gilroy – whose mother, the novelist Beryl Gilroy, migrated from British Guiana to London in 1951 – has recently defined British elites' post-war experience as a form of 'melancholia'. This he describes as 'an inability to face, never mind actually mourn, the profound change in circumstances and moods that followed the end of the Empire and subsequent loss of imperial prestige'.[46] British decline was also stirred by racial angst, as the 'dark million' of non-white British and Commonwealth citizens in Britain summoned the longstanding fear of white decline. The problem of 'coloured immigration' was a symptom of the long decay of a white society with an underlying disease. As the Labour MP Frank Tomney put it in the House of Commons in 1958, the 'coloured races will exceed the white races in a few years' time in the ratio of no less than five to one'.[47]

Imperial Crisis, Imperial Rebirth

Nonetheless, decline also presented an opportunity for imperial reimagining and rebirth. Despite the fact that the Commonwealth empire had spawned the problem of 'coloured immigration', British officials in the 1960s could not yet relinquish it as a vehicle for British post-war imperialism. Although the idea of an Anglo-Saxon white man's world had now been all but extinguished following international condemnation of apartheid in South Africa, South African withdrawal from the Commonwealth in 1961, and decolonisation in Africa, the promise of the Commonwealth empire was still simply too far-reaching to abandon.

Labour prime minister Harold Wilson was preoccupied with a British 'world role' throughout the 1960s, going so far as to announce publicly in 1965: 'Britain's frontiers are on the Himalayas'.[48] Upon election in 1964, Wilson insisted in the House of Commons that 'we cannot afford to relinquish our world role – our role, which for shorthand purposes, is sometimes called our "East of Suez" role'.[49] The phrase 'east of Suez' was taken from the line 'Ship me somewhere east of Suez', in Rudyard Kipling's 1892 poem, 'Mandalay'. In the 1960s, the 'east of Suez' role referred to the British military presence in the Persian Gulf, the Indian Ocean and Southeast Asia. Britain's naval base in Singapore was at the heart of the British commitment to the Cold War in Southeast Asia, and its defence costs had attracted criticism as 'a symbol of the Kiplingesque quality of our Far-Eastern policy', as Wilson admitted privately to US secretary of state Dean Rusk in 1966.[50]

Wilson's ambitions notwithstanding, the domestic narrative of Britain in the 1960s was one of crisis – the natural partner of decline. As Alec Cairncross, now a senior official in the Treasury, remembered years later, the 1960s was a 'decade of continuous crisis'.[51] The crises of the period were far from simply economic; they were plurally social and political, domestic and international. In addition to the Rhodesian crisis (1965 onwards), the Sterling crisis (1966) and the Kenyan Asian Crisis (1968), there were various other events that attracted the same definition, including the two failed attempts to enter the EEC (1963 and 1967), withdrawal from Aden and South Arabia (1967), the devaluation of sterling (1967) and political violence in Ulster (1968 onwards). Britain also had interests bound up in the outcome of the Six-Day War (1967) and the Biafran War (1967–70).[52] Immigration, race relations and domestic economic questions (the balance of payments and military spending) appeared to bleed into these international crises, as so many shades of the shadow cast by imperial decline.

The year 1967, in particular, was critical. A former Foreign Office official, Brian Crowe, remembered in a 2003 interview the significance of Aden as one of the major crises in a British crown colony: 'There was a general strike and a mutiny and British authority was being challenged and the Governor was apparently not coping. It was a huge crisis. People forget now. Aden was in the headlines.'[53] Seemingly events were combining in such a way as to put Britain on notice for political transition away from empire.

Military withdrawal from Aden bled into a parallel commitment to full withdrawal 'east of Suez' amid existing financial crises and recurring defence-spending reviews. Devaluation of sterling, for so long contemplated, finally became a reality on 18 November 1967 (the pound was devalued by 14.3 per cent to $2.40). Meanwhile, Britain made a second attempt to enter Europe ('[t]here is no real alternative to our joining the EEC', as one British diplomat admitted), although this ended in failure once again.[54] The apparent divestment of the imperial project was symbolised by the recent closure of the Colonial Office, now merged with the Commonwealth Relations Office to form the Commonwealth Office.

And yet, in the middle of this year of imperial decline and crisis, sections of the British state were working to reconceive empire. In April 1967 the Commonwealth Office and Foreign Office, making use of input from British high commissioners around the world, released a major report evaluating 'the value of the Commonwealth'. It reframed decolonisation as nothing short of a final realisation of a long-prized British world:

> Turning 'Empire' into 'Commonwealth' was a triumphant technique to cover the process of decolonialization. This both enabled us to extricate ourselves from colonial responsibilities with honour and psychologically cushioned the shock for the people of Britain in adjusting to a new era ... [I]f Britain still has a role to play in these major issues of rich and poor, coloured and white, the Commonwealth association provides us, and also Canada and Australia, with special opportunities for doing so. There is in the Commonwealth a complex of links, not only political, but economic, educational, administrative and professional, which are directly relevant. It would be a grave matter for us, both nationally and internationally, if we were seen to be throwing away a special asset which could give Britain a position of central importance in the world in, say, the last two decades of this century, out of proportion to her comparative economic and military strength.[55]

This was to take at face value the innumerable connections that new leaderships in the Global South had to Britain. To take a small sample from the educational category, the political leaders Forbes Burnham (Guyana),

Errol Barrow (Barbados), John Compton (St Lucia), Jomo Kenyatta (Kenya), Michael Manley (Jamaica), Veerasamy Ringadoo (Mauritius), Kwame Nkrumah (Ghana) and Pierre Trudeau (Canada) all studied at the London School of Economics; Seretese Khama (Botswana), Ratu Mara (Fiji), Malcolm Fraser (Australia) and Indira Gandhi (India) all studied at Oxford; and Tunku Abdul Rahman (Malaysia) and Lee Khan Yew (Singapore) studied at Cambridge.[56] The former Foreign Office official, Peter Hall, was no doubt serious when he claimed in a 2002 interview that the entire character of British relations with India in this period could be elucidated by such links: 'I think England paid a very heavy price in bilateral relations for Oxford University having, I believe, chucked Mrs Gandhi out, or certainly made life difficult for her as a result of some academic failure which was not forgotten. In contrast with her father who was rather proud of having been to Harrow and Cambridge, Mrs Gandhi was not.'[57]

Even in the former colony of Jamaica, British officials in diplomatic service believed in a sustained British imperial influence, whatever the evidence to the contrary. The deputy high commissioner in Kingston, R. G. Britten, wrote to London to confirm the vitality of the Common-wealth empire in the Caribbean. Despite some ill feeling in Jamaica over British immigration policies and 'racial discrimination in Britain', wrote Britten, Jamaicans retained 'an almost touching belief in British good faith, decency and rightmindedness. The Jamaicans look upon them-selves as something of a bridge between the Old World and the New – and the Old Commonwealth and the New … They set a high value on the Commonwealth connection.'[58]

As further evidence, Britten noted that Clifford Campbell, the first non-white governor-general of Jamaica, had led a congregation in a ren-dition of Rudyard Kipling's poem 'Recessional' at a Remembrance Day service in 1966. Britten also allowed himself some rumination over why it was – so he claimed – that Jamaicans accepted their Britishness as something 'almost dictated by a law of nature'. The 'ancestors of the great majority', he wrote, 'were brought here as slaves by the British, and as an act of deliberate policy were divorced from their cultural, linguistic and religious backgrounds. A society, in essence English with modifications governed by local conditions, thus developed from scratch, with almost all Jamaican institutions being either started by, or copied from, British counterparts.'[59]

Despite strong domestic elements – not least Enoch Powell – who believed that the empire could never be recaptured, others in government believed that it might be cleverly reimagined. At the same time as the military face of the post-war empire in the 1960s – the so-called 'east of Suez' role – was becoming synonymous with perceived domestic overreach, officials were able to turn to the Commonwealth as a wellspring of new conceptual and structural forms of post-war empire.

After Empire, a New Colony

Despite the fanfare over decolonisation in Africa in the 1960s, Britain in fact created a new crown colony in 1965, some 2,000 miles off the East African coast. In February 1964, it was decided that Britain and the United States would conduct a joint survey of certain islands in the Indian Ocean with a view to converting their territories into a military base. Designed to protect against perceived Soviet designs in the Indian Ocean, the islands were assessed in terms of their defence suitability and capacity for military administration. The United States wanted any such islands to be empty, and tasked Britain with making any necessary 'resettlement arrangements' for resident or indigenous populations on the islands. The United States agreed to cover building costs, and Britain agreed to secure the land itself and partition and administer the islands.

Surveys of the Chagos Archipelago and other small islands took place in July and August 1964. Terms were agreed in secret between Britain and the United States in April 1965. The whole endeavour of creating a new colony cost £10 million, of which the United States agreed to contribute half. The colonial governors of Mauritius and Seychelles, both of which were still under British colonial rule, were sent instructions on the partition of islands from their territories in October 1965. That same month, the British Indian Ocean Territory Order 1965 created the new colony in law.[60]

The British Indian Ocean Territory – the new crown colony – was made up of small islands previously administrated by the colonies of Mauritius and Seychelles. The entire rationale of the British Indian Ocean Territory was that it provided potential sites for 'transit, communications and support' in the context of the Cold War. After an initial US–British agreement on the terms and suitability of the territory, the British made the sites available to the US on lease for an initial period of fifty years 'for defence purposes'. Further agreements on terms between Britain and the United States were signed in December 1966. Staffed mostly by US military personnel, a naval communication facility on the Diego Garcia atoll in the Chagos Archipelago, part of the British Indian Ocean Territory, would finally come into operation in 1973.[61]

This relatively little-known episode – the creation of a new colony five years after the 'wind of change' – reveals much about post-war British imperialism under Labour's Harold Wilson and his successor, the Conservative leader Edward Heath. Those living on the islands that made up British Indian Ocean Territory in 1965 were indigenous Chagossian people, largely African or Malagasy in their origins, and descended largely from enslaved African people brought to the islands by French colonialists hoping to exploit a plantation economy in the late eighteenth century. British officials knew of a population of 'about 1,000' people living on the Chagos Archipelago in 1965, yet chose to believe that only a fraction of these 'could be regarded as having their permanent homes in Chagos', as an official in the pacific and Indian Ocean department of the Foreign and Commonwealth Office rationalised the situation in 1969.[62]

If Britain had recognised those living on the Chagos Islands as permanent inhabitants, it would have had a responsibility (under Chapter 11, Article 73 of the United Nations Charter) to ensure their advancement beyond direct colonial rule towards self-government. Instead, the British government gave out 'temporary residence permits' to indigenous Chagossian people on their own land, and declared them to be 'a migratory force' that had largely travelled from nearby Mauritius in order to find work as contract labourers – thereby circumventing Article 73, which only applied to permanent inhabitants of colonised territories.[63]

But declassified documents reveal that, privately, officials at the Foreign and Commonwealth Office knew that such claims were bogus, and worried that 'if the numbers and character of the Ilois [another name for Chagossians] became known to Parliament or in the UN', Britain would be 'forced to acknowledge a Charter responsibility to develop self-government and social services for an irremovable population.'[64]

Although the Chagossian people were in fact entitled to self-determination under international law, the United Nations failed to recognise this. Many of the Chagossian people were also now fully fledged British citizens (citizens of the United Kingdom and Colonies).

But this did not prevent colonial authorities from forcibly deporting some 1,500 to 1,800 people – 'uprooting them from their traditional homes', as the FCO put it – to Mauritius and Seychelles (each over 1,000 miles away) in the early 1970s.[65] In the eyes of British officials, the Chagossian people were 'simple islanders, not versed in the obscure problems of their national status', and could be forcibly removed at will.[66]

1968: A Phantom End to Empire

What was going on here? Harold Wilson's Labour government had presided over the latest phase of decolonisation. He was dealing with multiple crises and public sentiment calling for more domestically focused policies, yet in private British officials were busy reconceiving – yet again – an expansive British imperial role in the world, albeit in non-military terms. Meanwhile, Britain had just created a new, though very small, crown colony. As the American political scientist Kenneth Waltz put it in 1967, Britain had still not awakened fully to doubts about 'its ability to play a world role'. Instead, wrote Waltz, Britain's 'material weakness has led to an emphasis upon nonmaterial forces'. This new iteration of the British imperial imagination showed agility at adapting to new circumstances, privately reconceiving the shape of the Commonwealth empire once again and exploiting its longstanding presence in the Indian Ocean. Waltz's realist sensibility led him to condemn British pretensions; he wrote bluntly that it was 'a natural inclination of the weak to define influence in terms of moral force, for they have little of any other kind'.[67]

At the beginning of 1968, Harold Wilson was in need of a sop to those complaining of 'overstretch', and deliberately chose to relinquish the 'east of Suez' role. On 16 January 1968, the month before parliament debated the 1968 Commonwealth Immigrants Act, he declared to the House of Commons:

> We have accordingly decided to accelerate the withdrawal of our forces from their stations in the Far East ... and to withdraw them by the end of 1971. We have also decided to withdraw our forces from the Persian Gulf by the same date ... we shall by that date not be maintaining military bases outside Europe and the Mediterranean ... Again, by that date, we shall have withdrawn our forces from Malaysia and Singapore.[68]

Harold Wilson spoke of this military retrenchment, including the sacrifice of the prized naval base at Singapore, as equivalent to 'reassessing
our role in the world'.[69] 'What right does the Prime Minister think he
has irrevocably to abdicate Britain's role in the world?' asked Conservative politician Duncan Sandys, as if on cue.[70] But this declared transition
away from an imperial 'world role' was simply a device to curate an end
to empire without fully achieving it. Wilson had in fact written to US
president Lyndon Johnson the day before to reassure him that Britain was
not abdicating its role in the world. 'This does not mean', wrote Wilson to
Johnson of his planned announcement, 'a British withdrawal from world
affairs [but a] determination, once and for all, to hew out a new role for
Britain in the world at once commensurate with her real resources yet
worthy of her past'.[71]

In the public discourse of the day, the 'east of Suez' announcement
was taken at face value as the end of empire. A couple of weeks after
his announcement, in early February 1968, Wilson made a state visit to
Washington to meet with the Johnson administration. Reiterating the
commonly held view of the time, the *Spectator* noted in its coverage of
the visit that US president Johnson 'did not like Mr Wilson's East of Suez
cuts. Nor was he especially happy with the devaluation of sterling and the
attendant disorders in the financial markets'.[72]

During a state dinner in Wilson's honour, reported the *Spectator*, the
Americans 'had made him listen to "The Road to Mandalay"' in an apparent surprise humiliation. But, writing for the *New York Times*, American
journalist and winner of two Pulitzer Prizes, Anthony Lewis, claimed
that Wilson had been alerted of the Kipling rendition in advance and,
far from objecting, had noted that it was 'among his favourites'.[73] Lewis
summarised the occasion in terms of 'the continuing decline of Britain's
power since World War II', the withdrawal announcement amounting to
'stringent measures to abandon Britain's world role and drop the order
for American F-111's [military aircraft]'. Lewis ended on a reflective note,
remarking of Britain that it still had 'much to contribute after shedding
the military pretensions'. Soon afterwards, the British high commissioner
in Washington communicated to British foreign secretary George Brown
his perception that American officials saw the 'east of Suez' withdrawal
as the 'passing of an era'.[74]

When Wilson returned home from Washington, in mid February 1968,
he soon set about passing the second Commonwealth Immigrants Act.

That month, in protests at Nairobi airport, Kenyan South Asians drew comparisons between the recent relegation of British economic prestige and the planned tiering of British citizenship along racial lines. 'Wilson: your £ devalued, your passport devalued', read one protestor's placard at Nairobi airport.[75] Tellingly, the *Economist* used similar language the following month, suggesting that the 1968 Commonwealth Immigrants Act not only 'discredited the British passport' for those who were 'British and brown', but that it might also work to 'devalue it in the eyes of other people in other parts of the world'.[76] In a similar vein, the Goan writer Dom Moraes explained the popular hostility in Britain towards Kenyan South Asians in terms of a reaction to a loss of international status:

> The British people had only begun to realize in the last few months how completely Britain's power had slipped away. The realization had thrown a large segment of the population into a certain mood of xeno-phobia, and now as they beheld numbers of coloured people in turbans and saris, claiming to be British and calmly walking into their country, popular feeling flared up. We've enough coloured people here already, said the British, we don't want any more.[77]

The following month, March 1968, the Foreign Office was merged with the Commonwealth Office, in a demonstration of imperial down-sizing. Although the Foreign Office had expressed reservations as to the Commonwealth Office's idealism about the Commonwealth in 1967, now, in 1968, with 'east of Suez' commitments disavowed, officials in the merged FCO turned their hand once again to redrawing British imperialism.[78]

On 12 March 1968, a steering committee of permanent under-secretaries in the civil service held a meeting on the topic of British 'non-military means of influence' internationally. Its aim was to produce an interdepartmental consensus on a future world role. In his review of foreign policy Labour foreign secretary Michael Stewart put a positive spin on recent events, concluding that a British role in the world could persist despite its reduced 'military presence'.[79] 'We now need to be on the alert', Stewart concluded, 'to capitalize on these changes'.

In a document prepared for the defence and overseas policy commit-tee, Stewart and the Commonwealth affairs secretary, George Thomson, elaborated on this theme. Britain's turn to Europe (its planned entry to the EEC) counterintuitively prompted a reimagining of an imperial world role. 'We have now decided on a Europe-based policy'; yet, by a 'judicious blend of various non-military means', Britain might 'maintain our influence overseas' and preserve 'as far as we can our substantial remaining interests and assets outside Europe and North America'.[80] Britain would focus its efforts on the 'developing world', on the basis that it 'brings real returns in terms of direct British interests'.

The document went on to identify several categories of non-military influence, including diplomacy, student and professional 'exchanges', trade promotion, civil and military aid, and technical assistance (defined very broadly to include voluntary service overseas, civil and military exports, intelligence liaison, and even 'counter-subversion'). Within this scheme, Commonwealth states had supposed built-in advantages including a shared use of the English language and an orientation towards British institutions, standards and practices, as well as professional, educational and other links. The security of British trade and investment, however, required 'political stability' and 'favourable attitudes' to British political interests, and the 'prevention of the expansion of Soviet and Chinese influence'. Crucial to this global agenda was reputational power – namely, Britain's 'image' as racially tolerant and supportive of the United Nations, a complement to its leadership of the Commonwealth and the global Anglo-Saxon diaspora.[81]

What is astonishing here is the tenacity of British imperial faith that the world was forever hewn in the image of British institutions and law, sustained around the world by Anglo-Saxon blood. As we shall see in Chapters 5 and 6, the world had changed, the Commonwealth had changed, British racism was being held to account in the international public sphere – and yet British imperial idealism persisted. Astonishing too is the hypocrisy of these views when seen beside racially discriminatory immigration policies, the latest of which had been passed a mere month before the production of this document.

The commitment to the Commonwealth as the gateway to a 'world role' had never finally been abandoned, despite, or perhaps because of, impending 'east of Suez' retrenchment and planned entry into Europe. Reliance on the Commonwealth as the perennial home of British imperial ambition was allowed to continue. As the British Marxist historian Victor Kiernan wrote in 1969, the end of empire might be more suggestive of renewal than of forfeit within the imperial imagination. 'Loss of empire', wrote Kiernan, 'has set Europe free to begin finding a better confidence, inspired by a new consciousness of itself and a new relationship with its neighbours, and to recollect in tranquillity its adventures across the seven seas.'[82]

Despite the announced 'east of Suez' withdrawal, the British colonial presence in the Indian Ocean was set to continue, under the mask of the Cold War and 'the currently fashionable and generally overrated Russian menace to the Indian Ocean trade routes', as the *New Statesman* put it in 1970.[83] As we saw earlier, it was at this very time that the military base in the new colony known as the British Indian Ocean Territory was being prepared, and its indigenous population forcibly relocated. In yet another little-known episode, Britain orchestrated the ouster of Said bin Taimur in Oman in 1970, allowing for a centralisation of power in that country. Subsequent British involvement in state-building there led one historian to remark recently that Britain built the modern state of Oman 'almost from scratch' in the early 1970s.[84]

What is more, the 'east of Suez' withdrawal never took place. Although announced in 1968, to be completed three years later, it was subject to repeated deferral, and never fully carried out.[85] As the Foreign and Commonwealth Office briefed Wilson's successor, Conservative prime minister, Edward Heath, before a visit to the United Nations headquarters in New York in October 1970, there would remain a military presence 'east of Suez' as part of a new 'five power' defence arrangement.

'We shall be keeping', the FCO advised, 'a small number of frigates or destroyers' stretching as far as Hong Kong. This would consist of reconnaissance aircraft and helicopters and a battalion of ground troops stationed in Singapore, alongside those of Australia and New Zealand.[86] After all, Britain had 'substantial economic interests' in Southeast Asia, as well as military treaty commitments in the context of the Cold War that tied it to both Southeast Asia and the Persian Gulf. Whatever the declared end of an 'east of Suez' presence, the FCO concluded, 'British forces should remain in the area after 1971'.[87] Although Britain's naval Far East Command did finally leave Singapore in 1971, Britain retained surface vessels under the Five Power Defence Arrangements, set up in 1971 together with Australia, New Zealand, Malaysia and Singapore, until 1974. Britain retained military bases in the Maldives, Masirah and Mauritius until 1975–76, and to this day remains attached to the Indian Ocean region by way of the five-power commitments.[88]

But the idea persisted that Harold Wilson had ended the empire once and for all in 1968. The vast reduction in imperial scale and the shift towards development and other forms of structural power was mistaken for a true end to empire. Labour politician and Commonwealth aficionado Patrick Gordon Walker wrote in 1970 that the 'east of Suez' announcement was 'the most momentous shift in our foreign policy for a century and a half'.[89]

The pioneer political economist Susan Strange, for her part, lambasted Britain for not accepting its post-imperial fate sooner. 'Ten years ago', Strange wrote, 'we in Britain still thought of ourselves as one of the stronger and richer of the European countries.' But the 1960s had been years of 'political and economic transition' – a transition that 'was not at first recognised as the inevitable process that it surely is and was resisted instead of accepted'.[90] Despite going through an extended period of 'almost chronic' crisis from 1964 to 1968, Britain had remained hopelessly attached to 'associated ideas which no longer apply to Britain's changed situation, but have nevertheless proved remarkably hard to shed or modify', judged Strange.[91] These included the particular vices of 'clinging to traditional roles' outside Europe, as if Britain were a 'world policeman' or 'universal financial uncle', and indulging in 'the prestige of sterling and the solidarity of the sterling area as the main prop of the Commonwealth system'.[92]

One of the more fulsome accounts of imperial longing occurred when British diplomat Arthur de la Mare made his valedictory dispatch upon stepping down as high commissioner of Singapore, in October 1970. In his mind a front-line witness to the final end of empire, De la Mare used his moment of farewell to Singapore to remember the beginning of the end of empire in 1942. 'I heard of Singapore's surrender' – that is, the destruction of the military garrison at Singapore by the Japanese imperial army during the Second World War – 'on my birthday', wrote De la Mare, who would have been twenty-eight years old on 15 February 1942. His tenure as British high commissioner in Singapore, beginning some twenty-six years later, had been 'repellent because every day I am reminded of the shame of 1942'.

For the last two years, De la Mare had presided over 'a vast, lavish British military establishment' in Singapore. But this, De la Mare now conceded, had been little more than 'an attempt to expunge the shame of 1942, and the uncomfortable knowledge that we returned [to Southeast

Asia] on the back of the Americans, by a garish display of military extravagance, appropriate perhaps to the imperial days of Kipling but incongruous and unseemly in today's world'. Withdrawal from Singapore was now occurring, De la Mare seemed to imply, because British imperialism could no longer resist its past shame: 'history is too near, and the smell of our ignominy still hangs in the air'.[93]

More Decline, but No End to Empire

Despite the phantom imperial divestment of 1968, historians have been keen to jump on Harold Wilson's 'east of Suez' announcement of 16 January 1968 as a means of fixing in time the elusive moment of the end of empire. Ronald Hyam marks Wilson's statement as 'the effective termination of the British imperial-global cosmoplastic system'. Saki Dockrill calls it 'a landmark in Britain's twentieth-century history'. John Darwin similarly refers to it as 'the final collapse of the post-war campaign to remain a great power', marking out the 1970s as 'the first real post-imperial decade'.[94]

But other historians have suggested that this apparent 'end of empire' moment was more a political staging of change than a substantive transition. As one historian puts it, 'what mattered was what it looked like rather than what it actually was'.[95] There were certain domestic gains to be made in the performance.

Not unexpectedly, there was a new wave of British declinist literature in the wake of the 'east of Suez' announcement, including Max Beloff's *Future of British Foreign Policy* (1969), Correlli Barnett's *The Collapse of British Power* (1972), and F. S. Northedge's *Descent from Power* (1974).[96] British declinism conjured Britain's latest perceived loss of purpose back into the past, missing the ways in which European imperial interests had re-inscribed themselves in the present.

In 1971, the journalist Joe Rogaly captured declinist sentiment in his 'Society Today' column for the *Financial Times*:

> [W]e are in the unbreakable grip of History; [and] Britain is in a long and grand period of decline that will continue for an unknown period of years ahead. Nobody can say what will arrest this descent if anything ... No economist, or indeed sociologist, will readily admit to the

existence of national moods: it is like confessing to a belief in ghosts. But this ghost exists alright, and in our hearts most of us know it.[97]

Post-war Britain had moved from a 'fourth British empire' after 1945 to its disavowal amid decline and crisis, before shifting again into a more permanent, near-mystical state of decline. If the 'east of Suez' announcement signalled the end of empire, British entry into Europe – successful on its third attempt – was deemed by some to spell the utter eclipse of the British imperial imagination. When Britain finally entered Europe, on 1 January 1973, the *New York Times* assessed the state of the nation as follows: 'Britain in the 1970s is melancholy and uncertain. A second-rate power with a poignant – almost mystical – yearning to be taken seriously, the nation faces her strikes, labour unrest, problems in Northern Ireland and political division over entering the Common Market with a kind of bemused self-doubt.'[98]

Predictably, however, the senior Conservative politicians taking Britain into Europe did not see its entry in terms of a final imperial decline. Foreign secretary Alec Douglas-Home declared at the 1971 Conservative Party conference that the 'enlarged Communities' of Europe would be the future of British 'influence and stature' and 'authority and influence' in the world. If British imperialism was to be realised through non-military structures such as development, the European project would maintain imperial continuity and provide much-needed economic rejuvenation.[99]

The prominent British historian J. G. A. Pocock was unconvinced, however, and judged Britain's entry into Europe in 1973 in terms of its negative consequences for British sovereignty, and for the very coherence of Britishness itself. Even the *Oxford History of England*, he complained in 1975, opens with an 'express denial that the term "Britain" has any meaning'.[100]

What are the lessons of the never-ending end to the British empire? Whatever the event in view, political elites found a means of reinventing British imperialism. Decline and crisis were ultimately imperial themes, and often part of the process of imperial reawakening. This was an idealism that would not die. Certain senior British officials continued to see post-war world politics in terms of an imperial British-led Commonwealth. This centred on what the Commonwealth Office described as an imperial 'complex of links' in the British world. The irony, of course, was that the Commonwealth was also the source of non-white immigration.

5

Postscripts to Decolonisation

At the turn of the 1960s, Harold Macmillan became the first serving British prime minister to visit sub-Saharan Africa (specifically South Africa, Ghana, Nigeria, and the Federation of Rhodesia and Nyasaland), an indication that the diplomatic centre of gravity was shifting south. In office between 1957 and 1963, Macmillan is known for two phrases: one about the British people having 'never had it so good' (1957), a reference to post-war economic recovery, and the other about 'the wind of change' (1960), which referred to decolonisation in Africa.

The first phrase was uttered in Bedford, the second in a speech in Accra, and soon afterwards again in Cape Town. Macmillan's 'African tour' between January and February 1960 was captured in a memorandum prepared by his cabinet secretary, Norman Brook, which was circulated to ministers the following April. Brook's account, although not for the public, was self-conscious and manicured. Brook is credited with co-authorship of the 'wind of change' speech, and in 1960 was at the height of his powers. 'There is a golden rule for every ambitious civil servant' and 'every ambitious politician too', declared the *Daily Mail* in 1961. 'Don't cross Norman Brook.'[1]

Brook was used to travelling overseas with Macmillan, and had accompanied him two years earlier on a 'Commonwealth tour' of India, Pakistan, Ceylon, Singapore, New Zealand and Australia. The 'African tour', however 'exhausting' and 'arduous', had been 'a personal triumph for the Prime Minister and Lady Dorothy Macmillan', Brook began his account later that spring. It had also, Brook implies, been intrepid. Macmillan left London on 5 January 1960 and returned on 15 February, spending five days in Ghana, six in Nigeria, eight in the Federation of Rhodesia and Nyasaland in Central Africa, and ten in South Africa. 'In all, the Prime Minister travelled 13,360 miles by air, 5,410 by sea and about 800 by road', recorded Brook. He travelled mainly by air, using a chartered aircraft provided by British Overseas Airways Corporation – a British state-owned airline created in 1939 through a merger of Imperial Airways and British Airways – to make the initial journey between London and Accra.

Macmillan brought with him an eighteen-person entourage, including officials from the Colonial Office and the Commonwealth Relations Office, and his personal valet. The tour consisted of a relentless itinerary of informal sit-downs with prime ministers, luncheons with civic luminaries, and trips to local sites that showcased advances in economic development. Dorothy Macmillan often accompanied her husband, and also kept a number of separate engagements, visiting Red Cross headquarters, hospitals, schools and welfare institutions. Her programme had to be cut short at Ndola airport in Northern Rhodesia when she slipped on the stairs of an aircraft boarding ramp, 'cutting her leg severely'.[2]

Upon arrival in Accra, Macmillan, now sixty-six years old, was relaxed. There was no particularly important business to be done with Ghanaian prime minister Kwame Nkrumah or his ministers; instead Macmillan could focus on public relations with 'the ordinary people of Ghana'. One morning he visited Accra old town and was taken through the old market, where the 'market-women' were 'vociferous, and plainly sincere, in their greeting'. Unmanned by the 'genuine friendliness of the Ghanaians', who exhibited 'no trace of colour consciousness', he agreed to be taken out on a surfboat.

After a meeting with Nkrumah and opposition leaders at the residence of the British high commissioner, Macmillan attended 'a tea party' to meet representatives of 'various "Pan-African" bodies'.[3] One might presume this was the most challenging tea party Macmillan had ever attended, yet in Brook's breezy account, 'these supposed extremists listened with deference' to a series of 'cogent and skilfully phrased impromptus by the Prime Minister on the elements of democracy and the peculiar problems of multi-racial societies'.[4]

Macmillan's trip is remembered as a surrender to the reality of decolonisation – 'the wind of change'. His visit to newly independent Ghana was an indication of a new phase in international relations. But Britain at this time had its own interpretation of the spirit of the 'wind of change'. In the British imperial imagination, independence was not something granted, but something earned. In 1957, a draft resolution of the United Nations General Assembly in New York had asked Britain to comment on the question of Tanganyika – precisely, what was the estimated period of time before this colonial territory was 'guided towards self-government or independence' in accordance with the United Nations Charter? The British minister of state for foreign affairs, Allan Noble, was recalcitrant, telling the UN General Assembly that Britain was 'firmly opposed to any attempt to regulate the organic growth of constitutional development by setting arbitrary time-tables or time-limits'. It would 'decide on the pace of change in the light of experience gained at each stage and the readiness of the people of the Territory for the next step forward'.[5]

Macmillan signalled a change of heart from this established British policy line in his famous Cape Town speech, in which he said of African self-determination: 'We must accept it as a fact.'[6] But in Brook's account of Macmillan's meeting with Nkrumah in 1960, Macmillan speaks of his commitment to a British management of decolonisation. This was so with respect to the colony of Kenya and the protectorate of Uganda, which were far away from gaining independence – or so Macmillan thought:

> Even in Kenya, when the British first went there 60 or 70 years ago, conditions were so primitive that the potter's wheel was unknown. These considerations alone would mean that the pace of constitutional advance could not in any event be as rapid in those parts of Africa as it could in some of the West African territories. But, in addition, the problem was further complicated by the existence of racial minorities, whose interests must be safeguarded. This was not solely a problem of the white settler: in most of these territories there were large Asian communities too; and constitutional solutions must be found which took account of these minority interests.[7]

Britain was a tutor to colonial societies held in pupillage. Not only did African nationalism have to be submitted to British theories of staged 'constitutional advance', there was also the problem of race relations – indeed, in Brook's account this was Macmillan's main concern.[8] On his African tour Macmillan was, Brook declared, 'concerned throughout

with the problem of race relations – a problem of immense intellectual difficulty and one which can quickly arouse strong prejudice and
bitter controversy'.[9] The topic dominates the document, which contains
forty-three instances of the word 'race', sixty-four of 'racial', nineteen of
'multi-racial' and nine of 'race relations'.[10] Almost all these references to
race are made by Macmillan himself, or by Brook.

In a way, this was not so surprising. Britain was at this point suspended
between past and future policies on the question of so-called 'race relations'.[11] Until recently, the British had been committed to a policy of
'multi-racialism' – a euphemistic technique of colonial government in
which the claims of different 'races' were managed in partnership, with
the effect that black majorities were denied equal rights. Now the government, at least in principle, was committed to a policy that ensured that
the future constitutions of the colonies were held in common by peoples
of different races.

But such futures, including the end of direct imperial rule, could not be
rushed forward in time. As foreign secretary Selwyn Lloyd had intoned
to the UN General Assembly a few months before, 'the task of building
nations is not easy'. The reason 'it cannot always be quick' was due to a
certain 'special responsibility' keenly felt as a function of British imperial
noblesse oblige:

> In those territories where different races or tribes live side by side the
> task is to ensure that all the people may enjoy security and freedom
> and the chance to contribute as individuals to the progress and well-
> being of these countries. We reject the idea of any inherent superiority
> of one race over another. Our policy therefore is non-racial. It offers a
> future in which Africans, Europeans, Asians, the peoples of the Pacific
> and others with whom we are concerned, will all play their full part as
> citizens in the countries where they live, and in which feelings of race
> will be submerged in loyalty to new nations.[12]

The 'non-racial' idea promoted Britain's role in securing inclusivity in the
constitutional futures of former colonies, tidily erasing the very codes
of racial difference Britain had inculcated in its colonial administration.
Ian Buist, who was seconded to the colonial Kenyan government in 1954
from the Colonial Office, recalled what British multiracialism had meant
in practice, here describing the colonial police force in Kenya:

[T]he grades ran from 'Chief Inspector (European)' down to 'Assistant Inspector (European)' and below that was 'Chief Inspector (Asian)' and so on down to the 'Assistant Inspector (Asian)', and only then came 'Chief Inspector (African)'. This was ridiculous, and I was absolutely determined that we would abolish this straightaway. There was no question but that we would do it, but how to do it and integrate people without loss of status and feeling was quite important.[13]

On his African tour, Macmillan nevertheless saw himself as adapting to new realties based on stark colonial failures, such as 'a million French settlers' in Algeria whose occupation had led to years of anticolonial struggle. As Macmillan pointed out privately to the South African prime minister, it now looked as though the French had 'lost their struggle in Algeria'.[14] In other words, Macmillan's 'wind of change' speech was more descriptive than anything else.

His own private secretary, John Wyndham, later publicly referred to the 'wind of change myth', describing the phrase as 'a diagnosis and not a prescription'.[15] The reconstruction of the British view on decolonisation was tempered by a theory of constitutional timetabling or 'ripeness'. As Brook recorded with respect to Macmillan's trip to the Federation of Rhodesia and Nyasaland, Africans in Southern Rhodesia, although 'by and large a contented and peaceful community', had 'as yet scarcely achieved any organized political machinery for the expression of their views'.[16]

Even in Brook's carefully managed account of Macmillan in Africa, the new realities that were redefining international relations emerge. A diary entry for 14 January 1960 records that Macmillan faced protests in Lagos, including placards proclaiming 'Butcher Macmillan, go home' and 'MacNato, we who are about to die salute thee', among other slogans related to British policy in Central Africa, apartheid in South Africa, and the imprisoned anticolonial leaders, Hastings Banda and Jomo Kenyatta.[17]

The Ghanaian government provided a written submission to Macmillan on the general African situation, presenting it in terms of national self-determination, not race: 'Ghana believes that freedom for Africans on their native continent is essential for World Peace. The great wave of nationalism at present sweeping Africa is a fact which should be recognized; it is a force which no one can hold in check and therefore it should be co-operated with in the best interests of all concerned.'[18]

Even in 'multi-racial territories' facing the specific problems of 'minority communities', it was essential, declared Nkrumah's government, that the 'principle that the majority of the people, i.e., Africans, should form the basis of Government in these territories should be accepted'.[19]

At the Groote Schuur residence in Cape Town on 2 February, the South African foreign affairs minister, Eric Louw, who had recently represented South Africa at the United Nations, tried to recruit Macmillan's sympathies on the international condemnation of apartheid. As Louw described current events to Macmillan, an 'Afro-Asian group' was 'now canvassing in the United Nations the possibility of applying sanctions'.[20] South Africa was a member of the Commonwealth, and now faced the prospect of fellow Commonwealth member-states advocating against its racist policies.

Whatever Britain's imperial scheme for the Commonwealth, it was now becoming harder – if not impossible – to control. Upon Macmillan's return to London on 15 February 1960, his already famous speech appeared to be 'headed for a permanent niche in tomorrow's history books', as a bulletin of the Institute for African-American Relations put it.[21] The *Times of India* was much more phlegmatic about Macmillan's tour as a whole, placing it in the wider context of apartheid, the beginning of the first conference at Lancaster House in London to discuss the terms of Kenyan independence, and the imprisonment in Southern Rhodesia of Nyasaland leader, Hastings Banda.[22]

Another European making a tour of Africa in January 1960 was the Swedish economist and diplomat, Dag Hammarskjöld, who at this time was serving as the second secretary-general of the United Nations. Between 18 December 1959 and January 1960, Hammarskjöld made 'a long journey through Africa', as he told the press upon his return on 31 January at an airport in New York. 'I and my collaborators', he remarked, 'have visited some twenty-four countries, territories, or regions' where they met 'the majority, I think, of the national African leaders'.[23]

A few days later, at a press conference in New York on 4 February, Hammarskjöld referred directly to Macmillan's Cape Town speech, saying: 'That is not news'. Like Macmillan, he had been taken with 'this new national consciousness' among African political leaders, and in particular with 'their philosophy' regarding the United Nations.[24] He had made the 'strictly professional' tour of Africa for 'study', in order to improve his understanding of the new nations joining the UN. His conclusion was that 'Africa today is in one sense a unity', however differently refracted it was in its various lands.

Hammarskjöld saw the UN as a membrane of governance between colonial powers and their former colonial territories. In a rather involved metaphor, he once even quipped to the French minister of cultural affairs that the UN was like an Angostura bitters that kept the tonic of relations between former colonial powers and former colonies in good flavour.[25] The following year, 1961, Hammarskjöld died in a plane crash as he travelled to the Congo, in circumstances that remain unclear to this day.

A Shifting World

The African trips of Harold Macmillan and Dag Hammarskjöld in 1960 reveal a shifting centre of gravity in the post-war world. Decolonisation was the promise of a postcolonial world, and the realities of anticolonial agency meant that Britain could not control the destiny of the colonies. The attempts to reconceive British imperialism after 1945, the immigration controls on the right of entry into Britain in 1962, and ultimately the patrial-based system of control created in 1971, took place in sequence with dynamic changes in world politics in which African and Asian leaders among others helped define a post-war international public sphere.

British officials used the term 'coloured immigration' as a distancing strategy that belied the fact not only that so-called immigrants carried British nationality, but also that Britain was facing fierce debates on questions of colonial accountability internationally at the very same time as it was authoring immigration laws. In other words, immigration, despite being invariably presented as a domestic issue, was intertwined with the international politics and diplomacy of decolonisation.

The passage of the 1962 Commonwealth Immigrants Act coincided with the quickening pace of decolonisation in Africa, and the subsequent immigration acts of 1968 and 1971 were passed at moments when international debates on race, human rights and global social and economic equality were at their height. The point is not to argue for a direct causal association here, but to show that post-war immigration did not occur in a vacuum. Immigration was in fact a part of Britain's imperial gambit in the post-war world – an attempt to enjoy the benefits of national sovereignty at the level of immigration while at the same time taking advantage of perceived imperial influence globally.

This chapter introduces the ideas, relationships and arenas of discussion that helped to create a set of postcolonial international norms. By listening to the voices of new, formerly colonised states and their leaders, we can make better sense of post-war immigration during a time in world history when racial equality and accountability for colonialism were at the forefront of international debate.

It is too often overlooked that a new international environment characterised by deep concern about antiracism, anticolonialism and equality more generally placed constraints on, and drew explicit criticism towards British immigration policies, especially in relation to racial discrimination. For British officials, ideas of racial equality and human rights were not simply concerns for post-war immigration policy at home; they were also at the heart of international debates in which Britain was heavily implicated abroad. This was particularly true for a unique period between the late 1940s and the early 1970s, when the UN became a theatre for debate on these topics.

This wider international context enables much-needed light to be cast on the fate of the Commonwealth empire. Although it had been designed to be the very expression of British imperialism, newly joined Commonwealth states worked to drive the association away from Britain and towards an anticolonial internationalism. By the 1960s, the Commonwealth had become, as the phrase went, a 'multi-racial association' – no longer one of white-settler states plus Britain, but one that by 1960 included the new republics of India, Pakistan, Cyprus, and Ghana, as well as the 'dominion' of Nigeria (itself later a republic) and the Federation of Malaya (later Malaysia).

As far as Jawaharlal Nehru was concerned, as he announced to the Lok Sabha (the lower house of the Indian parliament) in 1955, the Commonwealth had taken 'a tremendous leap' following Britain's decision to allow a republican India to retain its membership. For Nehru, Indian membership in the Commonwealth did not mean that India would be 'subordinate to anybody'. Nehru noted that the hoped-for accession of an independent Gold Coast into the Commonwealth would be an even more significant step, commenting that it 'changes the entire character' of the Commonwealth. 'Here is a full-blooded African nation', remarked Nehru, 'for the first time being associated in this way'. It meant that 'the European character of the Commonwealth' would finally give way, in the wake of 'free Asian and African nations coming together' within it.[26]

By 1967, fourteen additional former British territories, now newly independent states, had joined the Commonwealth. British officials now saw the Commonwealth as being internally split into 'white' and 'non-white' elements. In 1967 the Commonwealth affairs secretary, Herbert Bowden, wrote to his colleagues in the cabinet that Britain was not only experiencing 'damaging intervention by the United Nations', but was also subject to 'violent and blackguardly attacks' by various Commonwealth leaders 'of African origin'. Diplomatic meetings with Commonwealth leaders in the 1960s had deteriorated so far as to resemble 'Britain clutching vipers to her bosom'.[27] Not only had Britain's punt on the Commonwealth led to the problem of post-war immigration; Commonwealth governments in Asia and Africa had not shied away from making their views about British policies felt.

The Makers of a New World

The British empire after 1945 was sustained by a longstanding assumption that there was a special British genius animating the future of world governance – that there was no entity better placed than imperial Britain to evolve the peoples of the world into harmonious cooperation, association and federation. Yet we can now acknowledge that ideas looking beyond the nation-state or towards international cooperation were hardly exclusive. There were alternative anticolonial visions of the future not simply at a national but at a transnational level.

A Pan-African Congress held in Chorlton-on-Medlock Town Hall in inner-city Manchester in October 1945, for example, not only demanded 'autonomy and independence' for 'Black Africa', but acknowledged a progression towards 'inevitable world unity and federation'. The prize of national sovereignty would secure freedom from direct imperial rule, but this was simply one stage in a movement towards world political unification. Notionally distinct 'groups and peoples' of the world would finally coalesce within a single political structure.

Organised among others by British Guiana–born Ras Makonnen, American-born W. E. B. Du Bois, Trinidad-born George Padmore, and future Kenyan leader Jomo Kenyatta, who had completed his education in London, the 1945 Congress rejected the supposed progressive character of British imperialism. The Western world was 'still determined to rule mankind by force', it declared. A short but respectful article in the *Manchester Guardian* declared that the some 200 delegates of the Congress represented 'virtually the whole coloured world'.[28]

Concerned with dimensions of British imperial rule in particular, the programme of the Pan-African Congress in Manchester made transnational connections between 'Imperialism in North and West Africa', 'Oppression in South Africa', 'The East African Picture', 'The Problem in the Caribbean' and 'The Colour Problem in Britain'. 'At the present moment there [are] many coloured people in Britain', noted Edwin Duplan, born in Gold Coast Colony and representing the Negro Welfare Centre based in Liverpool, at the opening session. Britain's black community had contributed 'a very major part' to the war effort and formed a sizable presence in places like Liverpool, Cardiff and Hull. Yet they found themselves 'victims of the colour bar'. 'One of the reasons why coloured people come to Britain is imperialism in our own countries', responded E. A. Aki-Emi, also born in Gold Coast Colony and representing the London-based Coloured Workers Association. It was a fact 'uncomfortable to live with', thought Aki-Emi, since, on the promise of and right to a livelihood in the imperial heartland, people had migrated to Britain only to face racial discrimination.[29]

The rest of the sessions at the 1945 Pan-African Congress moved seamlessly to consider different imperial situations and places. Its resolutions rejected imperial paternalism and 'pretentious constitutional reforms'.[30] The Special Branch police unit and MI5 each produced detailed reports of the proceedings, to be passed on to the Colonial Office. The MI5 report made particular note of 'well known negro extremists' in attendance.[31] Certain attendees of the conference, in particular Hastings Banda, Jomo Kenyatta and Kwame Nkrumah, went on to be synonymous with anticolonial resistance in Africa, and eventually became the leaders of Malawi, Kenya and Ghana, respectively.

The Pan-African Federation subsequently wrote optimistically to Labour prime minister Clement Attlee on behalf of the Congress to demand 'for the Colonial peoples the immediate right to self-determination'.[32] Pan-African ideas, already in circulation for several decades, by 1945 foreshadowed not simply liberation movements but attempts by postcolonial leaders to instil federation both across Africa as a whole and regionally within it.

The 1945 Pan-African Congress also had half an eye on the newly created United Nations, whose Charter came into force that same month, following a huge diplomatic conference in San Francisco earlier in the year. After the Congress, the African-American scholar, W. E. B. Du Bois, in his capacity as its international president, sent a memorandum to the new United Nations Secretariat, urging that 'representatives of the African colonial peoples' should be included in the activity of the new organisation.[33] This was a pressing concern given that African peoples were still largely colonised, and that just four African states – Egypt, Ethiopia, Liberia and South Africa – had been recognised as sovereign by the UN, the latter under white-minority rule.

The United Nations: Contesting the Post-War World

The original meaning of the term 'United Nations' referred to a declaration made upon American entry into the Second World War. The 'United Nations' were those powers joined in military alliance against Germany and Japan. Now established as a permanent organisation to promote international peace and security, the United Nations in its new form was realised at a San Francisco conference that ran for two months in 1945, where delegations from fifty nations participated, amounting to a total of over 3,000 attendees. The most pressing question for those wanting to end colonial rule was whether this new world organisation would support the anticolonial cause.

Some legal scholars argue that the UN Charter was not simply an international treaty, but served as a world constitution.[34] At first blush, its language appeared to support anticolonialism, referring to the 'principle of equal rights and self-determination of peoples'. The idea of 'self-determination' belonged to Western political philosophy, and a version of it had appeared in the 1941 Atlantic Charter, a public statement of Anglo-American war aims. The Atlantic Charter, the clear precursor to the UN Charter, had referred to 'the right of all peoples to choose the form of government under which they will live' – a turn of phrase that worried Churchill.[35]

What was more, the UN Charter embodied a principle of racial non-discrimination, declaring that the pursuit of freedoms globally applied to all people 'without distinction as to race, sex, language, or religion'. This clause was driven by India, Haiti and Uruguay, whose delegations spoke out against racial discrimination. India was included as a non-sovereign original member of the UN because of its previous membership of the now defunct League of Nations. The non-discrimination clause of the UN Charter built on a Chinese proposal (made during talks the year before) that a 'principle of equality of all states and all races shall be upheld'.[36]

Much like the rejected Japanese proposal on racial equality at the 1919 Paris Peace Conference, the Chinese proposal in the 1940s was a direct reference to long-standing anti-Chinese immigration laws across the Anglo-Saxon world, notably in Australia, Canada, New Zealand and the United States. But the Chinese proposal, a direct incursion on the sovereign discretion of states, was rejected in the final formulation of the UN Charter, principally by the United States, in favour of a short clause on non-discrimination.

Advocacy for a principle of universal racial equality in the UN Charter was also resisted by delegations from Australia and South Africa, which were keen that their prerogatives to pass immigration laws among other things should remain unchecked.[37] In its final form, the UN Charter showed the limits of its antiracism in its special emphasis in Article 2(7) on the privileges of the 'domestic jurisdiction of any state', ensuring that much of a member-state's domestic politics would be beyond the reach of the United Nations.

If the UN Charter's reference, in particular, to the 'self-determination of peoples' appeared to enshrine an anticolonial principle in international affairs and international law, there were other elements of the Charter that were more ambiguous on the question of colonialism. The UN Charter did not even mention colonialism or imperialism directly, but instead referred euphemistically to 'non-self-governing territories'.

Under the UN Charter, member-states of the United Nations that happened to be colonial powers had an obligation, expressed as a 'sacred trust', to the peoples within so-called 'non-self-governing territories', including to 'develop self-government' in each territory. 'Self-government' was the language of the British Colonial Office, and did not imply an end to empire. In an official gloss on the import of the UN Charter, the British

Foreign Office noted assuredly that it merely 'prescribes the principles of Colonial Administration', and did not 'empower the United Nations organisation to intervene' in colonial affairs per se.[38] As the colonial secretary, Oliver Stanley, publicly declared in 1942, Britain was 'pledged to guide Colonial people along the road to self-government within the framework of the British Empire.'[39]

The UN Charter directly replicated the language of British trusteeship and paternalism, deciding on behalf of colonised peoples where their constitutional destination lay, as if a grant of freedom made too soon would be an abdication of responsibility by an imperial parent. It was next to impossible to read the UN Charter in such a way as to imagine that it granted colonised peoples a right to self-government per se – still less a right to self-determination and the full autonomy that the term implied.

Instead, the UN Charter recognised self-government and self-determination as prized potential outcomes in a programme of concerted political action. Vijaya Lakshmi Pandit, Nehru's sister and the leader of a non-official Indian delegation to the San Francisco Conference, had spurned the interests that led to a colonialism-friendly UN Charter. 'Great Britain, France and the Netherlands', she declared in a statement in May 1945, 'all colonial powers, have proposed "self-government" as a substitute for "independence" … The British formula of "self-government" – an ancient weasel word – was deliberately designed and has long been used in India and elsewhere to offer the shadow but never the substance of independence to subject peoples.'[40]

The United Nations became something of an intermediating force between colonial and anticolonial forces that each claimed to speak for the destiny and well-being of colonial populations. The original members of the UN in 1945 included the United States, Britain, France, South Africa, Australia, New Zealand and Canada, as well as India, Egypt, the Philippines and Cuba. The British government certainly received the UN Charter, signed on 26 June 1945, as a victory for imperial civilisation. The UN was an affair of the 'Great Powers of the world, who have indeed taken the lead in this great enterprise', as lord chancellor William Jowitt told the House of Lords in August 1945.[41]

India's Global Voice

Within a year of the signing of the UN Charter, the still non-sovereign India marshalled its longstanding diplomatic reputation when its representative to the UN, Ramaswami Mudaliar, requested in June 1946 that the issue of 'treatment of Indians in South Africa' be included in the provisional agenda of the first session of the UN General Assembly.[42] South Africa had just passed the Asiatic Land Tenure and Indian Representation Act, a mandate for racial segregation.

By proposing that the United Nations consider racial discrimination in South Africa, India was not simply asserting itself on the world stage but testing the limits of the UN Charter. British and South African officials were convinced that the Indian request violated Article 2(7) of the Charter, which upheld domestic jurisdiction over internal affairs. Yet, to the general surprise of those involved, the Indian request was not thrown out at committee level, but included in the agenda of the second half of the very first session of the UN General Assembly, in late 1946.

Jawaharlal Nehru again nominated his sister Vijaya Lakshmi Pandit to lead the Indian delegation when the UN General Assembly convened in New York in late October. Pandit had by this time garnered a reputation for interventionist diplomacy and coruscating speeches. On 25 October 1946 she continued in this vein, declaring to the assembly that 'the treatment of Indians in the Union of South Africa' was not a marginal domestic matter but a pressing concern for 'civilised life' in the world. She positioned the United Nations as the conscience of the post-war world. 'Millions look to us', she declared, 'to resist and end imperialism in all its forms, even as they rely upon us to crush the last vestiges of fascism and nazism'. An end to imperialism spoke directly to 'the objects and purposes of the United Nations and of its Charter'.[43]

The manner in which the UN General Assembly now chose to interpret racial discrimination in South Africa would reveal its fitness for purpose. The whole world was watching. Pandit suggested that the 'progressive peoples of all countries – more particularly the non-European peoples of the world – who, let it not be forgotten, are an overwhelming section of the human race' would now see whether the United Nations would live up to its ideals or was prepared to forsake its purpose. What was remarkable about Pandit's speech was not simply the way in which it pivoted

India into the world as a diplomatic leader, but the way in which it cast racial discrimination and imperialism as a threat to peace and amicable relations between nations.

The British delegation was forced to choose sides between two Commonwealth partners, India and South Africa, and came down decisively in favour of South Africa. Rather than argue in favour of South African policies, Hartley Shawcross, the British attorney-general who was Britain's delegate, argued that India's challenge to South Africa was inadmissible under Article 2(7), and dismissed Pandit as a rhetorician.[44] Nonetheless, despite the protestations of South Africa, Britain and even the United States, the Indian effort succeeded. In December 1946 the UN General Assembly adopted a resolution on the 'Treatment of Indians in the Union of South Africa', rejecting it as a matter of domestic jurisdiction and instead declaring that South African policies did not conform to 'relevant provisions of the Charter', including its commitment to human rights. But this was more a diplomatic victory than anything that carried the power to force a change to South African policies.[45]

Indian activism at the United Nations in 1946 had shown that the UN Charter could be redeployed towards antiracist, and by extension anticolonial, ends. Although it did not mention colonialism directly, the Universal Declaration of Human Rights, approved by the UN General Assembly in December 1948, framed human rights as universal, extending them to the 700 million or so people living in colonial territories of various kinds in 1948. Although core UN member-states had always intended to expand on the UN Charter's commitment to 'fundamental human rights' and the 'dignity and worth of the human person' in the form of an international bill of human rights, the Declaration also bore the influence of anticolonial and antiracist thought. Articles 2 and 7 expanded on the UN Charter's commitment to non-discrimination.

The commitment to ending racial discrimination was built into the United Nations insofar as it referred to Nazi racial ideology. But in the drafting of the Universal Declaration of Human Rights, delegates raised instances of racial discrimination that implicated existing regimes, including the treatment of African-Americans in the United States, Indians in South Africa, and Africans in the British colonies of the Gold Coast, Nigeria and Rhodesia.[46]

When Jawaharlal Nehru addressed the UN General Assembly in Paris a month before the passage of the Declaration, he used the occasion to stress the 'evils of colonialism and of imperial domination'. Where 'racial inequality is practiced', he remarked, where 'it is a menace to world peace' and where it 'violates the principles of the United Nations Charter', it posed too great a threat to peaceful relations between states to be tolerated. He then spoke of the evolving forms of colonialism being refined by the British government, among other colonial powers. It was, he thought, 'an astonishing thing that any country should still venture to hold and to set forth this doctrine of colonialism, whether it is under direct rule or whether it is indirectly maintained in some form or other'.[47]

India's delegate to the UN commission that led to the Universal Declaration of Human Rights was the Gujarati feminist Hansa Mehta, who also helped to draft a programme of women's rights at the UN. Following Nehru's advice, she emphasised that human rights might help to resolve the inequities posed by regimes of immigration and citizenship following the migrations of the past. As recorded by historian Manu Bhagavan, Mehta declared to her fellow delegates at the UN committee in New York that 'during the past one hundred years, four million Indians had been transplanted to various parts of the world … As a result of this transplantation, numerous cases of denials of rights in law and equality and complicated questions of nationality and citizenship had arisen'.[48]

She and Nehru were optimistic – incorrectly, as it turned out – that these delicate questions might finally be solved by the United Nations and its international bill of human rights. Although several articles within the Declaration touched on questions of migration, nationality and racial discrimination, these were not framed in such a way as to interfere with states' right to determine who were its citizens (nationals) and to convene immigration controls for non-nationals. What was more, the Declaration was not a treaty, and contained no mechanisms of legal enforcement.

The British government felt that it had no choice but to support the Universal Declaration of Human Rights in the face of strong American commitment. British officials at the Foreign, Colonial and Commonwealth Relations offices felt a loss of control over the shape of the Declaration, but reassured themselves privately that it was designed 'solely as a Statement of Ideals', and related more to past Nazi atrocities than to the colonial present.[49] The British colonial secretary even recommended to colonial governors around the world that they publish the Declaration locally, though in the event many colonial officials stopped short of doing so. Regarding certain African colonies, officials in London soon conceded the hypocrisy of the idea: 'We can hardly expect to win the confidence of Africans by making statements of 'ultimate ideals' while in practice we take steps in precisely the opposite direction.'[50]

Whatever its implications for colonialism, the Universal Declaration of Human Rights was received in the West as a Cold War victory and the fruit of civilised Western leadership. American composer Aaron Copland was commissioned to write a work commemorating the adoption of the Declaration; the first performance of Copland's work took place in Carnegie Hall, New York, in December 1949. By way of an opening, English actor Laurence Olivier read sonorously and inimitably the full preamble to the United Nations Charter to an audience that included Eleanor Roosevelt.[51]

Contests over its symbolic meanings notwithstanding, the Declaration quickly became a new avenue for pursuing anticolonial ends within the structures of the United Nations. A further UN General Assembly resolution, in 1950, suggested that 'the right of peoples and nations to self-determination' might potentially be incorporated into the evolving UN framework for universal human rights. Then, in January 1952, a new resolution went further by upholding an underlying principle that 'all peoples shall have the right of self-determination', explicitly calling on colonial powers to concede this right to peoples in their colonial territories.

This finally made the idea of self-determination not simply an international objective under the United Nations, but an explicitly universal principle carrying anticolonial implications.[52] The idea of self-determination meant different things to different UN member-states. But the fiercest opponents of a universal article on self-determination were Britain, France and Belgium. Australia, New Zealand, Canada, the United States and the Netherlands also voted against the article on self-determination at the UN in January 1952.[53]

By the turn of the 1950s, antiracism at the United Nations was also beginning to amplify. If Indian activism at the UN in 1946 had raised the question of discrimination against people of 'Indian origin' in South Africa, the UN General Assembly would soon take up the question of South African racism per se – despite the South African government's argument that apartheid did not involve racial discrimination. A UN General Assembly resolution declared in December 1950 that 'a policy of "racial segregation" (apartheid) is necessarily based on doctrines of racial discrimination'.[54]

African–Asian Visions

Although Western powers were often the most powerful force at the UN General Assembly in the 1950s, Asian, Arab and Latin American member-states had already shown their capacity to rearticulate UN sentiment, particularly at the level of human rights. The Canadian jurist John Humphrey, the first director of the Human Rights Division in the UN Secretariat, noted in his diary that 'backward countries in revolt' would inevitably use the United Nations as a forum to promote 'their own ideas about rights'.[55]

Indian prime minister Jawaharlal Nehru was busy in this period cultivating partnerships and associative initiatives according to his own idealism and in implicit rejection of the Commonwealth, to which India remained attached. Nehru, like many others, remained bewitched by what he termed the 'ideal of world federalism', a hope that a 'One World' government might emerge. Having organised an Asian Relations Conference in 1947, Nehru was able to broker an informal alliance of Asian and African countries at the UN three years later. Nehru's commitment to Indian leadership in the post-war world was bearing fruit. 'The coloured people of the whole world are looking towards the tremendous moral influence of the nation of India', an unnamed African-American journalist told Nehru at a press conference in February 1950.[56]

A few years later, Nehru and other Asian leaders marshalled themselves to organise the Asian–African Conference for International Order, more commonly known as the Bandung Conference, in the Indonesian town of Bandung in 1955. Coalescing around a unifying idea of 'non-alignment' with or autonomy from Cold War allegiances, this six-day event afforded a more formal means of articulating ideals of anticolonialism, antiracism and solidarity. Bandung was, Nehru told the Lok Sabha a few days afterwards, an example of 'practical idealism'. 'We believe that from Bandung', he went on, 'our great organization, the United Nations, has derived strength.' It was clear that 'Asia and Africa must play an increasing role in the conduct and the destiny of the world organization'.[57]

In the following year, 1956, British foreign secretary Selwyn Lloyd was preparing to visit Nehru in New Delhi. The Foreign Office briefed him that it was 'inevitable that India should be against the colonial system in general, and that this attitude should be particularly evident in a forum such as the United Nations'.[58] Lloyd needed all the advice he could get.

'I've never been to a foreign country, I don't speak any foreign languages, I don't like foreigners', he had told prime minister Winston Churchill upon being offered the post of minister of state at the Foreign Office almost five years earlier.[59] It was inevitable, the Foreign Office brief continued, that 'Indian representatives at the United Nations' had been 'foremost in criticising the "evils of colonialism" and pressing the "right" of dependant people to self-determination'. Nehru's India had been steadfast in presenting India 'as a champion of coloured peoples everywhere'.

India had now established its own high commissions in Britain's remaining colonies, many of which had sizeable South Asian diasporas. The Indian high commissions were disseminating publications locally that were 'more than critical' of British colonial policies, the Foreign Office brief continued. Yet the Foreign Office remained hopeful that imperial Britain would be able diplomatically to stave off the criticisms of its former prized colony. Indian diplomats, even the redoubtable V. K. Krishna Menon, had been receptive to recent reformist efforts in British colonial administration. With 'suitable and tactful encouragement we may hope that India's understanding may grow', the Foreign Office concluded.[60] As we saw in Chapter 2, one diplomatic success Britain did have in this period was Nehru's cooperation in restricting the issuance of passports to certain Indians wishing to migrate to Britain.

The rise of the African–Asian bloc within the United Nations was a sign that Britain and other 'white' states would have increasingly less control over the international norms of the post-war world. Racially discriminatory immigration laws continued to be criticised in the international fora of the 1950s, and Canada, New Zealand and Australia each attempted to make their immigration policies more palatable to antiracist international sentiment. Even the notorious 'White Australia' government was attempting 'to achieve better relations with the Asian countries' and courting 'Asian statesmen', the *Manchester Guardian* reported in 1958.[61]

World Condemnation of Apartheid: 1960

African representation at the United Nations had risen to twenty-six member-states by the end of 1960. Sixteen new states joined the United Nations that year, all of which were African. From the following year onwards, African and Asian states held a numerical majority over 'white' states in the UN General Assembly. In 1960, there was a culmination of the steady interpretive transformation of the UN Charter into an anticolonial mandate. Adopted in December that year, UN General Assembly resolution 1514, known as the 'Colonial Declaration', asserted that 'the peoples of the world ardently desire the end of colonialism in all its manifestations'.

Using the language of human rights and the commitment to world peace enshrined in the UN Charter, the Colonial Declaration stated that peoples held in colonial dependency had a 'right to self-determination' and a 'right to complete independence' to the effect that colonial powers should now take immediate steps 'to transfer all powers to the peoples' in any dependant territories. Although eighty-nine UN member-states voted in favour of the Colonial Declaration, Britain abstained alongside the United States, Australia, New Zealand and South Africa.[62]

1960 had also been important in ways that went well beyond Harold Macmillan's famous 'wind of change' speech. In March 1960, the Sharpeville massacre perpetrated by the South African police, in which sixty-nine had been killed and 180 injured, led to international condemnation of apartheid in South Africa. The *New York Times* condemned the 'evil policy of apartheid', describing the 'horror of dozens of Africans being mowed down and killed by rifles and machine guns as the result of a protest'. The *Times of India*, meanwhile, described the events in terms of a 'racial crisis'.[63]

African and Asian states at the UN immediately referred Sharpeville to the UN Security Council. The British government was put in a deeply uncomfortable position. The Commonwealth was meant to showcase British imperial leadership in unifying a multiracial world, and yet deeply racist South Africa was a member of the Commonwealth. There were the additional complications that Britain and apartheid South Africa were trading partners and bound together by the 1955 Simonstown Agreement, a cooperative military arrangement including arms sales. To make things even more complicated, South Africa's white electorate voted to become a republic in a referendum in October 1960. This meant that, if South Africa wanted to remain in the Commonwealth as a republic, it would have to apply to do so.

This situation came to a head at the 1961 Commonwealth Prime Ministers' Conference, held in London. By this time, mirroring the United Nations, the Commonwealth association was no longer an expression of an imagined Anglo-Saxon world plus India, but a group that included India, Pakistan, Ceylon, Ghana, Malaya and Nigeria, as well as Canada, Australia, New Zealand and South Africa. British officials knew that apartheid would dominate the discussions in London; they worried that South African racism threatened the very existence of the Commonwealth, and by extension British imperial identity.

The Commonwealth Relations Office was particularly concerned about Ghana, Malaya and Nigeria, noting that 'the strong views of the Prime Ministers of all these countries about apartheid are well known and all have expressed them pretty freely in public'. It was more sanguine about the position of India, since Vijaya Lakshmi Pandit, now Indian high commissioner in London, had indicated that 'India would not take the lead in excluding South Africa from the Commonwealth'.[64] Harold Macmillan had written to Nehru urging him to remain open-minded on South Africa, since 'there is a real danger to the whole Commonwealth structure and the beginning of a break-up now'.[65]

Preparing Macmillan for a difficult occasion, the Commonwealth Relations Office reiterated that its position was that it wished 'to keep South Africa in'. The reasons for this included Britain's 'very large total investment (some £900 million)' in the country, a huge supplier of gold, among other things.[66] In the event, the conference at Lancaster House in London in March 1961 saw sustained protest against apartheid from half of the leaders of the Commonwealth, amid vows to make apartheid a permanent topic of discussion, to the extent that South African prime minister Hendrick Verwoerd was recorded in the final meeting declaring himself 'shocked by the spirit of hostility and in this last meeting even of vindictiveness shown towards South Africa'.[67]

A month after the London conference, in April 1961, the UN General Assembly passed another resolution condemning apartheid (although not mentioning Sharpeville directly), requesting that states take 'individual and collective action' against South Africa.[68] Significantly, Britain voted in favour. If the British imperial imagination believed that the Commonwealth was uniquely placed to usher into being a new world after 1945, it was now reckoning with a vast array of new ideas and initiatives to create a new world based on racial and other forms of equality and freedom from colonialism.

Britain was being shifted away against its will from the burden of empire by 'the burden of world opinion', as the American scholar and diplomat

Robin Winks put it the 1970s.[69] The international public sphere was being redefined by the African–Asian presence in both the United Nations and the Commonwealth. Given the imperial origins of both entities, this was a sea-change both rich and strange, depending on one's perspective.

Following the 1961 conference, South Africa duly became a republic, but withdrew its application to remain in the Commonwealth. Macmillan himself did not like the vast changes to the composition of the Commonwealth – now more African and less white. Reflecting on events to a colleague a year later, he remembered that it used to be 'like a small and pleasant house party'. Now it had become 'a sort of miniature United Nations', the African–Asian presence 'strongly organised', leaving 'the older members not knowing quite how to handle it'. The future of the Commonwealth looked uncertain. 'So the first question really is, is it worth it?', asked Macmillan. 'Would we', he wondered, 'be better to chuck it and regroup round the Crown: Canada, Australia and New Zealand and the United Kingdom?'[70]

The 'treatment of Indians' item secured by India in 1946 had remained on the UN General Assembly agenda annually (except for a single session) until 1962. In that year the item was merged with a separate India-led item on apartheid.[71] A UN General Assembly resolution of November 1962 exhorted member-states to enforce diplomatic, military and economic sanctions against South Africa. A UN Special Committee on Apartheid was also appointed. Following a UN Security Council resolution in August 1963 urging an arms embargo on South Africa, Harold Wilson's Labour government prevaricated on whether it would honour its 1955 contractual agreement to sell various types of military vessels and helicopters to South Africa, eventually stopping short of selling arms to the apartheid regime.

Rejecting Post-War British Imperialism

The longstanding British claim to expertise on federal innovation in world politics was now being challenged by leaders in Africa and the Caribbean. British federal visions were one of the devices by which Britain had sought to maintain its interests in a decolonising world. In the 1950s and early 1960s, Conservative politicians wanted to move East Africa towards a regional federation, building on the longstanding cooperation of British colonial governors there. An East African federation was regarded as a 'dream answer' and a 'wonderful prize' by senior Conservative politicians.[72] Federation in East and Central Africa was a bald attempt to protect white-settler interests, and in the early 1960s British politicians, keen on stewarding decolonisation, still saw federation as a preferred constitutional model.

But new postcolonial leaders in former British colonies took ideas of federalism towards more radically egalitarian goals. Eric Williams, prime minister of Trinidad and Tobago, proposed a federation for the West Indies, and Ghanaian prime minister Kwame Nkrumah proposed a Union of African States to help propel the new states out of postcolonial fragility. Although the West Indies Federation (1958–62) and the Union of African States (1958–61) did not last long, they revealed that visions of world order were being redeployed by a number of postcolonial leaders. As Jamaican prime minister Norman Manley remarked in a radio broadcast to a Caribbean audience in June 1960: 'Each of us alone is small in the world today. Because we are small, it is the simple truth that for us unity is strength.'[73]

To say that British officials resented the role of the United Nations in attempting to force the terms and timing of decolonisation is an understatement. From the UN Trusteeship Council to the UN Special Committee on Decolonisation, created in the early 1960s, British discontent against such efforts was best summed up in 1962 by Hilton Poynton, permanent under-secretary at the Colonial Office. 'I do not accept that the United Nations should have a right to meddle in our Colonial affairs', he wrote to colleagues.[74] The following year, a British diplomat, Clifford William Squire, reported to the Foreign Office that British diplomats, when confronted by the Special Committee on Decolonization, whose sessions were held in New York, were best advised to simply accept any criticism – to follow 'Confucius' advice to the girl about to be raped', as Squire put it.[75] Notwithstanding such resentment by certain British officials, the United Nations played an indirect role in overseeing British decolonisation. In 1966, Hilton Poynton wrote to the British minister of overseas development: 'The United Nations consistently confuse "independence" with "freedom" … Colonial status is not incompatible with a full guarantee of civil liberties.'[76]

But the powerful anticolonial voice in the UN General Assembly should not be taken to suggest that colonial powers like Britain gave up attempting to control new regimes of international governance. Despite the paramountcy of state sovereignty, the UN itself attempted to assume a role at the helm of new initiatives for global development, creating bodies such as the UN Technical Assistance Administration. At the beginning of the 1960s, the UN was offering new states in the Global South the opportunity to draw on 'expert' personnel to help build new state institutions, experimenting most heavily in Africa, Latin America and the Caribbean. This was accompanied by the 'training of nationals to assume as early as possible the responsibilities temporarily assigned to the internationally recruited staff', as the office of UN secretary-general Dag Hammarskjöld put it.[77] The UN Technical Assistance Administration was absorbed by the newly created UN Development Programme in 1965.

Although the UN's various efforts – all contained in a global language of development – were a challenge to British colonial paternalism, as well as a harbinger of new forms of global governance and dependency in a nascent postcolonial world, they were not unfavourable to colonial powers seeking to maintain their vested interests. Given that 'development' itself was among other things an imperial attempt to capture interests after the end of direct imperial rule, Britain was not alone in attempting to glut the new states with its own personnel in the name of delivering 'technical assistance' and various kinds of expertise into the public administration of the new states.[78] New states were winning their independence, but their state bureaucracies and institutions remained flooded with colonial administrators.

In a typically candid speech at New College, Oxford, rising Kenyan politician Tom Mboya acknowledged the frustrating irony that, because 'of the lack of trained men and women', independent African states had to 'depend on outside experts to help them run the countries'. Mboya spoke of development in terms of 'the dangers of neo-colonialism' and urged for 'equality' not dependence:

> If we are equal, only help us where we need help; stop being paternalistic. We need a continuing flow of technical, specialist, financial, and other types of aid. We will take it from you and from any other nations ready to offer aid with no strings attached. Do not grumble when we take it. We take it because we need it, and we take it because it is given free. Remember, we are also capable of gauging the ulterior motives of all those who offer to help us.[79]

That same year, the United Nations declared the 1960s to be the UN's first 'development decade', taking its lead from US president John F. Kennedy, who in his inauguration speech in January 1961 pledged his commitment to 'those peoples in the huts and villages of half the globe'.[80]

Anti-Racism at the Heart of World Politics

Like self-determination, human rights had entered the post-war world under the auspices of imperial power only to be pivoted towards anti-racist and anticolonial ends in the international public sphere of the 1950s and 1960s. As future president of Tanzania, Julius Nyerere, wrote in the late 1950s, the Universal Declaration of Human Rights had shown the colonial powers that 'Africans are "people" too, all of them, not just the most advanced ones'.[81]

The conscious international rejection of racial discrimination and segregation in the United States and apartheid in South Africa moved 'race' to the heart of the debate on what universal human rights meant in practice. States like Canada, among others, could no longer afford to ignore global censure on racial discrimination. As the Canadian immigration minister Ellen Fairclough told the Canadian parliament in 1962, the 'newly-emerging nations of the world will be watching with interest to see how sincere we are in applying our new immigration policy'. Canada had now to show the world that 'Canadians too realize that the winds of change are blowing'.[82]

A number of African states at the United Nations, including Mali and the Central African Republic, managed to propel existing antiracist sentiment into a commitment that racial discrimination should form the basis of international human rights law. A new United Nations instrument specifically banning racial discrimination would help to remedy 'one of the greatest tragedies of all times', as the delegate of the Philippines told the UN General Assembly, 'the iniquitous degradation of the human being by reason of the colour of his skin'.[83]

Racial inequality was a transnational reality, pointed out the Senegalese delegate, 'still the rule in the African colonial territories and in South Africa' and 'not unknown in other parts of the world'.[84] The time had come to crystallise the longstanding question of racial discrimination into the world's first legally binding international human rights treaty (for states electing to be bound by it). The UN's International Convention on the Elimination of all Forms of Racial Discrimination, as it was named, marked the start of international human rights law when it was adopted in 1965.

During the UN debate on the draft of this convention in November 1965, certain delegates directly took issue with the idea that human rights belonged to a special Western genius. Following the Canadian delegate's comment that human rights were a 'traditional Western concept', Waldo Waldron-Ramsey, the Tanzanian delegate, stated that 'the Western world clearly had nothing to teach the developing countries in the matter of human rights; indeed, it was the Western world that had given birth to colonialism and slavery, while the developing countries had suffered as a result'.[85] Waldron-Ramsey singled out Britain for being uncommitted to implementing international recommendations and decisions on racial discrimination – and on international trade, for that matter, as had been set forth at the UN Conference on Trade and Development in 1964. 'The record of the Western countries in the matter of human rights', Waldron-Ramsey declared, gave those countries 'absolutely no right to take a patronizing attitude towards others'.[86]

The British delegate in New York in 1965 charged with responding to Waldron-Ramsey was Dora Gaitskell, born near Riga before her family migrated to Britain, and of Russian Jewish descent. She was married to former Labour leader Hugh Gaitskell. She fought back, albeit rather defensively, declaring that connections to trade and development were hardly relevant, and insisting that racial discrimination was 'a very complex subject'. Playing an apparently pre-prepared trump card, she wondered 'how the Tanzanian representative could impugn the motives of the United Kingdom when at that very time there was a bill on racial discrimination before the House of Commons'. Prudently, given this international context, Harold Wilson's Labour government was at that time promoting what, the following month, would become the first domestic Race Relations Act.

Just over two weeks later, Gaitskell diligently affirmed the new international consensus on race. There was, she declared, 'a wide feeling among Member States that racial discrimination was the most urgent of human rights problems'. Britain itself was 'taking measures to deal with the problem at home', and the British government believed that 'it was high time for the United Nations to play a more active part in the implementation of those rights.'[87] Ironically, she made this statement in the process of justifying her decision to abstain from a vote to ensure a right for people in remaining colonial territories to be able to submit petitions individually to the UN's Committee on the Elimination of Racial Discrimination.

Led by the efforts of Ghana and the Philippines, the UN's International Convention on Racial Discrimination itself was nonetheless passed unanimously on 21 December 1965, some 106 states voting in favour. By this time, Asian and African states made up 54 per cent of the UN's overall membership. The concept of antiracism was cogent enough for those states willing to ratify the convention partially to restrict their sovereignty over domestic affairs.

If this history of the role of postcolonial states in the evolution of the norms of international human rights law seems obscure, it is because it has only recently received attention from historians. As one historian has recently noted, if a set of countries from the Global South were 'the driving force behind the breakthrough of universal human rights, how Western, then, is the concept?'[88]

The debates and votes on human rights on the international stage in the 1960s left Britain in the difficult position of defending its imperial record and immigration policies without wanting to be seen to disparage human rights. When senior Labour ministers suggested privately in 1967 that Britain might 'easily assume a leading, and even dominant, role [in the] field of human rights', they thought only of Europe, not of the wider international public sphere.[89]

On the international stage, it was another former British colony, Jamaica (independent since 1962), that became a diplomatic leader in the field of human rights in the 1960s. Future Jamaican prime minister Hugh Shearer proposed further human rights initiatives to the UN General Assembly in 1963, in order to target 'denials of human rights in whatever form and by whatever name – apartheid, segregation, Jim Crow, or colour prejudice'.[90] The subsequent efforts of Jamaica's UN ambassador, Egerton Richardson, on this front led to the first UN World Conference on Human Rights in Tehran in 1968, and secured 1968 as the first UN 'international year of human rights'. Meanwhile, Britain was playing catch-up to these developments. Although Britain ratified the UN's Convention on Racial Discrimination in 1969, it provided an interpretative gloss arguing that its Commonwealth Immigrants Acts of 1962 and 1968 had not involved racial discrimination either in principle or in practice.[91]

Holding Britain to Account

The second half of the 1960s saw Commonwealth membership increase further as more former British territories gained independence. These included Malta, Malawi and Zambia in 1964; Singapore and the Gambia in 1965; Botswana, Lesotho, Barbados and Guyana in 1966; Mauritius and Swaziland in 1968; and Fiji and Tonga in 1970. By the middle of the 1960s, no British official could claim that the Commonwealth remained the older 'Commonwealth empire' of the first half of the twentieth century. The claim that the Commonwealth was the expression of Britain's civilisational, constitutional and institutional claims on the world ignored current realities. Commonwealth Heads of Government Meetings, as they were called after 1969, were notorious in British eyes for their anti-colonial and antiracist sentiment.[92] Alongside debates on equitable trade arrangements, certain Commonwealth states criticised Britain for its stance on apartheid in South Africa and white-minority rule in Rhodesia.

Under British constitutional law, the white-minority government in Southern Rhodesia was a self-governing colony – an idea rejected by the UN General Assembly, which had suggested that it was a 'non-self-governing territory', insofar as it denied self-determination to the African majority.[93] Already a source of tension, Rhodesia became an international-relations disaster for Britain in 1965, when the white-settler Rhodesian Front unilaterally declared its independence from Britain on 11 November 1965. The very next day, the UN Security Council passed a resolution calling Rhodesia an 'illegal racist minority régime'. The basis of the illegality was that it denied its African majority self-determination. Eight days later, the Security Council passed another resolution calling the Rhodesian Front regime a 'racist settler minority'.[94]

In December 1965, Tanzania and Ghana both broke diplomatic relations with Britain over Rhodesia, despite both remaining in the Commonwealth. The *Times of India* described the situation in Rhodesia as a 'tragedy in the heart of Africa'. British promotion of white-settler interests had led to the 'illegal seizure of power by the white supremacists in that

colony in open defiance of world opinion'. It was true that the timing of
the Rhodesian move – one month before the adoption of the UN Convention on Racial Discrimination – could not have put it more out of step
with international norms. The only hope, declared the *Times of India*, was
for the UN to intervene, or for 'world opinion' to pressure Britain to use
military force to end the rule of the '220,000 white settlers' assumed to
be loyal to the regime.[95]

Between 1965 and 1970, there were six Security Council resolutions
on the rogue white-minority regime in Rhodesia. Britain vetoed one that
called for the use of force and the severance of all communications with
Rhodesia. Whatever the fury of Harold Wilson's Labour government
against Rhodesia's decision, it saw too many risks in using military force
against the Rhodesian Front; nor was military force against white British
'kith and kin' in Rhodesia seen as an attractive proposition.[96]

In 1965, the Commonwealth acquired a Secretariat – a Nigerian and
Ugandan suggestion – breaking the influence of London's Commonwealth Relations Office over the association, now enabling it to mirror the
organisational structures of the UN. Relations with Ghana were finally
restored in March 1966, and with Tanzania in July 1968. In 1966 the
Commonwealth Prime Ministers' Conference was held in Lagos; this was
the first time, Foreign and Commonwealth Office officials remembered a
few years later, that the conference had been held outside London – a sign
of loss of control for the British, for whom the 1966 conference was a 'low
point' in the Commonwealth that 'dealt solely with Rhodesia'.[97]

Indeed, Zambian president Kenneth Kaunda threatened to leave the
Commonwealth over Britain's failure to use force against Rhodesia.
Whether over the question of arms sales to apartheid South Africa or
white-minority rule in Rhodesia, British policies were eviscerated by
African leaders in particular, who used the Commonwealth to hold
Britain to account. In the words of one British diplomat, the experi-
ence of listening to Commonwealth discussions in the mid 1960s was
'not unlike that which I suffered through long hours of fruitless United
Nations oratory'.[98]

Despite the tenacity of a British imperial vision throughout this period,
the Commonwealth Office admitted to the cabinet in 1967 that many of
the countries in the Commonwealth now belonged not to Britain but to
the 'Afro–Asian world'.[99] At a Commonwealth Conference on Aid and
Development, held in Nairobi in May 1967, senior Kenyan politician

Tom Mboya poured cold water on any notion of British leadership. It was anachronistic to say that the Commonwealth was about Britain – 'our governmental systems are departing rapidly from the British model' – declared Mboya, suggesting instead that the association should consider solely questions of 'aid, technical assistance and export promotion'.[100]

British diplomat Crispin Tickell described Commonwealth leaders' sentiments in the following terms: 'the newer, darker ones feel obscurely that Britain should be morally obliged to pay for her imperialism by providing whatever sort of aid, protection or help they may require at any particular moment'.[101] What was more, the United Nations outshone the Commonwealth as an international grouping. As P. J. S. Moon, first secretary of the UK Mission to the UN, wrote to the Commonwealth Office in 1966, 'so far as the UN is concerned, the Commonwealth has already almost ceased to exist'.[102] But since Britain had wedded its nationality and its imperial identity to the Commonwealth, British officials had to live with the reality that African and Asian Commonwealth states might stage a mass departure, and keep imperial hope alive where possible.

India, too, increasingly used the Commonwealth to attack British policies. Jawaharlal Nehru, who had valued the Commonwealth association, died unexpectedly in 1964. Relations between Britain and India soured in the mid 1960s, when India and Pakistan went to war, and when, in 1966, Indira Gandhi, Nehru's daughter, came into power.[103] More of a realist than her idealist father, Indira Gandhi placed far less importance on India's Commonwealth link. This did not stop Harold Wilson's Labour government displaying in the 1960s 'a sort of hankering in a way for the great role Britain could play in the sub-continent', as Peter Hall, a British diplomat based in New Delhi between 1966 and 1969, recalled in a recent interview. Yet these attempts to influence Indian–Pakistani relations, Hall concluded, only proved that Britain could not, 'when push came to shove, influence Indian policies'.[104]

Despite Indira Gandhi's more muscular foreign policy and the waning of the African–Asian solidarities of the 1950s, the Indian government chimed with African states in using the Commonwealth as an arena in which to hold Britain to account. During a press conference in Allahabad in December 1968, Gandhi stated that Britain and India were divided on Rhodesia, calling it 'a very flammable issue [that] could set the whole of Africa on fire'.[105] Gandhi, the Foreign and Commonwealth Office warned prime minister Edward Heath in 1970, 'might take India out of the Commonwealth over the South African arms issue'.[106] Gandhi wrote to Heath directly in July 1970 to tell him that the 'total effect of your new approach to the Southern African question will be to re-enforce the racist regimes in Rhodesia and South Africa'.[107]

Like certain African leaders, Indira Gandhi was also concerned about the integrity of the Indian Ocean – in particular, South Africa's naval gateway to Indian Ocean waters. As Singapore's prime minister Lee Kuan Yew privately confided to Edward Heath in 1970, Tanzania's Julius Nyerere and Zambia's Kenneth Kaunda both believed that 'a section of the Conservative Party wanted to endorse apartheid'; nor did they believe the British government's 'arguments about defence in the Indian Ocean'.[108] If the Commonwealth was performing its presumed role in protecting world peace, this was not in deference to British policies but actively in resistance to them.

Gains and Losses

In 1970 the United Nations celebrated twenty-five years since the signing of the UN Charter. At the UN General Assembly in New York, Norwegian diplomat Edvard Hambro used the opportunity as acting chairman of the assembly to survey the past and present of world politics. If the origin moment of the United Nations in 1945 had upheld state sovereignty, he remarked, the 'ideology of national sovereignty' had been wielded as 'an instrument for national liberation' from colonialism, and 'remains in the minds of many as the ultimate guarantee'.[109] The month after Hambro's address, the UN held a ten-day commemorative session with newly elected prime minister Edward Heath in attendance.

The UN's 'anniversary declaration' acclaimed the role of the UN in bringing about the liberation of peoples from colonial rule.[110] The number of formerly colonised sovereign states had 'greatly increased', it declared, yet at the same time Namibia, Southern Rhodesia, Angola, Mozambique and Portuguese Guinea (later Guinea-Bissau) had thus far been denied self-determination 'in deliberate and deplorable defiance of the UN and world opinion'. The declaration also condemned 'racism and the practice of racial discrimination in all its manifestations', including 'the evil policy of apartheid', a 'crime against the conscience and dignity of mankind'.[111]

The year 1970 also marked the ten-year anniversary of the UN's Colonial Declaration – already a landmark in the history of decolonisation. With this in mind, the 1970 UN Programme of Action identified a paradox of decolonisation, recognising that 'although many colonial countries and peoples have, in the last ten years, achieved freedom and independence, the system of colonialism continues to exist in many areas of the world'.[112] It recommended that the UN Security Council 'continue to give special attention to the problems of southern Africa' – in particular 'the regimes of South Africa and Portugal and the illegal racist regime of Southern Rhodesia'. There ought, it continued, to be 'an embargo on [the sale of] arms of all kinds' to Rhodesia, Portugal and South Africa.

The FCO briefed Edward Heath that, if he found himself on the back foot during his attendance at the proceedings in New York, he should be ready to remind his audience that it was 'after all a Conservative Prime Minister who made the "wind of change" speech', and that Conservative governments had presided over independence for 'the majority of African States'. Since Britain had 'done more for decolonization' than any other country, Heath should not feel that he had to 'dissociate [the British] from the general desire to mark the progress from colonial status to self-determination and independence'.[113] The following January, however, after a decade on the UN's Special Committee on Decolonization, its anti-colonial and anti-British sentiment proved too much, and Britain finally and unceremoniously left the committee.

Despite these momentous changes in the international public sphere, the question of a British obligation to honour arms sales to apartheid South Africa was resurrected by Edward Heath as soon as he assumed office. This obligation was justified in the name of the Cold War – the Cape sea routes were seen as central to containing the threat of a Soviet naval presence in the Indian Ocean – and the 1955 British–South African agreement on military cooperation. The Commonwealth Heads of Government Meeting held in Singapore in January 1971, which focused squarely on the issue of British arms sales to South Africa, became a nadir in Commonwealth relations. Heath's insistence on asserting Britain's right and need to make such arms sales almost ended the Commonwealth once and for all. As the *Times of India* noted in its summary of Commonwealth sentiment the week before the start of the conference, 'Mr Heath must have a very poor appreciation of the situation in Africa if he genuinely believes that the Commonwealth can survive the exit of some members on the issues of the sale of British arms to South Africa.'[114]

Tanzania's Julius Nyerere and Zambia's Kenneth Kaunda attempted to use the 1971 meeting to repurpose the Commonwealth yet again by presenting a set of Commonwealth Principles along the lines of a United Nations declaration.[115] Their draft text sought to consolidate the antiracism of the Commonwealth and transform its function. 'We are committed to the principles of human equality and dignity, self-determination and non-racialism and will use all our collective and separate efforts to implement them', it declared.[116]

British foreign secretary Alec Douglas-Home pointed out to Heath the dangers of the draft text, having received a circulated copy. It contained 'traps' that 'blur the principle of non-interference in the internal affairs of other Governments'.[117] In the final event, the draft was adjusted to uphold the right of individual countries to make discretionary decisions.[118] The 1971 Commonwealth Principles may have been symbolic and legally non-binding, but they showed just how definitively the Commonwealth had left British imperialism behind.

Having survived this latest diplomatic skirmish, Heath agreed later in 1971 to supply seven WASP military helicopters to apartheid South Africa, the sale itself going through a couple of years later.[119] When Heath's decision became public knowledge, the Indian Ministry of External Affairs made a statement declaring that Heath was acting in a way that might break up the Commonwealth, and that 'any accretion to the military strength of South Africa' would 'reinforce its racist policies' and assist both 'the illegal racist regime in Rhodesia' and 'Portugal's colonial oppression of the peoples of Angola and Mozambique'.[120] In the event, however, no country left the Commonwealth in protest.

A Possible Postcolonial World?

The early 1970s saw the climax of trends within the international public sphere after 1945 towards anticolonialism and international equality. Following upheavals in the world economy and international monetary system from 1971 onwards, this period of decolonisation then gave way to a new phase in globalisation. Amid its finally successful bid to join Europe, Britain now faced a new set of economic crises.

Britain signed the Treaty of Accession to enter Europe on 22 January 1972, becoming a full member of the European Communities, including the European Economic Community, on 1 January 1973. Postcolonial efforts towards regional economic integration included the Organisation of African Unity and the Caribbean Free Trade Association (the Caribbean Community after 1973). But deepening European integration did not mark the end of imperial relations between former colonial powers and their former colonies. In reaction to the possible severing of preferential imperial trade arrangements, many postcolonial states sought 'associated status' with the European Economic Community under article 238 of the Treaty of Rome. In 1963, eighteen newly independent African states signed the Yaoundé Convention between the Community and the Associated African States plus Madagascar. This would be superseded by the Lomé Convention in 1975 between the Community and seventy-one African, Caribbean and Pacific states.

Just like the Commonwealth, the 'outward-looking' and 'enlarged Communities' of Europe were a political palimpsest superimposed on the relationships of an imperial past.[121]

As Britain prepared to join the European Economic Community, economies like Jamaica had to lobby for their trade preferences anew within the coming European framework. In 1970 the FCO felt sure that Jamaican prime minister Hugh Shearer was unlikely to pull out of the Commonwealth over arms sales to South Africa because of 'the likely repercussions on their own vulnerable economy, with its labour intensive agricultural industries (sugar and bananas)'.[122]

If today we see the early 1970s as a turn towards economic globalisation, for Britain and certain of its former colonies the impact of an enlarged European Economic Community was in a sense the latest episode in decolonisation, throwing up another round of diplomatic efforts, threats, and promises based on old colonial relationships. Just as Guadeloupe, Martinique and francophone West Africa sought special trade preferences with Europe through their relationship with France, the former colonial power, Jamaica and the Windward Islands sought special arrangements with Europe through their existing relationships with Britain. Yet dependence on preferential treatment by the European Economic Community was far from ideal, and worked against Global South solidarities.

Developing African and Asian countries had formed a bloc of almost a hundred states in the 1960s to contest inequalities in international trade and economic dependence on former colonial powers. This bloc used the second United Nations Conference on Trade and Development, held in 1968 in New Delhi, to set out a programme by which the least developed states would not suffer as a result of the deepening integration of global capital markets. Instead they pressed for a global preferential trade arrangement that would ensure that all developing economies had equal access to non-reciprocal tariff cuts granted by developed economies. The proposals for a 'New International Economic Order', adopted by the United National General Assembly in 1974, exhibited the sharpness of the struggle for economic equality in the early 1970s.

A New World Rising

By the early 1970s, the gains of a radically egalitarian agenda in the postwar international public sphere – particularly on the questions of race, self-determination and human rights – had been substantial. Indian legal scholar Ram Anand wrote passionately in 1972 of the 'new world' wrought by decolonisation. His sense of novelty about this new world was mixed with a measure of awe and agnosticism about the future. 'With the decay and destruction of colonialism', wrote Anand, 'scores of new nations with their teeming millions' had emerged as 'full-fledged members of the international society'.

The new states were well aware that they had been 'subjugated and colonised and lost their identity'. Whatever the outstanding problems of world poverty, inequality and the nuclear threat, the achievement of freedom from colonial rule could not be underestimated. 'It is an age of unbounded opportunity', wrote Anand, who believed that the old dualisms between Christian and non-Christian, civilised and uncivilised, developed world and developing world might be cast aside. This was the promise of a shared world on equal terms: 'We are completely involved in a world society which is physically one because we share a common destiny and constitute a universal community. We are living today through the birthpangs of this wholly new world. We are entering upon a new age in the history of man, an age which has no precedent in human experience.'[123]

These ideas were a measure of the hope for egalitarian change and the near-millennialist desire for universal solutions to questions of social and political rights. Despite Anand's optimism, the struggle between colonial and anticolonial powers at the time of his writing was not over. Angola and Mozambique only gained independence from Portugal in 1975. But the new internationalism had carved out new norms with respect to what was acceptable and what was not – unless states wanted to risk reputational damage.

Britain emerged from the period of decolonisation with its self-image thoroughly divested of grander imperial claims. Contradiction and hypocrisy notwithstanding, certain elements within the British state, particularly in the diplomatic service and the merged Foreign and Commonwealth Office, continued to keep watch over the imperial flame into the 1970s. Some of this is captured by a Foreign and Commonwealth Office internal document of 1968 setting out Britain's soft imperial power in the world. 'Britain's image', the document contended, was secured by its 'internal race relations policy', its 'support for United Nations and multilateral agencies' and the existence 'of old and strong British connection' in the Commonwealth and world, including with 'people of British stock' in Australasia.[124]

If reputational power was central to Britain's influence in the world, Britain's self-image was confused and ultimately self-deceiving. Britain's race relations policy was belied by its immigration policy; its support for the United Nations was belied by its record at the UN Special Committee on Decolonisation and by its imperial record generally. The Commonwealth had been all but disbanded over the issues of race, Rhodesia, apartheid South Africa, and – as the next chapter will explore – immigration.

6

Race and Immigration in a Decolonising World

The history of race is more a typology – a range of ideas – than a single idea. Race had more than one meaning in the twentieth century. At first sight, many of the statements on race in the early twentieth century seem overtly supremacist. Arthur Percival, the first Rhodes lecturer in imperial history at King's College London, wrote in his *Introduction to the Study of Colonial History* in 1919 that colonial history was 'the history of the inter-action of the European with the less civilized races'.[1] Meanwhile Hugh Egerton, the first Beit professor of colonial history at Oxford, wrote in 1910 of 'the sense of an unseen super-intending Providence controlling the development of the Anglo-Saxon race'.[2]

But at the same time, race and culture were often used as synonyms in this period, and supremacist racial thought was increasingly seen as a liability for international ideals. Was it the Anglo-Saxon race that was naturally superior, or was it Anglo-Saxon culture? Could a non-white person belong to Anglo-Saxon culture, especially having been apprenticed in Anglo-Saxon civilisation? To make things more complicated, eugenic ideas were also taken seriously in Britain in the first half of the twentieth century, alongside attempts to revitalise the empire in the face of military defeats and the growing strength of rival imperial powers.[3]

Bearing this in mind, what did it mean that successive British pre-war and post-war governments were attentive to 'people of British stock' in the territories of the empire, and to dilution of 'British stock' at home?

'Stock' traditionally referred to a line of ancestral descent, synonymous with the more explicit 'blood'. A supposed British blood group or groups inevitably recalled nineteenth-century ideas of higher, lower or 'pure' racial stocks. Yet 'British stock' also referred to assumptions about a British character or civilisation with less explicitly racial content. Certainly, as the twentieth century wore on, British political elites retained the phrase 'British stock', but also tended to favour more delicate terms like 'belonging', 'connection' and 'community' as its natural synonyms.

After the 1950s, immigration became both a proxy for and an avatar of racial consciousness among British political elites. British immigration policies also became notorious internationally, as an unreconstructed British racism came into direct opposition to the international effort to eliminate racial discrimination. From the international perspective of Britain's former colonies, the sum of British theory on immigration and the Commonwealth was a racism that refused to die.

Talking Racial Domination

One of the original progenitors of racial thought in Britain was the anatomist Robert Knox, who gave a popular lecture series on the 'races of men' in the middle of the nineteenth century. In one of his choice phrases, Knox argued that 'race is everything in human history', and that 'the races of men are not the result of accident'. Knox was particularly interested in 'the Saxon' – 'the dominant race on the earth' – and the Saxon subset, 'the Anglo-Saxon', a race that had proved itself 'all-powerful on the ocean'. Knox was concerned with the future of 'dark races' and the racial significance of world migration in the Anglo-Saxon world. With racial supremacy came ideas of racial mixing and decline. Given that Europeans were 'now flocking to Australia', among other places, the idea of 'the Saxon' being 'converted into the Red Indian' or the 'Anglo-Saxon into the Hindoo' had to be considered.

Although haunted by the idea of racial mixing, Knox was so confident in his conclusions as to lead him to be critical of empire. It was 'almost certain' that the 'dark races' faced 'ultimate expulsion from all lands which the fair races can colonize'. The Saxon race was adept at using 'conventions, treaties' and 'law' in 'robbing the coloured races of their lands and liberty'.[4] Knox's thought was a tonic to Victorian Britain's social and political confidence and imperial paternalism. Reporting on one of Knox's lectures at the Athenaeum Club in London in 1847, the *Manchester Guardian* told readers that nothing short of the 'mastery of the world' was at stake in Knox's theory of racial difference and conflict. His lecture received 'the loud applause of a very numerous and highly respectable audience', the newspaper concluded.[5]

As the nineteenth century drew on, fears of white decline amid 'Asiatic' migration began to deepen in various parts of the empire, kindling the racial preoccupations of immigration control in the white-settler colonies. Purportedly 'scientific' racial theories and so-called Social Darwinism also crystallised at the end of the nineteenth century, each distinct but the latter anticipating the ideas of eugenics. Eugenic ideas had some purchase on British culture in the first half of the twentieth century, and even led to experiments in colonial administration by doctors and scientists in Kenya. The *New York Times*, in 1930, was not unusual in referring to the London-based *Eugenics Review* as a credible journal.[6]

At the same time, though, by the early twentieth century unchecked racial patriotism came to be seen as a dangerous source of conflict in the world. Influential criticisms of the British empire also meant that many racial theories were distinctly out of favour among various leading thinkers on the constitution and future of British imperialism. Despite his own antisemitic economic theories, the influential socialist and economist J. A. Hobson wrote in 1909 that any definition of civilisation based on 'race and colour' was bound 'to sow a crop of dark and dangerous problems for the future'.[7]

The politician, diplomat and author James Bryce took up a similar theme in a 1915 lecture delivered at the University of London, entitled 'Race Sentiment as a Factor in History'. Bryce opened his discussion by acknowledging that theories of race had served only to reveal 'how little is scientifically known!' The idea of 'a really pure race' was bogus. Nevertheless, ideas of 'racial kinship' within national groups were fomenting existing national antagonisms into full-blown 'international hatreds'. If national groups continued to be understood as synonymous with unified racial groups, he was sure that 'racial consciousness will become more intense'. As racial consciousness increased, no political device could be expected to 'hold back the dogs of war'. Bryce's ideas garnered recognition from the *New York Times* in a review that explained the ongoing First World War in terms of the 'vanity' of racial consciousness.[8]

The Racial Genius of the British Empire

Other early-twentieth-century writers on the British empire were, by contrast, highly optimistic that 'race' could be contained by a progressive British imperialism. The theme of imperial solutions to world problems was taken up by the author, civil servant and former colonial administrator in South Africa, Philip Kerr. Kerr suggested that the very problem of racial antagonism in the world might be solved by the British empire. In his 1917 pamphlet *What the British Empire Really Stands For*, Kerr isolated two forces that 'threaten to make war a permanency in the world'. These were 'extravagant nationalism' and 'colour prejudice'. For Kerr it was the work of the empire to broker not simply a working constitutional settlement between Britain and its white-settler colonies, but between 'peoples who are of dark colour and of white colour'. The empire's tutelage in constitutional development held out promise of a future in which 'disputes between nations and disputes between black, yellow and white can be settled'. As long as the empire kept to its ideals, war could be averted, and even 'the ancient feud between East and West' might be held in balance.[9]

From the 1930s, a new term entered the lexicon: racialism. A 'racialist' was someone who made claims on the basis of perceived conceptions of race, whether for or against ideas of racial supremacy. The British empire was often positioned as the arbiter of race by British intellectuals; racial disputes were seen as a matter of colonial policy to be decided by British officials. But the imperial peace in places like Kenya was often disrupted by the racist atavism of white settlers. In 1945 Kenya's colonial governor remarked that he had witnessed 'much intemperate racialism' in Kenyan colonial legislative debates – by which he meant that Indian and African members of the colonial legislature were challenging their white-settler counterparts.[10]

The Anticolonial Rejection of Race

The African-American scholar and Pan-Africanist W. E. B. Du Bois predicted in 1903 that 'the problem of the Twentieth Century is the problem of the colour-line'.[11] His comment spoke to and anticipated not just the global reach of transnational white solidarity, but the sustained resistance of transnational black solidarity in the decades to come. The line of colour – a division between 'whiteness' and non-whiteness in the world – had split 'the ownership of the earth' into two, Du Bois wrote a few years later.[12] But Japan's military victory over Russia in 1905 was the global signal that 'yellow races' had 'crossed' the colour line and were 'awakening'. Du Bois felt certain that 'the black and brown races' would follow. 'The foolish modern magic of the word "white" is already broken', he concluded.[13]

In 1919, Japan attended the Paris Peace Conference having attained the status of a world power. The (albeit successful) attempt by Japanese delegates to insert a clause on equality into the Covenant of the League of Nations, in which no distinction could be made against alien nationals 'on account of their race', showed that race could be contested by a non-white power on the world stage.[14] Japan used its participation in the making of the international treaty to raise the question specifically of racial equality, most readily symbolised by anti-Japanese immigration laws in the United States.[15]

One observer in Paris was the Irish journalist and polyglot, E. J. Dillon, who was surprised at what he saw as the inclusivity of the attendees, whom he described as 'curious samples of the races, tribes, and tongues of four continents'. Paris had been turned into a 'trysting-place' for 'racial ambitions' and claims to sovereignty. Dillon noted the presence not simply of nations but of races, including 'Malays', 'Hindoos' and 'Negros and Negroids from Africa and America' who had come to Paris to 'watch the rebuilding of the political world system'. It was clear that the occasion at Paris was about a 'new ordering under the flag of equality'; yet this would inevitably, thought Dillon, be blocked by 'the hegemony of the Anglo-Saxon race' maintained by Britain and the United States.[16]

Making Race Count After 1945

The United Nations and UN Charter were created in direct opposition to 'the Nazi doctrine of racialism', as Jawaharlal Nehru put it in 1946.[17] There was a general acceptance that the lesson of Nazi racial crimes was that states urgently needed to place their national sovereignty within an international order. As prime minister Clement Attlee asked in the

House of Commons when presenting the UN Charter to parliament, 'can anyone deny that the kind of treatment that was meted out by Hitler and the Nazis to the Jews is a matter that far transcends a question of mere domestic jurisdiction?'[18] However, in the final version of the UN Charter, the sovereign rights of states were broadly upheld in Article 2(7).

The UN Charter mentioned 'race' in its very first article, indicating that a principle of non-discrimination was close to the heart of the purpose of the Charter itself. Three years after the Charter, the Universal Declaration of Human Rights referred in 1948 not just to 'race' discrimination, but also to 'colour' discrimination. In the drafting of the Declaration, an Indian representative and former mayor of Bombay, Minoo Masani, had successfully suggested that 'colour' be added to the forms of discrimination to be prohibited, since 'race and colour were two conceptions that did not necessarily cover one another'. Other Indian representatives attempted unsuccessfully to have 'caste' inserted into the Declaration, to give further substantive meaning to the text's antiracism.[19]

In June 1950, the United Nations Educational, Scientific and Cultural Organization (UNESCO) published a 'Statement on Race', proclaiming it to be 'the most authoritative statement of modern scientific doctrine on the controversial subject of race that has ever been written'. It was produced by a committee and wider transnational network of scientists and social scientists, including the British–American anthropologist, Ashley Montagu, and emphasised a common evolutionary stock (drawn from genetics and biology) and the social construction of race (drawn from insights from anthropologists, sociologists and psychologists). For 'all practical social purposes', the report stated, race was 'not so much a biological phenomenon as a social myth', since 'all men' were 'probably derived from the same common stock'. The *Times of India* summarised the report as an argument that 'no one of the races of mankind is mentally superior to another', while the *Manchester Guardian* carried the headline 'mental prowess is not racial'.[20]

A British Solution to the Colour Question

If, for many Western commentators, race had long been a usurping and atavistic category in international affairs, race and 'colour' were now increasingly associated with anticolonialism. The idea of racial identification between the 'coloured' races of the world was a source of inexhaustible threat. This line of thinking about the role of race in international affairs was taken up by the English historian E. H. Carr in his 1951 book, *The New Society*, a survey of the post-war world.

After the 'emancipation of Asia from the white race', Carr wrote, an anticolonial revolutionary movement was spreading to Africa. This burgeoning 'colonial revolution' was unlike its forebear, the French Revolution, in that the new revolutionary force in world politics was defined racially, and was distinct from other revolutionary forces like communism. It was 'a general revolt against political, economic and racial inequality'. Within this generalised revolt, 'colour is at least as important as communism'. Whatever the Russian stake in colonial revolution, Carr thought, it was important to emphasise race as a political category in itself, since 'Russia did not create the colonial revolution'.[21]

A more ambitious and febrile effort to judge the disruptive international influence of race and colour in the Commonwealth empire was made by Harry Hodson, editor of the *Sunday Times* throughout the 1950s and the son of a British anthropologist and sometime colonial civil servant in Bengal and Assam. Influenced by new studies in anthropology following a stellar academic career at Oxford, Hodson drew on ideas of 'race relations' in his contribution to the longstanding debate on British imperial solutions to racial problems in the world. 'There are two problems in world politics today which transcend all others', Hodson declared in 1950, the 'struggle between Communism and liberal democracy, and the problem of race relations.' Of the two, Hodson suggested that the 'problem of race relations is the more important'.

Hodson urged that more formal institutional efforts were necessary in Britain for the 'scientific and objective study of matters related to race and colour'. Race was complex. The most obvious difficulties were attendant on the 'passing away' of European imperialism, leaving a new reality in which the 'white people of the world are a smallish minority'. If European imperialism had 'created the problem of race relations', it also contained it by way of 'white or European supremacy'. But in the passing away of this stabilising force, the world faced 'those bloody conflicts which now abound, arising from the question of who is to rule in the white man's place, or share his power with him'. The question of South Africa was especially difficult due to its 'special race prejudices'.

Hodson was keenly aware that the current British policy of multiracialism was not theoretically equipped to manage constitutional futures amid the current racial antagonisms in world politics. The problem was much bigger than a simple 'white–black problem'. It was also an inter-group problem created by 'the presence of Asiatics in South and East Africa' and 'Muslim and pagan groups with different racial antecedents' in Nigeria. In places like Rhodesia, Kenya and Tanganyika, there was 'a settled white community' demanding 'a dominant share' in any future political settlement. In Malaya, power would eventually somehow have to be shared 'in some equitable way among Malays, Chinese, and Indians'.

Parliamentary democracy might suit a 'phlegmatic' people like the British, but more ingenious solutions had to be devised to accommodate, say, 'a mixed society of Bantus, Nilotes, Arabs, Indians, and Europeans'. But things could be worse in the Commonwealth empire, thought Hodson. The 'backwash from slavery' had not given the British 'a problem strictly comparable with that of the Negro in the United States'. But there was a more unpredictable and transnational threat: a simple 'rebuff to a West Indian cricketer in a London hotel' could trigger 'the sympathies and emotions of hundreds of millions of people who feel a sense of colour solidarity'.[22]

As a result of Hodson's efforts, the Institute of Race Relations was founded in 1952 under the wing of the research institution, Chatham House, maintaining an office with full-time staff at 36 Jermyn Street, London.[23] Its founders had courted British business interests in apartheid South Africa in order to gain support for the institute, and had also discussed their initial plans with the director of the South African Institute of Race Relations, G. Rheinallt Jones.[24] The founding director of the British Institute of Race Relations, Philip Mason, a former colonial civil servant in India, recalled that the institute was designed to be internationalist, focussed in particular on racial conflicts in South Africa, Rhodesia, Kenya and the Caribbean. '[I]t was the end of Empire that we considered', remembered Mason. Internal dimensions of 1950s Britain were supposedly hardly worthy of attention, since, as Mason remembered with respect to his and his colleagues' judgement in the 1950s, 'Britain was a tolerant society in which this kind of thing did not happen'.[25]

Immigration as Colour

The belief that race was more an international than a domestic problem would soon alter, as large numbers of people of colour migrated to Britain in the 1950s. What separates post-war immigration in Britain from its previous iterations is that 'coloured immigration' was treated as a wholly new phenomenon by Conservative and later Labour governments. Despite the existence of non-white communities in Britain, new arrivals of 'coloured immigrants' were deemed by British officials to bring the unique antagonism of 'colour' with them. The categories of race and colour were not to be confused with those of culture and religion. Some migrants were deemed culturally Anglo-Saxon and Christian, but still a cause of social unrest based on the bald fact of their 'colour'. In the pathology of immigration, race and colour were an insuperable problem threatening Britain's domestic balance. Between 1950 and 1961, 'coloured immigration' was discussed by British cabinet ministers on no less than thirty-seven occasions.[26]

If imperial theories of the Commonwealth were the solution to race internationally, the concept of 'race relations' was developed increasingly as a solution to domestic racial problems. 'Race relations', an imported concept from 1920s American sociology, began not as government policy, but as a form of knowledge promoted by British anthropologists and sociologists like Kenneth Little, Michael Banton and Sheila Patterson. The older, Cambridge-educated Little was trained in physical anthropology, and had in the early 1940s gone to Cardiff to study the physical features of mixed-race children, describing them in terms of a 'racial crossing' between 'pure Caucasoid stock' and 'Negroid genes', publishing his finding in the *Eugenics Review*.[27]

Little's thinking on race thereafter moved towards social questions, and his influence helped wed the fields of anthropology and sociology in Britain, as new research findings on 'race relations' and 'race' were cultivated at British universities, particularly Edinburgh, Oxford and the LSE in the 1950s. By 1959, Michael Banton, a student of Little's at Edinburgh University, was confidently able to present 'race relations' as a self-consciously progressive theory. The problems of racial difference were social and cultural, and were based in behavioural norms, not biology. 'The study of race relations', wrote Banton in his book, *White and Coloured*, 'may be regarded as one of the applied social sciences.'

Social-scientific analysis could be advanced towards the 'elucidation of particular problems' within race relations.[28]

These new ideas were heavily promoted by the Institute of Race Relations, to the extent that new concepts of 'pluralism' and 'integration' entered public and policy discourse in Britain in the late 1950s and 1960s. The emphasis here was on race relations as social betterment – a more considered and rigorous but no less idealistic project to the global racial solutions proffered by theorists of the Commonwealth empire.

Race in the 1960s: An Eschatology

In the minds of some Western observers, decolonisation in the 1960s had raised the spectre of a global race war. This sense of impending race war had been taken up as early as 1960 by the English historian Arnold Toynbee, who intuited that the world was in the process of being reconfigured in terms of 'racial majorities' and 'racial minorities'. Toynbee elaborated on this theme, asking if a 'race war' was 'shaping up' globally, in the *New York Times Magazine* in 1963.[29]

At the same time as race – 'coloured immigration' – had a cultivated association with social crisis and a breakdown of law and order at home, the Commonwealth continued to be projected as a solution to issues of race internationally. Patrick Gordon Walker, a former Commonwealth relations secretary and a member of Labour's shadow cabinet in the early 1960s, published a book in 1962 that argued that apartheid South Africa's departure from the Commonwealth would 'undoubtedly strengthen the Commonwealth as a force for race equality in the world'.

Gordon Walker believed that British imperialism in the form of the Commonwealth had shown itself to be uniquely self-effacing – so much so that an 'intimate inter-relationship' had been cultivated among 'Euro-Afro-Asian' peoples held within British association.[30] Two years later, having opposed the 1962 Commonwealth Immigrants Act, he would lose his parliamentary seat in Smethwick in the West Midlands to the Conservative Peter Griffiths, following the latter's notoriously racist local anti-immigration campaign.[31]

In the minds of British political elites in the 1960s, race was a domestic immigration problem that interacted with race as source of international political conflict. Labour leader Hugh Gaitskell had called the 1962

Commonwealth Immigrants Act, passed by Harold Macmillan's Conservative government, a 'plain anti-colour measure'. But, upon assuming
power under Harold Wilson in 1964, Labour promptly changed direction. Instead of repealing the 1962 Act, it maintained the now bipartisan
position that immigration control was 'indispensable', as Labour home
secretary Frank Soskice put it in 1964.[32] Ironically, Soskice himself had
only been naturalised in his early twenties; his father was an eastern
European Jewish immigrant who had been born near Kiev, migrating to
Britain in 1898.

Partly to mitigate its volte-face on immigration, Labour introduced a
Race Relations Act in 1965. This was both a product of the new theory
of race relations and an attempt to keep up with efforts to reform racial
discrimination at the United Nations and by the United States. The US
Civil Rights Act of 1964 and Voting Rights Act of 1965 dealt a significant
blow to the Jim Crow legal system.

Rhetorical commitments to repudiate racism in the international
public sphere reached a peak in the early 1960s, in the run-up to the
UN's International Convention on Racial Discrimination. The US ambassador to the United Nations, Adlai Stevenson, delivered a mea culpa at the
UN General Assembly in New York in 1963, but also asked: 'How many
members of the United Nations would validly claim that their societies
were free of discrimination based on race, religion, tribe or caste?' The
1963 UN Declaration on the Elimination of All Forms of Racial Discrimination asserted that 'any doctrine of racial differentiation or superiority
is scientifically false'.

Two years later, the Haitian representative to the United Nations, Alexandre Verret, condemned the 'theory of the inequality of human race',
identifying it as the philosophical evil of Europeans like French writer
Arthur de Gobineau and German philosopher Frederick Nietzsche and
'a whole series of sorcerers' apprentices who came after them'. Racism had
since been stoked by the 'controversial writings of specialists in anthropology or genetics'. But it was 'most gratifying', thought Verret, that the
UN's 1965 International Convention on Racial Discrimination had been
approved by nations in opposition to 'anti-Semitism, colonialism, Nazism
apartheid and all such'. These forms of racism were 'as degrading as the
minds that conceived them'.[33]

The challenge of eschewing racial discrimination also fell to new
postcolonial states that were now devising new constitutions and their

own laws on citizenship and immigration. On the eve of independence in Tanganyika, future president Julius Nyerere voiced his opposition in the National Assembly to the idea that Tanganyika's new citizenship bill should be racialised at the expense of Tanganyika's South Asians. 'If we are going to base citizenship on colour', he declared, 'we will commit a crime. Discrimination against human beings because of their colour is exactly what we have been fighting against.' Certain Tanganyikan parliamentarians, Nyerere felt, were 'preaching discrimination as a religion … they stand like Hitlers and begin to glorify the race. We glorify human beings, not colour.'[34]

Back in Britain, the Race Relations Act of 1965 turned out to be 'truly a whimper of a law', in the recent words of one historian.[35] Its scope was limited to written or spoken expressions of racial discrimination in places of public resort (pubs and hotels, for example), and was therefore not able to deal with complaints about employment, housing and the police. The report of the Race Relations Board – an institution established by the 1965 Act – stated that 70 per cent of the complaints it had received were 'about matters which fall outside the scope of the Act and the two largest categories have been employment and housing'.[36]

The 1965 Act was also derided by activists in Britain. Vishnu Sharma of the Indian Workers Association, who had lobbied for it through the Campaign Against Racial Discrimination, described it as 'toothless', while the London-based Sri Lankan activist Ambalavaner Sivanandan called it not just toothless but 'gumless'.[37] After 1965, these imperfect antidiscrimination laws were presented by successive British governments as the best solution to questions of race, and the natural rebuttal to accusations of 'racialism' amid new immigration policies. The simultaneous promotion of antidiscrimination laws and immigration control motivated by race made for a revealing contradiction throughout the 1960s.

Race inevitably affected all areas of social and cultural life, including sport. The British Empire Games had been renamed the British Empire and Commonwealth Games in 1954. In 1966, the games were held in Jamaica. In Kingston that year, the Games Federation voted on a Nigerian resolution to drop the word 'Empire' from the title of the games, the proposal passing by a large majority. Despite Rhodesia's unilateral declaration of independence from Britain, its official invitation to the games was not rescinded; but officials in Kingston warned the Rhodesian team's management that they would not be granted entry if they tried to participate.[38] Jamaica's *Daily Gleaner* reported meanwhile that Zambia was boycotting the 1966 games 'in protest over Britain's handling of the Rhodesian situation'.[39]

During the games, a Kenyan runner, Kipchoge Keino, became the first 'coloured athlete' to win the one-mile run, breaking 'a thirty-six year "colour bar" in sport', as the *Daily Gleaner* noted.[40] The *Manchester Guardian* described Keino's victory over a white Australian, Ron Clarke, with unguarded disappointment, writing that 'the sophisticated beauty of the Australian's running was trodden down and trampled by the uninhibited style of Africa'.[41] For Brisbane's *Courier-Mail*, individual races were a symbol of wider tension within the Commonwealth and the new international order. 'It was black man versus white man', the Australian newspaper reported, as 'the predominantly coloured crowd ... roared its applause as the Kenyan raced away in the closing stages'.[42] The *New Zealand Herald* quoted an Australian official at the games who considered Kingston's hosting of the event 'a death knell' for the games. 'African athletes', the official remarked, 'were rushing around the arena shouting "Africa for ever"'.[43]

Race Saturation in the Late 1960s

The Commonwealth Office advised government colleagues in 1967 that race was destined to be 'the most explosive problem in the world over the next half century'. Of the twenty-six member-states of the Commonwealth, the Commonwealth Office judged that eighteen were 'emotionally involved with racial issues'. These were India, Ceylon, Malaysia, Jamaica, Trinidad, Guyana and Barbados, in addition to African states.[44] That same month, April 1967, a highly influential report by the renowned public policy institute, Political and Economic Planning, published its findings on the extent of racial discrimination in Britain. It concluded that there was 'substantial discrimination' against black and brown minorities in employment, housing and the provision of services.[45]

Into this milieu, two of Britain's most active anti-immigration campaigners, Enoch Powell and Duncan Sandys, both of whom were experienced Conservative politicians, began to disseminate in British public life transnational theories of racial violence and conflict. Sandys, a former Commonwealth relations secretary, had been son-in-law to Winston Churchill. Jawaharlal Nehru once commented, upon meeting

Sandys, that he reminded him of the kind of Englishman who had put him in jail.[46] Since 1966 Sandys had been arguing in parliament that Britain had 'admitted many more immigrants of non-European stock than we have been able to assimilate'.[47]

His racial theories had been refined not only in various colonies, but during a visit to the United States in 1966. Two days after violence in Detroit in July 1967, Sandys gave a press statement reported by *The Guardian*. 'We read', he remarked, 'of race riots in America with detached sympathy. We do not seem to realise that the same will happen here unless we do something quickly about immigration.'

That same evening, 25 July, Sandys appeared on public television – on ITN's *News at Ten* – and was asked his opinion on 'coloured people'. He warned that 'when they get inflamed anything can happen'. He then turned to the imperilment of racial miscegenation, remarking that 'the breeding of half-caste children would merely produce a generation of mis-fits and create increased tensions'.[48] Sandys was not alone in reacting to the news from Detroit. The *Economist* described the events as fuelled by activists like Leroy Jones (later Amiri Baraka) and H. Rap Brown (later Jamil Al-Amin), who were interested only in 'black apartheid' and were 'obsessed by the black–white relationship'.[49]

An umbrella group of Caribbean antiracist organisations in Britain, the West Indian Standing Conference, reported Sandys's public comments as incitement to racial hatred (a dimension of the Race Relations Act of 1965), and Sandys was investigated for prosecution by the director of public prosecutions and the attorney general. His police file is closed until 2067.[50] Barbados-born Jeff Crawford, general secretary of the West Indian Standing Committee, complained to *The Times* the following month that pressure was being 'put on black leaders while white racialists are being allowed to continue their campaign unchecked'.[51]

Enoch Powell visited the United States for the first time in October 1967, soon after the Detroit riots, and subsequently monitored black-power activism and further violence in Chicago following the murder of Martin Luther King, Jr. If Powell's earlier military experience in colonial India had led to his theory of the Indian 'curse' of 'communalism', now brought to Britain by South Asian migrants, his American trip added a further transnational dimension to the threat of race. As the *New York Times* put it in 1968, Powell had 'discovered in America's racial crisis the ugly shape of things to come in Britain'. Powell's famous 'rivers of blood' speech, delivered in Birmingham in 1968 – elemental in its imagery of the whip, the pyre and foaming blood – was spurred not just by immigration, but in particular by the planned amendments to the Race Relations Act then being considered in parliament. For Powell, non-discrimination on racial grounds was a fateful surrender to communalism, and would inevitably provoke anarchy and chaos.[52]

Despite having just passed racially discriminatory immigration legislation in the form of the 1968 Commonwealth Immigrants Act, Harold Wilson's Labour government now amended the 1965 Race Relations Act, in spring 1968, extending antidiscrimination laws and creating a Community Relations Commission to promote 'harmonious community relations'. On 8 April 1968, it was announced in the House of Commons that the new Race Relations Act would 'make fresh provision with respect to discrimination on racial grounds'.[53] The 1968 Race Relations Act – expanding the existing protections into the areas of housing, employment, unions, banking, insurance, and goods and services – again mirrored antidiscrimination legislation in the United States, in this case the Civil Rights Act of 1968. In her recent survey of discrimination law in Britain, legal scholar Sandra Fredman came to the conclusion that both the 1965 and 1968 Race Relations Acts were 'weak and ultimately ineffective.'[54]

Treating controversies on race in terms of near-uncontainable forces, whether domestically or internationally, *The Times* felt compelled to publish nine articles between 4 and 16 March 1968 under the tagline, 'Black Man in Search of Power'. These articles were later extended and published as a 182-page book, *The Black Man in Search of Power: A Survey of the Black Revolution Across the World*. This series of articles by a team of investigative journalists opened with the contention that 'the relationship between coloured people and white people is fast developing into the world's dominant issue in the second half of the twentieth century'.

In an article on 6 March 1968, the team of *Times* reporters told readers they were watching Africa 'flounder towards racial war'; in America they were 'observing preparations for another long, hot summer' of race riots; and in Britain they noted the 'growing concern about racial tension'.[55] If the great revolutions of the past had been in England, the United States, France and Russia, a 'fifth revolution is being plotted' in order 'to claim for coloured people the privileges the whites have won'. The impact in Britain could not be overestimated. 'Never again will a British government be able to ignore the opinions here of a coloured minority on overseas questions in which it has an emotional interest', the reporters concluded.[56]

Their ultimate fear was that a new 'alliance uniting Indians, Africans, West Indians and Pakistanis' would be forged and mobilised 'under Maoist leadership'.[57] The *Times* reporters took care to include South Asians in their portrait of the idea of 'coloured identity' – a construct they judged to flow from America and Africa – remarking that it already existed among Indians and Pakistanis in Britain who paid 'lip service to the idea of integration' but looked 'inwards to their own closed social and religious communities and outwards towards their homelands'.[58] Immigration was not simply a question of domestic concern, since it was ensnared by global insurrectionary forces that used racial solidarity to unify themselves.

Politically active African-Caribbean and South Asian activists in Britain took a different view. Jagmohan Joshi, national secretary of the Indian Workers Association, stated that new achievements in political organising amounted to 'the first time in the history of race relations in this country that black people have come together against the onslaught of racialism'.[59] The Black People's Alliance, whose first national conference was held in the West Midlands in 1968, unified fifty political groups based on African and Asian identities, from the Indian Workers Association to the Caribbean Socialist Union. Despite various ideological fault lines, a political conception of blackness served as a unifying principle. When the London-based Black Liberation Front discussed its theory of 'revolutionary black nationalism' in 1973, it defined 'Black people' as 'all non-white peoples of African, Asian, Caribbean and Latin American origin who share the common enemy'.[60]

The Western preoccupation with race led to some remarkable reappraisals of British social and political life. The American journalist Harold R. Isaacs wrote in 1969 that the 'influx of black and brown immigrants from the Caribbean, India and Pakistan has produced a full-fledged white backlash in England'. Isaacs was writing about Britain not in isolation, but within global configurations of race. His intuition was that a threshold had been breached; people now lived in a world in which 'white dominance no longer exists, certainly not in its old forms'. There had been 'a painful rearrangement of identities and relationships' during the age of decolonisation, with many winners and losers. The 'prime threat' or 'prime fear' for Western onlookers was the prospect of 'racial confrontations leading to a universal race war that will drive the line of colour across all the other fields of conflict that now criss-cross the globe'. Whether the question was immigration or Rhodesia, 'African blacks and Asian browns could quite reasonably interpret Britain's behaviour as not so much weak as white'.[61]

Other commentators were more circumspect about the preponderance of race. The Caribbean-based political scientist Roy Preiswerk judged that 'the potency of racial considerations may have been exaggerated and must be evaluated relative to other factors'.[62] What was clear was that, to the same extent that political leaders and voices from the Global South heralded a new world based on egalitarian futures, Western onlookers were primed to see race and 'colour' as the quicksilver ingredient to ignite global conflict. Philip Mason, the first director of the Institute for Race Relations, argued in 1968 that race relations now consisted of three elements: the domestic, the international, and the study of race in other parts of the world. 'All these are linked', he wrote, 'events in one affect the other'.[63]

As the 1960s drew to a close, it was clear that race itself needed to be more carefully theorised as a category of world politics. James Rosenau, a professor of political science at Rutgers University, wrote *Race in International Politics* in 1970, aware that in international relations textbooks one found 'virtually no discussion of racial factors'. Inventively, the book is split into a dialogue between the author's 'moral conscience' and 'analytic conscience' – the former testifying to the intuitive reality of race, the latter raising doubts as to whether the nebulous concept of 'race' influenced relations and conflict between states in observable ways. 'The more one ponders the task of assessing the role of race in world politics', Rosenau wrote, 'the more staggering does it become. Where does one begin?' Was the problem 'empirical' – a matter of 'measuring the extent to which race operates as an independent variable' – or 'theoretical', a matter of 'determining the circumstances under which race may operate'?

Rosenau's 'moral conscience' proceeded to make its argument in favour of the self-evidence of race:

> Recently a chief of state broke down in tears while delivering a public speech at a United Nations conference on the treatment of blacks in Rhodesia. Now surely that is concrete evidence that race operates as a variable in behaviour at the international level! ... Look at the Congo, or Biafra, or the UN's condemnations of apartheid in South Africa.

Or consider the British efforts to obtain new policies towards Blacks in Rhodesia. Skin colour is even an issue in the Communist world, with the Chinese citing it as the basis for excluding the Russians from conferences.[64]

The 'chief of state' in question was Zambian president Kenneth Kaunda, who had paused in his speech at the UN after discussing, as the *New York Times* recorded, the 'duplicity and contradiction in the policy of those who profess to be the foremost advocates of freedom, liberty and the rule of law'.[65]

Rosenau's 'analytical conscience' responded in turn that the 'potency of race as a variable can be exaggerated'; more plausible variables were 'differences in resources, technology, and social organisation' in the Global North and South. When Rosenau's 'analytic conscience' had raised doubts as to whether race could be subject to 'systematic inquiry', his 'moral conscience' had retorted: 'You are inclined to the dispassionate because your skin is white. If you were black, you wouldn't be arguing for theoretical perspective'. Faith in 'a social scientific approach' to race was itself 'a form of racism' designed to salve 'your self-image as an open-minded liberal'.[66] Overall, Rosenau's book was as much a study of his own sensibility and its limitations as a study of external political worlds.

In 1972, the leadership of the London-based Institute of Race Relations was replaced by a new generation of researchers, most notably the historian Hugh Tinker and the writer Ambalavaner Sivanandan, who were keen to break with the past. Journalist Joe Rogaly wrote in the *Financial Times* in March 1972 that the Institute had been 'infiltrated by would-be revolutionaries and radicals who have sought, with some success, to turn it into a machine for propaganda against the government and capitalism'. It was a shame, thought Rogaly, that the London-based Institute could not replicate the job of the South African Institute of Race Relations, whose 'respect for the facts is so strong and its intellectual power so formidable'.[67]

The institute's new leadership under Sivanandan spoke explicitly in solidarity with anticolonial struggles in Angola and Mozambique.[68] In an interview many years later, Sivanandan recalled what to his mind was at stake in the struggle against the Institute's Council of Management in 1972. Above all, it was a movement towards public recognition that 'colonialism and immigration were part of the same continuum – that we were settlers and not immigrants, citizens not aliens. The purpose of my aphorism "we are here because you were there" was to capture the idea of the continuum in a sentence intelligible to all."[69]

By the early 1970s, political contests over race, the watchword of wider political struggles, had finally dampened British elite confidence that it could solve racial questions both domestically and internationally.

At the level of knowledge, institutional and government-backed ideas of 'race relations' now had to reckon with the beginnings of 'black studies' in the United States, and what would eventually be termed postcolonial theory. In a sign of the times, Victor Kiernan, a former British Communist and professor of modern history at Edinburgh University, wrote a book in 1969 whose American edition was titled, *The Lords of Human Kind: Black Man, Yellow Man, White Man.* Kiernan introduced a specific argument, made famous by Edward Said nine years later, about Europe's need for an 'other' in order to constitute itself.[70] As the *New Statesman* encapsulated Kiernan's argument, an idea of the 'mysterious East' and 'the inscrutable oriental' were necessary 'to preserve the European's everyday equilibrium'.[71] The following year, African-American novelist Toni Morrison published her first novel, *The Bluest Eye.*

Immigration: Racism in Law

Having followed the trajectory of race as an international category of politics, we can now turn to reactions to British immigration policies. British governments' justification for immigration control – that 'coloured immigrants' were a source of social unrest and a national burden – was seen not simply as transparently hypocritical from the perspective of newly decolonised Commonwealth states, but as unambiguously racist.

As we have seen, the letter of British nationality and immigration law did not mention race explicitly, but instead dealt in terms of the status of a given territory as a means of differentiating between and within classes of British nationality.[72] But as the 1960s drew on, the supposed racial neutrality of British immigration policies was increasingly harder to sustain given the new ubiquity of the subject of race in political life.

Despite its embattled place in the international public sphere, Britain had not fully relinquished the idea that it had something to teach the world about the management of supposed racial differences. As the Commonwealth Office declared in 1967, the fact that the 'multi-racial nature of the Commonwealth' acted as 'a bridge between white, black, brown and yellow' could not be denied, and was accepted by all Commonwealth states.[73]

By 1967, however, Britain could no longer pass immigration legislation without a thorough assessment of the potential diplomatic fallout. It was inevitable that former colonies, now equal sovereign partner states in the United Nations and Commonwealth, would see an underlying racist motivation in any new immigration legislation. In the run-up to the passage of the 1968 Commonwealth Immigrants Act – designed to stem arrivals of South Asian British citizens from Kenya – British officials scrambled to ascertain from various British high commissioners their thoughts on potential blowback from Commonwealth states.

Just as the British foresaw, some of the most damning diplomatic protests against the plans for racially discriminatory immigration legislation came from the Indian government. When Indira Gandhi came to power, in 1966, she immediately condemned Britain's immigration system. In the first instance, she wanted the flow of migration of Indian (Commonwealth) citizens to Britain to rest on specific bilateral arrangements. India 'deplores', wrote Michael Purcell of the Commonwealth Relations Office, the 'uniform system [of immigration] for the whole Commonwealth'.[74]

In 1967 there were cases of Commonwealth citizens from India who had flown to Britain for brief visits being turned away on arrival. In return, Gandhi's government was now threatening that some kind of control might have to be imposed on white British citizens entering India, unless Harold Wilson's Labour government made concessions.[75] The British high commissioner in New Delhi, John Freeman, found this prospect alarming, since what he described as 'the large and important British commercial community here' currently enjoyed free entry into India. Indian controls would mean 'the loss of this advantage over our trade competitors'.[76] The only thing to be done, recommended Purcell to colleagues, was to 'appear willing and forthcoming' in discussions with the Indian government, since Britain would never compromise its empowerment of immigration officials.[77]

Naturally, British officials anticipated that Gandhi's government would not take kindly to yet further immigration legislation – taking the form of the 1968 Commonwealth Immigrant Act – specifically targeting South Asian British citizens in East Africa. John Freeman wrote to London from New Delhi in October 1967 that the newly proposed immigration legislation would no doubt be 'considered here as discriminatory and there is no argument or inducement which would obviate the public and political outcry which would certainly follow'.[78]

Later that same month, the acting Indian high commissioner in London, D. H. Chatterjee, wrote back to colleagues in New Delhi telling them the British were considering legislation that would make its own South Asian British citizens in Kenya 'virtually "stateless"'.[79] As a result, the deputy secretary of the Africa division of the Indian Ministry of External Affairs, Shri Dareshah, met with John Freeman to find out more.

Freeman wrote back to London after the meeting that he had been able to keep the full truth from Dareshah by manipulating a distinction between '"controlling" the entry of UK citizens of Asian origin into the UK and "depriving" them of UK citizenship', as he put it – even though British officials were using the latter term in private. The whole affair was nonetheless bound to 'hurt our relations' with India, wrote Freeman, especially if Britain did not forewarn India if it did indeed to go ahead with racially discriminatory legislation.[80]

The British high commissioners in Pakistan and Singapore had similar concerns, the latter writing to London that the Singapore government 'might regard the proposed legislation as racialist' and impose 'counter-measures' that would cause 'difficulty to the British business community here'.[81] The British high commissioner in Kuala Lumpur was convinced that prime minister Tunku Abdul Rahman would 'feel strongly' about any 'racialist' immigration legislation. The proposed immigration legislation might be taken as 'a weakening of Commonwealth ties', undoing Malaysia's current commitment to the Commonwealth idea.[82]

The British high commissioner in Port of Spain, Trinidad, suggested that the Trinidadian government, too, would regard the proposed immigration legislation 'as one more sign of gradual dissolution of [the] Commonwealth'.[83] The Jamaican press, wrote the high commissioner in Kingston, was likely to view new immigration legislation as further proof 'that colour discrimination was the main motive of 1962 Act'. Any new immigration law would need careful presentation in Jamaica to show that it did not affect the existing prospects of Jamaican citizens wishing to gain access to Britain as Commonwealth citizens.[84]

Meanwhile, the British high commissioner in Gaberones, Botswana, wrote that the Botswanan government 'may object in principle to any legislation of the United Kingdom which may seem to promote extension of colour bar'.[85] The British high commissioner in Nairobi, Edward Peck, warned that the proposed immigration policy might provoke Kenyan 'counter-measures' that could include 'a drastic scaling down of British commercial and other visitors to Kenya', as well as measures designed to 'make life more difficult' for remaining British white settlers in Kenya.[86] Nor was the British high commissioner in Rawalpindi, Pakistan, very optimistic. His only thought was that the Pakistani government could be prevented from making too much negative public comment about the forthcoming immigration legislation by the threat of 'curbs' on the entry of Pakistani citizens into Britain, causing 'a loss to Pakistan of sterling remittances'.[87]

The only good news regarding the plan to pass the 1968 Commonwealth Immigrants Act, as the British saw it, came from Australia, New Zealand and Canada. The British high commissioner in Wellington wrote to London briefly, and happily, to say that the 'new regulations would not make it appreciably more difficult for New Zealanders to enter Britain'. But he also acknowledged that the New Zealand government 'could be expected to complain' if a revised quota system favoured non-European British nationals 'at expense of New Zealand citizens'.[88] The British high commissioner in Canberra was also content that the Australian government would not 'react in any way adversely'.[89] The British high commissioner in Ottawa wrote to say that the 'Canadian government are likely to sympathize', and in any case could hardly object, since 'their own immigration requirements are such as effectively to exclude unqualified Asian and African immigrants unless sponsored by near relations'.[90]

A few months after the passage of the 1968 Act, Indira Gandhi fielded doubts from Indian parliamentarians in the Lok Sabha as to whether India should remain in the Commonwealth. She singled out the corrosive effect of British immigration laws. Perhaps surprisingly, given the array of foreign policy issues standing between India and Britain at the time, Gandhi replied that the hostility to the Commonwealth within the Indian government was 'generated by the Commonwealth Immigration [sic] Act', over and above other points of disagreement such as Rhodesia, the Indian Ocean and South Africa.[91]

More than any other post-war immigration law, the 1968 Commonwealth Immigrants Act provoked international fury. Trying to take matters into their own hands, a group of South Asian British citizens in Kenya wrote to the head of the Commonwealth Secretariat in 1969 asking it to create a 'multilateral Commonwealth immigration policy' and assure 'the right of free entry into the UK for all British citizens', as Kenya's *Daily Nation* reported.[92] Meanwhile, Tanzanian president Julius Nyerere called the entry voucher system that attended the 1968 Act 'decadent racism'.[93]

When, in 1971, Britain decided to pass yet further immigration legislation, it again had to brace for the reactions of Commonwealth states. The newly merged Foreign and Commonwealth Office notified Commonwealth governments of the impending Immigration Act on 7 January 1971, telling them that it would give effect to 'a permanent and unified system of control over all immigration'.[94] The document was sent to Commonwealth cities familiar to the British public – Rawalpindi, Canberra, Accra – and many more less so, such as Nuku'alofa (Tonga), Maseru (Lesotho) and Bandar Seri Begawan (Brunei).

Such an exhaustive overhaul of immigration policy, the FCO advised Commonwealth governments, was justified because of 'the growth of the communities of immigrants' in Britain to over a million people. One concession was that there was to be 'no change in the position of Commonwealth immigrants already settled here and there is to be no question of forced repatriation' – the idea of repatriation having been hawked by Enoch Powell for some time.[95]

The following month, February 1971, the president of the Indian Journalists' Association invited the new Conservative home secretary, Reginald Maudling, to address the controversial immigration bill that Maudling would shortly be presenting to parliament. Addressing the association at a dinner in his honour, Maudling began his speech by alluding vaguely to the British empire. 'I have always felt', began Maudling, 'that the relationship between our two countries is a particularly long and deep and enduring and a rather baffling one as well.'

India, Maudling noted, was a 'vast sprawling continent' whereas Britain was a 'small over-crowded island'. Between the countries' peoples there were 'total differences of religion, of personal habits, appearance'. Both countries were now facing 'this baffling modern world' together with a shared belief 'in political democracy, in individual liberty' and in 'freedom before the law'. The 'Indian community in this country is now numbered in hundreds of thousands', Maudling continued, ready now to broach the delicate subject of immigration. 'People fear what they don't understand', he continued. This fact was 'at the bottom' of the problem of immigration. The native people of Britain had been made fearful 'by

the speed of change and by the concentration of change'. Nicely bypass-
ing the human rights implications of the 1968 Act and the forthcoming
1971 Act, Maudling then declared that it was in fact his country that had
secured 'the basic principle of non-discrimination', having passed two
race relations acts.[96]

When the full plans for the 1971 Immigration Act became publicly
known, the idea that Britain was about to split British nationality into
'patrials' and 'non-patrials' caused a furore in the Indian press and within
Indira Gandhi's government. The British high commission in New Delhi
wrote to London to say that the Indian press had pointed out with conster-
nation that 'patrials' will 'come mainly from the "white Commonwealth"'.
'The Indians', continued the high commission official, 'as well as anyone,
recognize a country's right to limit immigration, what they object to is
the use of racial criteria in determining priorities'.[97]

On 1 April 1971, Swaran Singh, the Indian minister of external affairs,
discussed the proposed 1971 Act in the Rajya Sabha, the upper house of
the Indian parliament. The FCO had noted the year before that Singh was
'capable of emotional anti-British outbursts' and lacked the stomach 'to
assert much restraining influence' on anti-British feeling in the Indian
leadership.[98] Britain's new immigration bill 'has racial overtones', Singh
declared; it introduced 'the concept of "patrials" as a privileged category
for purposes of immigration'.[99] The Indian government could 'not view
with favour any legislation which would have the effect of discriminating
against our nations, particularly on racial grounds'. What was more, Singh
continued, the legislation contained 'a number of new restrictive provisions such as compulsory registration with the police' and 'deportation
without trial or appeal'. In addition, an immigrant would 'no longer have
the right of registration as a citizen after five years' residence' in Britain.
Neither would a Commonwealth citizen be able 'to bring in his dependants until he passes a means test'.[100]

On 24 March 1971, Apa Pant, the new Indian high commissioner in
London, met with British officials and handed a written document to
home secretary Reginald Maudling.[101] Pant, whose father had been raja
of Aundh, a princely state in Maharashtra, had come of age as a Gandhian
nationalist, and then studied at Oxford. His memorandum was a studied
attack on Britain's proposed immigration bill and the hostile environment
it would create. The bill, he wrote, 'militates against the very spirit of the
Commonwealth' by 'turning Commonwealth citizens into aliens'.[102]

The 'concept of "patrials"', Pant continued, was 'unmistakably racialist' and 'breaks up the Commonwealth into white and non-white'. The use of police registration would lead to 'surveillance of Indian immigrants' and 'harassment of Commonwealth citizens', making 'the already tense police–immigrant relation more tense and intolerable'. The bill would not 'bring about racial harmony but instead 'add to racial tensions'. The proposed powers of deportation, including the provision stating that dependants would also automatically be deported, was 'harsh and inhuman'. Tying an immigrant to 'a specified employer for a specified period and in a specified area turns the worker into virtually a "brown/black" slave labourer and not an immigrant'. Where right of appeal exists, 'an immigrant can appeal only in absentia after he has left the country', Pant detailed breathlessly.

A few months later, on 3 June 1971, Maudling again met personally with Pant, telling him frankly: 'Her Majesty's Government were disturbed at the tone and language adopted in the aide memoire.' References to 'brown/black slave labour' were not the sort of language 'to see used between one friendly Government and another', Maudling averred. Pant replied by saying that the tone of his letter was 'caused not by animosity but by pain'.[103]

Following the 1971 Act, subsequent immigration rules were adjusted to expand the entry rights of British racial 'kith and kin' in Commonwealth states. Thomas Bridges, a private secretary in the FCO, worried to colleagues about the implications of surreptitiously adjusting the immigration rules in this way: 'The Indians will be quick to see changes in the immigration rules as based on discrimination on grounds of colour.'[104]

The new British high commissioner in New Delhi, Terence Garvey, was clear about the likely effect on Indian–British relations. 'We would', said Garvey – who was partial to cricket metaphors – 'queer the pitch for good if we gave visible preference to whites in the revised immigration rules.'[105] The adjusted immigration rules were duly criticised by Indian officials and the Indian press, including Surendra Pal Singh, the deputy minister of external affairs. An official within the British high commission in New Delhi wrote again to London to confirm that Indian politicians saw the new rules as opening the door 'to a class of mainly white grand-patrials'. Whatever diplomatic goodwill might exist between India and Britain on immigration, India would not risk 'association with racialist policies'.[106]

At various points during the 1960s and early 1970s, British immigration policies strained Commonwealth relations to their limits. British officials had presented race in the 1960s as a problem to be contained, or a threat to be invoked and intensified before being solved. Many British political elites believed that they had a special claim on the problem of race, having achieved, as the FCO put it in 1969, 'the orderly end of empire'.[107] Making up ideas about 'race' and trading in race-threat inflation were ways of stimulating the busy reformism of British liberal imperialism, searching always for new ways to instil imperial management of non-white people. The domestic need for immigration control at the same time compromised the international quest for reputational power. As the 1960s came to an end, India's role in mitigating immigration and the problem of South Asian British citizens resident abroad came to dominate British perspectives on immigration, race and the end of empire.

Part III. *Here and There*

South Asian Migration at the End of Empire

7

Inflating the Threat: The Global Immigration Crisis of 1967

In the early hours of Tuesday, 22 August 1967, a large yacht with a white hull anchored off a private pebble beach at Sandwich Bay, Kent. It lowered a dinghy that proceeded to make three trips to the shore, eventually leaving eight men on the shingle. The men wore gold bracelets and smart brown or blue suits. By chance, a young holidaymaker, Jane Styles, who was staying at the coastguard cottages nearby, had watched the whole thing, shielded from view by an outcrop of shrubs. At first she had dismissed the yacht as belonging to a rich local, but she became increasingly curious as she watched the dinghy make its repeated trips. Straining to see, she saw her worst fears confirmed. The men were coloured. She moved away and called the police. Police and immigration authorities took the men almost immediately into custody, though the yacht and its crew were never discovered despite an extensive search of land, sea and air.

A local resident, H. J. Butcher, saw a police officer questioning the men, one of whom he overheard saying: 'Long live Queen Elizabeth. We like your Queen.' They had no documents of any kind. They were refused admission to Britain and held at Canterbury Prison while arrangements were made for their repatriation. The men, it transpired, had travelled from Pakistan. They waited in Canterbury Prison while the Pakistani authorities arranged for the issue of fresh documents so that they could be returned.[1] During the interval, they were closely questioned about the methods by which they had arrived in Britain, and, as home secretary

Roy Jenkins told the House of Commons a few months later, 'a great deal of very useful information came into the hands of the police as a result'.[2]

The eight men – nameless and forgotten – were returned to Pakistan by air on 10 September 1967. Even if they had been in possession of the correct travel documents, they would still have been subject to the 1962 Commonwealth Immigrants Act. The *Economist* discussed the attempted entry of Commonwealth citizens from Pakistan by reference to Britain's long history of immigrant 'stowaways'. Although the 'number of Asians sneaking in by small boat across the Channel cannot be very large', it concluded, 'it is extremely annoying, and is run by some particularly nasty gangs of crooks, both British and Pakistani'. The incident at Sandwich Bay in August 1967 has all but vanished from the historical record. But the image of undocumented migrants arriving on a European coastline has an obvious contemporary resonance. In 1967, if a migrant without papers could evade detection for twenty-four hours, they were entitled to remain in Britain. This provision, and the 'clandestine immigration' it represented to British officials, was abolished early the following year in the 1968 Commonwealth Immigrants Act.[3]

The year 1967 would be one of the most eventful in post-war British history. In April of that year Harold Wilson's Labour government faced the first report of the Race Relations Board as well as the Political and Economic Planning report on the extent of racial discrimination in Britain. In June it reacted to the Six-Day War, and in July to the beginning of the Biafran War, confronting their implications for British trade interests. In November it received a second veto from French president Charles de Gaulle regarding British entry to the European Economic Community, and finally decided to devalue sterling and enact 'east of Suez' retrenchment in response to recurring crises. And in October and November, Britain made a hurried colonial withdrawal from Aden and South Arabia, having declared a state of emergency. Several of these events attracted the language of 'crisis'. One historian has recently described the colonial evacuation of Aden alone as 'the nadir in the popularity of the British Empire'.[4]

But in 1967 there was another episode taking place in secret among civil servants and officials in various government departments. British political elites were preoccupied by what they saw as the 'race crisis' now consuming Britain. The same House of Commons debate on 15 November 1967 that discussed the incident at Sandwich Bay also referred to 'Black Muslim speeches' being made in Britain; the work of Martin Luther

King, Jr. ('a most moderate coloured leader'); a need for further immigration restriction ('it is necessary and desirable to continue to restrict immigration into this country'); and the link between American and British racial problems. 'The more colour that is brought into the country', said Conservative MP Cyril Osborne, 'the greater the danger that the tragedies that did so much harm in America will be repeated here'.

Race and immigration clearly stimulated a range of sentiments among British politicians, notwithstanding the surrounding political distractions of the latter half of 1967. These included confusion ('what is race?'); fear ('[i]f we natives so behave as to deserve the hatred of immigrants, no attempts at bottling it up by law or punishing individual cases will save us or serve us'); the importance of rights ('persons lawfully within this country should be treated on the basis of the universal declaration of human rights'); a recognition of human dignity ('[o]nly now are the negroes in America beginning to get their legitimate legal rights as human beings'); and anger at antiracist activism ('unjustified mischief can and should be nipped in the bud').[5]

Immigration needed to be understood once and for all. Cyril Osborne, who had been campaigning in parliament against 'coloured immigration' since 1952, offered an economic explanation: 'Why do these immigrants come here? The United Nations estimates the income per capita in this country at 1,680 dollars a year. In India it is 89 dollars and in Pakistan it is 84. This is the honeypot to which these immigrants want to come. If I were a coloured man I should come here like a shot.' At the same time, Osborne acknowledged that immigration was related to the question of race, a more intractable global problem:

We should recognise that racial discrimination and tension is not merely a problem of black versus white, and that it is not always the whites who are at fault. It exists between Arab and Jew, Asian and African, between the Pakistani and the Indian, between the people of Ceylon and the Tamils. Good men and women throughout the world have struggled for the last 100 years to solve this very difficult problem. No one has yet found an answer to it.[6]

The debate in hand was about immigration control – specifically the provisions of control mandated by the 1962 Commonwealth Immigrants Act. Did this system of immigration control, some five years later, need repurposing? Quintin Hogg, a Conservative MP, offered his view. The threat of immigration had placed the 'sword of Damocles' over life in Britain. Living with the inadequacy of current immigration controls was an intolerable experience of imminent ruin.

To support his point, he referred vaguely to 'people of various origins' in East Africa, who had 'an absolute right of entry because they have, for historical reasons of one sort or another, a British passport'. Labour home secretary Roy Jenkins decided not to ignore the allusion to East Africa, acknowledging that the people in question were the various South Asian communities living in East Africa. 'These people', admitted Jenkins, 'are citizens of the United Kingdom and Colonies. This is the starting point which we must accept. Because of uneasiness about their position under African Governments in Kenya, Uganda and Tanzania they may wish to come to this country.'[7]

This led to more questions, and Jenkins tried to change the subject. But Conservative MP Duncan Sandys pressed him for answers, asking how many of these South Asians were British citizens. Jenkins gave a figure of 190,000 British citizens across Kenya, Uganda and Tanzania, conceding that 'the great majority have British passports in their possessions', and that those that did not were entitled to them by law. The situation did not amount to an immigration crisis, claimed Jenkins, because, despite these high numbers, East African South Asian British citizens were only coming to Britain at an annual rate of 6,000 – far from 'anything approaching a mass exodus'.

Under the 1948 British Nationality Act, these South Asians resident in East Africa – alongside Africans and many white settlers – had become citizens of the United Kingdom and Colonies. After Kenya, Uganda and Tanzania gained independence, many East African South Asians had not gained citizenship of these countries (the reasons for this are discussed below), and thus retained British citizenship. After independence in Kenya, Uganda and Tanzania, their British passports were now issued by British high commissions under British sovereign authority, with the effect that their passports were exempt from the controls of the 1962 Commonwealth Immigrants Act.

Clearly, Sandys continued, there would need to be new immigration legislation. 'We cannot', he reasoned, 'let in all who had any connection with the British Empire, through their parents and grandparents. We just have not got room in this small island.' These South Asians had got themselves 'a privileged back-door entry into the United Kingdom' that now had to be closed off. Paul Rose, a Labour MP, suggested that Sandys admit the racial motivations beneath his argument. 'I wonder how he would feel', asked Rose, 'if these 200,000 people, instead of being coloured British citizens who served the British Commonwealth and Empire in the past in East Africa, happened to be white Rhodesians?'[8]

The House of Commons debate on 15 November 1967, four days before the humiliating devaluation of sterling, closed finally with home secretary Roy Jenkins acknowledging that new immigration legislation would indeed need to materialise. The new legislation would take the form of the 1968 Commonwealth Immigrants Act that passed in late February, some three months after the debate. We now know that the parliamentary back-and-forth between Labour home secretary Roy Jenkins and the Conservative back-bencher Duncan Sandys on the question of East African South Asian British citizens had in fact been going on in private for some time.

Sandys had written to Jenkins in October 1966 asking him for figures of non-white British citizens around the world, including those in East Africa. Both of them were aware that a public disclosure of the situation, or a disclosure of plans for new immigration legislation, might trigger both a media panic and a rush to beat the ban, particularly on the part of Kenyan South Asian British citizens. Sandys had kept silent until October 1967, when he again privately pressed Jenkins to act, before finally raising the issue publicly in the House of Commons in late October, and then tabling an amendment on 31 October calling for new immigration legislation. By this point, despite playing the situation down in the House of Commons, Jenkins was asking Home Office officials to explore ways of creating administrative delays in granting new passports to East African South Asian British citizens before new immigration legislation was passed. He even explored with his staff whether the new legislation could be 'retrospective to the date of its announcement', thereby trapping East African South Asian British citizens who were at that moment (late 1967) migrating to Britain.[9]

Sandys was worried that the Labour government would fail to act on this latest immigration crisis. He need not have worried. As early as August 1967, when the number of monthly arrivals of South Asian British citizens from Kenya into Britain began to spike, various government departments were racing into action to deal with the problem. As we shall see, they not only confirmed an immigration crisis flowing from East Africa, but inflated the threat, representing it as a global immigration crisis involving millions of people with British nationality, including hundreds of thousands of fully fledged citizens around the world.

Evacuation from East Africa: Whites Only

In the late 1960s, East African governments, and in particular Kenya, were committing to majoritarian policies – 'Africanisation', as it was termed. The residence, employment and immigration status of non-Kenyan nationals was in doubt. It was unclear whether 'Africanisation' would move beyond positive discrimination in favour of ethnic Africans towards state-sponsored violence against Kenya's ethnic minorities. Kenyan president Jomo Kenyatta's promotion of Africanisation (a near-synonym for decolonisation) was often interpreted in racial terms. There was a slippage between non-Kenyans and non-Africans ('non-natives') in the political contests around Kenya's postcolonial future. For British officials, this posed not just a potential immigration crisis in Britain, but a threat to the safety of British citizens in East Africa, some of whom were white. Ethnic and economic fragilities in new postcolonial states were colliding with Britain's imperial structures of citizenship, which had not been dismantled but instead patched over with immigration controls.

As a matter of 'operational urgency', the consular and other departments within the British government conducted 'emergency planning' to assess the possibility of evacuating British citizens from East Africa in August 1967. The worst-case scenario was political violence against minority British citizens (white and South Asian) in East Africa – chiefly Kenya. At worst, Britain would need to carry out a military-assisted evacuation or protect local populations of British citizens by deployments of British troops.

What is remarkable in hindsight is that these contingency plans for evacuation were conducted in such a way as to distinguish between British citizens who had a 'definite connection with the United Kingdom' and those who did not.[10] It 'seems only common-sense', wrote one official, 'to limit rescue operations to those who actually belong to this country'.[11] In other words, the contingency evacuation plans distinguished between

white British citizens (white settlers in Kenya) and non-white British citizens (South Asians in Kenya) using political rather than legal definitions
of belonging. In this way, consular protection of British citizens in foreign
jurisdictions was planned under a logic of immigration control.

The initial surveys of British citizens (not British Protected Persons or
those with another type of British nationality) in East and Central Africa
used the terms 'essential' versus 'non-essential' to distinguish between
white-settler British citizens and South Asian British citizens. The surveys
were carried out by asking various British high commissioners in East
and Central Africa to report back to the Foreign Office quoting respective
numbers of citizens. The British high commissioner in Nairobi estimated
that there were some '120,000 Asian non-essentials' (British citizens) in
Kenya, against a European population that had recently stood at 45,000.[12]
In Uganda there were '22,000 Asian non-essentials' – this figure excluding
the thousands of South Asians in Uganda who were British Protected
Persons rather than British citizens – and 7,000 people belonging to 'the
European British community'. In Tanzania, it was estimated that there
were 'about 15,000 Asian non-essentials' (a later estimate indicates 'possibly 20,000') against '8,000 [white] British'. In Zambia, the acting British
high commissioner indicated that there were '6,000 Asian UK citizens'
and 'about 44,000 [white] British'. In Malawi, meanwhile, the high commissioner estimated that there were 'about 7,000 [white] British and
about 10,000 Asian UK citizens'.[13]

The conclusions of these evacuation plans for East and Central Africa
considered ways to rescue British white settlers and abandon South Asian
British citizens while at the same time minimising accusations of racial
discrimination. Perhaps they could limit evacuation to those citizens
who had registered with the relevant high commissioner's office? This
was an attractive solution, since it was assumed that 'most of the expatriate British community' had registered with the high commissioner's
office, while 'very few of the Asian UK citizens have done so'. Further
investigation, however, revealed that 'considerable numbers of expatriate
British' were not on the high commissioner's register despite appearing
on the local records of British area wardens. Nor could British personnel
simply advertise the evacuation as being limited to 'only those with an
obvious and close connection with Britain', since it would 'in practice
be administratively impossible to check individually perhaps several
hundred thousand claims to close connection'.[14]

What stands out here is the phrase 'close connection'. These plans were, it seems, anticipating the scheme of the 1968 Commonwealth Immigrants Act – some six months before it was tabled in parliament – specifically the tying of the right of entry to Britain to ancestral territorial connection to Britain. Officials concluded that the only 'feasible' solution was to recommend to ministers that any plans for an evacuation should reflect the fact that 'the European British have an obvious and definite connection and that the Asians have not'. On this basis, Foreign Office officials accepted that 'in practice, there is bound to be separate treatment for the British and for the Asians', despite the fact that legally they had an identical British citizenship.[15]

These discussions regarding a possible evacuation of British citizens in East Africa reveal that officials never anticipated respecting the right of entry into Britain of South Asian British citizens resident in East Africa or elsewhere. Instead, it appears that officials were defining the terms of seemingly inevitable future immigration legislation in such a way as to deprive South Asian British citizens of their rights of entry and residence. These South Asians had supposedly slipped through the net of the 1962 Commonwealth Immigrants Act, and the master distinction between white and non-white citizens formalised in 1962 would now need to be reasserted and made definitive.

As early as 31 August 1967, Michael Scott, head of the East and Central Africa department at the Commonwealth Office, reflected the growing official consensus across government departments when he wrote to Harry Bass, head of the consular department, that a 'definition of a close connection or definite connection with Britain will have to be devised' that could supersede 'the mere possession of the appropriate passport'.[16] The East African South Asians, although largely British citizens, had no 'positive connexions with this country', wrote Brian Heddy, head of the general and migration department in the Commonwealth Office, two weeks later. They 'might be considered not to belong to Britain in a true sense'.[17] But the problem remained that, despite their routine invocation of an informal understanding of who belonged and who did not, British officials' imagined scheme of 'close connection' was in 1967 'simply a verbal device for excluding non-whites', as one official put it.[18]

This distinction between white and non-white British citizens would also be maintained at the level of emergency communication during a possible evacuation. British high commissioners prioritised white settlers by drawing up 'civil plans' that included 'arrangements for transmitting warnings and advice to the British community in case of emergencies'. This included a system of communication between high commissions and wardens appointed in various areas. In certain cases, it was planned to 'deploy emergency wireless equipment … in respect of the European British', in addition to 'broadcasting over local systems or through the General Overseas Service of the BBC'. This non-military communication planning excluded East African South Asian British citizens, who were deemed to have their own 'Asian wardens' and 'Asian correspondents' separate from their white-settler counterparts. Supplying emergency communications equipment to South Asian British citizens would depend on the 'practicability and cost' with respect to each high commission.[19]

Officials also judged themselves 'unable, for security reasons, to take Asians into our confidence in advance'. This decision to keep South Asian British citizens in the dark about potential threats to them was probably influenced by fears of triggering South Asian migration to Britain. As the Commonwealth affairs secretary George Thomson warned British high commissioners two months later, 'any publicity about this subject tends to increase the flow of immigrants'.[20]

The instinct of the Foreign Office to protect white settlers over South Asian British citizens was all the more disconcerting given that officials believed the greater level of threat in East and Central Africa to apply to South Asian British citizens, not white settlers. The contingency plans for evacuation make no mention of projected violence against white settlers, but allude to various threats to South Asian British citizens. Depending on 'the severity of the emergency', there might be, in the worst case, 'prolonged major violence' or 'warfare' in Kenya, with 'Asians themselves and their property being attacked'. South Asian British citizens would be in an unpredictable situation, since 'once their shops were closed and their trading position vacated, they would be unlikely to be able to re-establish themselves'. In short, 'by leaving the country most of them would lose practically everything'.[21]

A Global Immigration Crisis

Evacuation plans for East and Central Africa served to focus attention on an acute problem: the larger numbers of South Asian British citizens in Kenya and Uganda, specifically. Yet the Foreign Office investigations in August 1967 also acknowledged that the 'problem' the British faced in East Africa was in fact spread globally. There were non-white British citizens – people who were 'racially Indians, Pakistanis, West Indians etc.', as Foreign Office officials vaguely averred – spread out around the world, particularly in Commonwealth countries. Some of these were dual citizens in their countries of residence, while others had no nationality 'other than their British nationality'. The Foreign Office worried that the deepening majoritarianism in Kenya was a sign that similar occurrences could happen elsewhere.[22]

The problem of non-white British citizens (citizens of the United Kingdom and Colonies) including those with dual citizenship, spread far beyond Africa, in almost every direction. In Malaysia, for example, there were 'perhaps 100,000 Asian UK citizens (mostly Indians)' and '1,000,000 dual UK/Malaysian citizens of Chinese race', compared to only '8,000 expatriate [white] British'. Some future emergency, such as 'civil war' or 'racial disorders', might cause Britain to have to assume responsibility for these people. In Singapore there were 'perhaps 20,000 Asian citizens', and 'possibly 6,000 expatriate British'. In Singapore, the feasibility of an evacuation would not be helped by the planned closure of the Singapore military base. 'After our base has been run-down', an official noted, 'it would be quite unrealistic to base our protection plans on flying in British troops, except in the worst case.'[23]

In Ceylon, there were, worryingly, 'an unknown number' of Tamils born in Malaya 'who have UK citizenship (and not Ceylon citizenship)'. These realistically might become a British responsibility given the likelihood of a 'racial war between Sinhalese and Tamils'. The question of Tamils in Ceylon who were either British nationals or 'potentially or actually British citizens' had been known to officials for some time, but was assumed to be a problem submerged by Indian–Ceylonese relations. The British high commissioner in Colombo had assured colleagues in November 1964 that 'this skeleton-in-the-cupboard' could probably 'now be regarded as safely buried', despite having given him 'some anxious moments during past years'.[24]

Other people around the world had retained their status as British citizens – 'citizens of the United Kingdom and Colonies' – because of technicalities within the rules for automatic acquisition of citizenship in new postcolonial states.[25] In Jamaica, as well as Trinidad and Tobago, many people had retained their status as British citizens because their father or grandfather had been born in 'some other West Indian territory which was still a colony', as one official explained. Others retained their status, but were now dual citizens because they had been born 'in what was still a colony' in the Caribbean, and yet had automatically gained the option of a new citizenship 'by virtue of their father's birth in the country acquiring independence'. In Trinidad, there were an estimated 290,000 dual British–Trinidadian citizens of 'West Indian race'.[26]

The Foreign Office report left for the consideration of ministers three possible avenues for solving the problem, whose global dimensions were for now superseded by the urgency of the situation in Kenya. Regarding the endangered British citizens overseas, the first option (a) was that Britain 'could accept the full commitment ... evacuating all UK citizens to Britain without discrimination'. A second option (b) was that the government could decide that 'because the commitment ... is impossibly large, and because there must be no discrimination on grounds of race, we must henceforth abandon any plans to rescue even the "white" British communities overseas'. A third option (c) was that the government could decide that only those 'able to show a recent close connection, should be evacuated to Britain'.

Officials at the consular department answered their own question in advice for ministers' consideration. They offered reasons why options (a) and (b) were unsuitable. Plan (a) clearly had to be rejected:

> It is the view of officials that to expose the British Government to bring to this country, at public expense, 380,000 Asians, 1,000,000 Chinese Malaysians, and 290,000 Trinidadians would be undesirable on several grounds ... Even if transport were available, the cost of passages would be perhaps £62 million, and the cost of resettling the communities in Britain would be very heavy and might last a long time.[27]

The rejected people are here referred to not in terms of their British citizenship, but of their ethnic and geographical characteristics. The second option was also to be rejected, but for the opposite reasons: 'It is the view of officials that course (b) is unrealistic, in that Parliamentary opinion, and public opinion in the country at large, would not accept a situation where the lives of "white" British were being lost and no attempt made by the British Government to rescue them.'[28]

On the report, the phrase '"white" British' has been crossed out and 'expatriate Britons' written by hand above the type. Again, the phrasing of the statement is revealing: British officials thought in terms of transnational white solidarity, not legal citizenship. The report then concluded that 'course (c) offers the only practicable, if unprincipled, way of approaching this very difficult question'.[29] Were a crisis to arise, option (c) would apply as much to places outside Africa as to East Africa. There was, for example, 'no practicable possibility of including non-white UK citizens in our evacuation plans for Malaysia, Singapore and Ceylon'.[30] Whites would be rescued, non-whites abandoned. As a Foreign Office official put it fatalistically, 'there seems no other course but to rule out any evacuation of Tamil UK citizens and plan only for the 1,500 or so expatriate [white] British'.[31]

In this way, Foreign Office officials were putting the Home Office and the cabinet on notice to draw up and pass the 1968 Commonwealth Immigrants Act. Without more decisive immigration legislation buttressing the master distinction between white and non-white British citizens, Britain would have no way of protecting its white diaspora in former colonies while simultaneously reneging on its responsibility towards non-white British citizens.

Such a blatant plan to discriminate racially against non-white British citizens provoked fewer misgivings than one might imagine – though the head of the consular department, Harry Bass, did raise some doubts as he submitted the report to Commonwealth Office colleagues and Major-General J. M. McNeill: 'A point which arises but is not touched on in the paper, is whether it is morally justifiable to evacuate Canadians, Australians and New Zealanders from the affected countries, as we shall certainly be expected to do, leaving non-white UK citizens behind?'[32]

It appears none of his colleagues took up this moral question. General Anthony Read, one of the military personnel who oversaw the consular department's report, passed over Bass's misgivings entirely. 'I would agree', he wrote, 'that Canadians, Australians and New Zealanders could be evacuated from these counties, leaving the non-white UK citizens behind'.[33] For his part, James Brian Unwin, then an official in the Commonwealth Office who would later become a deputy secretary in the cabinet, questioned the wisdom of assuming responsibility for Canadian (Commonwealth) citizens, since this might involve 'including Canadian negros' in a potential evacuation.[34]

White and Coloured: A Master Distinction

In August 1967 the Foreign Office had uncovered nothing short of a potential global immigration crisis, consisting of hundreds of thousands of non-white citizens of the United Kingdom and Colonies – a status that belonged to the age of empires but which Britain had allowed to persist into the age of decolonisation. These non-white British citizens were entitled – just like South Asian British citizens in Kenya – to passports issued under British sovereign authority by their respective British high commissions, and were thus free from the controls of the 1962 Commonwealth Immigrants Act.[35] Each of these citizens, were they to acquire a passport, would be free to settle in Britain. How likely this was to happen depended on political stability overseas; in the meantime, the situation provided a perfect source of threat to justify new immigration legislation.

The Foreign Office conceded that the government only had itself to blame, having been in the habit of making pledges to minority groups that they could retain British citizenship after the independence of the colony in which they lived. When, in 1957, the Federation of Malaya gained independence, certain groups were knowingly allowed to retain their status as British citizens. It was true, Foreign Office officials admitted, that 'an implicit undertaking had been given to the Queen's Chinese' – certain residents of the colonies of Penang and Malacca – that their 'connection with the Queen' and British citizenship 'would remain unaffected'.[36]

However serious the immigration threat, British governments and officials would not sacrifice the 1948 British Nationality Act, since it was the constitutional centrepiece of a supposedly British-led Commonwealth. Until 1967, British governments had bet that they could control the immigration and diplomatic problems that might arise from retaining an imperial scheme of British nationality into the age of decolonisation. It now appeared that they had lost this bet.

Dual British citizens (large numbers of whom were in the Caribbean, Singapore and Malaysia) might remain a sleeper problem, unless political upheavals meant that they were deprived of their citizenship of Malaysia or Trinidad, so that 'a very large problem for us could arise', as one official put it. In addition, there were other types of British national (British Subjects without Citizenship and British Protected Persons) in various parts of the world who, although subject to control under the 1962 Commonwealth Immigrants Act, might 'present a migration problem only if they are persecuted and expelled'.[37] There were also South Asians in India, Pakistan and Singapore eligible for registration as British citizens.[38]

The Madness of Imperial Citizenship

In the summer of 1967, British government officials from various departments, particularly in the Foreign, Commonwealth and Home offices, quickly tried to make sense of the potential global immigration crisis it had uncovered. One thing was clear: the imperial inclusiveness of British nationality law had led to the establishment of minority groups with British citizenship and nationality in newly independent states. Of all the colonial legacies in postcolonial states, this one was decidedly unwanted.

The crisis gave officials an opportunity to reflect upon the 1948 British Nationality Act and the full rights of citizenship it had conferred on people born in the colonies after the Second World War. It appeared, reflected Michael Purcell of the Commonwealth Office, that 'we had obviously made a big mistake' in passing the 1948 Act, which was equivalent to 'handing out British citizenship to large numbers of Asians who had never been, and at that time presumably had not the least intention of coming, to this country or having anything particularly to do with it. Having made this mistake, we have somehow now got to pay for it.'[39]

General Anthony Read wrote to his civilian colleagues that the 1948 Act had been based on 'the doctrine of *civis Romanus sum*'. While this had been 'no doubt appropriate when we were a great imperial power', there was 'no justification [for it] whatever nowadays'.[40] Obligations to British citizens notwithstanding, 'we must apply a little realism to the problem', Read went on. 'The immediate step', he wrote to Harry Bass, 'seems to be to deprive these persons of UK citizenship by whatever legal means may seem appropriate.'[41] Britain's empire had been reduced to a few 'small islands', and it could thus be seen to have 'no military or economic resources to help these people'. It would 'therefore be kinder to them, and kinder to us, to get rid of our responsibilities to them now'.

Some blame, thought Read, had to rest with these 'Asians' themselves: 'It is all very well for us to gather into our skirts those people who neither can nor will go back to the land of their forefathers nor assimilate themselves in their country of residence.'[42] This was a type of imperial thinking that had little to do with law and citizenship. It was a theory of racial predestination, in which different races 'belonged' in different places, recreating the geography of Britain's original colonial project.

In a less agitated appraisal of the law itself, the British high commissioner in Lusaka, Zambia, reflected that Section 1(3) of the 1948 Act – relevant to the ability of Commonwealth citizens to register as citizens of the United Kingdom and Colonies – had left 'a loophole' open to citizens of Ceylon, India and Pakistan who had migrated to remaining British colonies after 1948.[43]

British Diplomats of the World Unite

By late September 1967 some British officials were focused on potential diplomatic solutions to the problem in East Africa, while others were still trying to ascertain the global contours of the immigration crisis Britain potentially faced. The regions of concern included not just East Africa, but also the Caribbean and Southeast Asia.[44] On 25 September the Commonwealth Office wrote urgently to the British high commissioner in Port of Spain concerning 290,000 dual British and Trinidadian citizens resident in Trinidad and Tobago. Was there 'any likelihood' that the Trinidadian government might take steps in the foreseeable future to 'deprive them of [Trinidadian] citizenship?'[45] If these dual citizens lost their Trinidadian citizenship, Britain would be under considerable pressure to assume responsibility for them. An almost identical telegram was sent on the same day to the British high commissioner in Kuala Lumpur, this time with respect to dual British and Malaysian citizens 'of Asian origin'.[46]

The British deputy high commissioner in Singapore, Paul Holmer, wrote to London with bad news. Some 30,000 people – 'probably mostly of Indian or Pakistani origin' – had registered as citizens of the United Kingdom and Colonies between 1949 and 1959 in Singapore.[47] This might not give immediate concern but for the fact that, in accordance with plans to shut down naval operations in Singapore, there would be redundancies for those employed by crown services on 1 April 1968. 'It is therefore possible', wrote Holmer, 'that over the next two or three years some thousands of UK citizens' – among them some 'of Indian or Pakistani origin' – might 'leave Singapore with their terminal gratuities and make their way to the UK'.[48] These Singaporean South Asian British citizens, moreover, were politically active and 'strongly represented' in the Singaporean trade union movement.[49]

This news from Southeast Asia led the Commonwealth Office to conduct a further survey of the numbers of white and non-white British citizens in its former colonies around the world. After the scoping reports of August 1967, this was now truly a 'global problem'. Amid the upheavals of postcolonial politics following decolonisation, any 'signs of instability' should be taken as a forewarning of the potential migration of non-white British citizens to Britain.[50] The long ending of empire, it seemed, carried a sting in its tail.

On Friday, 6 October 1967, the Commonwealth affairs secretary, George Thomson, took the lead, writing to all British high commissioners to apprise them of the situation as it stood. Officials in London, Thomson wrote, had been considering the entry to Britain in recent months of increasing numbers of racially 'non-European' British citizens. Though it was not yet certain that the situation was 'acutely serious', ministers would shortly decide whether the 1962 Commonwealth Immigrants Act should be extended. Under the new legislation, the only British citizens free from immigration control would be those people who had been born, naturalised, adopted or registered in Britain – or one of whose parents or grandparents had been. The new legislation would stem the 'present flow of immigrants' from East Africa, mainly Kenya, but it would also, Thomson wrote, affect all those with 'similar status', including non-white British citizens in Malaysia, Singapore, Trinidad and Tobago, Jamaica and Cyprus. The total number of people around the world affected by the proposed new immigration legislation 'might reach one and a half million'.[51]

British officials were well aware, Thomson went on, that such legislation would be likely to 'provoke accusations of racialism' by various affected governments, and that Britain also 'might experience difficulties' in terms of violations of international human rights law. Writing on a Friday, Thomson gave his high commissioners until the coming Wednesday morning, 11 October, to report back with details of non-white British citizens in their respective jurisdictions and any potential diplomatic fallout. Without this, ministers would not have 'a comprehensive view of the whole position' before they decided whether to pass legislation.[52]

By the following Tuesday, the replies from British high commissions around the world started to come in. In the Congo, there were 'some hundreds of Asian UK citizens', but these had been told to leave Congo along with 'all other UK citizens' amid the political upheavals in the region. The British high commissioner in Gaberones wrote to London that the British citizens in Botswana were 'mainly Indian and Pakistani [origin] traders and South Africans', amounting to little more than 150 people. Thankfully, there had been '[l]ittle or no interest shown by this community in settling in United Kingdom'.[53]

The British high commissioner in Bathurst, the Gambia, declared that there were 'a negligible number' of Gambian British citizens 'of Lebanese origin'.[54] In Ghana, wrote the British high commissioner in Accra, there were 'no less than 600 United Kingdom citizens' – some of these were 'of Lebanese descent' but 'some of Asiatic'. The Ghanaian Lebanese British citizens would prefer to return to Lebanon, thought the British high commissioner, but the Ghanaian South Asian British citizens would most likely choose to go to Britain 'in view of employment possibilities'.[55] In addition there were 'a few' ethnically African dual citizens in Ghana. The British high commissioner in Freetown, Sierra Leone, wrote of 'approximately two to three hundred United Kingdom citizens in Sierra Leone' of 'Lebanese/Syrian origin' including 'a few Asians'. While the Sierra Leonean government merely 'tolerated' these diasporic communities 'for practical economic reasons', it might well protest future British legislation if it were 'to become the target for international criticism on racial grounds'.[56]

The British high commissioner in Zomba wrote that in Malawi there were 12,000 people 'including dependants' from the 'Asian community', of whom a large majority were British citizens, and the rest probably British Protected Persons. These were a commercial community with 'no effective organisations which might organise protests locally' if Britain were to deprive them of citizenship rights. A few Malawian South Asian British citizens had already 'been deported or declared prohibited immigrants' for trade infringements in Malawi; of these, 'one or two' had gone to Rhodesia or Zambia, and the remaining 'six or seven' had gone to Britain.[57]

From Malta, the British high commissioner reported the existence of white British dual citizens who had lost their Maltese citizenship when Malta abolished dual citizenship on 21 September 1967 – these would be unaffected by the proposed legislation. But there were also 'United Kingdom citizens of Maltese descent' who had not automatically qualified for Maltese citizenship upon independence, as well as a number of South

Asians who might well have registered as British citizens, having chosen not to become Maltese citizens. Although the ethnically Maltese British citizens would be deprived of entry to Britain by the proposed legislation, the Maltese government was unlikely to protest, because the Maltese saw themselves as white. The Maltese government and people 'feel strongly that they are European by race and culture. Unguarded remarks about their Arabic language, Moorish architecture or Arab blood give offence. They are in fact as much (or as little) European as the Sicilians.'[58]

In Cyprus there was a similar situation to that in Singapore, amid the proposed 'rundown' of British Sovereign Base Areas. About 5,000 employees of the bases, wrote the high commissioner in Nicosia to London, were 'Turkish Cypriots' who had obtained citizenship of the United Kingdom and Colonies by virtue of 'five years [of] Crown service'. The Cypriot government itself was unlikely to 'protest vigorously if at all' to the proposed legislation, however, since Cypriot (Commonwealth) citizens wanting to migrate to Britain tended to access without difficulty the employment vouchers necessary for entry.[59]

In Guyana, wrote the British high commissioner in Georgetown, there were 'approximately 1,200 persons' who were British citizens, 'mainly Chinese (about 1,000)' and 'Indians (about 150)'. These people had retained their status 'as a means of escaping to the United Kingdom in the event of, e.g. political unrest, economic or other discrimination against persons without Guyanese citizenship'. The Guyanese government was unlikely to complain about the proposed legislation, but there might well be criticism from Guyanese civil society 'about racial discrimination'.[60]

The British high commissioner in Port of Spain wrote to London that, in Trinidad, there were dual nationals and about 1,000 naturalised British citizens 'of Chinese extraction'. In general terms, the reaction of the Trinidadian government to new immigration legislation would 'inevitably be critical'.[61] In Jamaica, wrote the high commissioner in Kingston, there were 'a fair number of Chinese and a smaller number of Syrians and Lebanese' who had gained British citizenship by being naturalised or registered as such, while Jamaica was still a colony. There were also British citizens resident in Jamaica whose father or paternal grandfather had been born, registered or naturalised in an existing Caribbean colony, 'e.g. Cayman Islands [or the] Eastern Caribbean territories'. There were also 'illegitimate offspring' in Jamaica whose fathers or grandfathers might have been born in Britain. The British high commissioner in Bridgetown, meanwhile, wrote that, although there were 'many' non-white British citizens in Barbados, thankfully they were generally 'not aware of their exemption from control'.[62]

The British high commissioner in New Delhi, John Freeman, wrote to London with particularly bad news. He had 'no reliable figures [for] United Kingdom citizens of Indian origin resident in India', but surmised that those who did exist were 'exempt from control'. The true figure, he estimated, was 'probably in the order of thousands rather than tens of thousands'. Various other groups resident in India – Anglo-Indians, Chinese, and Armenian Jews – also had a claim to British status.[63]

A few days later, an article in *The Times* suggested that there might have been a leak about the global dimensions of non-white British citizenry. 'There are people', began the editorial, 'living abroad in almost every corner of the earth, who hold by right or can legally claim United Kingdom passports which allow them to enter the homeland' free from immigration control. The article went on to blame the 1948 British Nationality Act for potentially increasing Britain's non-white population 'possibly by a million, possibly by ten millions – nobody knows, not even the Government'.

It was a problem that had no easy fix, since new legislative 'control could hardly be framed to exclude only the Asians'. New legislation would also inevitably 'amount to a general ban' on hundreds of thousands of white 'overseas British', many of whom lived in the United States, Canada or Australia. The current situation, *The Times* editorial judged, was absurd, since 'the Rhodesian', although white, could 'hardly get a visitor's permit from the Home Office while a Sikh from Mombasa can walk in saying in effect "Civis Britannicus Sum"'.[64]

By this time – October 1967 – newspaper articles recording new 'immigrant' arrivals of South Asian British citizens from Kenya started to appear at least once a week. British public life was reaching its most fevered apprehension of racial crisis to date. At the same time, in secret, the efforts of British diplomats revealed the true cost of the end of empire in terms of immigration. But how real was the perceived threat? How many of the non-white British citizens in various parts of the former empire could realistically enter Britain? Were the figures correct?

For the next five years, officials' tally of the global numbers of non-white British citizens resident overseas fluctuated wildly. But events in East Africa – and particularly in Kenya, where South Asians were

deciding to migrate to Britain – meant that British officials took the
threat of a global immigration crisis very seriously, using it to rationalise
the exclusivism of the 1968 Commonwealth Immigrants Act. In early
1968, the Commonwealth affairs secretary, George Thomson, claimed
in a private diplomatic meeting that there were '3 ½ million' non-white
British citizens around the world, all of whom enjoyed 'the right to have
a British passport and to enter Britain'.[65]

This was the immigration crisis to end all immigration crises. But the
actual figure of British citizens without another citizenship of an independent Commonwealth state was far below Thomson's figure. In 1972
British officials estimated the number of British citizens around the world
'who hold no other citizenship' to be 250,000 people. Those in Malaysia
and Singapore 'presented no real problem because they have never shown
any wish to come to this country'.[66] Yet the spectre of a larger figure that
included dual citizens remained.

8

The Kenyan South Asian Crisis: No Entry for British Citizens (1968)

'Kenya is a great country and I am sorry to leave it, but there is no future if you are not a citizen.' These were the words of a young Kenyan South Asian British citizen who lived in Kenya until the age of eighteen, before migrating to Britain in 1967.[1] At the moment of Kenyan independence, in 1963, president Jomo Kenyatta had been at pains to present Kenyan citizenship as 'completely non-racial'. But the 1963 Kenya Citizenship Act stipulated that citizenship by registration – the only avenue to Kenyan citizenship for around 100,000 Kenyan South Asians resident in Kenya – required proof of 'African descent'.[2] Kenya then moved towards the kind of indirect racial discrimination in citizenship and immigration that was associated with Western countries and the white-settler Commonwealth states. In 1966 eight Kenyan South Asians were summarily deported, six on grounds of 'disloyalty' and two on grounds of 'national security'.[3]

Kenya's Immigration Act of 1967, announced in July and coming into effect that December, stipulated that 'the presence in Kenya of any person who is not a citizen of Kenya shall, unless otherwise authorized under this Act, be unlawful, unless that person is in possession of a valid entry permit or a valid pass'. The Act abolished existing permanent resident certificates and introduced twelve new classes of permit to cover all persons who were non-citizens, affecting the residence permits of Kenyan

South Asian non-citizens in particular.[4] Later in 1967, a Trade Licensing Act – this time curtailing commercial activities of non-citizens in various places – was agreed by the Kenyan parliament. The letter of these legal Africanisation measures distinguished simply between citizens and non-citizens, but in practice targeted the ability of non-citizen Kenyan South Asians to live and work in Kenya.

At other levels of the Kenyan state and society, a majoritarianism that played on a distinction between indigenous Kenyans and racial outsiders had deepened. Anti–South Asian sentiment figured prominently in popular political rhetoric. A state-controlled Kenyan radio platform scorned South Asians in 1967 as 'leeches' and 'swarms of locusts'.[5] The incentives – or necessity – for Kenyan South Asian British citizens to migrate to Britain were all too clear.

British officials conceded that Kenyan South Asians found themselves in a precarious situation. 'The Asians fear, with some cause', a Commonwealth Office official wrote to colleagues at the Home Office in 1967, 'that many of them will be refused new [residence] permits'.[6] Kenya's Immigration Act had caused Kenyan South Asians to experience a 'loss of confidence in their future', and was the 'immediate cause' of their decision to migrate to Britain. The indication was that any Kenyan South Asian who wished to remain in Kenya would have to satisfy the government that 'their presence is "of benefit to Kenya"', the British high commissioner in Nairobi wrote to London. Those Kenyan South Asians who worked as doctors, lawyers, architects and engineers received preferential treatment from the Kenyan government, and were allowed to stay.[7]

Kenya's task of building a postcolonial nation had led to a nativism in which the figure of the 'Asian' represented an unwanted colonial past. Although South Asians had lived in East Africa before the arrival of the British, many had been sent as indentured labourers or had migrated for economic reasons under the auspices of the British empire. 'To have a British passport in Kenya', a Kenyan South Asian named Bravin Sonangi told reporters at *The Times*, 'now is to be a second-class citizen. It is difficult even to get a place in school'. If it was still unclear how severe the Africanisation measures would become, the fears of Kenyan South Asians were enough for a small number of them to take matters into their own hands by migrating to Britain. If there was 'undoubtedly some panic among Asiatics in Kenya', Nairobi-based P. K. Bhakoo told *The Times*, this panic was 'understandable'.[8]

By the middle of 1967 there were (accurate) rumours circulating throughout the South Asian communities in Kenya that new British immigration legislation was soon set to appear, blocking their right of entry despite their British citizenship. The Gujarati-language Kenyan newspaper *Africa Samachar* had somehow picked up information about a new British immigration bill, possibly leaked by Kenyan officials and subsequently picked up by national Kenyan newspapers.[9] Between 1965 and 1967, the monthly average of arrivals of East African South Asian British citizens into Britain had amounted to 540 people. But from July 1967 this monthly number of arrivals increased to 896 people in July, 1,493 in August and 2,661 in September.[10]

In September 1967, *The Guardian* declared to its readers that the number of 'Asian immigrants entering Britain from East Africa outside the control of the [1962] Commonwealth Immigrants Act has risen sharply'. Ministers were now considering 'how to close this perfectly legal gap in the 1962 Act'.[11] If the political atmosphere in Kenya was an uncomfortable one for South Asians, the atmosphere in Britain was only somewhat better.

Some young Kenyan South Asian British citizens came to Britain ahead of their parents. Malkeet Singh Wasson migrated to Britain from Kenya in 1964 as a seventeen-year-old. His parents and sister planned to join him. Wasson had little sense that the process of reuniting his family would be far from easy – 'I feel as though my brain was going to burst', he later said of this process.[12]

Another Kenyan South Asian British citizen who migrated to Britain before the 1968 Commonwealth Immigrants Act was Prabhaben, who 'came here with my children ahead of my husband, because he thought that if I didn't we might lose our right to enter Britain'. She rented a room in London, but was evicted after two weeks because 'I used to fry *pooris*' and her landlord 'didn't like the smell'. Prabhaben then found another room in Willesden Green, and a job at a local laundry. In reference to her employment, she remarked: 'There is a colour bar, that is for certain. First the pay. Indians get less. Oh yes, the whites get more.'[13]

Jayant Patel had been a cashier at Nairobi city council before migrating to Britain in 1967, buying a newsagents near Tottenham Court Road. Another migrant from Kenya before the 1968 Act was Bhagawan Soaham, who at first struggled to maintain his grocery shop in Wandsworth. 'White people told him face to face that he had lost customers because he was coloured', reported *The Times*. But by the late 1960s, Soaham made clear, 'white people know him and many of them are his clients'.[14]

Kenya's resident South Asian British citizens, numbering around 120,000 people, were 'the detritus of empire', as a Conservative Party researcher put it at the time.[15] Although full British citizens, these South Asians in Kenya were at the epicentre of what the British government privately conceived to be a global immigration crisis. The only ways to prevent such a crisis would be to influence events in former colonies diplomatically or pass new immigration legislation.

This legislation took the form of the 1968 Commonwealth Immigrants Act, which was the first immigration law specifically designed to target non-white British citizens not resident or born in Britain. Although they had identical citizenship to prime minster Harold Wilson himself, as citizens of the United Kingdom and Colonies, their guaranteed rights of entry and residence were removed. Astonishingly, Britain allowed its primary form of nationality to be disconnected from a right of entry into Britain. Although the letter of the 1968 Act operated according to an ultimate logic of territory, not race, this was in reality a case of indirect racial segregation at the level of citizenship.

British officials continued to search for a diplomatic solution to the problem of Kenyan South Asian British citizens even after the 1968 Act, which did not remove South Asians in Kenya of their British citizenship per se; nor did it fully abolish their right of entry into Britain, but instead restricted it. The 1968 Act dramatically restricted the flow of migrating citizens, but stopped short of blocking it outright. The British government attempted to recruit both Jomo Kenyatta's Kenya and Indira Gandhi's India, among other states, to the project of making migration to Britain so administratively difficult as to leave Kenyan South Asian British citizens with no other option than to seek residence and nationality outside Britain. Kenyan South Asian British citizens found themselves buffeted principally between the governments of Britain, Kenya and India, subjected to and accused on all sides of various degrees of betrayal.

An Imperial Puzzle: South Asians in Kenya

For British officials in 1967, Kenyan South Asians represented a puzzle of decolonisation. Kenya had been independent for four years, so why were these Kenyan South Asians not citizens of Kenya? This and similar questions again forced British officials to take stock of prior colonial experiences, projecting themselves back into their prior motives and decisions, and in other ways projecting themselves forward into new imperial futures adjusted to the pressing realities of decolonisation.

South Asians were a sizable minority in East African countries. It was a known anomaly within British officialdom that most Kenyan South Asians had not become citizens of Kenya. As a report of the Committee on Commonwealth Immigration, a Home Office division, recorded in 1967, it had been originally assumed that all British citizens resident in crown colonies, ethnicity notwithstanding, would lose their British status when independence was granted to a given colony, since any British citizens would automatically become citizens of the new postcolonial state at independence. They would only retain British citizenship if their 'father or father's father', was born, naturalised or registered in Britain itself, or in a colony that currently remained under direct British rule.[16]

But many thousands of South Asian British citizens and British Protected Persons in East Africa had not lost their British status. When successively Tanganyika (as Tanzania), Uganda and Kenya approached independence, 'their governments wanted to exclude as many Asiatics as possible from automatic acquisition of the new citizenship', as the Committee on Commonwealth Immigration put it in 1967. Accordingly, the new independence constitutions of those countries conferred citizenship not simply on the basis of a person having been born in the territory, but 'only if one parent had also been born there'. This successfully 'excluded from citizenship many people of Asiatic race' whose parents had been born in India, Pakistan or Ceylon. Out of a population of 176,613 South Asians resident in Kenya – 2 per cent of the total Kenyan population – only around 40,000 had automatically become Kenyan citizens upon independence.[17]

As one British official bluntly noted in August 1967, many East African South Asians were 'full-blown UK citizens' because of 'the restrictive citizenship laws' of newly independent East African countries.[18] These East African citizenship regimes based on ancestral descent had ironically been negotiated with British officials during the transition to independence, and prefigured the descent-based rules on 'connection' and British citizenship in the 1964 British Nationality Act. They also foreshadowed the rules of ancestral descent formalised in subsequent British immigration legislation in 1968 and 1971.[19]

Tanzania, Uganda and Kenya gave South Asians, like other British citizens, the right, where eligible, to be registered as citizens of their respective countries within two years of independence, on the condition that they renounced their British citizenship (citizenship of the United Kingdom and Colonies) or any other citizenship. Dual citizenship was not allowed. 'Only a few thousand Asiatics took advantage of this facility', the report of the Committee on Commonwealth Immigration noted regretfully.[20]

Later estimates recorded that only around 20,000 Kenyan South Asians applied to register for Kenyan citizenship between 1963 and 1965, out of a total population of 176,613.[21] The majority of Kenyan South Asians had opted to retain British citizenship, believing their right to enter Britain was secure. There were various considerations that militated against South Asian British citizens taking up Kenyan citizenship. Registration for Kenyan citizenship required a £200 deposit per applicant, among other requirements. Once secured, Kenyan citizenship by registration could be revoked at the discretion of the Kenyan Ministry of Home Affairs within seven years.[22]

Beyond this, the administrative realities of citizenship by registration were oppressive in both Kenya and Uganda. As one historian has put it, the citizenship-by-registration offer to South Asians resident in Uganda was a 'humiliating and useless game by the authorities, who would periodically order all of them to reapply, fill in new forms, pay new fees, and then, once again, simply not process their applications'.[23] For Kenyan South Asians, it was easier simply to keep their Kenyan permanent resident certificates and retain British citizenship. Kenyan South Asian British citizens could still, if eligible, naturalise as citizens of Kenya after the two-year period following independence had expired, but this process was subject to administrative delays.

In 1967, Home Office officials acknowledged that the many thousands of South Asians who had chosen not to register for Kenyan citizenship had taken that course because they suspected that life would be 'made difficult' for them in the future. Carrying a British passport had immediate benefits in terms of the British consular protection it afforded, as well as the future option of migration, since Kenyan South Asian British citizens were not subject to the 1962 Commonwealth Immigrants Act.[24]

'Asians' in Kenya: British, African or South Asian?

Kenyan South Asian British citizens appeared at first glance to belong to at least three different states. Resident in Kenya, legally British citizens, and carrying ancestral ties to South Asian countries, they bridged a fault-line between the colonial and postcolonial worlds. Many Kenyan South Asians had also in principle been made Indian citizens when the 1950 Indian constitution had granted Indian citizenship to persons outside India if they, either of their parents, or any of their grandparents had been born on Indian soil.[25]

However, in order to secure this acquisition of Indian citizenship by descent, such persons needed to register with Indian diplomatic representatives in their country of residence – in this case, Kenya. But those eligible had tended not to register. Some Kenyan South Asians would recall that, in the early 1950s, they had been urged by Apa Pant, the first Indian high commissioner in Nairobi, to identify with Kenya, not India, by taking up the citizenship of Kenya Colony and becoming British citizens. India's 1955 Citizenship Act soon removed the possibility of dual citizenship. The complexities of Kenya and India's succession from colonial to independent states meant that certain South Asians did not know their citizenship status. Prem Bhatia, the Indian high commissioner in Nairobi, recalled in a memoir that, in the mid 1960s, he occasionally 'ran into a citizen of India or a stateless person. Some in the latter group did not even know that they had no legal status whatsoever.'[26]

The British high commissioner in Nairobi privately conceded that the idea that Kenyan South Asians were now exploiting a 'loophole' in British nationality law by migrating to Britain was inaccurate. If Kenyan South Asians owed their British citizenship to a technicality, 'it is a technicality to which the British Government was a party at the time of the granting of independence and we have been daily reaffirming our responsibility over the past four years by issuing British passports'.[27] In the same vein, the British high commissioner in Kampala wrote to London that the 'key factor' in South Asian British citizens' decision 'not to leave East Africa at independence' was 'the deliberate wording of previous United Kingdom legislation'. To suggest otherwise was 'highly disingenuous'.[28]

Immigrants, Imperialists, Labourers or Capitalists? South Asians in Kenya

Why were South Asians being marginalised by the Kenyan government? In Kenya, South Asians occupied a position of economic security relative to Africans, a security associated with their integration within Kenyan colonial institutions over a number of decades. South Asians held significant purchase within Kenyan public institutions, as well as a 'virtual monopoly of trade, including the retail trade in remote trading centres throughout the country', as Tom Mboya, now Kenyan minister for economic planning and development, put it in a private letter in 1967.[29] The prominence of South Asians in Kenya was unmistakable. As Jeanne Hromnik, the daughter of J. M. Nazareth, a Kenyan politician from a Goan family, recently recalled:

> The Kenya of my youth was overwhelmingly Indian. We were the people who poured out of offices and places of business at closing time. Our names were on all the big shops in Government Road in Nairobi and all down the length of the Indian Bazaar and into the main municipal market. River Road was infested with us. We were the shopkeepers, the artisans, the clerks, the contractors, the mechanics, the bankers, businessmen, accountants, lawyers, doctors, teachers, civil servants.[30]

Political decolonisation had not been accompanied by economic redistribution in favour of ethnically African Kenyans. Although redistributive or socialist policies were less valued by the Kenyan government than in various other African states, the Kenyan South Asian business community was nevertheless seen not just as capitalist, but as an endogamous network of economic interests. There was certainly truth to the charges of relative inequality between South Asians and Africans. At the time of independence, 59 per cent of Kenyan South Asians had received at least nine years of schooling – a level of education received by only 4 per cent of Africans; 18 per cent of employed South Asians earned more than £750 a year in the private sector, while only 1 per cent of Africans earned more than £600.[31]

The outsized economic success of a small number of South Asians made their communities a ready symbol of failed economic uplift among ethnically African Kenyans after independence. Portraits of South Asians in East Africa at this time play on themes of their isolation, stubbornness and corruption. As the American writer Paul Theroux put it in 1967, in East Africa 'nearly everyone hates the Asians. Even some Asians say they hate Asians. The British have hated the Asians longest. This legacy they passed to the Africans, who now, in Kenya for example, hold the banner of bigotry high.'[32]

The figure of the 'Asian' had become a dangerously immutable image of mercenary commercialism. Sections within the Kenyan state and society also charged South Asians with willingly sustaining in postcolonial Kenya the old imperial racial hierarchy in which the 'Asian' was positioned between the 'European' and the 'African'. Nor had Asians contributed enough to the struggle for *uhuru* (freedom) from British colonial rule. The extent to which a racial exclusivity among South Asians was a direct legacy of British colonial rule remains a point of debate among social historians. Colonial administration in Kenya had instilled a tripartite segregation between whites, South Asians and Africans at every level of civic and legal life.

The playwright and theatre director Jatinder Verma was born in 1954 to a Punjabi Hindu family, and grew up in Nairobi, Kenya Colony. In a 1989 lecture, he reflected on the imperial racial divisions created in colonial East Africa: 'Not only were native Africans dispossessed of their lands but Indian labour, without which the colony could not have been developed, was alienated from the product of their sweat. Apartheid thus came to be established in British East Africa.'

These racial segregations entrenched in the formation of British East Africa led to particular social experiences of an imperial racial conscious-ness in Kenya Colony. As Verma remarked of his experience:

> Growing up in Kenya before its independence, I was most intimately aware, of course, only of my own community: in school, at home, at play, Indians surrounded my consciousness. Africans were servants and Whites [were] Gods on Earth. I cannot ever remember having talked to a White, certainly never touched one … English was our 'native' tongue; in schools, we sat for 'Senior Cambridge' exams; admired English films; dressed in English fashion (shorts and frocks for boys and girls, trousers and dresses for men and women); went for walks in English parks and Arboretum.[33]

These distinctions were also maintained in the economic sphere. One Kenyan South Asian recalled that he had been hired in 1960 as a trainee by an international oil company with an office in Nairobi. A fellow white British trainee was paid $120, he was paid $80, and an African trainee was paid $50.[34]

The homogenising social effects of colonial administration masked significant heterogeneity among South Asians in East Africa, encompassing economic as well as caste and religious distinctions. Although Kenyan South Asians tended to be lumped into major subgroups as Khojas, Bohras, Lohanas and Patidars, they were made up of diverse Hindu, Muslim (Sunni, Shia and Ismaili), Goan Catholic, Sikh and Jain communities. A majority came from places in Gujarat, Punjab, Kutch, Maharashtra and Goa. Some Kenyan South Asians were the descendants of indentured labourers; others were economic migrants.

There was also a long history of South Asian welfarism in Kenya that had extended to all Kenyans. There was, furthermore, a rich history of shared political participation between South Asians and Africans before independence, as well as Kenyan South Asian engagement with anticolonial nationalism in Kenya and India. Pockets of South Asians had also supported Mau Mau fighters in the 1950s.[35]

It was certainly easier for British officials to conceive of Kenyan politics in racial rather than political terms in the late 1960s. The British deputy high commissioner in Nairobi wrote to London that 'the deeply held emotional view of the vast majority of Africans' was 'to see the Asian go'.[36] Edward Peck, the British high commissioner, also believed that Kenyan policies were about race, not wider distinctions between Kenyan citizens and non-citizens. Even if South Asians gave up British citizenship and obtained Kenyan citizenship, this would 'not necessarily protect them since pressure is frankly for Africanization rather than Kenyanization'.[37]

In other words, protection ultimately entailed being ethnically African, not holding Kenyan citizenship. Peck saw the South Asians' predicament in similar terms to that of white European settlers. If South Asians were reluctant to leave Kenya, it was because, like white settlers, they 'enjoy a relatively high standard of living in an equable climate'. Equally, it was assumed that South Asians, 'like the Europeans', felt that more Africans in government-aided secondary schools, a dimension of Africanisation, would 'result in a drop in standards'.[38]

The reality was somewhat more complicated. On the one hand, race and Africanisation had a symbolic relationship, and Kenyan president Jomo Kenyatta had come under criticism 'for not Africanizing fast enough', as the British deputy high commissioner in Nairobi put it in a telegram to colleagues in London.[39] At face value, Africanisation – of land, commerce and the state – was about guarding against the competition posed by South Asians and Europeans in Kenya. The racial symbolism of Africanisation was a salve for national disunity and a general experience of economic malaise among different African ethnicities in Kenya. But within Kenya's ruling African National Union (KANU) party, race was ultimately only one political dimension of a more complex effort to consolidate the Kenyan state.

Kenyatta's political regime was beholden not just to Africanisation, but also to an economic pragmatism that refused to sacrifice foreign capital, aid and technical assistance (in 1968 only four of the fifty biggest private companies in Kenya were run by Africans, such was the preponderance of foreign capital).[40] Kenyatta took every opportunity to show that, despite the importance of British–Kenyan relations to his presidency, he intended to make an example of Kenyan South Asian British citizens.

In a private meeting with Commonwealth affairs secretary George Thomson in 1967, Kenyatta told him in a 'characteristically frank but stern outburst that, so far as he was concerned, the fewer "Indians" remained in Kenya the better'.[41] Apparently Kenyatta's plan was for South Asians to 'return' to India – although this suggestion may have been an attempt to appease British officials.

The British high commissioner in Nairobi, Edward Peck, wrote to London that Kenyatta had warned against the British government continuing to issue passports to 'so many Asians', and instead 'suggested we should close our doors to them'. In Peck's paraphrase of Kenyatta's views, South Asians had proved their 'lack of loyalty to Kenya by clinging, where possible, to their United Kingdom passports'. South Asians would integrate neither in Kenya nor in Britain; for Kenyatta the 'only solution was for them to return to "India" where they rightly belonged'.[42] Because South Asians were in the habit of travelling to India for long periods before returning to Kenya, Kenyatta had come to see them as a serious domestic immigration problem.[43]

A Long, Cold Lonely Winter

After the summer of 1967, the 'Kenyan Asian Crisis', as it would soon be termed in Britain, unfolded as a sequence of diplomatic bluffs between the British and Kenyan governments. Jomo Kenyatta's officials indicated to Harold Wilson's, and vice versa, that they were serious about forcing another jurisdiction to assume responsibility for South Asian British citizens resident in Kenya.

Harold Wilson's officials treated the situation as an immigration crisis, and explored ways to prevent further arrivals of South Asian British citizens from Kenya into Britain as a matter of priority. The required immigration legislation, British officials worried, might entail breaking international law. At the diplomatic level, British officials scrambled for ideas by which to persuade another government, whether in Africa or elsewhere, to assume responsibility for its citizens, claiming that they did not 'belong' in Britain. Meanwhile, British officials continued to try to measure the global scale of the future immigration crisis it might face.

As the month of September 1967 began, the arrivals of South Asian British citizens into Britain from Kenya continued apace, increasing almost two-fold from the month before.[44] The British high commission in Nairobi warned London on 5 September that the number of Asians leaving Nairobi on 'one way air tickets to London' had increased from an average of around sixty a week to 'an estimated 400–500 a week'. High commissioner Edward Peck blamed the increased numbers on the effects of the 1967 Kenya Immigration Act, and 'a rumour circulating throughout the Asian community' that new British immigration legislation was set to appear on 15 September.[45]

As Kenya's *East African Standard* reported on the same day, knowledge of impending immigration legislation in Britain designed to 'clamp down on the immigration of Asians' had 'spread like wildfire through Kenya's Asian community and caused a sudden sharp rise in the number of Asians travelling to Britain'. Flights from Nairobi to London were 'overbooked in the coming weeks', and South Asian British citizens had been 'turning up at the airport for several nights past, queuing up in the hope of buying a cancelled seat'.[46]

The Commonwealth Office wrote back to Peck that he should not speak publicly again on the number of South Asian British citizens leaving Kenya. The Home Office was keeping count of migrant arrivals, but this should not be made public. 'A close watch is being kept', wrote the official. At this time – early September 1967 – officials at the Commonwealth Office were hoping that the 'exodus' of South Asian British citizens from Kenya to Britain was overstated and that Britain would be able to avoid legislation that would be, as it told Peck, 'highly embarrassing to HMG since it would be openly discriminatory'.[47]

The Commonwealth Office now began to feed to local Kenyan newspapers informally the idea that the Home Office was baffled by the rumour of impending immigration legislation. Accordingly, on 7 September 1967, Kenya's *Daily Nation* carried the headline: 'Asian Fears Mystify British Government'. High commissioner Peck was left in a difficult position. When quizzed directly by the Kenyan press, he was – as he gingerly admitted to the Commonwealth Office – 'obliged to admit that these Asians would not be subject to British immigration control if they travelled to the UK'.[48]

Meanwhile, on 10 September, a *Sunday Express* headline in Britain declared that there was 'a threatened invasion of 100,000 coloured immigrants into Britain – an invasion which, under present law, Britain is powerless to stop'. With a mendacity that echoed that of British officials, the article went on to declare a paradox: these 'coloured immigrants' were 'Indians and Pakistanis' who somehow 'hold British passports and therefore cannot be barred from entering Britain'. These passports were '"full" British passports', meaning that 'legally [their holders] have as much right to live in Britain as people born in London or Leeds'.[49] On 13 September, Brian Heddy, head of the general and migration department in the Commonwealth Office, wrote resignedly to Leslie Monson, deputy under-secretary for Commonwealth affairs, that 'increasing numbers' of Kenyan South Asian British citizens were migrating to Britain 'with a view to permanent settlement'. Because of Africanisation and the new immigration law in Kenya, these South Asians had landed 'on our door steps with no other "home" to go to'.

British officials had little room for manoeuvre since, Home Office officials noted, 'well over 100,000' Kenyan South Asian British citizens had already managed to obtain a British passport. This was set to continue, as some 1,300 passports per month, emblazoned with 'United Kingdom of Great Britain and Northern Ireland', were being issued in Nairobi to South Asians at this time.[50] This meant that it 'would be quite ineffectual' to ask Commonwealth affairs secretary George Thomson to 'stop the issue of passports' to South Asian British citizens in East Africa altogether.[51] Instead, the Home Office explored with the Commonwealth Office what 'could in the meantime be done administratively to stem the flow'.[52] The British high commission in Nairobi immediately set up administrative screens to the processing of passports for South Asians. Kenyan South Asians began to appeal to the Indian high commission in Nairobi that they were encountering difficulties in getting their British passports renewed or replaced, and in getting dependants added to passports at the British high commission.[53]

By mid September, British officials were increasingly resigned to high numbers of arrivals at English airports. The migration of South Asian British citizens from Kenya to Britain was a beat-the-ban rush, and was comparable, as Brian Heddy put it, to the 'massive new wave of coloured immigrants' that had 'occurred a few years ago, immediately prior to the passage of the [1962] Commonwealth Immigrants Act'. Only this time, to Heddy's mind, the domestic context was far worse, amid 'a background of rising unemployment and economic stringency'.[54]

Immigration officers were now pouring over passports at ports of entry like London Airport (later Heathrow), making a note of indirect routes through India or Pakistan. However, because 'the people concerned are not subject to control', acknowledged the Committee on Commonwealth Immigration, 'there is a limit to the amount of information immigration officers can properly seek to obtain'. Nor could they ascertain if the newly arrived East African South Asian British citizens intended to settle permanently. A 25 per cent increase in 'women and children' among arrivals, and a 50 per cent increase in arrivals of 'children' as a separate category, indicated the worst.[55]

Some immigration officers did their best to create a hostile environment for arriving migrants. Jagdish Solankia, a seventeen-year-old child of a Kenyan South Asian British citizen, was held in detention for six days at Heathrow airport, on the grounds that he should have travelled with both parents.[56] This increased scrutiny of migrants led to very precise counts of arrivals. The Department of Education even wrote to the Home Office regarding the 'noticeable increase' in South Asian children entering British schools.[57]

British officials were now becoming desperate: What could be done, short of new immigration legislation, to stop these people migrating? One Commonwealth Office official suggested that Britain might consider 'offering compensation in the form of £X to Asian UK citizens' in exchange for having them instead 'emigrate to India or Pakistan and possibly to other countries, e.g. conceivably Canada or the United States'.[58] Perhaps British officials could still exert enough diplomatic pressure on Kenyatta and his ministers to force them, if not to roll back, then at least delay the effects of any majoritarian policies. Equally, a British cabinet minister should be sent to East Africa to win governments around, taking care not to imply that Africanization was illegitimate.[59]

The only other solution was to convince the Indian and Pakistani governments to take in South Asian British citizens from Africa (and in the future from Malaysia and Ceylon, if necessary). This, too, seemed like an unpromising avenue, since – as Leonard Allinson, an official in the Commonwealth Office, put it – the entire effort to ban East African South Asian British citizens from entry to Britain 'would undoubtedly cause great offence in the Indian sub-continent, particularly in India'.[60] Indian and Pakistani governments would judge the whole affair as 'designed to force the Asians on to them'. In general, the charges of 'race and colour' prejudice and 'second-class citizenship' would be 'difficult to rebut'.[61]

On 27 September 1967, the British high commissioner in New Delhi, John Freeman, reported to colleagues in London that Indira Gandhi's government was indeed unlikely to oblige. Subsequently, an unnamed British official remarked to *The Times* that new immigration legislation would produce 'a rift in Indo-British relations far more serious than anything experienced in the past, including the strains during the Indo-Pakistan conflict'.[62]

Nor was the British deputy high commissioner in Rawalpindi, Pakistan, very optimistic about Pakistani help in terms of support for new immigration legislation or the mass acceptance of East African South Asian British citizens into Pakistan. 'I'm sorry this is such a negative reply', he wrote back to London.[63] The Pakistani foreign secretary, S. M. Yusuf, regarded 'the problem of Asians in East Africa as a British headache', the British high commissioner in Rawalpindi subsequently wrote. It did not help, he continued, that the 'British Press is deliberately taking an anti-Pakistani line', chronicling 'the misdemeanours of Pakistani immigrants'.[64]

But David Cole, a civil servant based at the British high commission in New Delhi, eventually wrote to colleagues in London with a more optimistic view. Cole believed that, despite the long-held and publicly declared view of Indian governments that its overseas diaspora (in Africa and elsewhere) should identify with their countries of residence and take up local citizenship, Indian officials knew that, in practice, it was 'not easy for Indians to obtain local citizenship even if they should want to'.[65] Cole was certainly correct about India's professed divestment of overseas Indians. Nehru commented in 1953 that his government had 'rather gone out of our way to tell our people in Africa … that they can expect no help from us, no protection from us, if they seek any special rights in Africa that are not in the interests of Africans'.[66]

But Cole believed that India was saying one thing but doing another with respect to the members of its diaspora without Indian citizenship. Perhaps India might be willing for Kenyan South Asians, although legally Britain's responsibility, to return to the home of their ancestors were the British to force their hand. Indian officials often betrayed their belief, wrote Cole, that 'no matter what kind of passport they hold, persons of Indian origin abroad tend to retain their religious, cultural and family links with India'.[67] Besides, Kenyan South Asian British citizens, in their capacity as Commonwealth citizens under Indian law, were free to enter India without visa restrictions. Furthermore, under India's 1955 Citizenship Act, they were free to register as Indian citizens after having been resident in India for six months, if either of their parents or any of their grandparents had been born in India prior to independence.

Indian politicians were also monitoring the situation in Kenya closely. Surendra Pal Singh, India's deputy minister for external affairs, declared in the Lok Sabha on 22 May 1967 that the policy of the Indian government 'has always been to urge citizens settled in foreign countries to identify themselves with the aspirations of the indigenous population in the countries of their domicile and to take up citizenship of these countries'.[68] But Cole was not incorrect, in the sense that India had long used diplomatic channels to advocate for diaspora rights – recall its advocacy at the United Nations on behalf of South African South Asians – whether in Africa or, more recently, in Ceylon and Burma.

As Surendra Pal Singh remarked in a 5 June speech in the Lok Sabha, modifying the Indian position somewhat, there was 'no bar against entry into India of any person of Indian origin (including those holding British passports) who wishes to come to this country of his own volition'.[69] Whatever action Britain took, it would need India to be as cooperative as possible, since if it forced South Asian British citizens to go to India as a temporary solution to their attempt to migrate to Britain, they would not be going of their own volition.

Racially Encoding British Citizenship

By late 1967, the numbers of arrivals of South Asian British citizens from Kenya showed no sign of abating, but were up almost fourfold from their monthly average since 1965. After its exhaustive global racial census of British citizenship, Harold Wilson's Labour cabinet was resolved by late 1967 that new immigration legislation would most likely be necessary. Nor did Jomo Kenyatta roll back his anti–South Asian policies when he learned – in October 1967, if not before – of British plans to block the entry of Kenyan South Asian British citizens into Britain by way of a new immigration law.

British officials planned for a scenario in which its diplomatic efforts would be prioritised, and that only failing these efforts should it pass what would be its most transparently discriminatory immigration law to date. At the same time, they could not make any plans for new immigration legislation public since, as Commonwealth affairs secretary George Thomson put it in private correspondence, 'any publicity about this subject tends to increase flow of immigrants'.[70]

The new immigration legislation would need to succeed in restricting large numbers of Kenyan South Asian British citizens from entering Britain while simultaneously upholding the entry rights of white settlers in Kenya and other former colonies. The legal device for achieving this was the introduction of ancestral territorial connection to Britain as a condition of unrestricted entry. Once in place, the new law would not only stop large numbers of migrants from Kenya, but also the some 1.5 million non-white British citizens (citizens of the United Kingdom and Colonies) in various former colonies around the world, particularly in Africa, the Caribbean, South Asia and Southeast Asia, who held an automatic right of entry into Britain, depending on their passport.

Although under the proposed new immigration law some white British people would come under immigration control if removed from Britain by three or more generations – these included some white people of British descent in Africa and Argentina – this could not be helped.

As Michael Scott, head of the East and Central Africa department at the Commonwealth Office, noted, the new immigration legislation 'might exclude some "white" British people' who had gained Kenyan citizenship, but 'the number is, I believe, very small'.[71]

The task at hand was dealing with the legal, domestic and international implications of passing racially discriminatory legislation. Brian Heddy, head of the general and migration department in the Commonwealth Office, conceded correctly that the 1968 Commonwealth Immigrants Act would 'probably constitute an entirely new precedent because hitherto no measures have presumably been taken to restrict the entry into this country of a class of persons who are beyond dispute "Citizens of the United Kingdom and Colonies", and are at the same time neither citizens of some other Commonwealth country'.[72]

The move was bound to 'raise thorny problems' relating to citizenship and international human rights law, not to mention the implications for Indian–British and Pakistani–British relations, and foreign relations more generally.[73]

An annex to a Home Office memorandum for ministers set out the international human rights treaties that were in conflict with what would become the 1968 Commonwealth Immigrants Act. Article 3(2) of the Fourth Protocol of the European Convention on Human Rights stipulated: 'No one shall be deprived of the right to enter the territory of the state of which he is a national'; Article 12(4) of the International Convention on Civil and Political Rights stated: 'No one shall be arbitrarily deprived of the right to enter his own country'; and Article 5(d) of the International Convention on Racial Discrimination provided not simply that a person carried the right 'to return to his country', but that this right should be upheld 'without distinction as to race'.[74] Importantly, however, Britain had not yet ratified any of these treaties (at the time of writing, it still has not ratified the Fourth Protocol).

The only official to register any protest against the formulation of the new immigration law was Michael Purcell of the Commonwealth Office, who referred to the idea that East African South Asians somehow 'do not belong' in Britain as 'a complete botch and a really classic piece of Home Office sophistry'.[75] The legal implications were stark, spurring Purcell to write: 'I think it is quite impossible to provide any convincing justification for denying entry to anyone who is at present legally a full UK citizen.'[76] Nevertheless, even Purcell was convinced that 'something must be done ... the question is how else we can protect this country from a further major influx'.[77]

There was also the question of statelessness. Harold Wilson's officials were under no illusion as to what might happen to South Asian British citizens under the new immigration controls. If South Asians left Kenya for Britain, they would be turned away on arrival, and then Kenyan officials 'might refuse them re-entry on return'.[78] India and Pakistan only accepted migrants of South Asian origin who had decided to settle in South Asia of their own volition – in other words, not under the duress of deportation, expulsion or another form of migration forced by another government. This meant that Kenyan South Asian British citizens 'would not, on present practice, be admitted to India or Pakistan', and 'would have no right of entry into any country at all', as the Commonwealth Office put it.[79]

Under the new legislation, Kenyan South Asian British citizens would not have automatic entry rights to any state. This would put them, in the opinion of Michael Purcell, in 'a worse position than a stateless alien, who is at least protected by some United Nations Convention'.[80] But the British high commissioner in Lusaka pointed out correctly that the affected Kenyan South Asians would continue to hold British citizenship: 'Although such a person would not be stateless in the citizenship sense he would be homeless because there would be no country in which he would have an inalienable right of residence'.[81] A similar misgiving was expressed by the British high commissioner in Kampala, who argued that the proposed legislation would 'create a new class of stateless person'.[82] While described as retaining a nationality, the Kenyan South Asian citizens of the United Kingdom and Colonies were in reality rendered stateless by the 1968 Commonwealth Immigrants Act.

At the same time as the new immigration legislation was taking shape, British officials planned to pursue informal diplomatic solutions aggressively. British officials would try to force the hand of India and Pakistan, making them accept South Asian British citizens. This might work, but it would depend above all on the Kenyan government, since, if Kenya decided to deport Kenyan South Asian British citizens in their thousands all at once, Britain would be forced to assume responsibility for its citizens facing deportation.[83] In any event, it could be expected that some South Asians with the means of travel, having no other citizenship, would be forced to ignore any entry controls and travel to British airports.

The Razor's Edge

Between August 1967 and January 1968, 11,605 South Asian British citizens migrated to Britain from East Africa, according to Commonwealth Office figures.[84] In today's terms a small figure, it was enough at the time to spin Harold Wilson's Labour government into a full emergency, amid the wider crises of late 1967. If Wilson's cabinet was playing for time before passing the new immigration legislation – hoping still for a diplomatic solution – things were taken out of its hands when Conservative MP Duncan Sandys submitted a private member's bill in the House of Commons.

Kenyan travel agents, Kenya's *Daily Nation* reported, were being 'swamped with requests' for charter flights from Nairobi to London, at an average of £50 a seat, and were already booked until the end of February. Six charter flights were leaving for London each week in early February, but the number of daily flights soon rapidly increased.[85] Thousands of Kenyan South Asians now 'grabbed, on the spur of the moment, their last chance of getting into the country of which they had been invited to become citizens', as the *Economist* recorded a few weeks later.[86]

On 8 February, Kenya's *Daily Nation* declared on its front page: 'Asian Exodus Steps Up', recording that Sandys was determined 'to stem the flow of Asian immigrants into Britain from Kenya' by way of a private member's bill.[87] The Kenyan press was covering developments before British newspapers, and before Sandys's bill was publicly tabled in the House of Commons on 12 February. The new immigration legislation was now impossible to deny. Sandys's motion called for the government to 'introduce immediate action to curtail the flow of immigrants into Britain', and was supported by fifteen Labour MPs.[88]

British cabinet ministers decided to send a former colonial governor of Kenya, Malcolm Macdonald – who a few years before had called African politicians 'utterly inexperienced and helplessly immature' and 'rather like children playing at being statesmen' – on a special mission to Nairobi on 18 February. He was to convince Kenyatta to restore South Asians' confidence about their future in Kenya, and thus stem the 'panic flight' to Britain. This mission, despite Macdonald's diplomatic relationship with Kenyatta, ended in failure. Though he was personally against the 1968 Commonwealth Immigrants Act, Commonwealth affairs secretary George Thomson was then sent in secret to Nairobi to plead once again with Kenyatta – an effort that predictably also ended in failure.[89]

Jomo Kenyatta was under enormous political pressure – engulfed in 'a period of crisis', as Kenya's *Daily Nation* put it in early February – and was speaking unambiguously about Kenyan South Asians as having little claim to Kenya, rationalising their migration to Britain. The 'current exodus of Asians from Kenya', Kenyatta told a KANU party rally in Limuru in early February, 'had come about because they wanted to remain in privileged positions in the country'. 'Knowing that India and Pakistan are over-populated', he went on, 'and the people there are like swarms of locusts and are faced with a shortage of food, they have decided to pack up and migrate to the United Kingdom.'[90] Kenya's *East African Standard* also reported Kenyatta's speech in paraphrase: 'He asked Asians and Europeans to respect African rule and Africans. If any of them hated Africans, he would be told to leave Kenya.'[91]

Britain's Diplomatic Plea to Indira Gandhi

Diplomatic efforts in Kenya having failed, everything now rested on South Asian governments, particularly India, agreeing to accept as many Kenyan South Asian British citizens as possible in the immediate future as a stop-gap solution. The Commonwealth Office sent John Freeman – the British high commissioner in New Delhi and a former journalist and editor of the *New Statesman* – to make a last-minute plea to Indira Gandhi. The diplomatic centre of gravity in the eyes of British officials was no longer Nairobi, but New Delhi.

In a diplomatic skirmish that would go on for at least the next seven years, well beyond Harold Wilson's tenure as British prime minister, the Indian government maintained that in principle it had no responsibility for British citizens, notwithstanding their South Asian ancestry. But it had yet to be seen whether, in practice, India would allow Kenyan South Asians (those among them deemed to be connected to India rather than Pakistan) to enter India en masse. More than this, Britain hoped that Indira Gandhi's government would collude in the political manoeuvring required to ensure that Kenyan South Asian British citizens would settle in India, and give up on waiting to be allowed to enter Britain.

The *Times of India* declared its support for the Indian government to adopt an inclusive policy. If the task of 'keeping Britain white' was preoccupying British politicians, India's task was to 'make a declaration that its own doors will always be open to the people of Indian origin'. India could not 'run away from the fact that all these people once migrated from this land', the newspaper declared on 19 February.[92]

Indira Gandhi's early foreign policy is generally remembered to have been more strategic and pragmatic than Jawaharlal Nehru's. Yet she maintained at a basic level her father's ideas of friendship in foreign relations, meaning that she was unlikely to involve India in a sovereign dispute between Kenya and Britain. 'We accept the freedom of nations to choose their own destiny; we do not seek to interfere in the affairs of others', as she had declared in a speech two years previously.[93] At the same time, sections of the Kenyan South Asian community carried significant political capital in terms of their caste background, education, urban experience and economic standing – characteristics within the Indian diaspora that had long enjoyed patronage by the Indian state.

British officials throughout this period saw Indira Gandhi as a difficult case. A 'personality note' on Gandhi spoke of her 'unhappy childhood', a consequence of constant travel, a mother 'not in the best of health', and her father, Nehru, 'frequently in jail'. Like her father, Gandhi was supercilious, born 'with a strong sense that in this world it is for the Nehrus to give the orders and for the rest of humanity to carry them out'.[94] Her personality was 'complex'. She was 'wilful, petulant, hereditarily imperious', though not without personal charm.[95] Also like her father, she was a socialist, though 'more doctrinaire and pro-Soviet'. Using British aid 'either as stick or carrot' against Gandhi was judged to be 'of no use'. When the US government had suspended aid to India, 'Mrs Gandhi told them to go to hell', remembered a sometime British high commissioner in New Delhi in this period.[96] Those close to her were no better. Foreign secretary T. N. Kaul nursed a 'love/hate complex' about Britain. P. N. Haksar, soon to become Gandhi's principal secretary, had picked up the 'Moscow-orientated leftism' that had been 'popular in some circles' in Oxford, Cambridge and London Universities during the 1930s.

In their meeting in Delhi, Indira Gandhi told Freeman that, while she might sympathise with the British position, 'you must see that it is almost equally difficult for us'. As T. N. Kaul explained to Freeman two days later, the number of 'people of Indian origin living in other countries' around the world was probably higher than the publicly stated figure of under 5 million, and might be as high as 10 million people – and therefore the

Indian government really 'could not countenance any measures which might encourage them to seek refuge in India'.

While India tended to look sympathetically on elderly people who 'might want to come back to their ancestral home for the last years of their life', it would not simply 'accept large numbers of UK citizens' just because Britain 'sought to wash its hands of them'. India would not 'pull British chestnuts out of the fire', Kaul went on. It might provide East African South Asian British citizens with 'temporary shelter, say for a matter of months', but it would not simply take them off British hands. All in all, Kaul told the British high commissioner, the proposed racially discriminatory legislation promised to be 'very serious' for Indian–British relations, and moreover 'could be expected to have repercussions elsewhere in the Commonwealth'.[97]

Revealing a non-public commitment to supporting Kenyan South Asian British citizens, India deployed its own last-minute diplomatic offensive with both the Kenyan and British governments. Rather half-heartedly, Indira Gandhi sent a young junior minister, Bal Ram Bhagat, minister of state for external affairs, to Nairobi to assuage Kenyatta's views on his Indian-origin non-citizens. This did not go well.[98]

Gandhi also charged S. S. Dhawan, the Indian high commissioner in London, to meet with Commonwealth affairs secretary George Thomson in London on 21 February to try to get him to call off the 1968 Commonwealth Immigrants Act. Although himself opposed, Thomson made the predicable argument that the roughly 120,000 Kenyan South Asian British citizens represented 'an impossible number for a small island to absorb'. Dhawan remained unflappable in maintaining Gandhi's bluff, and even went so far as to suggest that India's dictating the fate of its overseas diaspora in various countries would be so dangerous as to recall 'Hitler and his alleged responsibility for the Sudeten Germans'.[99]

The fact that so many Kenyan South Asians had retained British citizenship was, argued Dhawan, 'a tribute to Britain and the British way of life'.[100] Dhawan also accused British officials in Kenya of stirring 'anti-Indian feelings among the Africans'.[101] When Dhawan firmly reiterated his government's position – 'India could not accept any legal or moral responsibility' – Thomson pleaded his case, claiming that the true figure of non-white British citizens around the world was 3.5 million, all of whom 'had the right to have a British passport and to enter Britain'.[102]

On 22 February the British government finally announced its long-planned new Commonwealth Immigrants bill. The final decision by ministers to bar non-white British citizens by way of an update to legislation that apparently concerned 'immigrants', or those with citizenship of a Commonwealth state, was a skilful, if transparent, way of eliding the fact that the majority of the people concerned held British citizenship only.

A Deadline to Entry

February 1968 was full of speculation as to whether the British government would actually go through with blocking its own citizens from entry into Britain. After the announcement of the new immigration bill, thousands of Kenyan South Asian British citizens rushed to migrate and 'beat the ban', in a movement widely described in British, Kenyan and Indian newspapers as a 'panic exodus'.

During late February, in anticipation of the 1 March deadline, Kenyan South Asians camped out at Nairobi airport in a last-gasp attempt to migrate to Britain. The airport authorities shuttered the gates, and occasionally even called in paramilitary riot police to quell the crowds, some of which were relatives come to say goodbye to travellers. As David Wood, a reporter with *The Times* wrote from Nairobi: 'About a thousand ticket-holders packed the steaming main hall. Crying children, clutching dolls, and old women were manhandled through the entrance to take their places in the queues at the counters. Several people fainted in the crush. British reporters were threatened by Sikhs.'[103]

Towards the end of February 1968, almost two dozen flights were leaving Nairobi every day, conveying around 750 people per day to Heathrow. Some 10,000 Kenyan South Asian British citizens are thought to have entered Britain within two weeks.[104]

In London, a coalition of antiracist groups – including the Joint Council of the Welfare of Immigrants, the Campaign against Racial Discrimination and the Indian Workers Association – organised a march from Hyde Park to Downing Street against the new immigration bill. 'Thousands of marchers', *The Times* declared on its front page on 25 February 1968, have 'swamped Whitehall to protest the new measures to curb immigration'. Among them were some 3,000 South Asians already resident in Britain. 'Scuffles' broke out with police, and a man and a woman were arrested.

Placards bore captions including 'Callaghan out – go to South Africa' and 'Is your passport black or white?'. As the march progressed, men waiting nearby were reported to have shouted in counter-protest: 'Send them back'.[105]

A Scottish woman, Heather Harvey, became briefly famous after she destroyed her own British passport outside Downing Street. 'I do this as a protest because our passports have been devalued by this Bill', she told the crowd, trying to tear up her passport. The Indian writer Dom Moraes recorded what happened next: 'Curiously enough, however, passports are among the most durable of British products. It wouldn't tear. She then set fire to it, but the effect of this symbolic act was somewhat weakened when it was discovered that the passport was in any case out of date and the lady had a new one at home.'[106]

The Home Office called on the president of the Board of Trade, Anthony Crosland, asking him 'to urge airlines to slow down their activities in bringing in Asians'. He replied that he had 'no power' to deny the charter flights of the state-owned British Overseas Airways Corporation, or any other British airline. Meanwhile the charter flights of Egyptian-owed airlines were protected by the Bilateral Air Services Agreement. On 26 February 1968, Crosland did oblige in denying permission for an Air Congo charter flight carrying South Asian British citizens from Central Africa to land in London.[107]

Although all Britain's diplomatic efforts prior to the 1968 Commonwealth Immigrants Act had ended in failure, Harold Wilson's Labour government had decided to press ahead with legislation anyway, citing the threat of 'grave social problems and an intolerable strain on housing and schools'.[108]

Dom Moraes, who was approaching his thirtieth birthday in spring 1968, recalled the last-minute arrival of Kenyan South Asians in Britain in an article for the *New York Times*:

Every scheduled flight to London was booked solid, charter planes buzzed to and fro between England and Africa. Daily they came in their hundreds, a brown tide scumbling over London Airport, turbaned fathers, mothers with castemarks and saris, doe-eyed children. They came with trunks and baskets, pathetic sacks tied with rope, satchels, cardboard cartons and all the goods they could carry. Gratefully they stepped onto British soil, glad that the odyssey was over and they had reached a place they could call home. They were astonished to be confronted by a prolonged roar of fury from the British population.[109]

Up until the very last moment, Kenyan South Asian British citizens remained hopeful that the legislation would not be passed. Although the 1968 Act received royal assent on 1 March, a group of South Asian British citizens was turned away at Nairobi airport on 29 February by airport officials demanding 'special entry' vouchers. 'We all heard this morning that the bill would be delayed … we thought we could get in', one of the group told the *New York Times*.[110]

This apparent recruitment of airport officials in Kenya in the policing of migrants' documentation did not last. Nonetheless, the following day the 1968 Act was officially in effect. Now the only British citizens with an automatic right of entry into Britain were those who had been – or whose parent or grandparent had been – born, naturalised, adopted or registered as British citizens in Britain itself. *The Times* now turned on the 1968 Act, calling it 'probably the most shameful measure that Labour members have ever been asked … to support'.[111]

But the 1968 Act more generally carried support. On 3 March Peregrine Worsthorne, deputy editor of the *Sunday Telegraph*, wrote an article titled, 'Race: Who Should be Ashamed?' It was accompanied by a cartoon version of Hokusai's 'The Wave' and depicted an ocean wave of turbaned Indians cresting above three wooden paddle boats. The boats were inscribed 'India (not to be used in this emergency)', 'Britain' and 'Kenya', respectively. With a carefree diction for which he would later become notorious, Worsthorne defended the newly passed act and reminded readers that 'the Africans and Asians who want to come here are not black and brown Englishmen. They are as alien to us, as immigrants, as we were alien to them, as imperial administrators.' Though careful to argue that it was 'not racialist to oppose large-scale immigration', Worsthorne suggested that 'the British people [no longer] feel responsible for "lesser breeds without the law"'.[112]

London Is the Place for Me

Despite the 1968 Act, thousands of South Asians from Kenya had managed to migrate to Britain in 1967 and early 1968 to begin a new life. One of the migrants who only just beat the 1 March deadline was former Nairobi resident Jatinder Verma, whose Punjabi Hindu family were 'all British citizens by birth', as he recalled years later. Aged fourteen in 1968, Verma had been told by his mother to prepare for travel to London in January that year. He accompanied her to buy blankets and scarves in preparation for the English winter. By February his family were 'racing to get into the country before 1 March'.

When he finally left his home in Nairobi with his parents and sisters on the evening of 13 February, Verma saw a vast caravan of lights from other vehicles stretching out towards Nairobi airport. At the airport there was 'a kind of bedlam that I had never experienced'. It was 'absolutely full of people' and unclear who were airport officials, who were travellers and who were well-wishers come to say goodbye to their relatives. Amid the melee Verma and his mother and sisters became separated from his father.

The young Verma arrived in Britain on 14 February on an Ethiopian Airlines flight that landed at Heathrow. Walking down the aeroplane stairs, he 'for the first time saw my own breath'. Having cleared the airport's immigration checks together with his mother and sisters, Verma boarded a bus to his aunt's house in Holloway Road, north London. Although Verma's mother tongue was English, together with Punjabi, he could not follow the bus conductor's idiomatic speech. For the first time, Britain felt like a foreign place. From the bus window he saw council workers clearing bins. 'These were white workers and it completely collapsed my worldview', remembers Verma. 'Even though I had lived through independence', he went on, 'there was still a view that the whites were the Gods, then come the Asians and Africans.'[113]

Again turning his hand to journalism, Bombay-born Dom Moraes interviewed another young arrival from Kenya, a teacher named Arvind Patel and his wife, referred to only as 'Mrs Patel', in spring 1968. 'It is so sad', she began. 'At home the Africans were not liking us because our traders were exploiting them, but here they do not like us for the colour of our skin', she told him. Her husband Arvind had got work initially as a kitchen porter in London, and then the couple had moved to the north of England in search of a teaching post for him. Arvind Patel described to Moraes the difficulties they faced in general terms: 'I am, how would you say, a classified person; I am an immigrant. Now I know that I am not British … And we who are here, how can we prove ourselves? Shall

I paint myself white? If there was another country to go to, I would go there, but there is no other country.'[114]

Other newly arrived migrants experienced similar difficulties. Mahendra Shah told *The Times* that he had 'found trouble finding somewhere to live because of my colour'. 'Too many people', he continued, 'seem to think we have come here illegally.'[115]

The Commonwealth Office estimated in March 1968 that the Commonwealth Immigrant Acts of 1962 and 1968 denied automatic entry into Britain to around 132,000 South Asian British citizens and British Protected Persons in Kenya alone. The exact numbers were always changing. As an official in the migration and visa department admitted, even the figures for South Asians who had migrated to Britain were unreliable: 'I am still not happy with them since in most cases we started from an inspired guess.'[116] At the same time, Kenya's majoritarian policies were beginning to tell on South Asian communities. The Kenyan immigration department notified employers that non-citizens whose applications for work permits had been rejected should be relieved of duties by 8 March.[117]

A crucial part of the political and legal justification of the 1968 Act was that it was not an outright ban on the entry of British citizens without ancestral territorial connection to Britain, but merely a regulation of that entry. The solicitor-general, Arthur Irvine, was forced to defend the legality of the act in the House of Commons. Although conceding that there was a 'principle in international law' that a state 'has a duty to admit its nationals in any circumstances, without qualification', he averred that the 1968 Act was 'not a refusal of entry Bill'.[118]

In order to uphold this, the Home Office created 1,500 'special vouchers' per year for entry into Britain. These were given to South Asian 'heads of household' who were 'under the most immediate pressure to leave' East Africa. The quota of special entry vouchers accounted for just 1 per cent of the total population of Kenyan South Asian British citizens, although each 'head of household', whether a man or woman, had the right to bring their dependants. The figure of 1,500 was decided, as Heath Mason, assistant under-secretary at the newly merged Foreign and Commonwealth Office put it, 'more or less by guess and by God'.[119] The quota of 1,500 was for the whole of East Africa, but Kenyan South Asian British citizens initially received the largest share. In 1968 alone, there were 2,572 applications for these, of which 1,468 were granted; by 31 March 1969, 2,608 people were waiting for their vouchers to be processed.[120]

'Human Shuttlecocks'

At this time, and for years afterwards, East African South Asian British citizens were referred to as 'human shuttlecocks' and 'migronauts' by British newspapers. They were so called because they often tried to fly to Britain, were denied entry at arrival, and – rather than try to return to East Africa – waited in a neighbouring European country in the hope of retrying. They were, as the *Sunday Telegraph* put it, 'suspended in stateless limbo'.[121]

Babu Mehta, a Kenyan South Asian British citizen whose family was already in Britain, had attempted to join them from Nairobi after the legislation had taken effect on 1 March. 'When I applied for the visa, they refused me. They said you can't join the family until you get your turn … so I had to stay back.' Without a voucher that would have secured his right of entry, Mehta travelled to London regardless, and was briefly imprisoned: 'We were put all together with other criminals.' Eventually he was deported to Nairobi, where he continued to attempt unsuccessfully to gain an entry certificate. Despite this, he decided again to try to travel to his family in Britain:

> We went to Uganda, and from Uganda they sent us back again to Nairobi, and this time the Kenyan government didn't accept us. They send us back to Entebbe, and at Entebbe they sent us back to Addis Ababa, and from Addis Ababa we went back to England, and from England they sent us back to Kenya. Again in Kenya they didn't accept us so they sent us back to London, again they sent us from London to Nairobi, and the last time they sent us back from Nairobi to London, and this time they accepted us.[122]

In cases like Mehta's, involving families that had been split apart, ad hoc concessions were sometimes made by the British government, especially in those cases that had gained publicity. In other cases, families remained separated.[123]

Rather than increase the number of entry vouchers, the newly merged Foreign and Commonwealth Office instead refocused its efforts on trying to convince third countries, particularly India and Pakistan, but also Zambia, to accept Kenyan (and more generally East African) South Asian British citizens now largely barred from entry to Britain. Yet another round of bluffs between governments ensued, most acutely between Britain and India once again.

The problem, wrote Stanley Croft of the migration and visa department to colleagues, was that 'these countries refused to admit them for residence unless they were assured of re-admissibility elsewhere'.[124] In other words, these third countries wanted a legal assurance from Britain that all persons coming into their respective countries would be able to move onwards to Britain if they wished – thereby cleverly ensuring that, if the British government wanted to use their territories as a transit camp for its own citizens, it would have to reaffirm those citizens' right of entry in principle.

India insisted that it would only accept South Asian British citizens if the British high commission in Nairobi endorsed their passports with an entry certificate into Britain. With this in place, the Indian government would not block their entry into India, and they could leave for Britain if they so wished. On 6 March, to force Britain's hand on this point, India introduced visa restrictions specifically for citizens of the United Kingdom and Colonies whose passports showed Kenya as their place of residence. Only with an endorsed passport could South Asian British citizens from Kenya gain a ninety-day visa, which could then be extended. To qualify for a British-passport endorsement, and thus an Indian visa, a Kenyan South Asian British citizen technically had to establish a condition of need (in reality statelessness) 'through the cancellation of his residence permit, or the withdrawal of his right to work or trade' in Kenya.[125]

These terms were agreed between India and Britain on 25 July. In the period leading up to this, India had not attempted to turn away the hundreds of South Asian British citizens who made the decision or were forced to leave Kenya.[126] The Indian high commissioner in Nairobi, Prem Bhatia, recalled in his memoir that, in early 1968, he had been instructed to issue Indian visas only in cases of emergency, on compassionate grounds. But he used this discretionary power to admit hundreds of South Asian British citizens with temporary Indian visas on 'patently flimsy' grounds.[127]

Terrified that, after a brief sojourn in India, these South Asians would travel on to Britain and make good on their endorsed entry certificates, the British high commission in Nairobi made Kenyan South Asians sign a 'declaration' that they wished to settle permanently in India.[128] The

British were happy to pressurise Kenyan South Asians in this way, and knew that there would be future diplomatic opportunities to try to stop India, Pakistan and Zambia from repatriating them to their legal homeland, Britain. Many South Asian British citizens living in Kenya were now subject to forms of administrative regulation or punishment from India, Britain and Kenya. For those with the means of travel and whose residence permits had been invalidated by the 1967 Kenyan Immigration Act, India was now possibly the easiest of the three countries in which to establish immediate residency after 1 March 1968.

Remains of the Day

Tens of thousands of South Asian British citizens remained in Kenya, left with no choice but to navigate the restrictions imposed on them by new Kenyan legislation. Under Kenya's now active Immigration Act of 1967, the residence permits of many Kenyan South Asians had been invalidated – 'their presence here is illegal', as the British high commissioner put it in 1968.[129] Employment restrictions had also come into force. One Kenyan South Asian British citizen, Jaswinder Singh, was asked soon after the 1 March deadline what he intended to do. 'I can work for another two years', he told a reporter from the New York Times. 'After that maybe I can work for another two years. After that who knows?'[130] The Times reported in December 1969 that some 10,000 applications by Kenyan South Asians to naturalise as Kenyan citizens were being 'administratively delayed' by the Kenyan government.[131]

Many South Asian families with British citizenship simply left East Africa (or India) without an official entry voucher to Britain. They often travelled to European destinations hoping to move onwards to Britain. Having no access to European states and carrying effectively useless British passports that were rejected at British ports of entry, clutches of families remained stranded for considerable periods between airports.

When Uganda replicated Kenya in passing a Trade Licensing Act (1969) and an Immigration Act (1970) targeting South Asian non-citizens, several thousand Ugandan South Asian British citizens also became in reality stateless, though they continued to be described as British citizens. Airlines were by this time no longer providing direct flights to Britain.

One group of Ugandan South Asian British citizens, having tried in vain for eighteen months to gain special entry vouchers from the British high commission in Kampala, in desperation flew in 1970 to Europe.

They had 'no other choice' but to try to 'push our way into England', the group wrote to a migrant organisation in London. Attempting to travel through Austria, they were 'pulled out of the train' near the border. They eventually ended up in front of the British deputy high commissioner in Belgrade, but were told that 'he couldn't do anything' since he had been instructed not to issue them any special entry vouchers. 'We are on the road since last 15 days and now we are penniless … we have take [sic] a loaf of bread and water and we are sleeping on the pavement of theatres and sometimes on benches', their letter to the Joint Council for the Welfare of Immigrants continued.[132]

While dozens of comparable stories of British citizens failed to reach public attention, the case of Ranjan Vaid did gain publicity in 1970. A South Asian British citizen from Kenya, Vaid left Nairobi airport on 6 February 1970 for Frankfurt; from there, she flew on to Britain, but without an entry voucher was sent immediately back to Frankfurt. After being ferried between German airports, whose officials in turn disclaimed responsibility for her, she was eventually sent back to Nairobi, where she was promptly returned to Germany.

Debating her case in the House of Commons, home secretary James Callaghan remarked that the government would not give in to Kenyan South Asian British citizens trying to 'jump the queue', but agreed to allow Vaid entry to Britain for three months.[133] This contradicted a speech Callaghan had made in late February 1968, when he indicated that any Kenyan South Asian British citizen who appeared in Britain, having lost their residency and livelihood in Kenya, would not in practice be turned away.

That same month, February 1970, several other Kenyan South Asian British citizens without entry vouchers were detained in Canterbury Prison before being deported to the port of Calais; others on various occasions were detained at Heathrow airport or Pentonville Prison pending deportation. There were often protests in an attempt to gain attention. A group of five Kenyan South Asians and one Ugandan South Asian – all British citizens – were removed by French police in early March 1970, having staged a sit-in at the entrance to the British consulate in Paris.[134] According to officials' figures published by the British government, 1,235

South Asian British citizens travelling from either East Africa or India were turned away on arrival in Britain between 1970 and 1972.[135]

As late as 1976, a group of 107 East African South Asians with British status (seventy British citizens and thirty-seven British Protected Persons) staged a seventeen-hour sit-in on a Pan-American Airways plane at Palam airport, Delhi, when they were refused travel to London. The group had travelled from East Africa to Bangkok, and thence to India, on a flight whose next stop-over was in London. They were removed by some 200 Indian policemen.[136] There were still large numbers of East African South Asian British citizens living in India in the second half of the 1970s. In 1976 there were 5,290 'heads of household' in the queue for special entry vouchers, some of whom had been 'waiting for years' according to British officials.[137]

For those thousands of South Asian British citizens who stayed in Kenya after 1 March 1968, political conditions did not worsen greatly in the early 1970s, even as many of them crossed into illegal residency. This was partly because Britain had increased the number of annual entry vouchers for East African South Asian British citizens from 1,500 to 4,500 in 1971, and to 3,000 thereafter (simultaneously reducing the number of entry vouchers for citizens of Commonwealth states), the majority of these being earmarked for Kenyan South Asians. This signalled a commitment that Britain was slowly phasing in Kenyan South Asian British citizens, and gave the Kenyan government less incentive to prosecute South Asians in violation of the new laws regarding non-citizens.

But this was a hopeless situation for many, and in April 1971 the *New York Times* reported that a group of nine South Asian British citizens had been conducting a 'sleep-in' outside the British high commission in Nairobi in protest for several weeks.[138] By this time, the article went on, Kenyan South Asians were living 'in a no man's land between statelessness and non-citizenship', without work permits and dependent upon forms of charity. In 1976 there were still at least 17,000 South Asian British citizens in Kenya.[139]

The initial actions of Indira Gandhi's government in early 1968 towards actively blocking the entry and settlement of Kenyan South Asian British citizens in India had been a part of a diplomatic strategy to force the British government to accept its own citizens. In the event, following the 1968 Commonwealth Immigrants Act, India allowed large numbers of East African South Asian British citizens to settle in India.[140] In public, however, Gandhi was careful to maintain India's longstanding policy that, in principle, it encouraged 'people of Indian origin who have made their home in other countries to become full and loyal citizens of those countries', as she put it in a July 1968 interview.[141]

Yet there was some public awareness of India's actions. In 1969 India's *National Herald* wrote of India's 'self-sacrificing cooperation to enable Britain to resettle within her own boundaries her own Asian citizens in East Africa'. The situation was breathlessly absurd, wrote the Indian journalist Narain Singh, since 'it has been stressed times out of number that these Asians in Kenya and Africa cannot be classified as "immigrants" at all. Britain of her own free will admitted them into her full citizenship status: the most elementary canons of justice ordain that they be admitted into Britain without the slightest objection.' Singh pointed out that the Indian government had that year offered to stop Indian (Commonwealth) citizens migrating to Britain altogether if this would induce Britain into accepting its own Kenyan South Asian citizens.[142]

At a press conference in Nairobi on 12 March 1970, officials from the British, Indian and Kenyan governments revealed the extent of migration of South Asian British citizens from East Africa to India. They announced that, since late 1968, some 12,500 families had migrated to India, of which 9,000 intended to become Indian citizens. In 1973, officials at the Home Office and FCO estimated that the total figure of South Asian British citizens in India who had left East Africa was 'as high as 25,000'. Indian officials, for their part, would only admit to the much lower figure of 3,000 people.[143]

It seems that Indira Gandhi's government did not want to publicise the fact that it had had its hand forced by Harold Wilson's government in 1968. In its year of crisis, Harold Wilson's Labour government had seemingly won its diplomatic skirmish involving the lives of non-white British citizens. This was a pyrrhic victory, given the human rights implications of the 1968 Act and the way in which it removed from British citizens an irreducible minimum of nationality. Prem Bhatia, the Indian high commissioner in Nairobi, gave his final thoughts on 'the panic exodus' of late 1967 and early 1968 in his memoir. The crisis had been 'a tragedy of miscalculation, bad faith and incalculable human suffering'.[144]

9

The Ugandan South Asian Crisis: Making British Nationality a Global Responsibility (1972)

Five years after the global survey of non-white British citizens resident in former British territories, and four years after the height of the crisis that saw South Asian British citizens arrive from Kenya, another episode occurred that confirmed British officials' very worst fears. In 1967 the Foreign Office had imagined some future political upheaval akin to majoritarian policies in Kenya that would again force Britain to assume consular responsibility for non-white British citizens – or, worse, trigger a migration of non-white British citizens to Britain.

This is exactly what happened in 1972 in Uganda, when Ugandan president Idi Amin deported en masse Uganda's South Asian population, many of whom were either British Protected Persons or British citizens (citizens of the United Kingdom and Colonies). The 'Ugandan Asian Crisis', as it was styled at the time, again forced Britain to confront the reality of non-white people with British nationality resident outside Britain.

Most histories of the 1970s begin with some reference to crises in the world economy at the start of the decade. The early 1970s saw the end of the secular post-war boom in economic growth. The end of the Bretton Woods fixed-exchange-rate system in 1971 (itself a watershed in post-war international monetary policy) and the beginning of a huge oil-price spike in 1973 led to a deepening of world economic interdependencies and the beginning of a new phase in post-war economic history.

But, for many former European colonies, the early 1970s were simply a continuation of a struggle for more equitable trade arrangements and the fight to make decolonisation more substantive. At the commemorative session of the United Nations in 1970, the terms of the 'second development decade' were debated in such a way as to demonstrate the influence of a coalition among 'developing' countries. The strategy document on development recommended to the UN General Assembly pointed out that 'the level of living of countless millions of people in the developing part of the world is still pitifully low'.[1]

Foreign and Commonwealth Office officials saw the claims of developing countries on questions of trade and aid as part of a 'communist thesis that western aid is simply reparation for past colonialist exploitation'.[2] The original draft of the strategy document on development was infused, they averred, with 'communist propagandist theses on colonialism, apartheid, disarmament' and 'sovereignty over natural resources'.[3]

In 1970 Britain had a new Conservative prime minister, Edward Heath, who was seemingly determined to see Britain enter Europe, economic integration in Europe having proved successful. Britain was included in the European Communities' membership negotiations beginning in June 1970. This enlargement was to include Denmark, Ireland, Norway and (for the third time of asking) Britain. Heath's successful diplomatic intervention with the new French president, Georges Pompidou, on 21–22 May 1971 indicated that Britain would finally enter Europe. This was three months before president Richard Nixon announced that the US dollar would be devalued and no longer pegged to gold, ending the Bretton Woods fixed-exchange-rate system.[4]

The disruptive economic events of the early 1970s triggered a new round of late declinist accounts of Britain's post-war fate. These accounts expressed an exceptionalism that had long refused to see Britain as simply ensconced in a lattice of regional and global economic and political relationships. The upheavals in international monetary policy affected the international status of sterling and Britain's existing Sterling Agreements. The use of sterling as a currency of international reserve decreased, especially as oil trade was increasingly denominated in dollars.[5] For developing countries, these critical events might have provided opportunities for change. As I. G. Patel, the then governor of the Bank of India and about to assume the role of deputy administrator of the UN Development Program, wrote at the time, for developing countries, 'the year 1971 led to a welcome recognition of the importance of their being fully involved in the discussion on international monetary reform'.[6]

Economic questions also pervaded British–East African relations at this time. In the shadow of former imperial hopes to build upon common economic arrangements within colonial East Africa, British officials now navigated Julius Nyerere's *ujamaa* (socialist and nationalisation policies) in Tanzania, Ugandan president Milton Obote's socialist declarations, and Jomo Kenyatta's African-first capitalism in Kenya.

Of these relationships, British governments had been by far most dedicated to Kenya as a British showcase of decolonisation, a partner in British trade and investment, and a country with a long British white-settler history. Thousands of South Asian British citizens remained in Kenya, and Kenyatta's government was able to maximise this situation to generate diplomatic bargaining power with respect to British aid. Uganda, meanwhile, had been a British protectorate, not a crown colony, and had not been cultivated by British white settlers.[7]

The territory of Uganda had originally been targeted by British imperial agents as part of a long political interest in the headwaters of the Nile. Uganda was fertile and richly watered. British colonial economic policy had focused on commercial agriculture, and used South Asian immigrant labour to grow an agrarian economy around commodities like cotton, wheat, coffee, cocoa and rubber. South Asians – the intermediary in the imperial economy – would be used to secure and marshal future commercial opportunities.[8]

A Coup in Uganda

On the morning of 25 January 1971, a senior member of the Ugandan military, Idi Amin, moved to oust president Milton Obote by occupying Kampala, the Ugandan capital. Obote was at the Commonwealth Heads of Government Meeting in Singapore, where he was strongly criticising Edward Heath over his apparent readiness to sell arms to apartheid South Africa. As early as that July, military forces attached to Amin had murdered several thousand Acholi and Langi soldiers. The Amin regime is estimated to have been responsible for the deaths of some 300,000 people in episodes of state-sponsored violence.[9]

There was a lurid fascination with Amin's personal excesses that seemed to confirm the worst eschatological visions of decolonisation offered by British imperialists a generation before. Foreign media styled Amin as both buffoonish and deeply threatening – the avatar of an ancient African violence, amid a swirl of rumours about cannibalism and engorged sexuality. Amin's growing reputation for 'black racism' – which would only grow when he made positive comments about Hitler – was used by Western newspapers as a way of distracting attention from international definitions of racism that associated it closely with colonialism and white-minority rule.

Amin had served with a British colonial regiment, and was judged by a senior British colonel to be 'thick and unintelligent', 'almost illiterate' and 'a bully'.[10] Complexities within the Ugandan state were overlooked, Amin's personality dominating British attention. Initially, remembered FCO officials in 1972, Amin had maintained good relations with Israel, which had given him 'a good deal of help in military training and in other ways'. Then, after his first visit to Muammar Gaddafi's Libya in mid February 1972, he 'began an ardent flirtation with the Arab countries'.

In March 1972, having 'turned suddenly' on the Israeli government, Amin made sure that 'all the Israelis were sent packing' from Uganda, and their embassy was closed down in just a few days. In the eyes of the FCO, Amin had clearly 'fallen further under Arab influence and his general behaviour has become ever more unbalanced and unpredictable'. At this time, Amin turned away from his personal links with the British empire towards Libya, France, Saudi Arabia and the Soviet Union.[11]

Amin was also publicly committed to vanquishing economic inequities and commercial exclusions in Uganda. By declaring 'economic war' on Uganda's South Asians in 1972, Amin was signalling a set of African-first policies akin to those in Kenya. Horace Campbell, a young Jamaican political scientist who was living and working in Kampala in 1973, wrote that Pan-Africanists should not be duped by Amin's signalling, urging them to make a distinction between 'crass black nationalism and serious anti-imperialism'.[12]

More Asians, More Problems

On 12 October 1971, some eight months after assuming power, Amin ordered an ad hoc census of all South Asians in Uganda to be conducted.[13] Then, on 6 December, Amin summoned chosen South Asian 'elders' (including Muslims, Hindus, and Catholics with Goan ancestry) to an 'Asian Conference' at the international conference centre in Kampala.[14] He indicated his hope to the South Asian delegates that 'the wide gap' between Asians and Africans in economic and social life would 'narrow down, if not disappear altogether, so that all of us, whether citizen or non-citizen, African or non-African, can live a happier life in the Republic of Uganda'.

The carefully prepared speech then moved to Amin's particular view of Ugandan South Asians. They had received 'special treatment' from the 'policies of the colonial government', allowing them to establish themselves firmly 'in all the main towns and trading centres' of Uganda protectorate. If some Ugandan South Asians had been 'vital to the development of this country' – in particular those who were judges, magistrates, doctors, engineers, teachers or accountants – others had shown 'total disloyalty'. South Asian importers, retailers and wholesalers were notorious for abusing exchange-control regulations, for 'under-cutting African traders' and keeping company accounts in indecipherable 'Gujarati writing'. As a community, Uganda's South Asians had 'not shown sufficient faith in Uganda citizenship', many carrying British passports.[15]

Soon afterwards, Amin's increasingly fervid confrontation with foreign elements and populations within Uganda came to focus on South Asians. In the early months of 1972, Amin had, as an official in the FCO's East Africa department put it, been 'blowing hot and cold on the Asians, sometimes threatening them, sometimes reassuring them that they were welcome to stay in Uganda'.[16] By the summer, things would change decisively.

On the morning of 4 August, in the town of Tororo in eastern Uganda, near the Kenyan border, Amin addressed a group of army recruits in the parachute regiment, telling them about a dream he had had the night before. He had received a numinous message in the dream that South Asians, having 'milked' Uganda, now had to leave.[17] When this story became public, its impression of Amin's capriciousness ensured that it

was widely reported. As always with Amin, alternative rumours circu-
lated as to his motives, including his having tried to marry a Ugandan
South Asian woman, only to be rebuffed. The FCO, for its part, believed
Amin to be 'much influenced by occult advisers'.[18]

Publicly, Amin was simply maintaining a commitment to economic
redress begun by Milton Obote against national 'economic sabotage'
allegedly perpetrated by Ugandan South Asians.[19] Amin's invective represented an intensification of the existing and longstanding resentment
against South Asians in East and Central Africa, where, as the FCO put
it, there were 'Asian-baiters' among both 'the man on the street' and 'some
members' of African parliaments.[20] As a former British high commissioner in Kampala, James Hennessey, remembered in 2018, when Amin
'kicked out the Asian business community', it was 'a very popular move
because they'd been lording it up and down the streets of Kampala in their
saris and in their Indian shops while the Ugandans were really dirt poor'.[21]

The Life of an Expulsion Order

Mahmood Mamdani, now a prominent political scientist, was a twenty-
six-year-old graduate from a Gujarati Muslim family living in Kampala
when he heard news of Amin's decree the following day:

> Saturday, 5 August 1972 was one of the more pleasant Kampala eve-
> nings. I had gone to dinner at the home of a university colleague. There
> were four of us – an African, two Arabs and myself, an Asian … It
> was eight o'clock in the evening, news time. 'Let's listen to Amin', my
> host suggested. The television was switched on. There he was, a big
> burly he-man … We sat down in the living room, sipping our beers
> and our gin and tonics, watching Amin. Life was good. Then it came.
> 'The Asians must leave', in so many words … 'Asians came to Uganda
> to build the railway. The railway is finished. They must leave now …
> Asians have discriminated against Africans' … Unable to stand it any
> longer, my host switched the television off. Blank stares, expressions of
> disbelief.[22]

On other occasions Amin suggested that South Asians who failed to
comply would be held in 'camps'. He subsequently toured potential

military sites in the towns of Bombo, Nakasongola, Nakaseke, Bugiri and Kabamba, apparently for this purpose.[23]

The Conservative British government – especially prime minister Edward Heath, home secretary Robert Carr and foreign secretary Alec Douglas-Home – now had to make a decision. Amin's expulsion order was reported as a clear statement that 'Asian British passport holders' were required to leave the country within three months.[24] This was the very nightmare British officials had been dreading since 1967.

Not only was Amin singling out South Asians with British nationality, as opposed to South Asians per se, his reference to 'Asian British passport holders' was vague.[25] This might force Britain to take responsibility not only for any British citizens among Uganda's South Asians, but also for the large number of British Protected Persons, given that Uganda had been a British protectorate. In terms of the entitlements it carried, a British Protected Person was a far lesser status than citizenship of the United Kingdom and Colonies (British citizenship).[26] The severity of the threat against Ugandan South Asians was also decidedly greater and less predictable than the corresponding situation in Kenya in 1967. There would be far less room for diplomatic manoeuvre – perhaps none at all. There was also a resident white British community of some 7,000 people in Uganda, around 1,000 of whom were teachers, while others were financed by the Overseas Development Administration.[27]

The timing could hardly have been worse for Edward Heath's Conservative government, which had just settled a 'crippling national coal strike', as the *New York Times* put it, some five months before.[28] By chance, on 3 May, Heath's government had agreed to raise the number of 'special entry vouchers' for East African South Asian British citizens to 3,500 per year, at the request of India's external affairs minister, Swaran Singh. This was a 'global figure' of vouchers, inclusive of East African South Asians now in India or Pakistan.[29]

Despite the 1968 Commonwealth Immigrants Act, between 1 March 1968 and 30 June 1972, some 36,711 East African South Asian British citizens had been admitted into Britain under the voucher system; this figure was much higher than the number of vouchers because of the right of voucher-holders to bring their dependants.[30] The new situation in Uganda might mean yet more non-white British citizens, and even British Protected Persons, in Britain at a time when the domestic influence of Enoch Powell's anti-immigration campaigning was close to its height, and Heath's government was embroiled in a number of additional crises. Amin's announcement had come at a time, as the *New York Times* reported, when Britain was 'wrestling with multiple problems of labour strife, near-war in Ulster and general economic stagnation'.[31]

A New Humanitarianism

The British government's decision was a remarkable and unexpectedly accountable one. By contrast to Harold Wilson's Labour government in 1967, Edward Heath's ministers almost immediately publicly accepted in principle their responsibility for Ugandan South Asians with British nationality if Amin followed through with his expulsion order. Three days after Amin's expulsion order was reported, foreign secretary Douglas-Home declared in the House of Commons that his government 'accept a special obligation for these people', declaring there to be 'some 57,000 British citizens in Uganda'.[32] Douglas-Home here obfuscated the fact that most Ugandan South Asians were likely to be British Protected Persons, not British citizens (his figure also turned out to be an overestimate).

This was a noteworthy decision, not least because public support in Britain for non-white immigration was extremely low. An August poll recorded that only 6 per cent of respondents believed that Britain should accept 'Ugandan Asians with British passports' for immediate settlement.[33] At the same time, however, the Heath government decided to frame the event not simply as an expulsion of those carrying British nationality, but as a humanitarian and refugee emergency.

This was a deft, if perhaps transparent act of political imagination. The decision to present Amin's expulsion order as a humanitarian and refugee emergency would particularly bear fruit when Amin later extended his expulsion order to include some 26,657 South Asian Ugandan citizens, making it easier to conflate now stateless former South Asian Ugandan citizens with Ugandan South Asians with British nationality.[34] In the months that followed, the British government appeared to want to have it both ways, projecting British nationality as a global humanitarian responsibility, yet often demarking the limits of settlement in Britain on the basis that certain Ugandan South Asians (those that were stateless, for example) were not Britain's domestic responsibility.

A New Way to Pay Old Debts

Having almost immediately positioned Uganda's South Asians with British nationality as 'refugees' in August 1972, despite the numbers of British citizens among them, Heath's officials now began to reach out to other countries both inside and outside the Commonwealth, asking them to share the humanitarian burden of settling Ugandan South Asians. The British government also referred the situation to the United Nations, soliciting the intervention of UN agencies and fora. This was a way of turning the solidarity and antiracism of the UN and the Commonwealth towards British interests, after over a decade of muddled attempts by British officials to manage trends in post-war internationalism. In his memoir several decades later, Edward Heath cleaved to the same humanitarian vein he had cultivated in 1972. Ugandan South Asians were 'unfortunate people' whom Britain 'had a moral duty to accept' as a 'civilized nation'.[35]

International awareness of humanitarian emergencies – a consequence of both natural disasters and political episodes – was burgeoning rapidly in the early 1970s. The wars in Biafra, Vietnam and Bangladesh, as well as a catastrophic earthquake in Peru in 1970, had brought the reality of displaced populations into greater focus. Under the ambitious Sadruddin Aga Khan, the office of the United Nations High Commissioner for Refugees (UNHCR) had begun to play a larger role in these episodes – not least in Bangladesh, where nearly 10 million refugees had crossed into India in 1971.[36]

In the West, a particular image of people in the so-called Third World was gaining currency, fuelled by the accounts of Westerners bearing witness to Third World suffering. Margery Perham, for example, who became famous late in life for her interest in Biafra, offered the following portrait in 1970:

> The Biafran appeal to our emotions came from the repeated pictures, not only of dead or dying men and women, but, even more penetrating, of small children with swollen stomachs and stick-like limbs who sometimes appeared to look straight at the viewer with a last cry for help. The charitable organisations reproduced such images in their appeals and offered the public some alleviation to the anguish of pity by giving them the opportunity to assist the courageous air-lift of supplies and devoted helpers.[37]

It was in this appreciating currency of humanitarianism that Heath's government now sought to trade. As T. Fitzgerald, a Home Office official, wrote to C. P. Scott at the Foreign and Commonwealth Office in August 1972, 'it seems preferable to accept the UKPHs [United Kingdom Passport Holders] from Uganda on the basis that they are "refugees" whether or not they are technically refugees'.[38] The UN's 1951 Refugee Convention had defined a refugee as a person, among other things, 'outside the country of his nationality' or 'not having a nationality'. This definition, in other words, could not be applied to Ugandan South Asians with British nationality.[39]

Comparisons between East African South Asian British citizens and those affected by the Biafran War had been made as early as 1970. Praful Patel, secretary of the Committee on UK Citizenship, an advocacy group with bipartisan party-political support, was quoted in the *Sunday Telegraph* asking whether the problems faced by East African South Asian British citizens had to 'reach Biafran proportions' before Britain would reconsider its entry-voucher system.[40] Taking its cue from Heath's government, the British media throughout 1972 obligingly referred to Ugandan South Asians as 'refugees' – the *Daily Telegraph* described them as 'Uganda's Huguenots' – despite the fact the many of them were either British citizens or British Protected Persons.[41]

At 11 a.m. on Tuesday 8 August, foreign secretary Alec Douglas-Home told his cabinet colleagues that Britain 'could not disclaim responsibility for British passport holders, even if we so wished'. Instead, said home secretary Robert Carr, Britain would mobilise 'world opinion' and perhaps organise an 'international conference' to urge Commonwealth and other states to assist in resettling Ugandan South Asian British passport holders, here implicitly including both British citizens and British Protected Persons.[42] One thing that had not changed since 1967 was the occupant of the position of cabinet secretary, Burke Trend, symbolic of civil-service continuity across governments.

The following day, 9 August, the British high commissioner in Kampala, Richard Slater, managed to secure a meeting with Amin, together with the Indian high commissioner and the Pakistani ambassador. Amin confirmed his expulsion order, specifying that all South Asian British passport holders had ninety days to leave (the deadline was 8 November). There were to be a small number of exceptions for those indispensable to the Ugandan government and economy.[43] Meanwhile, the British high commissioner in New Delhi wrote to London to say that he understood that 'nationals of India, Pakistan and Bangladesh would also be included' within the scope of Amin's expulsion order. That same day, the FCO was also made aware of reports of 'beatings up and especially of rape' of Ugandan South Asians, but decided not to make these claims public 'for lack of substantiation'.[44]

Mahmood Mamdani remembered the days of August 1972 as full of 'endless decrees' issued by Amin, harassment and arbitrary arrests, as a 'mass depression set in' among all Ugandan South Asians.[45] Officials at the Foreign and Commonwealth Office now tried to make sense of the legal status of the various communities among Ugandan South Asians. The FCO estimated in August that the entire South Asian community in Uganda amounted to nearly 80,000 people, based on a 1969 Ugandan census. Prior to independence in 1962, Uganda had been a British protectorate, meaning that a birth in Uganda conferred the status of British Protected Person – a status that had never conferred unrestricted right of entry to Britain. However, via clauses in the 1948 British Nationality Act (Section 12(3) and Section 6(1)), many Ugandan South Asians had been able to register as citizens of the United Kingdom and Colonies, and thus had right of entry to Britain prior to 1968. Some South Asian British citizens now resident in Uganda had acquired that status in Kenya, or by birth in pre-independence India, and had subsequently migrated to Uganda.

The opportunity for Ugandan South Asians to become naturalised Ugandan citizens after the two-year registration period after independence was in practice impeded by administrative challenges that made it almost impossible to take up. Richard Slater, the British high commissioner in Kampala, believed that 'from about mid-1965 the Ugandan government have approved virtually no applications for Ugandan citizenship on behalf of Asians', sometimes refusing even to 'take delivery of applications'. Nevertheless, nearly 27,000 South Asians had become Ugandan citizens either automatically or during the two-year registration period after independence.[46]

An estimated 6,000 Ugandan South Asians were Indian and Pakistani citizens. This left around 40,000 Ugandan South Asians with British status as either British Protected Persons or British citizens. The Home Office estimated in 1968 that there were as many as 30,000 South Asian British citizens (citizens of the United Kingdom or Colonies) in Uganda, though this may have been a slight overestimate.[47] It subsequently transpired that a few thousand of the overall South Asian population resident in Uganda in 1969 (close to 80,000), whether Ugandan citizens or non-citizens, appeared to have left the country between 1969 and 1972, when Uganda emulated Kenya in passing Africanisation policies targeting South Asian non-citizens.[48]

There were early indications that the British government's initial response to the situation was being favourably received internationally. On 11 August, a *New York Times* editorial declared that the British government 'has acted with honour and courage in accepting responsibility for an estimated 50,000 Asians holding British passports who have been abruptly ordered out of Uganda'. The editorial judged Heath's decision to be 'a humanitarian action' but conceded that 'London's duty was clear', since South Asians affected by Amin's 'impetuous' expulsion order had 'settled in Uganda under British colonial rule and had been permitted to retain their British citizenship when Uganda gained its independence'.[49]

Privately, Britain maintained at this stage an indirect line of communication with the Ugandan minister of internal affairs, Ernest Obitre-Gama, who was at the time planning a coup against Amin, drawing on loyalist members of the Ugandan army spread across Sudan and Tanzania. This line of communication with the Obote-loyalist opposition to Amin came from Shariq Arain, a former Ugandan politician of Punjabi ancestry.[50]

A Diplomatic Offensive

British officials were gathering as much information as possible before launching a vast diplomatic offensive. FCO officials would first try to manoeuvre Amin by threatening to renege on pledged aid, leveraging the fact that Britain received £20 million in Ugandan imports, mostly coffee, in 1971. They also pointed out to Amin that Britain had over 1,000 'technical assistance' personnel in Uganda, as well as military and police training teams.[51]

This strategy was deemed to be a cogent one. The FCO learned that Peter Nkambo Mugerwa, the Ugandan attorney general, had privately confided to international lawyer Elihu Lauterpacht – his former law professor at Trinity College, Cambridge – that Amin's order had been 'triggered off' by a realisation that he could not spend a pledged £10 million in British aid in an unrestricted way. Nkambo Mugerwa and his office had 'done their best as lawyers', Nkambo Mugerwa wrote to his former professor, to mitigate the expulsion order by ensuring exceptions for those in certain professions.[52]

British high commissions in Africa now began to deluge the Foreign and Commonwealth Office with African political reactions to Amin's expulsion order. The reactions of East and Central African governments were most significant. The influential and widely respected Tanzanian president Julius Nyerere thought that Amin's expulsion order was unpleasant, and he remained faithful to Obote. Kenya's president Jomo Kenyatta reacted by closing the Kenyan–Ugandan border in order that no South Asians were displaced into Kenyan territory.[53] Hastings Banda, the Malawian president, reportedly told the British high commissioner in Blantyre that he, like Jomo Kenyatta, felt that Amin was 'crazy' and that 'it was most unlikely that anyone could influence him'.[54]

Other anti-Amin government reactions were informally recorded from Nigeria, Cameroon, Botswana and Liberia. The Cameroonian president, Ahmadou Ahidjo, was reportedly 'much displeased with Amin over the Asians'.[55] Quett Masire, the vice-president of Botswana, told British foreign secretary Douglas-Home in London that the whole of Botswana 'was deeply depressed at events in Uganda'.[56] William Tolbert, the Liberian president, told a BBC journalist he believed that the 'Uganda situation was an internal affair' but that he had sent a letter to Amin by way of a personal envoy to ask that Amin 'do everything possible to reduce intolerable inconvenience and human suffering'.[57] The Iranian foreign affairs minister, Abbas Ali Khalatbari, told Douglas-Home that he sympathised, and that his government 'had a very similar problem' arising from the Iraqi government's expulsion of Iranians.[58] It was even reported – via Solomon Pratt, the Sierra Leonean minister of external affairs, who was making a tour of Latin America – that Fidel Castro thought Amin's expulsion order was 'inhumane'.[59]

One of the more egregious examples of British imperial underhandedness in this period came from a representative of the Conservative right-wing association, the Monday Club, who telephoned the British government's resident clerk with a message for the home secretary on the evening of 11 August. The Monday Club wanted home secretary Robert Carr to move all Ugandan South Asian British passport holders to an island within the British Indian Ocean Territory as a means of forcing the Indian and Pakistan governments into taking them for settlement. Henry Downing, the head of the migration and visa department, took this suggestion seriously enough, though he doubted its legality.[60]

In framing the situation in humanitarian terms, Britain had to be careful to assume just the right amount of responsibility to encourage other countries to help. Over the next few months, there was a British 'campaign to keep the Ugandan problem in the international limelight', as Frederick Mason, the permanent British representative to the UN in Geneva, put it to a colleague at the FCO.[61] In mid August, Edward Heath started to write personal letters to various heads of state. He wrote to Haile Selassie, emperor of Ethiopia, that the 'humanitarian questions arising from President Amin's recent decision' were 'bound to cause immense human suffering'. He wanted Selassie to personally intervene with Amin. 'I should be most grateful', Heath wrote, 'if Your Imperial Majesty felt able to help by using the very great influence and authority which I know you to possess'.[62]

Heath wrote separate but identical messages to Indira Gandhi, Zulfikar Ali Bhutto, the president of Pakistan, and Sheikh Mujibur Rahman, prime minister of Bangladesh, expressing his hope that 'we must all do everything that is in our power to persuade President Amin to think again. If we fail, we shall need to consult urgently together about the arrangements that will have to be made to handle the exodus. But may I urge you to approach President Amin personally'.[63] In the event, efforts to intercede with Amin by the United Nations, the Organisation of African Unity and Mobutu Sese Seko, president of Zaire, came to nothing.[64]

British politician Geoffrey Rippon travelled to Kampala and immediately held a press conference about his diplomatic mission to intercede with Amin, conveniently forgetting British treatment of the Kenyan South Asians four years before. 'We will accept our responsibility', he remarked, 'and we have a responsibility which we have always accepted for people who hold UK passports. We have got to do what we can to protect them.'[65]

Over the same weekend, the chairman of the Natal Indian Congress publicly stated that South Africa should admit some Ugandan South Asians for settlement. But the South African minister of the interior, Connie Mulder, threw cold water on the idea, telling the South African press that 'this would be a radical departure from policy on immigration', and would have to be discussed with other ministers. Mulder's personal opinion, he told the *Rand Daily Mail*, was that 'South Africa had never permitted black immigrants'.[66] The South African prime minister, John Vorster, would reject the idea out of hand, publicly insisting without reference to citizenship that the 'Asians who must leave Uganda are the responsibility of India'.[67]

In the middle of August, the British high commissioner in Kampala, Richard Slater, wrote to London to request experienced legal staff to field the rush of enquiries and applications for British passports and confirmation of British status.[68] South Asians with Ugandan citizenship, meanwhile, had to face the offices of the immigration division of Uganda's ministry of internal affairs. Mahmood Mamdani remembers the process of administrative reprisal by which South Asians were forced to 'verify' their claim to Ugandan citizenship:

> [A]ll citizen Asians were asked to come and queue up at the Immi-gration Office and verify their citizenship claim. Proper 'documentary evidence' had to be presented. This meant that besides passports, the birth and marriage certificates of both the individuals concerned and their parents must be produced. A process of summarily invalidating citizenships began. If your father was born in East Africa and was over 50 years old, he was most unlikely to have a birth certificate at all. You were then said to have 'insufficient documentary evidence' and your claim to Uganda citizenship declared false.[69]

Reports would later emerge of South Asians with Ugandan citizen-ship having their Ugandan passports torn up, or stamped as 'void' or 'unacceptable'.[70]

India's minister of external affairs, Swaran Singh, declared in the Lok Sabha on 15 August that he could not 'accept in India the British passport holders who are squarely the responsibility of the British Government'. India was fresh from a vast refugee emergency in Bengal and war with Pakistan, amid the creation of the new state of Bangladesh.[71] Yet, predict-ably, officials at the Foreign and Commonwealth Office were exploring the idea that Britain would ask India to accept Ugandan South Asian British passport holders 'on a permanent basis' in exchange for 'a cash payment towards the cost of re-settling the Uganda Asians in India'.[72]

This was soon rejected as unlikely to work. Terence Garvey, British high commissioner in New Delhi, worried that any 'offer of financial induce-ment' to India to take British passport holders in Uganda 'would invite rejection as involving trade in human flesh'. At this time, mid August, the FCO was confident that India would accept Ugandan South Asians with British status already 'aboard ships and unable to return to Uganda'.[73]

A similar process of bluffs between India and Britain that had occurred during the so-called Kenyan Asian crisis was now applied to Ugandan South Asians. On 14 August the Indian high commission in Nairobi set out a similar process to the one that had operated in 1968: if Ugandan South Asians with British nationality wanted to enter India, they would need a British endorsement – 'a guarantee of admission to the UK and onward ticket … even if the persons involved professed their intention to settle in India' – before being issued an Indian visa.[74] Such British entry certificates expired after six months, but could be renewed by the British high commissions in India (in Bombay, for example). This device was designed to reassure the Indian government that Britain bore 'continued responsibility' for the people concerned, and from Britain's perspective to ensure that India extended the visas of Ugandan South Asian British passport holders, keeping them away from Britain.[75]

British officials viewed this new system of entry certificates as purely for presentational purposes. They would not allow the persons concerned actually to enter Britain – such entry certificates were 'of no value' for 'settlement in the UK' or for 'travelling direct'.[76] The existing system of special entry vouchers, created in 1968, would in principle be the only means of entering Britain, and would only be offered to British citizens. British officials in any case made the renewal process of the new ad hoc entry certificates difficult, asking Ugandan South Asian British passport holders detailed questions about their future intentions, as well as telling them they could not renew their British entry certificates indefinitely, and should therefore renounce their British status and take up permanent residence in India.[77]

As in previous years, India was poised to accept, as an official in the FCO's South Asian department put it, 'a very considerable number' of South Asian British citizens and British Protected Persons from Uganda. As before, the Indian government avoided drawing public attention to its role, and did not advertise the number of people with British nationality it had accepted. Unlike in the Kenyan episode, it avoided a formal British–Indian agreement akin to the one made in July 1968.[78] British and Pakistani officials also set up an identical system involving visas for entry into Pakistan and entry certificates for Britain.[79]

On 19 August, Amin announced that even Ugandan South Asians with verified Ugandan citizenship had to leave Uganda, yet contradicted himself three days later. 'It doesn't make sense', one twenty-year-old Ugandan South Asian told the *Times of India* on 20 August, the 'only thing to do is to take a one-way ticket to India'.[80] Amin made subsequent declarations explaining that his term 'British Asians' included all Ugandan South Asians, since all had at some time been 'British subjects' (this was inaccurate), whether or not they ever held British passports.[81]

Here Amin matched Britain's own imperial vision of belonging during this period, but defined the ultimate place of origin to be the imperial homeland, not the place of ancestral connection. Amin claimed there was no such thing as a Ugandan Asian stateless person – 'he will doubtless say that they are all UK nationals', as an official in the FCO's United Nations department subsequently put it.[82] Amin's personal theory of belonging was uninterested in law, but there was a legal technicality that presented itself to the Ugandan government for the purpose of depriving thousands of South Asian Ugandan citizens of their citizenship.

Technically, if a Ugandan South Asian who had gained Ugandan citizenship automatically or during the two-year period after independence failed to renounce their British citizenship within three months, they lost their claim to the former.[83] Evidence of tardy declarations of renunciation, known for several years to the Ugandan government, was now brought up and used to bolster Amin's statements. Although the number of now-stateless Ugandan South Asians was less than that of Ugandan South Asians with British nationality, the presence of the former lent itself to portrayals of Amin's expulsion order as a refugee crisis.

A few days later, at the end of August, Edward Heath wrote again to Indira Gandhi, invoking the spirit of the Kenyan crisis, asking her to accept as many Ugandan South Asian British passport holders as possible, implying that they would simply 'stage through India before coming on to Britain'.[84] This contradicted the administrative efforts of British officials to make any migration from India to Britain as hard as possible. Despite the claims of successive British governments, maintained since 1968, that East African South Asian British citizens mostly wished to return to South Asia, in private British officials were convinced that they would try to enter Britain. As Terence Garvey, the British high commissioner in New Delhi, put it, 'the grass looks greener in England than in Gujarat'.[85] Indira Gandhi was not forthcoming in her reply, and did not reveal that she had in fact already written to the presidents of Zaire, Tanzania, Kenya, Zambia, Nigeria and Sierra Leone arguing against Amin's actions as an instance of racial discrimination.[86]

On 4 September, Indian external affairs minister, Swaran Singh, declared in the Rajya Sabha that India's stance on racial discrimination meant that it had to act in an inclusive way. Singh argued this case by blending rhetorical stances on ancestral solidarity, humanitarianism and human rights: 'India has always responded with sympathy and humanity to those who have suffered and sought shelter here. We cannot deny it to our own kith and kin. We must stand firm in support of human rights and … the dignity of man and the equality of all races.'[87]

C. C. Desai, a former Indian high commissioner in Pakistan, entered the debate to say that India seemed 'to have an uncanny knack for two things – receiving things without kicking back and unlimited absorption of immigrants from abroad'. 'Every person of Indian origin' in East Africa, Desai argued, whether he was an Indian or Ugandan citizen, a stateless person, or a British passport holder, 'must be permitted to come to this country and have the right to settle'. That very morning he had read that there were marches taking place in Britain, 'what are called *morchas* in our country', protesting against the entry of Ugandan South Asian British passport holders into Britain. The marches in question, which took place in London, were organised by the National Front, which supplied placards reading: 'Enoch was Right: Stop Immigration.'[88]

Piloo Mody, a Parsi architect and MP for Godhra, felt similarly: India should accept all Ugandan South Asians 'with open arms and do whatever we can to extend hospitality', just as India had done 'in respect of Bangladesh refugees'. Swaran Singh did not contradict these comments – which rather simplified India's strategic responses to the refugees from Bangladesh the year before – but made it clear that his hesitation was based in a reluctance to supply 'a very easy way for the British government to get out of their responsibility to receive the British passport holders'.[89]

The Indian government subsequently prepared Air India flights and ships from Mombasa to Bombay to transport Ugandan South Asians with Indian citizenship, notifying the British high commission in New Delhi that it had surplus capacity on its ships if Britain wished to dovetail its evacuation efforts with India's.[90] As soon as Indian officials were satisfied that Britain was serious in its intention not to debar Ugandan South Asian British citizens and British Protected Persons from entering

Britain, it loosened its ad hoc visa regime, and the Indian high commission in Kampala began to endorse for entry to India all Ugandan South Asians willing to become permanent Indian citizens.[91]

Bangladesh and Pakistan had been less positive in their diplomatic signals to British officials than India, but were still expected to take in sizeable numbers.[92] An official at the British high commission in Kampala had been able to discuss the Pakistani stance with a Pakistani representative in 'a back room' of a Muslim girls' school in Kampala's old town. Happily, it appeared Pakistan had already issued around 700 visas to Ugandan South Asian British passport holders, and that 'the eventual total of those going to Pakistan could rise to 4,000'.[93]

By 7 September, the British high commission in Kampala had cleared some 3,000 families for evacuation by air to Britain.[94] Whatever the successful arrangements with third countries, Britain was faced with an airlift of some 35,000 Ugandan South Asians with British nationality, who would have to fly from Entebbe 'at a rate of 700 a day' if Britain was to meet Amin's deadline.[95] Just as in Kenya in early 1968, South Asian British citizens and British Protected Persons were faced with administrative and logistical chaos. As Mahmood Mamdani recalled of September, 'thousands of people streamed into the city from the country and hundreds daily queued in front of the British high commission'.[96]

Airlines (BOAC, British Caledonian and East Africa Airways) had to work around the fact that expellees had only forty-eight hours to leave once they had finalised their paperwork and received clearance for Britain.[97] Announcements about the evacuation were being made via the *Uganda Argus*, and failed to reach people in more rural areas. Those outside Kampala were frightened to travel into the capital, and needed an escort to protect them against roadblocks manned by Ugandan soldiers. One group of South Asians was reluctant to board any aircraft, in the belief that a bomb might have been planted on it.[98] South Asians coming to Britain were told they would pay their own fares; in those cases where families could not afford travel costs, they were asked to sign an undertaking to repay the amount.[99]

Meanwhile, by September, Britain's diplomatic offensive was in full operation. A huge amount of activity was focused on having third countries relieve the burden of resettlement both for Ugandan South Asians made stateless and for those with British nationality. By mid September, Britain had – as foreign secretary Alec Douglas-Home explained to the

British high commissions in Vienna and Bern – approached over fifty governments, including all European Economic Community countries except Ireland, 'for help in settling the Asians'.

Douglas-Home was desperate, admitting that 'even a token number of Asians would be of real help to us'. So far, offers had come in from Malawi, Bolivia, Mauritius, Iran, Malaysia and Fiji. The Canadian government had 'made a most encouraging response', offering to take 6,000 people.[100] UNHCR head Sadruddin Aga Khan was spearheading the transport of 'about 1,000' Ismaili Ugandan British passport holders to Iran.[101] West Germany soon made a public offer to settle 1,000 Ugandan South Asians with British nationality.[102] As before, India was 'a special case', and might take 'up to 20,000'.[103]

At a September press conference at the State House in Zomba, Malawian president Hastings Banda made public his intention 'to do something practical' to help both Britain and Ugandan South Asians. He was not 'pro-Asian' – 'I have spoken openly against Asians for their practices in business' – nor 'an extreme lover of Britain', but he had considered the situation 'on humanitarian grounds' and was ready to accept up to 1,000 skilled South Asian British citizens from Uganda. Banda sympathised with the fact that 'the majority of British people, particularly the working class, resented being flooded with foreigners, particularly those who were not white in colour'. The current situation was far removed from Banda's own time in Britain. When he had for a time practised medicine in Willesden, north-west London, there 'wasn't a single black person … Mine was the only black face they saw in that part of London.'[104]

Eric Williams, the prime minister of Trinidad and Tobago, was less impressed with Britain's framing of the crisis. Addressing fellow party members of the People's National Movement in Port of Spain in September, Williams declared that Trinidad would not help Britain at a time when 'our own West Indians are finding it increasingly difficult to get admitted to a number of countries, especially in Britain with its open unadulterated and ambiguous racialisms'.[105]

The government of British Honduras (later Belize) offered to accept twenty-five families – making no distinction as to whether these would be Ugandan South Asian British passport holders or stateless persons – 'provided they are agriculturalists'.[106] Jamaica, too, was willing to accept 'small numbers of professional people'. Guyana had shown interest in taking in a few more – 'ten doctors', to be precise – and Sweden, Norway and Denmark appeared poised to accept 'token numbers', as a British official put it.[107]

US senator Ted Kennedy told the *Chicago Sun-Times* on 10 September that he wanted the Nixon administration to grant asylum to a reasonable number of Ugandan South Asians.[108] The US ambassador in London, Walter Annenberg, subsequently wrote to Douglas-Home that Nixon had approved 'the admission of up to 1,000 Ugandan Asians to the United States'.[109] The Swedish newspaper, *Svenska Dagbladet*, reported on 12 September that the Swedish foreign affairs minister, Krister Wickman, had indicated at a meeting of the Swedish United Nations Association that Sweden, in response to a British request, would give assistance 'in some form' to Ugandan South Asians with British passports.[110] An offer to settle 300 Ugandan South Asians with British nationality in Sweden was made soon afterwards.[111]

Every type of persuasion was being explored. The Austrian government, for example, was reminded by British officials of 'the generosity of Britain in accepting Austrian refugees into Britain in 1938' and 'Hungarian refugees in 1956'.[112] On 13 September, foreign secretary Douglas-Home wrote to New Zealand's prime minister, Keith Holyoake, to thank him for 'your government's decision to admit 230 Asians from Uganda for settlement in New Zealand' – 'your example will, I am sure', Douglas-Home continued, 'be followed by others'.[113] Neighbouring Australia, however, was unwilling to make 'a blanket exception', as the FCO put it, to its immigration rules.[114]

By September, Britain had a range of public and private offers to accept Ugandan South Asian British citizens and British Protected Persons from various countries, including Austria, Belgium, Bolivia, British Honduras, Canada, Denmark, Fiji, France, Germany, Guyana, Iran, the Netherlands, Mauritius, New Zealand, Singapore and Sweden. Italy had said no to permanent settlement, and Norway had yet to decide. Afghanistan, Australia, Iran, Kuwait and Malaysia had declared themselves open to a limited number of skilled Ugandan South Asians with British nationality. The United Arab Emirates, for its part, expressed an interest in 'doctors, engineers and possibly teachers', while Singapore asked for 'anyone with experience of servicing aircraft' or those with industrial investment capital of £20,000.[115] France would look 'favourably' upon visa applications from Ugandan South Asians.[116]

Some offers of 'private employment' for Ugandan South Asians with British nationality had also been made by Dominica, Ethiopia and the British Solomon Islands.[117] When an offer came in from the Falkland Islands, a British colony, asking for 'doctors, teachers, artisans, domestic servants and farm workers', foreign secretary Douglas-Home notified British officials in Kampala that any Ugandan South Asians with British nationality who wished to go to British territories – in particular Bermuda, Virgin Islands, Cayman Islands, Seychelles and Gibraltar – should be 'sent to the territory concerned for consideration'.[118] Britain knew that if Ugandan South Asians with British nationality stayed in a third country for over two years, they would have to make a fresh application for an entry certificate to Britain, which 'we would not be under an obligation to grant' if they ever wanted to move onwards to Britain, as Henry Downing at the migration and visa department remarked.[119]

In Geneva, on the evening of 12 September, Frederick Mason, British permanent representative to the Geneva Office of the United Nations, asked John F. Thomas, director of the Intergovernmental Committee for European Migration (ICEM), for help. The ICEM – today known as the International Organization for Migration – agreed to facilitate a placement and settlement programme for Ugandan South Asian British citizens and British Protected Persons in various Latin American countries – specifically Brazil, Argentina, Ecuador, Uruguay, Chile, Colombia and Bolivia. The ICEM eventually secured the cooperation of Argentina, Colombia, Ecuador and Uruguay in offering to resettle Ugandan South Asians with British nationality. In order for the ICEM to classify them as 'displaced persons', their transit accommodation would need to be in Europe, since they could not be so described if they were brought to Britain.[120] ICEM officials subsequently asked European governments if they would be able to accommodate in-transit Ugandan South Asians, blurring the line between Ugandan South Asian 'refugees' and Ugandan South Asians with British nationality.

Italy quickly offered to provide transit camps, and Belgium offered to grant temporary residence to thirty families with British nationality. British officials planned to give these thirty families, now referred to as 'transit refugees', collective – as opposed to individual – entry certificates, believing that this would give them 'less temptation to change their mind and opt for the UK after all'.[121] The charitable organisation that would be facilitating their temporary stay in Belgium asked the ICEM director to ensure that 'all transit refugees should be the sort of people who would respect the furniture and equipment of the rented accommodation'.[122] Meanwhile, M. Pierre Schneiter, special representative to the Council of Europe for national refugees and over-population, offered to appeal to member-states of the Council for help.[123] To Schneiter's mind, the problem ought to be solved 'in a spirit of European solidarity', as he put it to the European Committee of Ministers.[124]

With assorted third-country offers nominally in place, the FCO now worked hard to manage the crisis on the ground in Uganda in such a way that Ugandan South Asians with British nationality might choose to leave for a third country instead of Britain.[125] British authorities invited third-country delegations to Uganda for the selection of willing Ugandan South Asians with British nationality for removal.[126] Ministers resolved that it should be emphasised to them that the welcome in Britain would be 'less inviting and less congenial than in a number of the other countries now offering to receive them'. There were particular areas within Britain that did not want them.[127]

Ugandan South Asians with British nationality were pre-warned of 'green' and 'red' areas within Britain, the latter already being 'congested' with immigrants. The red areas included Birmingham, Bradford, Huddersfield, Wolverhampton, Leicester and the 'whole of inner London', as well as the outer London boroughs of Brent, Ealing, Haringey, Hounslow and Waltham Forest. Leicester City Council even advertised in the *Ugandan Argus* on 17 September that no South Asian should attempt to come to Leicester.[128] Though the arrangements between Britain and India remained unpublicised, the FCO was very hopeful that many Ugandan South Asian British citizens would choose – through fear, genuine desire or administrative inconvenience – to go to India. Mahmood Mamdani remembered that these warnings had the opposite of the intended effect: 'Most people had by then heard of England and of London. But now they knew there was some place called Leicester, where there were numerous Asians. All those who had been undecided as to where to go ... after reading of the hostile reactions of the British public in general, started making arrangements to go to Leicester.'[129]

The FCO was adamant that Britain, having accepted responsibility for Ugandan South Asians with British nationality, would not accept any stateless South Asians (Ugandan citizens who had had their citizenship administratively stripped), despite the fact that this contradicted the presentation of all Ugandan South Asians as 'refugees'.[130]

When asking third countries to settle Ugandan South Asians, Britain blurred the line between those who were stateless and those who were British citizens or British Protected Persons.[131] As it turned out, several countries indicated that they 'would give preference to stateless persons' over Ugandan South Asians with British nationality, or at least began to distinguish between British citizens and stateless persons.[132] The Belgian government agreed to take a second group of 'thirty families' of Ugandan South Asian stateless persons – and 'refugees within the meaning of the Geneva Convention' – for permanent settlement.[133] The Netherlands was willing to help with stateless persons upon request from the United Nations High Commissioner for Refugees.[134] In addition, the Danish Ministry of Foreign Affairs confirmed that Denmark would settle 'about 40' Ugandan South Asian stateless persons in Denmark, as well as an unspecified number of 'old or handicapped Asians' whether stateless or with British nationality. Belgium, Guyana and the Netherlands specified that they were only concerned to assist Ugandan South Asian stateless persons, not those with British nationality.[135]

Back to the United Nations

The plan of the British government was that it would mobilise the UN General Assembly on the question of South Asians in Uganda, in something of a reversal of Britain's embattled position in the General Assembly. Accordingly, on 27 September, Colin Crowe, the British permanent representative to the UN, wrote to the UN's general committee to propose that Amin's expulsion order be officially included in the agenda of the current session of the General Assembly, since the matter was 'of concern not only to the governments immediately involved but to the international community as a whole'.[136]

The issue could still be debated in the meantime. In New York that same day, foreign secretary Alec Douglas-Home addressed the UN General Assembly. Paying tribute to 'those who have come forward with offers of help', he urged member-states to 'show your good neighbourliness by sharing some of the practical problem of resettling these unhappy people'.

The situation in Uganda was a question that struck at the very core of human fellow-feeling: 'There are human problems, rights and feelings which should have equal consideration. The Uganda government should be called upon to change its policy and treat these people with humanity and not with contempt.'[137]

Uganda's foreign minister, Joshua Wanume Kibedi, dismissed Douglas-Home's appeal, noting that Britain was trying to internationalise a problem that was a bilateral matter between Uganda and Britain, and ultimately within Ugandan domestic jurisdiction. A few days later, the Ugandan permanent representative to the UN clarified the Ugandan view: 'What is the history of this problem? … During the time of British rule in Asia and Africa, the United Kingdom, when it ruled the subcontinent of India, systematically encouraged the exodus of citizens of Indian extraction from the Indian subcontinent to various territories under its jurisdiction at that time.'[138]

The Ugandan Mission to the UN went further, circulating a document within the General Assembly that drew comparisons between Amin's expulsion order and Harold Wilson's Commonwealth Immigrants Act of 1968. The 1968 Act, it claimed, was 'a racist device put in the way of British people of black and brown races', but not 'those British citizens whose parents and grandparents were from the British Isles'. 'Why', it asked, 'should a White Briton from South Africa, Zimbawe or Hong Kong be able to enter Britain any time he wishes while his counterpart from Asia is refused or frustrated when he tries to gain entry?'[139]

On 2 October, the Costa Rican minister of foreign affairs, Gonzalo Facio Segreda, announced in the General Assembly that, just as Costa Rica condemned 'apartheid and other odious forms of discrimination which men of the white race practice against those of the black race', it also condemned 'new manifestations of racism which have led majority groups of the black race to commit odious discriminatory acts against human beings of another race'. As a 'token of good faith', Costa Rica was prepared 'to receive on its soil a group of inhabitants of Uganda who are victims of the discriminatory acts'. This action, continued Facio Segreda, followed the UN secretary-general's 'humanitarian appeal' on behalf of Ugandan South Asians for third countries 'to contribute to the asylum provided to those who have been expelled'.[140]

Neither India nor Pakistan spoke out against Uganda until India's external affairs minister, Swaran Singh, addressed the General Assembly on

3 October.[141] Echoing Britain's positioning of the question, Singh declared that the effects of Amin's expulsion order were 'essentially humanitarian in character'. India was 'doing all it can' to help. Since 'racial discrimination' was 'an evil to be fought we, all of us, cannot but oppose it, whatever form it may take'.[142]

Despite these acknowledgements of the situation in Uganda, British efforts at the UN General Assembly came to little. There was no resolution, and the British proposal for inclusion of an item on 'International Implications of the Expulsion of the Asian Community in Uganda' on the General Assembly agenda was not even put to a vote in order to save British face, given the lack of support from other states.[143]

Shutting Out the Stateless

The fate of stateless South Asians in Uganda was yet to be resolved. The UNHCR – the international agency best placed to deal with stateless persons – had been waiting for events at the General Assembly to play out. In late September, UNHCR officials finally tried to enter Uganda in order to assume responsibility for Ugandan South Asian stateless persons. They met with resistance from the Ugandan government, but finally one of their representatives, Anatole Komorsky, was granted entry into Kampala, where he set up a UNHCR office.[144]

It did not help that Sadruddin Aga Khan, the religious leader of Uganda's South Asian Ismaili community, also led the UNHCR.[145] Komorsky tried to win Uganda's cooperation by offering UNHCR financial assistance to Amin in order to mitigate Uganda's pre-existing problem of Sudanese refugees (Uganda also housed refugees from Zaire and Rwanda), but to little effect.[146]

A bigger problem was that the UNHCR, under its own rules, was not permitted to issue Ugandan Asian stateless persons with identity documents for travel, since, as an internal FCO report put it, 'stateless refugees do not come within the responsibility of the UNHCR until they leave their country of origin'.[147] The FCO was reluctant to issue identity documents of any kind to Ugandan South Asian stateless persons in Uganda, fearing that to do so would 'weaken our case that they are an international rather than a UK responsibility'.[148]

The FCO was especially anxious that stateless South Asians might arrive in Britain before the UNHCR had commenced its work.[149] Britain knew that refusing to issue documentation to Ugandan South Asian stateless persons would leave those among them with fewer resources very vulnerable – 'the poorer sort must simply accept their fate', in the words of Peter Scott, assistant under-secretary for foreign and Commonwealth affairs.[150] At the end of September, most Ugandan South Asians had yet to leave Uganda, and the FCO began to turn the blame on the UNHCR head, Sadruddin Aga Khan, claiming that he did 'not seem to have realised the extreme urgency of the situation'.[151]

In a meeting held at the FCO in London, Charles Mace, UN deputy high commissioner for refugees, asked Britain to assume responsibility for processing stateless persons, given the impasse. To reassure him, the FCO's Peter Scott claimed that Britain 'acknowledged a responsibility' specifically towards former British citizens who had renounced their status to acquire Ugandan citizenship, only subsequently to have been made stateless by administrative means under Amin's expulsion order.[152] In the end, it was decided that Britain would issue 'certificates of identity' to Ugandan South Asian stateless persons, but on the understanding that in doing so Britain was acting 'as the agent of the UNHCR'. Stateless persons had to complete a form in order to gain such certificates, which asked among others things for the person's height, 'colour of hair' and any 'special peculiarities'.[153]

The fear on the part of British officials that the UNHRC would not provide help was unwarranted. The Red Cross, the UNHCR and the ICEM began their work in October, the Red Cross taking over the provision of travel documentation to stateless Ugandan South Asians, the ICEM arranging flights, and the UNHCR underwriting costs.[154] The UNHRC eventually assumed responsibility for some 4,500 Ugandan South Asian stateless persons, and took up the offers, originally solicited by the ICEM, of transit centres in Italy, Belgium, Spain, Malta and Austria (offers from Greece and Morocco were not taken up).[155] Sometimes these transit centres consisted of boarding houses, youth hostels and hotels, and in other cases they were military barracks, such as the Tigne barracks in Sliema, Malta.[156]

These transit camps – whose original purpose had in fact been to house Ugandan South Asians with British nationality designated for migration to Latin America – were not altogether successful. In February 1973, some 2,000 Ugandan South Asian stateless persons were still in these camps, and it was not until autumn 1974 that each person secured settlement in a willing third country.[157]

After their sojourn in European transit camps, the largest numbers of Ugandan South Asian stateless persons ended up in Canada (2,160 people), India (1,500) and the United States (1,620). Smaller numbers were accepted by Pakistan (800) and Sweden (344), and smaller numbers again by the Netherlands, Austria, Belgium, Denmark, Norway, New Zealand, the United Arab Emirates, Iran and ICEM-affiliated Latin American countries.[158]

The distinction made between Ugandan South Asian stateless persons and Ugandan South Asians with British status, though legally sound, negatively affected many Ugandan South Asian families. It was not untypical for one member of a family to be stateless without permission to enter Britain, and another already to be in Britain as a British citizen or British Protected Person.[159] Under pressure to reunite families, Britain also accepted small numbers of stateless persons on an ad hoc basis. If Britain's ambitions at the UN General Assembly had come to nothing, it had successfully avoided taking in large numbers of stateless persons. Charles Mace, the UN deputy high commissioner for refugees, had even worried during his private meeting in London with the FCO's Charles Scott that there might be an 'allegation that the [UN] Secretary-General and the UNHCR were acting at British behest', were news of such private meetings to leak.[160]

Despite the various offers from third countries, it is unclear how many Ugandan South Asians with British nationality took up the offers from third countries, given the various restrictions placed upon acceptance – though there were confirmed migrations of small numbers to Germany, Sweden, Argentina, Brazil, Colombia, Malawi, Fiji, the British Solomon Islands, the Seychelles, the Netherlands, Mauritius, New Zealand, Sweden, Switzerland and the United States.[161] As it turned out, India and Canada, of all the third countries mobilised, admitted the largest numbers – some 4,800 Ugandan South Asian British citizens and British Protected Persons going to the former and at least 6,000 to the latter.[162]

Coming to Britain: Citizens, Protected Persons, Immigrants or Refugees?

Edward Heath's Conservative government had successfully internation-alised what it conceived to be an immigration crisis, but also accepted its responsibility for the some 28,608 Ugandan South Asians with British nationality, as well as a tiny minority of stateless persons, who migrated to Britain in 1972–73.[163] After delaying the evacuation for over a month, in its search for third-country commitments to offset its burden, British authorities finally started transporting Ugandan South Asians with British nationality in late September. Between 18 September and 9 November, there were 419 flights carrying Ugandan South Asians into Heathrow, Gatwick, Glasgow, Manchester and (most often) Stansted airports.

Regarding the 7,000 white British residents in Uganda at the time, con-siderably more care was taken. Although Amin's expulsion order did not extend to white British residents, contingency plans for their evacuation were drawn up in September, including the use of military force in a worst-case scenario. Some eighty white British people resident in Uganda had been detained by Ugandan authorities on 17 September, but all were released within five days.[164] The British high commission in Kampala had advised the white British community in Uganda to 'thin out' its numbers, something made easier by the fact that, by September, 'most children had gone back to boarding school' in Britain, and 'numbers of wives had in fact accompanied them'.[165] Secretly, Britain arranged with Zaire, Sudan, Kenya and Tanzania that any white British 'refugees' from Uganda would be given shelter there if things deteriorated.[166] Some 3,000 white British 'belongers' had been surreptitiously airlifted out of Uganda by the time Amin declared, in December, that they also had to leave.[167]

Despite virulent British public opposition to further 'coloured immi-gration', Edward Heath presented the arrival of Ugandan South Asians as a testament to the generosity of the British people: 'They have refused to be scared into supporting the attitude of meanness and bad faith towards the refugees. They have responded in accordance with our tradition of honouring our obligations and holding out a friendly hand to people in danger and distress'.[168]

Processing the 'Refugees'

The careful framing of Ugandan South Asians with British nationality as refugees allowed Edward Heath's government to set up a Uganda Resettlement Board, designed to ensure the 'orderly' reception of Ugandan South Asians, and their 'dispersal as widely as possible throughout the country', as was publicly declared upon its creation in late August 1972.[169] The Board was a collaboration between the Home Office, the Department of Environment and the Ministry of Defence (MoD).

The MoD earmarked a number of disused army and Royal Air Force barracks spread widely around the country to be repurposed as 'resettlement centres', each of which could accommodate upwards of 500 people. Close to the village of Stradishall, near Bury St Edmunds in Suffolk, was a Royal Air Force base that had ceased to operate in 1970. It was ideal, since it was close to Stansted Airport. Soon other former military barracks in rural locations were found – a total of sixteen in all from Devon to Warwickshire, Kent to Lincolnshire, and Dorset to Gwynedd.[170] Upon arrival at British airports, incoming South Asians were bused directly to these main resettlement centres with the help of local volunteers. One Ugandan South Asian woman, Raxa, remembered her arrival years later:

> We came to Gatwick airport. It was really nice actually when we came. There were people there to help us, to greet us. They brought us warm coats and clothing because … over there you just wear a dress … We hadn't even seen a coat there. Here, it was really freezing all the time … They asked us if we had any relatives or anybody staying here but at that time we didn't know anybody, so we said no. They took us to Greenham camp … for a couple of days and then they moved us to another one. I think it was somewhere in Wales.[171]

Also among the arrivals, Mahmood Mamdani recalled his first experiences in Britain. Carrying a sitar, Mamdani was ushered onto a bus by a volunteer after his plane landed. He was to be taken to the resettlement centre in Kensington Barracks, London. He remembered a conversation he had overheard on the bus:

> A little boy asked his mother:
> 'Mother, who are they?'

'They are refugees, darling.'

'What's he carrying, Mother?'

'It's an *Indian* instrument, darling. Now why don't you be quiet, dear?'[172]

Some of these military barracks – in rural Lincolnshire, Dartmoor, and a remote coastal village in Wales – were by design far away from existing South Asian communities. These were hardly fit for accommodating families, and there were problems with respect to water supply, kitchen facilities and central heating.

The Board officials were unsure as to 'what sort of food the refugees ate and whether it would be possible to encourage them to change their diet quickly'. A catering service was commissioned to service Stradishall camp on the basis that it had 'done the catering for the Hungarian refugees in 1956'. One camp administrator believed the food should be 'a compromise between European and Oriental', and should avoid 'controversial items such as pork'. In all but one of the military barracks, the dining hall was in effect racially segregated, with staff dining facilities designated as 'European Dining Rooms'.[173]

Although the Uganda Resettlement Board was answerable to the Home Office, the Foreign and Commonwealth Office provided initial advice on the selection of civil servants and camp administrative staff. On FCO recommendation, the final colonial governor of Uganda, Walter Coutts, was brought into the selection process; he chose Richard Turnbull, the last colonial governor of Tanganyika, as head of 'airport reception arrangements'. In 1959 Turnbull had warned Harold Macmillan's government of a spectre of insurrection if it decided to keep to its plan to give Tanganyika independence in 1970, saying it would lead to 'a combination of Mau Mau and the Maji-Maji rebellion, with the modern techniques of guerrilla warfare and fifth column activities'.[174] Turnbull's colonial credentials, in other words, were impeccable.

A former colonial administrator in Kenya, R. A. Wilkinson, was chosen in turn to manage accommodation for the resettlement programme. Wilkinson, in consultation with Turnbull and Coutts, made further hires from among former colonial administrators in Kenya. Brigadier Geoffrey Beyts, appointed as the administrator for the Greenham Common resettlement centre, had served in the British Indian army from the 1920s to the 1940s, set up as a farmer in Kenya in the late 1940s, and was employed in the Kenyan colonial administration throughout the 1950s.[175] Meanwhile Charles Cunningham, chairman of the Uganda Resettlement Board, was a longstanding Home Office official who had experienced the rising numbers of South Asian arrivals in the late 1950s.

Within the resettlement centres, it was decided that there should be 'education of the refugees' in British customs and behaviour. This programme of education included lectures on topics such as 'our system of government', 'sports and games in Britain', and, ironically enough, 'the police, the law and the citizen'.[176] A carefully regimented programme of 'refugee' assimilation and centre maintenance was established. This was particularly senseless given the level of British imperial acculturation in East Africa. One young Ugandan South Asian explained to the *Observer* that, at his school, he had been 'taught in English from the start. In fact, I failed Gujarati in the Senior Cambridge [exam]. I did Macbeth, Dickens and Tennyson. I wasn't taught Indian history, but the history of the British Empire.'[177]

The colonial men administrating the Uganda Resettlement Board and the camps found fault with their charges, labelling some 'trouble makers' and 'uncooperative residents'. The FCO recorded that a Sergeant Bussey, head of the resettlement centre in Maresfield, had notified his colleagues that six South Asians (four Ismailis and two Hindus), were 'causing trouble', and should be deemed 'uncooperative residents'. It turns out these men were refusing to 'take their proper share of camp cleaning tasks' and had begun a petition to protest their being financially charged for accommodation and food.[178] The men in turn wrote a letter to Bussey: 'We are most grateful to the British Government for the assistance provided ... But we are most hurt by the insults that we had from you without any reason. We have self-respect, and it is very very dear to us, dearer than our lives.'[179]

The task of promoting resettlement in third countries continued within Britain. In order to maximise the third-country options, the 'offers and opportunities' in other countries were 'advertised widely' in the resettlement centres by way of notices, leaflets, posters and films. In addition, embassies and high commissions from various countries were invited 'to supply literature and information' within the resettlement centres on the living and working conditions of their respective countries. Delegations of officials from Sweden, New Zealand and Germany visited various resettlement camps between October and November 1972.[180]

One official from the Uganda Resettlement Board later recorded that he himself had processed 184 Ugandan South Asians with British nationality (excluding any accompanying dependants) who decided to take up these offers from third countries, including Argentina, Brazil, Colombia, Germany, the Netherlands, India, Mauritius, New Zealand, Norway, Sweden, Switzerland and the United States.[181] The Home Office later recorded that, by the end of 1973, 1,004 Ugandan South Asians with British nationality, excluding dependants, had chosen to leave Britain for other countries having been processed by the Uganda Resettlement Board. A further 216 persons had been accepted for departure.[182]

The final report of the Uganda Resettlement Board recorded that its resettlement centres housed 21,987 people for varying periods of time. The endeavour of the Board had been to keep the new migrants far away from urban centres, both on arrival and in the future. This 'policy of dispersal' meant that Ugandan South Asians were encouraged to settle away from immigrant 'red areas'. The Board conceded, however, that after their stay in the resettlement centres, 'many have gone, against our advice, to areas in which housing is difficult and the social and educational services are under strain'.[183]

Those Ugandan South Asians who were earmarked for settlement in particular areas within Britain were connected with local government–mandated associations, such as the Wandsworth Council for Community Relations (WCCR), charged with the integration of 600 Ugandan South Asians. The WCCR was created as a part of the local infrastructure of the 1968 Race Relations Act, and drew on local volunteers and church groups to provide Ugandan South Asians with clothes and household goods. A core focus of the WCCR's work was to provide English-language tuition classes and guidance about English life and culture in the form of local visits and outings.[184] As a whole, the assumption that Ugandan South Asians were refugees distracted attention away from the events and migrations from Kenya some four years before. The reality that British nationality remained imperial receded still further from public understanding.

Lessons from Uganda

The British government managed to frame events in Uganda as above all a refugee crisis. In December 1972, the FCO prepared a statement to be sent to European Economic Community states, the UN secretary-general, the UN High Commissioner for Refugees, and the governments of the United States and Canada. 'We gratefully acknowledge', it declared, 'the assistance we have received from a number of Commonwealth and other Governments, particularly the Governments of India and Canada, in dealing with the Uganda situation. We believe that any future problems of this nature can only be tackled by international action.'[185]

Edward Heath also wrote personally to Jomo Kenyatta and Indira Gandhi, remarking to the latter that his government had 'faced up to our responsibilities'.[186] But Amin's expulsion order had revealed the limits of British immigration legislation. Despite the 1968 Commonwealth Immigrants Act and the 1971 Immigration Act, Britain had been forced into accepting almost 30,000 non-white people with British nationality.

Imagining future political episodes that might lead to comparable situations, FCO officials in early 1973 used the term 'refugee problem', replacing the term 'coloured immigration', which had been in use since the 1950s.[187] The most immediate problem was represented by the 105,000 or so South Asians left in Kenya (35,000 of whom were British citizens); around 70,000 South Asians remained in Tanzania (between 15,000 and 20,000 of whom were British citizens); and around 14,000 South Asians remained in Malawi, nearly all of whom possessed British passports. In addition, there were up to 25,000 South Asian British citizens from East Africa in India.[188]

If immigration legislation was effectively powerless in episodes of political upheaval akin to Uganda in 1972, it was essential that diplomatic arrangements with third countries remained robust. This was hardly going to be easy. In the first week of 1973, the Canadian prime minister Pierre Trudeau wrote to Heath that 'in the event of a further expulsion' in East Africa, he would not be able to 'accept any of their number as immigrants into Canada. Public opinion in Canada had proved definitely hostile to the refugees from Uganda'.[189] But British officials were determined that there could be 'no more Ugandas', as one official summarised the opinion of home secretary Robert Carr later that month.[190]

A Final Mission to India

At the heart of everything was India. If India decided to repatriate its South Asian British citizens, or refused to take in more in the event of a new crisis, Britain would have no choice but to accept them. Heath's government decided in January 1973 to send the brigadier-turned-banker Toby Low, known as Lord Aldington, who was prized as a political fixer, on yet another diplomatic mission to persuade Indira Gandhi to retain and accept as many East African South Asians with British nationality as possible.

Low was chairman of the Port of London Authority, and had already played a role in the national dockers' strike the year before. Low's mission to India was kept secret from the Select Committee on Race Relations and Immigration, whose members were by chance visiting India at the time, including Gujarat, in order 'to learn what they could about [Ugandan] expellees'.[191] Low's trip to meet Indira Gandhi in New Delhi was disrupted by Gandhi's busyness; she was in middle of an official visit from the Polish prime minister, and had developed a 'filthy cold'.[192] Upon meeting her finally for forty-five minutes on 13 January, he referred to Britain's non-white population in terms of 'communalism' – a gesture towards Britain's imperial past in India that he bizarrely thought Gandhi might appreciate.

Low had been instructed to be blunt, and to tell Gandhi that the 'only eventual answer to the problem of race would be for people to go where they belonged'.[193] He pleaded Britain's case by telling Gandhi that there were now probably a million South Asians in Britain. The meeting was a failure, and Low himself was left somewhat nonplussed, reporting to the British high commission in New Delhi that 'she is not the most talkative person'.[194]

Low then met with the external affairs minister, Swaran Singh; but the only obliging comment Singh made was to suggest that Heath's government had displayed 'more concern for human aspects' in Uganda than Harold Wilson's Labour government had shown in Kenya in 1968. To close out this latest round in Indian–British diplomacy, Gandhi wrote to Heath on 22 January 1973 in vaguely cooperative terms, but reminded him that Amin's expulsion order had 'imposed great strains on us' at a time when India faced 'enormous difficulties' of its own.[195]

Having failed to convince Indira Gandhi to accept large numbers of South Asians with British nationality in the event of a future expulsion from anywhere in the world, and East Africa in particular, the Cabinet Office drew up a four-stage operational contingency plan in the event of future expulsions. This represented the fruit of the country's experience since 1968.

It used a broad repertoire of state action – from emergency evacuation plans to rescue white British 'belongers' to ideas to prevent airlines and ocean liners from bringing non-white people with British nationality to Britain. Following the Ugandan example, any future crisis would be presented as an international refugee situation. There would be an 'international appeal' to third countries to accept non-white people with British nationality – particularly India, Pakistan, the United States, Canada, Australia and New Zealand. Furthermore, the UN High Commissioner for Refugees, the UN General Assembly, and the UN Security Council would be mobilised 'to criticise the expelling country'.[196]

By April 1974, Britain had admitted over 100,000 East African South Asian British citizens and British Protected Persons during the preceding nine years.[197] Despite the extraordinary lengths British governments had gone to in order to keep their own citizens out of the country since 1968, a combination of factors, including a recognition of an underlying right of entry and the right to bring dependants, meant that the East African South Asians came to constitute one of the largest cohorts of post-war migrants to Britain.

Britain may have joined Europe in 1973 – long understood to be a final capitulation to the end of empire – but the FCO remained unreconstructed in its imperial vision of racial belonging and non-belonging. The problem of non-white British citizens was to persist throughout the 1970s, until British citizenship was finally overhauled in 1981.

In 1973, the FCO recorded the presence of some 400,000 'tea estate coolies' in Sri Lanka who held a form of British nationality ('although very few in fact hold United Kingdom passports or have shown any interest in obtaining one'). There were 120,000 people in British Honduras (soon to be renamed Belize) with British nationality (political disruptions in this region 'would necessarily produce a significant refugee problem'). In addition, there were some 470,000 people in the Caribbean with British nationality. In Southeast Asia, it was possible that episodes akin to what had unfolded in Uganda might occur in Malaysia or Hong Kong, with their large populations of people with British nationality.[198] None of these people was white. If this ongoing circumstance was an unintended consequence of decolonisation, it was also a result of British design, since the imperial commitment to the Commonwealth had knowingly sustained the British nationality of millions of non-white people around the world.

Epilogue

Mandatory training is being introduced for new and existing members of staff to ensure everyone working in the Home Office understands and appreciates the history of migration and race across this country.

Home Secretary Priti Patel on the Windrush
Lessons Learned Review, July 2020

Immigration and the end of empire were deeply connected. British nationality remained imperial at the same time as Britain's imperial power was taken away. British officials experienced the twin processes of immigration and the end of empire in ways that were preoccupied with race and maintaining Britain's imperial purchase on the world. The refrain of the so-called immigrant in this period, *we're here because you were there*, spoke to a political, historical and legal reality, no matter how disavowed and denied.

Post-war politics was transnational. Britain could not come to know its domestic identity without reference to its international status. The problem was that for many British officials, politicians and various other elites, the only way they knew to conceive of the international was in imperial terms. The post-2016 debates around Britain's decision to leave the European Union, for instance, betrayed a faith that Britain might effortlessly restore its Commonwealth links, making good on trade and any number of other partnerships within a Commonwealth realm. Euphemisms for colonialism inevitably followed. Britain enjoyed a shared history with many states around the world; the possibilities were endless.

Many of these arguments were out of date in 1960. They speak to a historical failure to reckon with an imperial past – a failure that has diffused itself evenly throughout the post-war decades. British sovereign power, so reduced in the first twenty-five years after 1945, came to be focused on the body of the immigrant. The immigrant could be moved across or stopped at borders according to a racial theory of belonging derived from the experience of empire. The fact that these immigrants were bearers of British nationality was a source of pained historical self-reckoning for British officials in the 1960s and early 1970s.

For non-white British and Commonwealth citizens, the implications of British immigration laws in this period were nonetheless immediate, far-reaching and, for some, catastrophic. The varieties of and important distinctions between experiences are too many to count. Some, like the Chagossians, who were forcibly removed from their homes, had few resources to protect themselves from the British state. South Asians in Kenya, meanwhile, found that a British government was prepared to pass an immigration law specifically to block their migration.

The recreation of historical narratives often relies on state archives. The power of the state to omit from the archive and euphemise or destroy the past means that there are always things that are kept from view. The historian Richard Drayton has tried to obtain files related to decolonisation and Cold War proxy operations in British Guiana. 'When Kenyan historians requested documents in the past', Drayton wrote in *The Times* in 2012, 'they were told repeatedly by the FCO that they had been destroyed, only for the FCO, under judicial pressure, to yield them. It is to be hoped that the FCO will at some point "discover" its British Guiana archive.'[1] The potential for historical redress extends, of course, to the history of race and migration in Britain, and might include a reckoning of the full history of discrimination against non-white British and Commonwealth citizens in the context of immigration.

The hostile environment created by the 1971 Immigration Act has become a rationale for the British state that is every bit as immovable as the refusal to examine its imperial past, still less its post-1945 imperial ambitions. The close relationship between immigration, British identity and the imperial past will not be broken until this reckoning takes place. The experiences of those affected by the 2018 Windrush scandal capture with terrible consequence the distorted relationship the British state has long had, and continues to have, to its past. The idea that the Windrush generation was welcomed by governments, and that British traditions of rights and rule of law were gifted to colonial populations who then migrated to Britain as so many pupils gone to meet their teacher, are national superstitions exposed by the hostile environments of past and present. In the struggle between imperial idealism and a reactionary nativism, so perceptible in British governments in the 1960s, it is a British nativism that has recently made its hostility the more loudly known.

None of what is described in this book is very far in the past; as the saying goes, it is not even past. Much ink has been spilt on British national identity, yet a simple reality is often kept just out of reach: others have been made to carry its burden. As British national identity could no longer draw on a direct imperial presence in the world, it became more pressed to find a new form of expression. Immigration and sovereignty, or decline and crisis, are themes of a national identity that is better able to look outwards than within.

Dreams of an imperial Commonwealth, and simultaneously the maintenance of a hostile environment for migrants, appear to live on without apparent contradiction. Sarah O'Connor, who migrated to Britain from Jamaica when she was six, was told she was an immigrant in 2018, after living in Britain for fifty-one years. Her experience reminded her of the racism she had faced in the 1970s: 'It feels like it has become a hostile country again.'[2] In this history, and this present, there are the less and the more deceived.

Acknowledgements

Having the opportunity to read and write at length is a great blessing. I'm grateful to be able to convey my thanks here.

Thank you to Leo Hollis, my editor at Verso, for many considerable improvements and helpful suggestions throughout this process. My gratitude also goes to the wider team at Verso.

Thank you to my colleagues in the Department of Sociology at the London School of Economics. In particular I would like to thank Chetan Bhatt, Nigel Dodd and Louisa Lawrence for their support over several years. I would also like to thank the LSE Library staff, in particular Ellen Wilkinson and Heather Dawson. My sincere thanks also go to the staff and archivists at the British National Archives.

Several people have offered thoughts and commentary on parts of this book. The initial idea and encouragement to write the book came in conversation with my former colleague, Vineet Thakur, who has over many discussions helped bring to life some of the core ideas I explore. I would also like to thank my colleague at LSE, Bronwen Manby, for reading an early version of this book and offering countless insights over several years. For their comments and thoughts, my thanks also go to Poppy Cullen, Antara Datta, Alison Harvey, Eva-Maria Muschik, Kalathmika Natarajan, Ben Richardson and Catherine Schenk. For sharing his experiences so generously, my thanks also go to Jatinder Verma.

Needless to say, any errors contained within the book are my own.

This book has been driven forward by the memory of my paternal grandparents, Shantaben Patel and Dahyabhai Patel, whose lives were deeply affected by the events contained within it. Their home, which in the later years of their life was in London, I remember as a perennial place of peace.

To my dear friend Mayer Abraham, I cannot say thank you enough. What little I know I learned from you. I also give my warmest thanks to Lina Abraham, Joseph Abraham and Benjamin Abraham.

I would also like to thank David Drews for his support, encouragement and unique insightfulness. I am extremely grateful to you, David.

Finally, a huge thank you to Dani for her invaluable comments on this book and for sharing the process with me. It means the world to me, Dani, thank you.

Notes

Introduction

1 A 1970 census records 'Black and Asian' communities at 1.2 million. See Ian Spencer, *British Immigration Policy Since 1939: The Making of Multi-Racial Britain* (London: Routledge, 1997), p. 146; Randall Hansen, *Citizenship and Immigration in Post-War Britain: The Institutional Origins of a Multicultural Nation* (Oxford: Oxford University Press, 2000), p. 3; Peter Stevens and Gill Crozier, 'England', in Peter A. J. Stevens and A. Gary Dworkin, eds, *The Palgrave Handbook of Race and Ethnic Inequalities in Education* (Basingstoke: Palgrave Macmillan, 2014), p. 262.

2 1948 British Nationality Act §1(2).

3 A. V. Dicey, *The Law of the Constitution*, ed. J. W. F. Allison, vol.1 (Oxford: Oxford University Press, 2013), p. 434, n. 43.

4 1962 Commonwealth Immigrants Act §1(2a).

5 'The Cost of Whiteness', *Economist*, 2 March 1968.

6 See A. V. Dicey, 'A Common Citizenship for the English Race', *Contemporary Review*, vol. 71 (1897), pp. 457–76.

7 1981 British Nationality Act §1(1).

8 Salman Rushdie, in Michael Reder, ed., *Conversations with Salman Rushdie* (Jackson: University Press of Mississippi, 2000), p. 78.

9 See Gerard-René de Groot and Oliver W. Vonk, *International Standards on Nationality Law: Texts, Cases, Materials* (Oisterwijk: Wolf Legal, 2016), pp. 7–12. See also Reiko Karatani, *Defining British Citizenship: Empire, Commonwealth and Modern Britain* (London: Frank Cass, 2003), p. 17.

10 HC Deb. 7 July 1948, vol. 453, col. 455; Reiko Karatani, *Defining British Citizenship*, p. 124.

11 Nirad C. Chaudhuri, *The Autobiography of an Unknown Indian* (London: Macmillan, 1951).

12 Cited in Bronwen Manby, *Citizenship in Africa: The Law of Belonging* (Oxford:

Hart, 2018), p. 11–12. See also Paul Weis, *Nationality and Statelessness in International Law* (Alphen aan den Rijn: Sijthoff & Noordhoff, 1979), pp. 65–70.

13 See Hannah Arendt, *The Origins of Totalitarianism* (Cleveland/New York: Meridian, 1962), pp. 296, 278; Stephanie DeGooyer, Alastair Hunt, Lida Maxwell and Samuel Moyn, *The Right to Have Rights* (London: Verso, 2020), p. 1.

14 John Stuart Mill, 'A Few Words on Non-Intervention', in *Dissertations and Discussions*, vol.3 (London: J. W. Parker, 1875), pp. 167–71.

15 See Alison Kesby, *The Right to Have Rights: Citizenship, Humanity, and International Law* (Oxford: Oxford University Press, 2012), p. 44.

16 Cited in ibid., p. 41.

17 Henry Hopkinson, Minister of State at the Colonial Office, HC Deb. 5 November 1954, vol. 532, col. 827.

18 'United Kingdom Passport Decision', *The Times*, 12 August 1967. See Richard Plender, *International Migration Law* (Dordrecht: Martinus Nijhoff, 1988), p. 150.

19 Nelson Mandela, *Long Walk to Freedom* (London: Little Brown, 1994), p. 346.

20 See 'Cabinet: Conclusions of a Meeting of the Cabinet', 15 February 1968, CAB/128/43.

21 Cited in Sandra Fredman, *Discrimination Law* (Oxford: Oxford University Press, 2011), p. 229.

22 John Darwin, *Britain and Decolonisation: The Retreat from Empire in the Post-War World* (Basingstoke: Macmillan, 1988), p. viii.

23 Stuart Hall, *Familiar Stranger: A Life Between Two Islands* (London: Penguin, 2018), p. xiv.

24 Ibid., pp. 198–9.

25 Zadie Smith interview on *Writers & Company*, CBC Radio (2017), available at https://www.youtube.com/watch?v=L1OSTD6wA4A&t=2304s.

26 Kimberly McIntosh, Jason Todd and Nandini Das, *Teaching Migration, Belonging, and Empire in Secondary Schools*, TIDE and the Runnymede Trust (2019), pdf available at runnymedetrust.org.

27 Interview with Rozina Visram by Arts Asia Heritage (2016), available at youtube.com/watch?v=MHpYiIvPFDk.

1. Immigration and the White Man's World

1 Rozina Visram, *Asians in Britain: 400 Years of History* (London: Pluto, 2002), pp. 1–2.

2 See Peter Fryer, *Staying Power: The History of Black People in Britain* (London: Pluto, 2018), p. 9. See also Imtiaz Habib, *Black Lives in the English Archives, 1500–1677: Imprints of the Invisible* (Hampshire: Ashgate, 2008).

3 See Daniel Gorman, *Imperial Citizenship: Empire and the Question of Belonging* (Manchester: Manchester University Press, 2006), p. 159; Todd M. Endelman, *The Jews of Britain, 1656 to 2000* (Berkeley: University of California Press, 2002), pp. 127–9.

4 Patrick Manning, *Migration in World History* (New York: Routledge, 2002), p. 149.

5 Gary Magee and Andrew Thompson, *Empire and Globalisation: Networks of People, Goods and Capital in the British World, c. 1850–1914* Cambridge: Cambridge University Press, 2010), p. 231. See also Adam M. McKeown, *Melancholy Order: Asian Migration and the Globalization of Borders* (New York: Columbia University Press, 2008).

6 David Northrup, *Indentured Labour in the Age of Imperialism, 1834–1922* (Cambridge: Cambridge University Press, 1995), pp. 3, 53. For women migrants in the indenture system, see the same work, pp. 74–8, and Gaiutra Bahadur, *Coolie Women: The Odyssey of Indenture* (London: Hurst, 2013).

7 Adam McKeown, 'Global Migration 1846–1940', *Journal of World History*, 19: 2 (2004), p. 158.

8 Marjory Harper and Stephen Constantine, 'Introduction: The British Empire and Empire Migration, 1815 to the 1960s', in Marjory Harper and Stephen Constantine, eds, *Migration and Empire* (Oxford: Oxford University Press, 2010), pp. 3, 5.

9 See also Ashutosh Kumar, *Coolies of the Empire: Indentured Indians in the Sugar Colonies, 1830–1920* (Cambridge: Cambridge University Press, 2017), p. 133.

10 David Northrup, *Indentured Labour in the Age of Imperialism*, pp. 4, 44.

11 Hugh Tinker, *A New System of Slavery: The Export of Indian Labourers Overseas* (London: Oxford University Press, 1974), pp. 236–87.

12 Of this 20 million, 13.5 million migrated to the United States, around 4 million to Canada, 2 million to Australia and New Zealand, and around 750,000 to southern Africa. W. David McIntyre, *The Commonwealth of Nations: Origins and Impact 1869–1971* (Minneapolis: University of Minnesota Press, 1977), p. 40.

13 W. David McIntyre, *The Commonwealth of Nations*, p. 40.

14 Stephen Constantine, 'British Emigration to the Empire-Commonwealth since 1880: From Overseas Settlement to Diaspora?', *Journal of Imperial and Commonwealth History*, 31: 2 (2003), pp. 19–20.

15 Marjory Harper and Stephen Constantine, 'Introduction: The British Empire and Empire Migration, 1815 to the 1960s', pp. 3, 5.

16 Cited in Bill Schwarz, *The White Man's World – Memories of Empire vol. 1* (Oxford: Oxford University Press, 2011), p. 79.

17 See James Brown Scott, 'The British Commonwealth of Nations', *American Journal of International Law*, 21: 1 (1925), p. 97.

18 Edward Gibbon Wakefield, 'A Letter from Sydney', cited in Angela Woollacott, *Settler Society in the Australian Colonies: Self-Government and Imperial Culture* (Oxford: Oxford University Press, 2015), p. 41.

19 Myra Willard, *History of the White Australia Policy until 1920* (London: Frank Cass, 1967), pp. 21–3. See also Marilyn Lake and Henry Reynolds, *Drawing the Global Colour Line: White Men's Countries and the International Challenge of Racial Equality* (Cambridge: Cambridge University Press, 2008), p. 20.

20 R. A. Huttenback, 'The British Empire as a "White Man's Country": Racial Attitudes and Immigration Legislation in the Colonies of White Settlement', *Journal of British Studies*, 13: 1 (1973), p. 131.

21 See Alison Bashford, 'Immigration Restriction: Rethinking Period and Place from Settler Colonies to Postcolonial Nations', *Journal of Global History*, 9: 1 (2014), pp. 26–48.

22 Henry Parkes, speech at Federation Conference, Parliament House, Melbourne, 6 February 1890, cited in Sally Warharft, ed., *Well May We Say: Speeches that Made Australia* (Melbourne: Black Inc., 2004), pp. 6–7.

23 Cited in Benjamin Mountford, *Britain, China, and Colonial Australia* (Oxford: Oxford University Press, 2016), p. 240.

24 Cited in Huttenback, 'The British Empire as a "White Man's Country": Racial Attitudes and Immigration Legislation in the Colonies of White Settlement', p. 116.

25 Ibid., p. 111.

26 Jonathan Klaaran, *From Prohibited Immigrants to Citizens: The Origins of Citizenship and Nationality in South Africa* (Cape Town: UCT, 2017), p. 17. See also Sally Peberdy, *Selecting Immigrants: National Identity and South Africa's Immigration Policies, 1910–2008* (Johannesburg: Wits University Press, 2009).

27 See Sankaran Krishna, 'A Postcolonial Racial/Spatial Order: Gandhi, Ambedkar and the Construction of the International', in Alexander Anievas, Nivi Manchanda and Robbie Shilliam, eds, *Race and Racism in International Relations* (London/New York: Routledge, 2015). See also Kalathmika Natarajan, 'Entangled Citizens, Undesirable Migrants: The Imprint of Empire and Afterlives of Indenture in Indian Diplomacy (1947–1962)', PhD thesis, University of Copenhagen, 2019, pp. 18–20.

28 Cited in Jeremy Martens, 'A Transnational History of Immigration Restriction: Natal and New South Wales, 1896–97', *Journal of Imperial and Commonwealth History*, 34: 3 (2006), p. 332. See also Marilyn Lake and Henry Reynolds, *Drawing the Global Colour Line*, pp. 125–33.

29 Cited in Daniel Gorman, 'Wider and Wider Still? Racial Politics, Intra-Imperial Immigration and the Absence of an Imperial Citizenship in the British Empire', *Journal of Colonialism and Colonial History*, 3: 3 (2002). See also Arthur B. Keith, *Responsible Government in the Dominions*, vol. 3 (Oxford: Clarendon Press, 1912).

30 See Benjamin Mountford, *Britain, China, and Colonial Australia*, pp. 245–6.

31 27 February 1897, CO 179/197 and draft of telegram dispatched to the Governor of Natal, 13 January 1897, CO 179/187. Both cited in Lake and Reynolds, *Drawing the Global Colour Line*, p. 128.

32 See Roger Daniels, 'The Growth of Restrictive Immigration Policies in the Colonies of Settlement', in Robert Cohen, ed., *The Cambridge Survey of World Migration* (Cambridge: Cambridge University Press, 1995), p. 40.

33 R. A. Huttenback, 'The British Empire as a "White Man's Country": Racial Attitudes and Immigration Legislation in the Colonies of White Settlement', *Journal of British Studies*, 13: 1 (1973), pp. 117–18.

34 Cited in Mountford, *Britain, China, and Colonial Australia*, p. 242.

35 See Radhika Mongia, *Indian Migration and Empire: A Colonial Genealogy of the Modern State* (Durham, NC: Duke University Press, 2018), p. 133.

36 Cited in Peter Cochrane, *Best We Forget: The War for White Australia* (Melbourne: Text, 2018), p. 183.

37 A. V. Dicey, 'A Common Citizenship for the English Race', *Contemporary Review*, 71 (1897), pp. 467, 476. See also Paul Rich, *Race and Empire in British Politics* (Cambridge: Cambridge University Press, 1990), p. 13.

38 Frederick Lugard, *The Rise of Our East African Empire*, vol. 1 (London: William Blackwood, 1893), p. viii.

39 Ibid., pp. 488–90.

40 Cited in Sana Aiyar, *Indians in Kenya: The Politics of Diaspora* (Harvard: Harvard University Press, 2015), pp. 33–4.

41 Ibid., p. 29; Anaïs Angelo, *Power and the Presidency in Kenya: The Jomo Kenyatta Years* (Cambridge: Cambridge University Press, 2020), pp. 3–4.

42 Winston Churchill, *My African Journey* (Toronto: William Briggs, 1909), pp. 20–1.

43 HC Deb. 2 May 1905, vol. 145, col. 756.

44 Cited in Alison Bashford and Catie Gilchrist, 'The Colonial History of the 1905 Aliens Act', *Journal of Imperial and Commonwealth History*, 40: 3 (2012), p. 410.

45 Ibid., pp. 410–12, 434 n. 96.

46 HC Deb. 2 May 1905, vol. 145, col. 787.

47 1905 Aliens Act, §1(3d).

48 See Louise London, *Whitehall and the Jews, 1933–1948: British Immigration Policy, Jewish Refugees and the Holocaust* (Cambridge: Cambridge University Press, 2000), pp. 16–18.

49 Lothrop Stoddard, *The Rising Tide of Color Against White World-Supremacy* (New York: Charles Scribner's Sons, 1921), pp. 268, 251.

50 Cited in Rieko Karatani *Defining British Citizenship: Empire, Commonwealth and Modern Britain* (London: Frank Cass, 2003), pp. 79–80.

51 'Should Resist Entry of Chinese', *The Province* (Vancouver), 1 October 1913.

52 See Vineet Thakur and Peter Vale, *South Africa, Race and the Making of International Relations* (London: Rowman & Littlefield, 2020), p. 7.

53 HC Deb. 2 May 1905, vol. 145, col. 731.

54 A. G. Hopkins, 'Rethinking Decolonisation', *Past and Present*, 200 (2008), p. 212.

55 1914 British Nationality and Status of Aliens Act §1(a).

56 HC Deb. 13 May 1914, vol. 62, col. 1199.

57 E. F. W. Gey van Pittius, *Nationality within the British Commonwealth of Nations* (London: P. S. King & Son, 1930), p. 163.

58 See Hugh Johnston, *The Voyage of the* Komagata Maru*: The Sikh Challenge to Canada's Colour Bar* (Vancouver: University of British Columbia Press, 1989).

59 See Vineet Thakur, Chapter 3, *India's First Diplomat: V. S. Srinivasa Sastri and the Making of Liberal Internationalism* (Bristol: Bristol University Press, 2021).

60 Alfred Zimmern, *The Third British Empire* (Oxford: Oxford University Press, 1926), pp. 66–70.

61 Lionel Curtis, *The Commonwealth of Nations: An Inquiry into the Nature of Citizenship in the British Empire, and into the Mutual Relations of the Several Communities Thereof*, part I (London: Macmillan, 1916), p. 625–6.

62 For Curtis's ideas of federal unity and a hierarchy of political development, see Vineet Thakur and Peter Vale, *South Africa, Race and the Making of International Relations*, pp. 31, 65, 66, 74, 155. See also, John Darwin, 'Was There a Fourth British Empire?', in Martin Lynn, ed., *The British Empire in the 1950s: Retreat or Revival?* (Basingstoke: Palgrave, 2006), pp. 19–20; Marilyn Lake and Henry Reynolds, *Drawing the Global Colour Line*, p. 348.

63 See W. David McIntyre, *British Decolonization, 1946–1997: When, Why and How did the British Empire Fall?* (Houndsmills: Macmillan, 1998), p. 16.

64 See Jeanne Morefield, *Empires Without Imperialism: Anglo-American Decline and the Politics of Deflection* (Oxford: Oxford University Press, 2014), p. 132.

65 Alfred Milner, 'Credo', *The Times*, 27 July 1925.

66 See W. David McIntyre, *The Commonwealth of Nations: Origins and Impact 1869–1971* (Minneapolis: University of Minnesota Press, 1977), p. 321.

67 Cited in Patrick Thornberry, *The International Convention on the Elimination of All Forms of Racial Discrimination: A Commentary* (Oxford: Oxford University Press, 2016), p. 15.

68 Naoko Shimazu, *Japan, Race and Equality: The Racial Equality Proposal of 1919* (London: Routledge, 1988), pp. 18–19, 83–4, 167–9. See also A. W. Brian Simpson, *Human Rights and the End of Empire: Britain and the Genesis of the European Convention* (Oxford: Oxford University Press, 2004), p. 124.

69 'Racial Discrimination and Immigration', 10 October 1921, FO 371/6684. Cited in Paul Gordon Lauren, 'First Principles of Racial Equality: History and the Politics and Diplomacy of Human Rights Provisions in the United Nations Charter', *Human Rights Quarterly*, 5: 1 (1983), p. 2.

70 See Patil to Secretary in the Ministry of External Affairs, Government of India, Government of India, 31 May 1956, DO 133/147, p. 137; Deborah L Hughes, 'Kenya, India and the British Empire Exhibition of 1924', *Race and Class*, 47: 5 (2006), pp. 73–4.

71 See Laura Tabili (1994), 'The Construction of Racial Difference in Twentieth-Century Britain: The Special Restriction (Coloured Alien Seamen) Order, 1925', *Journal of British Studies*, 33: 1 (2006); Kenneth Little, *Negros in Britain: A Study of Racial Relations in English Society* (London: Routledge, 1972), pp. 85–9; Kathleen Paul, *Whitewashing Britain: Race and Citizenship in the Postwar Era* (Ithaca: Cornell University Press, 1997), p. 113.

72 Cited in Patil to Secretary in the Ministry of External Affairs, Government of India, 31 May 1956, DO 133/147, p. 132.

73 See Hugh Tinker, *Race, Conflict and the International Order: From Empire to the United Nations* (London: Macmillan, 1977), p. 20.

74 See opening section to the 1931 Statute of Westminster.

75 See John Darwin, 'The Dominion Idea in Imperial Politics', in Judith M.

Brown and William Roger Lewis eds., *The Oxford History of the British Empire, Vol: IV: The Twentieth Century* (Oxford: Oxford University Press, 1999).

76 C. Rajagopalachar and J. C. Kumarappa, eds, *The Nation's Voice: Being a Collection of Gandhiji's Speeches in England and Sjt. Mahadev Desai's Account of the Sojourn (September to December, 1931)* (Ahmedabad: Navajivan, 1947), p. 130.

77 See Anita Inder Singh, 'Keeping India in the Commonwealth: British Political and Military Aims, 1947–49', *Journal of Contemporary History*, 20: 3 (1985).

78 Cited in ibid., p. 472. See also A. G. Hopkins, 'Rethinking Decolonisation', p. 226.

79 See Marie Lall, *India's Missed Opportunity: India's Relationship with the Non Resident Indians* (Aldershot: Ashgate, 2001), p. 53; interview with K Shankar Bajpai by Philip Murphy, Institute of Commonwealth Studies (2013), available at: https://commonwealthoralhistories.org.

80 Cited in Sunil Purushotham, 'Jawaharlal Nehru, Indian Republicanism, and the Commonwealth', in Saul Dubow and Richard Drayton, eds, *Commonwealth History in the Twenty-First Century* (Basingstoke: Palgrave Macmillan, 2020), pp. 155–6.

81 Cabinet Official Committee on Commonwealth Relations, 'India's Future Relations with the Commonwealth', 22 February 1949, cited in Singh, 'Keeping India in the Commonwealth: British Political and Military Aims, 1947–49', p. 475.

82 Ibid.

83 See Sunil Purushotham, 'Jawaharlal Nehru, Indian Republicanism, and the Commonwealth', p. 154.

84 Krishnan Srinivasan, 'Nobody's Commonwealth? The Commonwealth in Britain's Post-Imperial Adjustment', *Commonwealth & Comparative Politics*, 44: 2 (2006), p. 260.

85 See W. David McIntyre, 'Commonwealth Legacy', in Judith M. Brown and Wm Roger Lewis eds., *The Oxford History of the British Empire, Vol: IV: The Twentieth Century* (Oxford: Oxford University Press, 1999).

86 See Rieko Karatani, *Defining British Citizenship*, p. 114.

87 Elspeth Huxley, 'British Aims in Africa', *Foreign Affairs*, 28: 1 (1949), p. 49.

88 Cited in Schwarz, *White Man's World*, p. 115.

89 Eileen Fletcher, 'Kenya's Iron Curtain', *Africa Today*, 3: 6 (1956), p. 5. See also HC Deb. 31 October 1956, vol. 558, cols. 1418–21.

90 Andrew Thomson and Meaghan Kowalsky, 'Social Life and Cultural Representation: Empire in the Public Imagination' in Andrew Thomson ed., *Britain's Experience of Empire in the Twentieth Century* (Oxford: Oxford University Press, 2012), pp. 283–4.

91 '"A Vile, Brutal Wickedness": The Murder of the Ruck Family by Mau Mau Terrorists in Kenya, A Shocking Crime Redeemed Only by the Heroism of an African Houseboy', *Illustrated London News*, 7 February 1953. See also Wendy Webster, *Englishness and Empire 1939–1965* (Oxford: Oxford University Press, 2007), pp. 124, 129; Elizabeth Buettner, *Europe after Empire: Decolonization, Society, and Culture* (Cambridge: Cambridge University Press, 2016), p. 52.

92 See Bruce Berman, *Control and Crisis in Colonial Kenya: The Dialectic of Domination* (Athens, OH: Ohio University Press, 1996), p. 130; Donald Rothchild, 'Kenya's Minorities and the African Crisis over Citizenship', *Race & Class*, 9: 4 (1968).

93 Patil to Secretary in the Ministry of External Affairs, Government of India, 31 May 1956, DO 133/147, p. 138.

94 Elspeth Huxley, 'British Aims in Africa', p. 49.

95 Kathleen Paul, *Whitewashing Britain: Race and Citizenship in the Postwar Era* (Ithaca, NY: Cornell University Press, 1997), pp. 30–4.

96 Cited in Matthew Jordan, '"Not on Your Life": Cabinet and the Liberalisation of the White Australia Policy, 1964–67', *Journal of Imperial and Commonwealth History*, 46: 1 (2018), p. 177.

97 Cited in ibid.

98 Cited in ibid., p. 178.

99 HL Deb. 24 April 1967, vol. 282 col. 398.

100 See Stephen Constantine, 'Waving Goodbye? Australia, Assisted Passages, and the Empire and Commonwealth Settlement Acts, 1945–72', *Journal of Imperial and Commonwealth History*, 26: 2 (1998), p. 193.

101 'The Commonwealth as a British Interest', O'Leary to Walker, 30 November 1966, DO 193/79, cited in S. R. Ashton and Wm Roger Louis, eds, *British Documents on the End of Empire: East of Suez and the Commonwealth 1964–1971* (London: Stationery Office, 2004), part II, p. 354.

102 'The Value of the Commonwealth to Britain', 24 April 1967, CAB 129/129, cited in Ashton and Louis, *British Documents on the End of Empire*, part II, p. 421.

103 Barnes, 15 June 1968, FCO 37/99, p. 15.

104 'Synopsis of Tour', Central Office of Information, 24 June 1968, FCO 37/99, pp. 36–47.

105 See Dhananjayan Sriskandarajah and Catherine Drew, *Brits Abroad: Mapping the Scale and Nature of British Emigration* (London: IPPR, 2006) – pdf available at ippr.org. See also Migration Watch UK, 'Net Migration Statistics', at migrationwatchuk.org.

2. Beyond Windrush

1 Walter Bagehot, *The English Constitution* (London: Chapman & Hall, 1867), p. 5.

2 Amanda Bidnall, *The West Indian Generation: Remaking British Culture in London, 1945–1965* (Liverpool: Liverpool University Press, 2017), p. 123.

3 See Tom Fleming, *Voices Out of the Air: The Royal Christmas Broadcasts 1932–1981* (London: Heinemann, 1981), p. 72.

4 Cited in Krishnan Srinivasan, 'Nobody's Commonwealth? The Commonwealth in Britain's Post-Imperial Adjustment', *Commonwealth & Comparative Politics*, 44: 2 (2006), p. 261.

5 Labour Party, *European Unity: A Statement by the National Executive Committee of the British Labour Party*, cited in Elizabeth Buettner, *Europe after Empire:*

Decolonization, Society, and Culture (Cambridge: Cambridge University Press, 2016), p. 73.

6 Iain Dale, ed., *Conservative Party General Election Manifestos, 1900–1997* (Abingdon: Routledge, 2000), p. 109.

7 'British Empire Gets New Nationality Act', *New York Times*, 1 January 1949.

8 Richard Plender, *International Migration Law* (Dordrecht: Martinus Nijhoff, 1988), p. 24.

9 See Laurie Fransman, Adrian Berry and Alison Harvey, Chapter 3, *Fransman's British Nationality Law* (London: Bloomsbury Professional, 2011). See also Reiko Karatani, *Defining British Citizenship: Empire, Commonwealth and Modern Britain* (London: Frank Cass, 2003); Randall Hansen, 'The Politics of Citizenship in 1940s Britain: The British Nationality Act', *Twentieth Century British History*, 10: 1 (1999).

10 Randall Hansen, *Citizenship and Immigration in Post-War Britain: The Institutional Origins of a Multicultural Nation* (Oxford: Oxford University Press, 2000), p. 5.

11 For the figure of forty-seven colonies for the purposes of 'and Colonies' in the 1948 Act, see government document, 'UK and Colonies' – pdf available at assets.publishing.service.gov.uk.

12 HL Deb. 7 July 1948, vol. 453, cols. 393–4.

13 Ibid., col. 392.

14 HL Deb. 11 May 1948, vol. 155, cols. 762, 786.

15 HL Deb. 11 May 1948, vol. 155, cols. 786–7, 793.

16 Cited in Karatani, *Defining British Citizenship*, p. 76.

17 'South African Question at Commonwealth Prime Ministers' Meeting: Briefings by Sir N. Brook for Mr Macmillan', 1–11 March 1961, PREM 11/3535. Cited in Ronald Hyam and Wm Roger Louis, eds, *The Conservative Government and the End of Empire, 1957–1964: British Documents on the End of Empire*, part I (London: Stationery Office, 2000), p. 420.

18 Elizabeth Quigley, 'Scotland's Debt to Forgotten Belize Lumberjacks', BBC News website, 2 February 2019, available at bbc.co.uk.

19 See Ian Spencer, *British Immigration Policy since 1939: The Making of Multi-Racial Britain* (London: Routledge, 1997), p. 18.

20 'Arrival in the United Kingdom of Jamaican Unemployed', 18 June 1948, CP (48)154, CAB 129/38.

21 This was the calypso singer, Lord Kitchener (Aldwyn Roberts). Cited in Paul Arnott, *Windrush: A Ship Through Time* (Stroud: History Press, 2019).

22 See Foreign Labour Committee to Cabinet, 14 March 1946, CAB 134/301. See also Kathleen Paul, *Whitewashing Britain: Race and Citizenship in the Postwar Era* (Ithaca: Cornell University Press, 1997), p. 193 n. 18; Randall Hansen, *Citizenship and Immigration in Post-War Britain*, p. 8; James Hampshire, *Citizenship and Belonging: Immigration and the Politics of Demographic Governance in Postwar Britain* (Basingstoke: Palgrave Macmillan, 2005), p. 60. On labour recruitment from the Caribbean, see Ian Spencer, *British Immigration Policy since 1939*, p. 156.

23 These recruitment schemes included the Polish Resettlement Act, the European Volunteer Workers Program (known as Westward Ho!), the Official Italian Recruitment Scheme, the Private Domestic Worker Scheme, the Blue Danube scheme and the North Sea scheme. The figure of 215,000 appears in J. A. Tannahill, *European Volunteer Workers in Britain* (Manchester: Manchester University Press, 1958), pp. 5–6. The figure of 345,000 appears in Paul, *Whitewashing Britain*, p. 64 (see also pp. 64–89). See also Tony Kushner and Katherine Knox, *Refugees in An Age of Genocide: Global, National and Local Perspectives during the Twentieth Century* (London: Frank Cass, 1999), pp. 217–40; Diana Kay and Robert Miles, 'Refugees or Migrant Workers: The Case of the European Volunteer in Britain (1946–1951)', *Journal of Refugee Studies* 1: 3–4 (1988), p. 214. On Jewish refugee entry, see Louise London, *Whitehall and the Jews, 1933–1948: British Immigration Policy, Jewish Refugees and the Holocaust* (Cambridge: Cambridge University Press, 2000), pp. 12, 252.

24 HC Deb. 14 February 1947, vol. 433, cols. 757–8.

25 HC Deb. 11 November 1948, vol. 457, col. 1721.

26 See Zig Layton-Henry, *The Politics of Immigration: Immigration, 'Race' and 'Race' Relations in Post-War Britain* (Oxford: Blackwell, 1992), p. 14; Ian Spencer, *British Immigration Policy*, pp. 40, 156–7.

27 See Elizabeth Buettner, *Europe After Empire*, p. 257. See also A. J. Stockwell, 'Leaders, Dissidents and the Disappointed: Colonial Students in Britain as Empire Ended', *Journal of Imperial and Commonwealth History*, 36: 3 (2008), pp. 487–501.

28 Adil Jussawalla, 'Indifference' and Sillaty K. Dabo, 'Some Contexts of Blackness', both in Henri Tajfel and John L. Dawson, eds, *Disappointed Guests: Essays by African, Asian, and West Indian Students* (London: Oxford University Press, 1965), pp. 69, 129.

29 Chikwenda Dwariaku, 'The Paternal Posture', and Patricia Madoo, 'The Transition from "Light Skinned" to "Coloured"', both in Tajfel and Dawson, *Disappointed Guests*, pp. 55–6, 78.

30 Dom Moraes, *My Son's Father: An Autobiography* (London: Secker & Warburg, 1968), p. 115.

31 Ibid., pp. 119, 129–30.

32 See 'I Was Deported Because … ' (interview with George Bowrin in *Caribbean News*, June 1956); 'Ship's Log – December 19, 1955', in Carole Boyce Davies, ed., *Claudia Jones: Beyond Containment* (Banbury: Ayebia Clark, 2010), pp. 16–17, 193. See also Carole Boyce Davies, *Left of Karl Marx: The Political Life of Black Communist Claudia Jones* (Durham/London: Duke University Press, 2007), p. 92.

33 Syed Ali Baquer, 'The File of Regrets', in Tajfel and Dawson, *Disappointed Guests*, p. 108.

34 Cited anonymously in Tajfel and Dawson, *Disappointed Guests*, p. 143.

35 The origin of this anecdote is a later-published diary by a Conservative MP. See Ian Gilmour, *Inside Right: A Study of Conservatism* (London: Hutchinson, 1977), p. 134; Ian Gilmour and Mark Garnett, *Whatever Happened to the*

Tories: The Conservative Party Since 1945 (London: Fourth Estate, 1997), p. 78.

36 See Ian Spencer, British Immigration Policy since 1939, p. 176 n. 60.

37 HC Deb. 5 November 1954, vol. 532, cols. 821, 825, 827.

38 'Colonial Immigrants', Cabinet memorandum, 2 September 1955, CAB 129/77/13. Cited in Ann Dummett and Andrew Nicol, Subjects, Citizens, Aliens and Others: Nationality and Immigration Law (London: Weidenfeld & Nicolson, 1990), p. 180.

39 Swinton to Salisbury, 7 April 1954, CAB 124/1191. Cited in Spencer, British Immigration Policy since 1939, p. 65.

40 See Kalathmika Natarajan, 'Entangled Citizens, Undesirable Migrants: The Imprint of Empire and Afterlives of Indenture in Indian Diplomacy (1947–1962)', PhD thesis, University of Copenhagen, 2019, pp. 136–73.

41 Ian Spencer, British Immigration Policy since 1939, p. 47.

42 Rashmi Desai, Indian Immigrants in Britain (Oxford: Oxford University Press, 1963), pp. 31–3.

43 Claudia Jones, 'The Caribbean Community in Britain', in Boyce Davies, ed., Claudia Jones, pp. 164, 174.

44 See Drew Middleton, 'Race Riots Erupt in London Again', New York Times, 3 September 1958; '"Lynch him!" Cries as Coloured Man is Chased', Manchester Guardian, 2 September 1958; 'Thirteen Arrests After New Racial Clash: Crowd of 400 in London Struggle', Manchester Guardian, 1 September 1958. See also Tony Moore, Policing Notting Hill: Fifty Years of Turbulence (Hook: Waterside, 2013), pp. 37–52.

45 Cited in E. J. B. Rose et al., Colour and Citizenship: A Report on British Race Relations (London: Oxford University Press, 1969), p. 214. Zig Layton-Henry argues that the riots 'put black immigration on the national political agenda'. See Zig Layton-Henry, Politics of Immigration, p. 73.

46 Cabinet Commonwealth Migrants Committee, 17 May 1961, CAB 134/1469. Cited in Spencer, British Immigration Policy since 1939, p. 121.

47 Adil Jussawalla, 'Indifference', pp. 130, 132.

48 Donald Wood, 'A General Survey', in J. A. G. Griffith, Judith Henderson, Margaret Usbourne and Donald Woods, eds, Coloured Immigrants in Britain (London: Oxford University Press, 1960). See also Panikos Panayi, An Immigration History of Britain: Multicultural Racism since 1800 (Harlow: Pearson, 2010), pp. 41–2.

49 Stephen Barber, 'A Passage to England', Sunday Telegraph, 17 November 1961. See also Kalathmika Natarajan, 'Entangled Citizens, Undesirable Migrants', p. 165.

50 Douglas-Home to all High Commissioners, 21 April 1958, DO 35/7987. Cited in Spencer, British Immigration Policy since 1939, p. 92.

51 'Keeping Britain White', Economist, 17 February 1968.

52 Kath Kazer, 'The Pakistani Community in Britain', May 1971, FCO 37/970, pp. 87–105.

53 Dom Moraes, 'The Lost Tribes of Kenya', in From East and West: A Collection of Essays (Delhi: Vikas, 1971), p. 29.

54 Adil Jussawalla, 'Indifference', p. 132.
55 Susunaga Weeraperuma, 'Colour and Equality', in Tajfel and Dawson, *Disappointed Guests*, p. 121.
56 These ideas are explored fully in Chapters 4, 5 and 6, below.

3. A Hostile Isle

1   Ian Spencer, *British Immigration Policy Since 1939: The Making of Multi-Racial Britain* (London: Routledge, 1997), pp. 118–19.
2   Elspeth Huxley, *Back Street New Worlds: A Look at Immigrants in Britain* (New York: William Morrow, 1964), pp. 171, 180.
3   'British Nationality and Immigration', 3 July 1968, FCO 37/99, p. 19.
4   Ian Spencer, *British Immigration Policy since 1939*, p. 127. In 1967, the former civil servant Nicolas Deakin interviewed successive home secretaries Rab Butler and Henry Brooke, both of whom stressed the importance of the Commonwealth in the delay on the decision to introduce restrictive immigration legislation (ibid., p. 187, n. 131).
5   HC Deb. 16 November 1961, vol. 649, col. 695.
6   'Immigration: Memorandum by the Secretary of State for Commonwealth Relations', 2 September 1955, CAB 129/77 CP (55) 113. Cited in A. N. Porter and A. J. Stockwell, eds, *British Imperial Policy and Decolonization, 1938–64*, vol. 2 (London: Palgrave Macmillan, 1989), p. 383.
7   See Laurie Fransman, Adrian Berry and Alison Harvey, *Fransman's British Nationality Law* (London: Bloomsbury Professional, 2011), pp. 1,029–30.
8   1962 Commonwealth Immigrants Act §1(2a–b).
9   See Kalathmika Natarajan, 'Entangled Citizens, Undesirable Migrants: The Imprint of Empire and Afterlives of Indenture in Indian Diplomacy (1947–1962)', PhD thesis, University of Copenhagen, 2019, p. 153.
10 'Commonwealth Migrants', 6 October 1961, CAB 129/107.
11 The workings of the 1962 Act are best explained in Ann Dummett and Andrew Nicol, *Subjects, Citizens, Aliens and Others: Nationality and Immigration Law* (London: Weidenfeld & Nicolson, 1990), pp. 180–4.
12 Claudia Jones, 'The Caribbean Community in Britain', in Carole Boyce Davies, ed., *Claudia Jones: Beyond Containment* (Banbury: Ayebia Clark, 2010), p. 174.
13 L. Monson, 15 September 1967, FCO 37/19, p. 88; 'Legislation to Control Entry of UK Citizens of Asian Origin into this Country', 21 September 1967, FCO 37/19, p. 72. See also Ann Dummett and Andrew Nicol, *Subjects, Citizens, Aliens and Others*, p. 198; Randall Hansen, *Citizenship and Immigration in Post-war Britain: The Institutional Origins of a Multicultural Nation* (Oxford: Oxford University Press, 2000), p. 168. For discussion of the Southern Rhodesia (British Nationality Act 1948) Order, see HL Deb. 25 November 1965, vol. 270, col. 119.
14 Ian Spencer, *British Immigration Policy since 1939*, pp. 133, 135. See also Randall Hansen, *Citizenship and Immigration in Post-War Britain*, pp. 228–31.

15 Godfrey Elton, *Imperial Commonwealth* (New York: Reynal & Hitchcock, 1946), p. 444.

16 Paul Knaplund, review of *Imperial Commonwealth* by Godfrey Elton, *American Historical Review*, 52: 3 (1947), pp. 507–8.

17 Godfrey Elton, *The Unarmed Invasion: A Survey of Afro-Asian Immigration* (London: Bles, 1965), p. 87.

18 Ibid., pp. 7, 63.

19 Ruth Glass, 'The Dark Million', letter to the editor, *The Times*, 1 February 1965.

20 'Asian Immigration', 29 November 1967, FCO 37/21, p. 11.

21 'Immigration Control', 23 February 1971, FCO 37/324, p. 146.

22 'Ministry of Labour's Proposal to Restrict the Issue of Category A Employment Vouchers', 1 November 1967, FCO 37/20, p. 75.

23 Ibid., p. 77.

24 Ibid.

25 'Racial Conflict: Prospects for a Balanced Society', *The Times*, 12 December 1969. On the pledge given to Kenyan South Asians in 1963, see Randall Hansen, 'The Kenyan Asians, British Politics, and the Commonwealth Immigrants Act of 1968', *Historical Journal*, 42: 3 (1999), pp. 809–34. See also Peter Brooke, *Duncan Sandys and the Informal Politics of Britain's Late Decolonisation* (London: Palgrave, 2018), p. 230.

26 Randall Hansen, *Citizenship and Immigration in Post-War Britain*, pp. 169–75. See also James Hampshire, *Citizenship and Belonging: Immigration and the Politics of Demographic Governance in Postwar Britain* (Basingstoke: Palgrave Macmillan, 2005), p. 35; Ann Dummett and Andrew Nicol, *Subjects, Citizens, Aliens and Others*, p. 183.

27 For a fuller account, see Chapter 8, below.

28 On the so-called 'pledge' given to Kenyan South Asian British citizens, see Peter Brooke, *Duncan Sandys and the Informal Politics of Britain's Late Decolonisation*, pp. 229–30.

29 'Incomers From Kenya', *The Times* editorial, 13 February 1968.

30 David Wood, 'Rapid Rise in Influx From Africa', *The Times*, 16 February 1968.

31 Sana Aiyar, *Indians in Kenya: The Politics of Diaspora* (Harvard: Harvard University Press, 2015), p. 277.

32 Colin Legum, 'Jenkins Warning Alarms Asians', *Observer*, 24 September 1967.

33 Randall Hansen, *Citizenship and Immigration in Post-War Britain*, p. 161, n. 39.

34 HC Deb. 27 February 1968, vol. 759, cols. 1,246–7.

35 See HC Deb. 27 February 1968, vol. 759.

36 HL Deb. 29 February 1968, vol. 289, col. 1017.

37 'Immigration Legislation: Memorandum by the Secretary of State for the Home Department', 12 February 1968, C(68)34, CAB 129/135.

38 Cabinet meeting, 22 February 1968, CC(68), CAB/128/43.

39 1968 Commonwealth Immigrants Act §1.

40 'United Kingdom Passport Holders (UKPH) in East Africa: European Commission on Human Rights', 25 April 1974, FCO 50/503, p. 215.

41 See Chapter 8, below.

42 Cited in David Steele, *No Entry: The Background and Implications of the Commonwealth Immigrants Act, 1968* (London: C. Huret, 1969), p. 247.

43 'Panic and Prejudice', *Times* editorial, 27 February 1968. See also 'The Cost of Whiteness', *Economist*, 2 March 1968.

44 For the full story of the subsequent crisis of South Asian British citizens and British Protected Persons in Uganda in 1972, see Chapter 9.

45 Conservative Manifesto, *A Better Tomorrow* (1970), cited in Hansen, *Citizenship and Immigration in Post-War Britain*, p. 192.

46 'Bangladesh: Immigration into Britain', 29 March 1973, FCO 37/1204, p. 110.

47 Ibid., pp. 105, 108.

48 'The Pakistani Community in Britain', May 1971, FCO 37/970, pp. 87–105.

49 Ann Dummett and Andrew Nicol, *Subjects, Citizens, Aliens and Others*, p. 217.

50 Randall Hansen, *Citizenship and Immigration in Post-War Britain*, p. 195.

51 HL Deb. 18 October 1971, vol. 324, cols. 428–71.

52 'It's Bad Enough to be Black, Man, but Who'd be a Non-Patrial?', *Economist*, 27 February 1971.

53 'Immigration Act: Notes on Sections', 2 November 1971, FCO 50/404, p. 175. See Laurie Fransman, Adrian Berry and Alison Harvey, *Fransman's British Nationality Law*, pp. 223–4.

54 'Immigration', 19 December 1972, FCO 37/1117, p. 32.

55 HC Deb. 25 January 1973, vol. 849, col. 655.

56 Ibid. For the different rights afforded to Commonwealth citizens (British subjects), 'patrials' and 'grandpatrials', see Richard Plender, 'The New Immigration Rules', *Journal of Ethnic and Migration Studies*, 2: 2 (1973), pp. 168–76.

57 'Immigration Bill: The Patrials Clause and Anglo-Indians', 12 March 1971, FCO 37/763, p. 128.

58 See T. C. Hartley, 'When Is a Patrial Not a Patrial?', *Modern Law Review*, 39: 3 (1976), pp. 347–9. The non-white patrial in question relates to *R v. Secretary of State for the Home Department, Ex parte Phansopkar*.

59 'Immigration Bill: Notification of Commonwealth Governments', 7 January 1971, FCO 37/763, p. 188.

60 'Immigration Bill: Notification of Commonwealth Governments', 7 January 1971, FCO 37/763, p. 187; 'Immigration Act: Guidance Note', 2 November 1971, FCO 50/404, p. 171.

61 Ann Dummett and Andrew Nicol, *Subjects, Citizens, Aliens and Others*, p. 222.

62 See James Read, 'Some Legal Aspects of the Expulsion', in Michael Twaddle, ed., *Expulsion of a Minority: Essays on Ugandan Asians* (London: Athlone, 1975), p. 198.

63 'Immigration: Entry of Dependants', 6 April 1973, FCO 37/1204, p. 139.

64 'Immigration', 10 December 1974, FCO 37/1414, p. 66.

65 'Immigration: Entry of Dependants', 6 April 1973, FCO 37/1204, p. 137.

66 See Randall Hansen, *Citizenship and Immigration in Post-War Britain*, pp. 229–30, 238.

67 'Bangladesh: Immigration into Britain', 29 March 1973, FCO 37/1204, p. 105.

68 'Approach to Europe: Conclusions of a Cabinet Meeting Held at Chequers', 20 April 1967, CC 26(67) CAB 128/42. Cited in S. R. Ashton and Wm Roger Louis, eds, *British Documents on the End of Empire: East of Suez and the Commonwealth 1964–1971* (London: Stationery Office, 2004), part II, p. 34.

69 To be exact, thirty-one were declared admissible, thirty-eight inadmissible, and 174 struck out during an eight-year period finally concluding on 9 October 1978. See Marie-Bénédicte Dembour, *When Humans Become Migrants: Study of the European Court of Human Rights with an Inter-American Counterpoint* (Oxford: Oxford University Press, 2015), p. 64 n. 15.

70 Cedric Thornberry, 'Asians Accuse Britain of Violating Human Rights', *Guardian*, 7 October 1970.

71 See *East African Asians v UK*, European Commission on Human Rights, 14 December 1973; Sandra Fredman, *Discrimination Law* (Oxford: Oxford University Press, 2011), p. 229.

72 Anthony Lester, 'The Overseas Trade in the American Bill of Rights', *Colombia Law Review*, 88: 3 (1988), p. 550.

73 'Cabinet: Ministerial Committee on Immigration and Community Relations', 13 December 1974, FCO 37/1414, p. 28–9. See also Anthony Lester, 'Thirty Years On: The East African Asians Case Revisited', *Public Law*, Spring 2002, pp. 52–72; Marie-Bénédicte Dembour, *When Humans Become Migrants*, pp. 62–5, 86–91; Richard Plender, 'European Commission of Human Rights: Decision on Admissibility of Applications by East African Asians Against United Kingdom', *International Legal Materials*, 10: 1 (1971). For further detail, see Chapter 8, below.

74 'Memos Presented to UK Official: Virginity Tests', *Times of India*, 9 February 1979. See Evan Smith and Marinella Marmo, *Race, Gender and the Body in British Immigration Control: Subject to Examination* (London: Palgrave Macmillan, 2014).

75 HC Deb. 7 May 1980, vol. 984, col. 488.

76 Conservative Political Centre, *Who Do We Think We Are? An Inquiry into British Nationality Law by a Conservative Study Group Under the Chairmanship of Edward Gardner, QC MP* (London: Conservative Political Centre, 1980), p. 5.

77 See Laurie Fransman, Adrian Berry and Alison Harvey, *Fransman's British Nationality Law*, pp. 21–2; Gina Clayton, Caroline Sawyer, Rowena Moffat, Georgine Firth, Helena Wray, *Textbook on Immigration and Asylum Law* (Oxford: Oxford University Press, 2016), p. 86.

78 HC Deb. 5 November 2002, vol. 392, col. 147.

79 Home Office internal memo, 19 June 2002. Cited in Colin Yeo, 'Citizens in Waiting: The Case for Reforming Citizenship', in Kimberly McIntosh, ed., *From Expendable to Key Workers and Back Again: Immigration and the Lottery of Belonging in Britain* (London: Runnymede Trust, 2020), p. 15 – pdf available at runnymedetrust.org. See also Laurie Fransman, 'Commonwealth, Subjects and Nationality Rules', in R. Wolfrum, ed., *Max Planck Encyclopedia of Public International Law* (Oxford: Oxford University Press, 2009).

4. The Persistence of Empire

1 See John Darwin, *Britain and Decolonisation: The Retreat from Empire in the Post-War World* (Basingstoke: Macmillan, 1988), p. 334; Wm Roger Louis, 'The Dissolution of the British Empire', in Judith Brown and Wm Roger Louis, eds, *The Oxford History of the British Empire: The Twentieth Century* (Oxford: Oxford University Press, 1999), pp. 329–54.

2 Frederick Cooper, *Decolonization and African Society: The Labor Question in French and British Africa* (Cambridge: Cambridge University Press, 1996), p. 248.

3 See Michael Collins, 'Decolonization', in John Mackenzie, ed., *The Encyclopedia of Empire: Volume 2* (Oxford: Wiley-Blackwell, 2016), p. 2.

4 John Darwin, 'The Fear of Falling: British Politics and Imperial Decline since 1900', *Transactions of the Royal Historical Society*, 36 (1986), p. 42.

5 Keith Hancock, *The Wealth of Colonies* (Cambridge: Cambridge University Press, 1950), p. 17. See also Wm Roger Louis, 'Sir Keith Hancock and the British Empire: The Pax Britannica and the Pax Americana', *English Historical Review*, 120: 488 (2005), p. 961.

6 Keith Hancock, *Perspective in History* (Canberra: ANU, 1982), p. 164. Cited in Louis, 'Sir Keith Hancock and the British Empire: The Pax Britannica and the Pax Americana', p. 959.

7 Alec Cairncross, *Years of Recovery: British Economic Policy 1945–51* (Abingdon: Routledge, 1985), pp. 5–10, 276.

8 George Orwell, *The Complete Works of George Orwell*, vol. 5, *The Road to Wigan Pier* (London: Secker & Warburg, 1986), p. 148. See also Ina Zweiniger-Bargielowska, *Austerity in Britain: Rationing, Controls, and Consumption, 1939–1955* (Oxford: Oxford University Press, 2000); Kenneth O. Morgan, *Britain since 1945: The People's Peace* (Oxford: Oxford University Press, 2001), pp. 65–70; Elizabeth Buettner, *Europe after Empire: Decolonization, Society, and Culture* (Cambridge: Cambridge University Press, 2016), p. 41.

9 See Camilla Schofield, *Enoch Powell and the Making of Postcolonial Britain* (Cambridge: Cambridge University Press, 2013), pp. 55, 78.

10 Keith Hancock, *Perspective in History*, p. 55. Cited in Louis, 'Sir Keith Hancock and the British Empire: The Pax Britannica and the Pax Americana', p. 961.

11 Attlee cited in A. N. Porter and A. J. Stockwell, *British Imperial Policy and Decolonization, 1938–64*, vol. 1 (London: Palgrave Macmillan, 1987), p. 59; Winston Churchill, 'Speech at a Conservative Mass Meeting, Llandudno, 9 October 1948', in Randolph S. Churchill, ed., *Europe Unite – Speeches: 1947 and 1948* (London: Cassell, 1950), pp. 417–18. See also Alec Cairncross, *Years of Recovery*, p. 11.

12 See Nicolas J. White, 'Decolonization in the 1950s: The Version According to British Business', and Sarah Stockwell, 'African Prospects: Mining the Empire for Britain in the 1950s', in Martin Lynn, ed., *The British Empire in the 1950s: Retreat or Revival?* (Basingstoke: Palgrave, 2006), pp. 77–99, 100–21; Catherine Scheck, *Britain and the Sterling Area: From Devaluation to Convertibility in*

the 1950s (London: Routledge, 1994); Charles Feinstein, 'The End of Empire and the Golden Age', in Peter Clarke and Clive Trebilcock, eds, *Understanding Decline: Perceptions and Realities of British Economic Performance* (Cambridge: Cambridge University Press, 1997), p. 218.

13 See Nicolas J. White, 'Decolonization in the 1950s: The Version According to British Business', p. 101. See also A. G. Hopkins, 'Rethinking Decolonisation', *Past and Present*, 200 (2008), p. 224.

14 See Ashley Jackson, *War and Empire in Mauritius and the Indian Ocean* (Basingstoke: Palgrave, 2001), p. 181.

15 Keith Hancock, *Wealth of Colonies*, p. 5. For 'invisible empire', see Keith Hancock, *Survey of British Commonwealth Affairs*, vol. 2, part I (Oxford: Oxford University Press, 1940), p. 27.

16 D. A. Low and J. M. Lonsdale, 'Introduction: Towards the New Order, 1945–63', in D. A. Low and Alison Smith, eds, *History of East Africa*, vol. 3 (Oxford: Oxford University Press, 1976). See also Sarah Stockwell, *The British End of the British Empire* (Cambridge: Cambridge University Press, 2018).

17 HC Deb. 3 December 1954, vol. 535, col. 489.

18 David R. Devereux, 'Britain, the Commonwealth and the Defence of the Middle East 1948–56', *Journal of Contemporary History*, 24: 2 (1989); John Darwin, 'Was There a Fourth British Empire?', in Lynn, *The British Empire in the 1950s*, p. 16. See also Martin Lynn, 'Introduction', in Lynn, *The British Empire in the 1950s*, p. 6.

19 Krishan Kumar, 'Empire, Nation, and National Identities', in Andrew Thomson, ed., *Britain's Experience of Empire in the Twentieth Century*, (Oxford: Oxford University Press, 2011), p. 318.

20 George Padmore, *Africa: Britain's Third Empire* (London: Dennis Dobson, 1949), pp. 9–10.

21 Cited in Leslie James, *George Padmore and Decolonization from Below: Pan-Africanism, the Cold War, and the End of Empire* (London: Palgrave Macmillan, 2015), p. 184.

22 See Chapter 5, below.

23 Doris Lessing, *The Four-Gated City* (St Albans: Panther, 1972), p. 304.

24 'Future Constitutional Development in the Colonies', Report by the Chairman of the Official Committee on Colonial Policy (Norman Brook), 6 September 1957, CPC (57) 30, CAB 134/1556. Cited in Cooper, *Decolonization and African Society*, p. 395.

25 S. R. Ashton, 'Keeping Change within Bounds: A Whitehall Reassessment', in Lynn, *The British Empire in the 1950s*, p. 44.

26 Wm Roger Louis, 'Public Enemy Number One: The British Empire in the Dock at the United Nations, 1957–1971', in Lynn, *The British Empire in the 1950s*, pp. 194–5.

27 Other dates include: the Seychelles (1976), the British Solomon Islands (as Solomon Islands, 1978), the Gilbert Islands (as Kiribati, 1979), the Ellice Islands (as Tuvalu, 1978), and British Honduras (as Belize, 1981). See A. W. Brian Simpson, *Human Rights and the End of Empire: Britain and the Genesis*

of the European Convention (Oxford: Oxford University Press, 2004), pp. 1,085–6.

28 See Alison Smith and Mary Bull, 'Introduction' to a special issue on 'Margery Perham and British Rule in Africa', *The Journal of Imperial and Commonwealth History*, 19: 3 (1991), p. 1.

29 Prudence Smith, 'Margery Perham and Broadcasting: A Personal Reminiscence', *The Journal of Imperial and Commonwealth History*, 19: 3 (1991), p. 199.

30 Perham wished this book, which never appeared, to be titled 'Dear Mr Mboya'. Patricia Pugh, 'Margery Freda Perham: 1895–1982', *Proceedings of the British Academy*, vol. 111 (Oxford: Oxford University Press, 2001), p. 630.

31 Margery Perham, Reith Lectures, 1961 – Lecture 6: 'Prospects for the Future', broadcast 21 December 1961, BBC Home Service, p. 6 – pdf available at downloads.bbc.co.uk.

32 Margery Perham, Reith Lectures, 1961 – Lecture 3: 'The Politics of Emancipation', broadcast 30 November 1961, BBC Home Service, p. 1 – pdf available at downloads.bbc.co.uk.

33 Margery Perham, Reith Lectures, 1961 – Lecture 5: 'The Colonial Account', broadcast 14 December 1961, BBC Home Service, p. 7 – pdf available at downloads.bbc.co.uk.

34 Margery Perham, Reith Lectures, 1961 – Lecture 6, p. 7.

35 Margery Perham, Reith Lectures, 1961 – Lecture 3, p. 1.

36 Margery Perham, Reith Lectures, 1961 – Lecture 6, pp. 6–7.

37 Max Beloff, *Britain's Liberal Empire 1897–1921: Volume 1 of Imperial Sunset* (Basingstoke: Macmillan, 1987), p. 1. See also HC Deb. vol. 645 cols 928–31, 31 July 1961.

38 Max Beloff, *Britain's Liberal Empire 1897–1921*, pp. 4, 6.

39 'Future Defence Policy', 17 June 1963, D(63)22, CAB 131/28. See also Richard Aldous and Sabine Lee, '"Staying in the Game": Harold Macmillan and Britain's World Role', in Richard Aldous and Sabine Lee, eds, *Harold Macmillan and Britain's World Role* (Basingstoke: Macmillan, 1996).

40 Cited in Krishnadasa Gowda, *The European Common Market and India: Basic Issues Re-Examined* (Mysore: Rao & Raghavan, 1962), p. 118.

41 Cited in Peter Brooke, *Duncan Sandys and the Informal Politics of Britain's Late Decolonisation* (London: Palgrave, 2018), p. 33.

42 'New Power Arising', *Spectator*, 14 December 1962. See also Douglas Brinkley, 'Dean Acheson and the "Special Relationship": The West Point Speech of December 1962', *Historical Journal*, 33: 3 (1990).

43 Anthony Sampson, *Anatomy of Britain* (London: Hodder & Stoughton, 1962), p. 620.

44 Arthur Koestler, ed., *Suicide of a Nation? Enquiry into the State of Britain* (London: Macmillan, 1963), p. 14.

45 Perry Anderson, 'Origins of the Present Crisis', *New Left Review*, I/23 (1964), p. 35.

46 Paul Gilroy, *After Empire: Melancholia or Convivial Culture* (London: Routledge, 2004), p. 98. See also John Solomos, Bob Findlay, Simon Jones and Paul

Gilroy, 'The Organic Crisis of British Capitalism and Race: The Experience of the Seventies', in Centre for Contemporary Cultural Studies, *The Empire Strikes Back: Race and Racism in 70s Britain* (London: Hutchinson, 1982), p. 23.

47 HC Deb. 5 December 1958, vol. 596, col. 1589.

48 Patrick Kealty, 'Premier Pledges Support for India', *The Guardian*, 11 June 1965. See also John Darwin, 'British Decolonization since 1945: A Pattern or a Puzzle?', *The Journal of Imperial and Commonwealth History*, 12: 2 (1984), p. 191.

49 HC Deb. 16 December 1964, vol. 704, col. 424.

50 'South-East Asia: Record of a Conversation between Mr Wilson and Mr Rusk about Britain's Commitments in South-East Asia', 10 June 1966, PREM 13/890. Cited in S. R. Ashton and Wm Roger Louis, eds, *British Documents on the End of Empire: East of Suez and the Commonwealth 1964–1971* (London: Stationery Office, 2004), part I, p. 92. Wilson also refers to Kipling in his memoirs; see Harold Wilson, *The Labour Government 1964–1970: A Personal Record* (London: Penguin, 1971), p. 497.

51 Alec Cairncross, *Managing the British Economy in the 1960s: A Treasury Perspective* (London: Macmillan, 1996), p. 263.

52 See Chibuike Uche, 'Oil, British Interests and the Nigerian Civil War', *Journal of African History*, 49: 1 (2008); Robert McNamara, 'Britain, Nasser and the Outbreak of the Six Day War', *Journal of Contemporary History*, 35: 4 (2000).

53 Diplomatic Oral History Programme, transcript, Sir Brian Lee Crowe, 15 October 2003, p. 14 – pdf available at https://www.chu.cam.ac.uk/archives/collections/bdohp/.

54 These words on Britain's second application to join the EEC were made by Saville Garner; see 'EEC', Garner to Bowden, 26 April 1967, FCO 20/14. Cited in Ashton and Louis, *British Documents on the End of Empire*, part II, p. 23. On devaluation, see S. R. Ashton, 'Introduction' in Ashton and Louis, *British Documents on the End of Empire*, part I, p. xli.

55 'The Value of the Commonwealth to Britain', 24 April 1967, C(67)59, CAB 129/129. Cited in Ashton and Louis, *British Documents on the End of Empire*, part II, pp. 421, 428.

56 See Ruth Craggs, 'Subaltern Geopolitics and the Post-Colonial Commonwealth, 1965–1990', *Political Geography*, 65 (2018), p. 53.

57 Diplomatic Oral History Programme, interview transcript, Sir Peter Hall, 8 November 2002, p. 12, pdf available at https://www.chu.cam.ac.uk/archives/collections/bdohp/.

58 'The Commonwealth as a British Interest', Britten to Walker, 12 December 1966, DO 193/79. Cited in Ashton and Louis, *British Documents on the End of Empire*, part II, p. 380.

59 Ibid. Cited in Ashton and Louis, *British Documents on the End of Empire*, part II, pp. 376, 379.

60 'British Indian Ocean Territory', 11 February 1969, FCO 37/387, pp. 95–6; 'Additional Supplementary and Background Notes for Question by Mr Tam

Dalyell dated 17 November [1970]: Additional Background Note', FCO 37/632, p. 138.

61 'British Indian Ocean Territory', 27 March 1969, FCO 37/387, p. 21.

62 'BIOT Working Papers: Paper no. 3: The Problem of the People Living in the Chagos Archipelago', Pacific and Indian Ocean Department, FCO 37/388, pp. 137, 138.

63 Ibid., p. 139.

64 'British Indian Ocean Territory', 21 March 1969, FCO 37/387, p. 24–5.

65 'BIOT Working Papers: Paper no. 5: Evacuation & Resettlement of Inhabitants of Chagos Archipelago', Pacific and Indian Ocean Department, April 1969, FCO 37/388, p. 156. See Stephen Allen, *The Chagos Islanders and International Law* (Oxford: Hart, 2014). Allen points out that the Chagossian population's right of self-determination became binding on Britain as customary international law in 1970 following the adoption of United Nations General Assembly resolution 2625.

66 'BIOT Working Papers: Paper no. 5: Evacuation & Resettlement of Inhabitants of Chagos Archipelago', Pacific and Indian Ocean Department, April 1969, FCO 37/388, p. 143. See also 'Security of the Indian Ocean: Brief by the Foreign and Commonwealth Office', 30 December 1970, FCO 37/544, p. 14.

67 Kenneth Waltz, *Foreign Policy and Democratic Politics: The American and British Experience* (Boston/Toronto: Little Brown, 1967), p. 241.

68 HC Deb. 16 January 1968, vol. 756, cols. 1580–1.

69 Ibid., col. 1577.

70 Ibid., col. 1603.

71 Foreign Office to Washington, 15 January 1968, PREM 13/1999. Cited in Ashton and Louis, *British Documents on the End of Empire*, part I, p. 138. See David M. McCourt, 'What Was Britain's "East of Suez Role"'? Reassessing the Withdrawal, 1964–1968', *Diplomacy & Statecraft*, 20: 3 (2009).

72 John Graham, 'Wilson in America – 2', *Spectator*, 7 February 1970, p. 169.

73 Anthony Lewis, 'US and Britain: Still a Very Special Relationship', *New York Times*, 11 February 1968.

74 Dean to Brown, 12 March 1968, FCO 46/42. Cited in Ashton and Louis, *British Documents on the End of Empire*, part I, p. 137.

75 See Peter Brooke, *Duncan Sandys and the Informal Politics of Britain's Late Decolonisation*, p. 118.

76 'The Cost of Whiteness', *Economist*, 2 March 1968.

77 Dom Moraes, '"Shall I Paint Myself White?" The Kenyan Asians Find that Some People with British Passports are More Equal than Others', *The New York Times*, 5 May 1968.

78 See S. R. Ashton, 'British Government Perspectives on the Commonwealth, 1964–71: An Asset or a Liability?', *The Journal of Imperial and Commonwealth History*, 35: 1 (2007), p. 89.

79 'Non-Military Means of Influence in the Persian Gulf, South-East Asia and Australia', 18 March 1968, FCO 37/238, pp. 7–8.

80 'Non-Military Means of Influence in Australasia/South East Asia and the

Persian Gulf Area: Outline of a Memorandum for the DOP Committee by the Foreign Secretary and the Commonwealth Secretary', 12 March 1968, FCO 37/238, p. 21.

81 Ibid., pp. 22–4.

82 Victor Kiernan, *Lords of Humankind: Black Man, Yellow Man, White Man* (Boston: Little, Brown, 1969), p. 322.

83 Alun Chalfont, 'Escape from Simonstown?', *New Statesman*, 11 December 1970, p. 795.

84 James Worrall, *Statebuilding and Counterinsurgency in Oman: Political, Military and Diplomatic Relations at the End of Empire* (London: I.B. Tauris, 2018), p. 111. See also Abdel Razzaq Takriti, *Monsoon Revolution: Republicans, Sultans, and Empires in Oman, 1965–1976* (Oxford: Oxford University Press, 2016), p. 193.

85 See Ashley Jackson, 'Empire and Beyond: The Pursuit of Overseas National Interests in the Late Twentieth Century', *English Historical Review*, 122: 499 (2007), pp. 1,360.

86 'Visit of the Prime Minister to the United Nations 19–24 October 1970', 13 October 1970, FCO 7/1835, p. 9.

87 'East of Suez (Including Soviet Naval Expansion): Brief by Foreign and Commonwealth Office', 13 October 1970, FCO 7/1833, pp. 25–6.

88 See Ashley Jackson, 'The Royal Navy and the Indian Ocean Region since 1945', *RUSI Journal*, 151: 6 (2006).

89 Patrick Gordon Walker, *The Cabinet: Political Authority in Britain* (New York: Basic, 1970), p. 122.

90 Susan Strange 'Sterling and British Policy: A Political View', *International Affairs*, 47: 2 (1971), p. 315.

91 Susan Strange, *Sterling and British Policy: A Political Study of an International Currency in Decline* (Oxford: Oxford University Press, 1971), p. 47.

92 Susan Strange, 'Sterling and British Policy: A Political View', p. 304.

93 'Farewell to the Lion City: Valedictory Despatch from Sir A. de la Mare to Sir A Douglas-Home', 2 October 1970, FCO 24/885. Cited in Ashton and Louis, *British Documents on the End of Empire*, part I, pp. 391–2.

94 See Ronald Hyam, *Britain's Declining Empire: The Road to Decolonisation, 1918–1968* (Cambridge: Cambridge University Press, 2007), p. 397; Saki Dockrill, *Britain's Retreat from East of Suez: The Choice between Europe and the World?* (Basingstoke: Palgrave, 2002), p. 209; John Darwin, 'British Decolonization since 1945: A Pattern or a Puzzle?', p. 191; John Darwin, *Unfinished Empire: The Global Expansion of Britain* (London: Penguin, 2012); John Darwin, *Britain and Decolonisation*, p. 324.

95 Shohei Sato, *Britain and the Formation of the Gulf States: Embers of Empire* (Manchester: Manchester University Press, 2016), p. 58.

96 See Ian Hall, *Dilemmas of Decline: British Intellectuals and World Politics, 1945–1975* (Berkeley, CA: University of California Press, 2012). For a discussion of how decline relates to the post-war social-democratic settlement, see Emily Robinson, Camila Schofield, Florence Sutcliff-Braithwaite and Natalie

Thomlinson, 'Telling Stories about Post-War Britain: Popular Individualism and the "Crisis" of the 1970s', *Twentieth Century British History*, 28: 2 (2017), p. 269.

97 Joe Rogaly, 'Britain at the Bottom of the League', *Financial Times*, 12 January 1971.

98 Bernard Weinraub, 'The New Anatomy of Britain: By Anthony Sampson', *New York Times*, 18 June 1972.

99 'Opposing Voices, But Entry to Europe Wins Backing of a Huge Majority', *The Times*, 14 October 1971.

100 J. G. A. Pocock, 'British History: A Plea for a New Subject', *Journal of Modern History*, 47: 4, p. 601.

5. Postscripts to Decolonisation

1 *Daily Mail*, 28 November 1961. See Ian Beesley, *The Official History of the Cabinet Secretaries* (Abingdon: Routledge, 2017), pp. 16, 158–9.

2 'Prime Minister's African Tour – January–February, 1960', Cabinet Secretary to Cabinet, 12 April 1960, C(60)66, CAB 129/101, p. 4.

3 These associations included the African Affairs Centre, the National Association of Students Socialist Organisation, the Ghana Trades Union Congress and the All-African People's Conference Secretariat.

4 'Prime Minister's African Tour', p. 7.

5 'Report of the Fourth Committee', UN General Assembly, eleventh session, 661st plenary meeting, 26 February 1957, A/PV.661, p. 1,225.

6 Speech reproduced in Harold Macmillan, *Pointing the Way 1959–1961* (London: Macmillan, 1972), p. 156.

7 'Prime Minister's African Tour', p. 16.

8 Ibid.

9 Ibid., p. 4.

10 Ibid. By way of contrast, 'communist' is only mentioned seven times, and 'communism' four times.

11 See Ritchie Ovendale, 'Macmillan and the Wind of Change in Africa, 1957–1960', *Historical Journal*, 38: 2 (1995), pp. 455–77; L. J. Butler and Sarah Stockwell, 'Introduction' in L. J. Butler and Sarah Stockwell, eds, *The Wind of Change: Harold Macmillan and British Decolonization* (Basingstoke: Palgrave Macmillan, 2013), p. 2.

12 UN General Assembly, fourteenth session, 798th plenary meeting, 17 September 1959, A/PV.798, p. 23.

13 Diplomatic Oral History Programme, interview transcript, John Latto Farquharson (Ian) Buist, 8 April 2008, p. 11 – pdf available at https://www.chu.cam.ac.uk/archives/collections/bdohp/.

14 'Prime Minister's African Tour', p. 140.

15 John Wyndham, 'The Wind of Change Myth', *Sunday Times*, 10 May 1964.

16 'Prime Minister's African Tour', p. 61.

17 Ibid., p. 34.

18 Ibid., p. 18.

19 Ibid.

20 Ibid., p. 141.

21 'Macmillan Trip Clarifies British Policy', *Africa Report*, 5 (1960), p. 12.

22 See G. K. Reddy, 'UK Premier for Ghana: African Tour to Begin Today', *Times of India*, 5 January 1960; 'Mr Macmillan's African Tour: Apartheid Issue to be Ignored', *Times of India*, 11 January 1960.

23 Dag Hammarskjöld, 'Airport Statement on Return from African Trip', UN Press Release SG/895, 31 January 1960, reproduced in Andrew Cordier and Wilder Foote, ed., *Public Papers of the Secretaries-General of the United Nations: Volume IV: Dag Hammarskjöld: 1958–1960* (New York/London: Columbia University Press, 1974), p. 522.

24 Dag Hammarskjöld, 'From Transcript of Press Conference', UN Note to Correspondents no. 2108, 4 February 1960, reproduced in Cordier and Foote, *Public Papers of the Secretaries-General of the United Nations*, p. 526.

25 See Eva-Maria Muschik, 'Managing the World: The United Nations, Decolonization, and the Strange Triumph of State Sovereignty in the 1950s and 1960s', *Journal of Global History*, 13 (2018), p. 134.

26 Jawaharlal Nehru, speech in the Lok Sabha on the 1955 Citizenship Bill, 5 December 1955, in Jawaharlal Nehru, *India's Foreign Policy: Selected Speeches, September 1946–April 1961* (New Delhi: Ministry of Information and Broadcasting, Government of India, 1961), p. 157

27 'The Value of the Commonwealth to Britain', 24 April 1967, C(67)59, CAB 129/129. Cited in S. R. Ashton and Wm Roger Louis, eds, *British Documents on the End of Empire: East of Suez and the Commonwealth 1964–1971* (London: Stationery Office, 2004), part II, pp. 442, 449.

28 'Pan-African Congress', *Manchester Guardian*, 15 October 1945, pp. 22–7. See also Hakim Adi, *Pan-Africanism: A History* (London: Bloomsbury, 2018), pp. 122–7.

29 Cited in George Padmore, *History of the Pan African Congress* (London: Hammersmith Bookshop, 1947), pp. 1–15.

30 Ibid.

31 'Report by the Special Branch of the Metropolitan Police', 8 November 1945, MEPO 38/91. Cited in W. O. Maloba, *Kenyatta and Britain: An Account of Political Transformation 1929–1963* (Cham: Palgrave Macmillan, 2018), p. 93.

32 See ibid., pp. 98–9.

33 Cited in Adi, *Pan-Africanism*, p. 126.

34 See, for example, Bardo Fassbender, 'Rediscovering a Forgotten Constitution: Notes on the Place of the UN Charter in the International Legal Order', in Jeffery Dunoff and Joel Trachtman, eds, *Ruling the World? Constitutionalism, International Law, and Global Governance* (Cambridge: Cambridge University Press, 2009), pp. 133–48.

35 For Churchill's resistance to this phrasing, see A. W. Brian Simpson, *Human Rights and the End of Empire: Britain and the Genesis of the European Convention* (Oxford: Oxford University Press, 2004), pp. 179–80.

36 Ibid., p. 242.

37 See Lorna Lloyd, '"A Most Auspicious Beginning": The 1946 United Nations General Assembly and the Question of the Treatment of Indians in South Africa', *Review of International Studies*, 16: 2 (1990), p. 131.

38 'A Commentary on the Charter of the United Nations', Foreign Office report (1954). Cited in Manu Bhagavan, *The Peacemakers: India and the Quest for One World* (London: Palgrave Macmillan, 2013) p. 45.

39 HC Deb. 13 July 1943, vol. 391, col. 48.

40 Statement by Pandit, 20 May 1945, cited in Manu Bhagavan, *The Peacemakers*, p. 44.

41 HL Deb. 22 August 1945, vol. 137, col. 105.

42 See Raphaëlle Khan, 'Between Ambitions and Caution: India, Human Rights, and Self-Determination at the United Nations', in A. Dirk Moses, Marco Duranti and Roland Burke, eds, *Decolonization, Self-Determination, and the Rise of Global Human Rights Politics* (Cambridge: Cambridge University Press, 2020), p. 215. See also Vineet Thakur, *Jan Smuts and the Indian Question* (Scottsville: University of KwaZulu-Natal Press, 2017), p. 54.

43 UN General Assembly, first session, 37th plenary meeting, 25 October 1946, A/PV.37, pp. 732–3.

44 See Lorna Lloyd, '"A Most Auspicious Beginning": The 1946 United Nations General Assembly and the Question of the Treatment of Indians in South Africa', p. 147.

45 UN General Assembly resolution 44, 'Treatment of Indians in the Union of South Africa', 8 December 1946.

46 See Johannes Morsink, *The Universal Declaration of Human Rights: Origins, Drafting, and Intent* (Philadelphia: University of Pennsylvania Press, 1999), p. 96.

47 Jawaharlal Nehru, 'Firm Adherence to Objectives', speech in the UN General Assembly, 3 November 1948, in Nehru, *India's Foreign Policy*, p. 164.

48 Statement by Hansa Mehta on 27 January 1947. Cited in Bhagavan, *The Peacemakers*, p. 87. See also Raphaëlle Khan, 'Between Ambitions and Caution: India, Human Rights, and Self-Determination at the United Nations', pp. 222–6.

49 Foreign Office, 23 March 1948, FO 371/72803. Cited in Simpson, *Human Rights and the End of Empire*, p. 419.

50 The colonies in question were Gambia, Gold Coast and Sierra Leone. 'Secret and Non-Secret Circulars to Governors', 28 March 1949, FO 371/78945. Cited in ibid., p. 458.

51 John Kenton, 'Human Rights Declaration Adopted by UN Assembly', *New York Times*, 11 December 1948. On Aaron Copland's work, *Preamble for a Solemn Occasion*, see Mark Philip Bradley, 'Approaching the Universal Declaration of Human Rights', in Akira Iriye, Petra Goedde and William Hitchcock, eds, *The Human Rights Revolution: An International History* (Oxford: Oxford University Press, 2012), pp. 327–8.

52 See Mary Ann Heiss, 'Privileging the Cold War over Decolonization: The US

Emphasis on Political Rights', in Moses, Duranti and Burke, *Decolonization, Self-Determination, and the Rise of Global Human Rights Politics*, pp. 36–7.

53 See Antonio Cassese, *Self-Determination of Peoples: A Legal Reappraisal* (Cambridge: Cambridge University Press, 1995), pp. 48–52.

54 UN General Assembly resolution 395, 'Treatment of People of Indian Origin in the Union of South Africa', 2 December 1950.

55 Cited in Roland Burke, 'From Individual Rights to National Development: The First UN International Conference on Human Rights, Tehran, 1968', *Journal of World History*, 19: 3 (2008), p. 279.

56 Jawaharlal Nehru, 'Principle of Universality', speech in the Lok Sabha, 18 November 1953, and 'Asia and Africa Awake', speech at the concluding session of the Bandung conference, 24 April 1955, in Nehru, *India's Foreign Policy*, pp. 169, 271. For the 1950 press conference, see Middleton to MacGillivary, 25 January 1954, DO 133/147, p. 184.

57 Jawaharlal Nehru, 'The Bandung Conference', speech in Lok Sabha, 30 April 1955, in Nehru, *India's Foreign Policy*, p. 279. See also Manu Bhagavan, *The Peacemakers*, pp. 116–21.

58 'Brief for the Foreign Secretary's Visit to New Delhi, March 1956', DO 133/147, p. 143.

59 Selwyn Lloyd, *Suez 1956: A Personal View* (London: Jonathan Cape, 1978), p. 4.

60 'Brief for the Foreign Secretary's Visit to New Delhi, March 1956', DO 133/147, pp. 143–5.

61 John Douglas Pringle, 'The White Australia Policy: Locking the Doors Against Asia', *Manchester Guardian*, 29 September 1958.

62 UN General Assembly, fifteenth session, 947th plenary meeting, 'Declaration on the Granting of Independence to Colonial Countries and Peoples', 14 December 1960.

63 'The Tragedy at Sharpeville', *New York Times* editorial, 22 March 1960; 'Africans Asked to Gather by White Policemen: Sworn Affidavits by Firing Victims', *Times of India* editorial, 26 March 1960.

64 'Membership of South Africa as a Republic: UK View', CRO briefing, 22 February 1961, CAB 133/261. Cited in Ronald Hyam and Wm Roger Louis, eds, *British Documents on the End of Empire: The Conservative Government and the End of Empire, 1957–1964* (London: HMSO, 2000), part I, p. 417.

65 Macmillan to Nehru, 6 January 1961, PREM 11/3393. Cited in Hyam and Louis, *British Documents on the End of Empire*, part I, p. lxxv.

66 'Membership of South Africa as a republic: UK view', CRO briefing, 22 February 1961, CAB 133/261. Cited in Hyam and Louis, *British Documents on the End of Empire*, part I, p. 415.

67 'South Africa's continued membership of the Commonwealth: Minutes of Six Meetings of Commonwealth Prime Ministers', 15 March 1961, CAB 133/251. Cited in Hyam and Louis, *British Documents on the End of Empire*, part I, p. 449. See also Saul Dubow, 'The Commonwealth and South Africa: From Smuts to Mandela', *The Journal of Imperial and Commonwealth History*, 45: 2 (2017).

68 UN General Assembly resolution 1598, 'Question of Race Conflict in South Africa Resulting from the Policies of Apartheid of the Government of the Union of South Africa', 13 April 1961, A/RES/1598.

69 Robin Winks, 'On Decolonization and Informal Empire', *American Historical Review*, 81: 3 (1976), p. 542.

70 'Reflections on Commonwealth and Other Changes in the Post-War World: Personal Telegram (Reply), Mr Macmillan to Mr Menzies', PREM 11/3644, 8 February 1962. Cited in Hyam and Louis, *British Documents on the End of Empire*, part I, p. 664.

71 See Vineet Thakur, 'The "Hardy Annual": A History of India's First UN Resolution', *India Review*, 16: 4 (2017).

72 These are the words of Malcolm Macdonald and Iain Macleod, respectively. See 'Introduction', in Hyam and Louis, *British Documents on the End of Empire*, part I, p. liii. See also Martin Lynn, 'Introduction', in Martin Lynn, ed., *The British Empire in the 1950s: Retreat or Revival?* (Basingstoke: Palgrave, 2006), p. 5.

73 Cited in Adom Getachew, *Worldmaking after Empire: The Rise and Fall of Self-Determination* (Princeton: Princeton University Press, 2019), p. 128. For postcolonial federal ideas, see p. 109 of the same text.

74 Poynton, 9 May 1962, CO 936/727. Cited in Wm Roger Louis, 'Public Enemy Number One: The British Empire in the Dock at the United Nations, 1957–1971', in Lynn, *British Empire in the 1950s*, p. 188.

75 C. W. Squire, 29 May 1963, FO 371/172591. Cited in Louis, 'Public Enemy Number One: The British Empire in the Dock at the United Nations, 1957–1971', p. 212, n. 69. Years later, Squire would write a doctoral thesis on the British occupation of Indonesia at the School of Oriental and African Studies in London.

76 'The United Nations and Colonies', Poynton to Greenwood, 6 January 1966, CO 967/434. Cited in Ashton and Louis, *British Documents on the End of Empire*, part II, p. 59.

77 'Technical Assistance in Public Administration: Provision of Operational, Executive and Administrative Personnel: Note by the Secretary-General', UN General Assembly, fifteenth session, 22 November 1960, A/4589.

78 See Sarah Stockwell, *The British End to the British Empire* (Cambridge: Cambridge University Press, 2018).

79 Tom Mboya, 'Tensions in African Development' (1961), in *The Challenge of Nationhood: A Collection of Speeches and Writings by Tom Mboya* (New York/Washington: Praeger, 1970), p. 32.

80 See UN General Assembly resolution 1710, 19 December 1961. See also, 'The Kennedy Inauguration', *Life*, 27 January 1961, p. 24.

81 Julius Nyerere, 'The Entrenchment of Privilege', *Africa South*, 2: 2 (1958), p. 88. Cited in Bonny Ibhawoh, 'Seeking the Political Kingdom: Universal Human Rights and the Anti-colonial Movement in Africa', in Moses, Duranti and Burke, *Decolonization, Self-Determination, and the Rise of Global Human Rights Politics*, p. 45.

82 Cited in Sean Brawley, *The White Peril: Foreign Relations and Asian Immigra-tion to Australasia and North America 1919–1978* (Sydney: University of New South Wales Press, 1995), p. 290.

83 Moreno Salcedo, UN General Assembly, eighteenth session, 1261st plenary meeting, 20 November 1963, A/PV.1261, p. 9. See Paul Gordon Lauren, *The Evolution of International Human Rights: Visions Seen* (Philadelphia: Univer-sity of Pennsylvania Press, 2011), p. 247.

84 UN General Assembly, third committee, seventeenth session, 1167th plenary meeting, 30 October 1962, A/C.3/SR.1167, p. 168.

85 UN General Assembly, twentieth session, third committee, 1345th meeting, 17 November 1965, A/C.3/SR.1345, p. 327. See also Steven Jensen, *The Making of International Human Rights: The 1960s, Decolonization, and the Reconstruc-tion of Global Values* (Cambridge: Cambridge University Press, 2016), p. 118.

86 UN General Assembly, twentieth session, third committee, 1345th meeting, 17 November 1965, A/C.3/SR.1345, p. 326.

87 UN General Assembly, twentieth session, third committee, 1363rd meeting, 2 December 1965, A/C.3/SR.1363, p. 431.

88 Steven Jensen, *The Making of International Human Rights*, p. 4. For the role of Ghana, the Philippines and other states in the debate leading to the conven-tion, see pp. 117–26 of the same text.

89 'Approach to Europe: Conclusions of a Cabinet Meeting Held at Chequers', 20 April 1967, CC 26(67) CAB 128/42. Cited in Ashton and Louis, *British Docu-ments on the End of Empire*, part II, p. 34.

90 UN General Assembly, third committee, eighteenth session, 1228th plenary meeting, 4 October 1963, A/PV.1228, p. 3. Cited in Jensen, *The Making of International Human Rights*, p. 80. For Jamaica's diplomatic contribution to international human rights in the 1960s more generally, see pp. 69–101 of the same text.

91 See United Nations Treaty Collection, Depository, Status of Treaties, Interna-tional Convention on the Elimination of All Forms of Racial Discrimination. Available at treaties.un.org.

92 See David W. McIntyre, *The Significance of the Commonwealth, 1965–90* (Bas-ingstoke: Palgrave, 2001), p. 28.

93 See James Crawford, *The Creation of States in International Law* (Oxford: Clar-endon, 2007), p. 609.

94 See David Raic, *Statehood and the Law of Self-Determination* (The Hague/London/New York: Kluwer Law International, 2002), p. 129.

95 'Tragedy in Rhodesia', *Times of India*, 13 November 1965.

96 See 'Rhodesia: Brief by Foreign and Commonwealth Office', 13 October 1970, FCO 7/1833, p. 22. See also Ruth Craggs, 'Subaltern Geopolitics and the Post-Colonial Commonwealth, 1965–1990', *Political Geography*, 65 (2018), pp. 46–56; Philip Murphy, '"An Intricate and Distasteful Subject": British Planning for the Use of Force against the European Settlers of Central Africa, 1952–65', *English Historical Review*, 121: 492 (2006), pp. 746–77; Carl Watts, 'Killing Kith and Kin: The Viability of British Military Intervention in

Rhodesia, 1964–5', *Twentieth Century British History*, 16: 4 (2005); Elizabeth Buettner, *Europe after Empire: Decolonization, Society, and Culture* (Cambridge: Cambridge University Press, 2016), p 68. On the Commonwealth and Rhodesia, see W. McIntyre, *The Significance of the Commonwealth, 1965–90* (Basingstoke: Palgrave, 2001), p. 29.

97 'Commonwealth Prime Ministers' Conference: Brief by Foreign and Commonwealth Office', 13 October 1970, FCO 7/1833, p. 109.

98 Ibid. See also Lorna Lloyd, *Diplomacy with a Difference: the Commonwealth Office of High Commissioner, 1880–2006* (Leiden/Boston: Martinus Nijhoff, 2007), pp. 224, 231.

99 'The Value of the Commonwealth to Britain', 24 April 1967, CAB 129/129. Cited in Ashton and Louis, *British Documents on the End of Empire*, part II, p. 420.

100 Tom Mboya, 'Aid and Development in the Commonwealth', in *The Challenge of Nationhood*, p. 241.

101 'Commonwealth Prime Ministers' Conference: Minute by CCC Tickell on Constructive Ideas that Might Emerge from the Singapore Conference', FCO 59/571, 29 May 1970. Cited in Ashton and Louis, *British Documents on the End of Empire*, part II, p. 447.

102 'The Commonwealth as a British Interest', P. J. S. Moon to R. Walker, 5 December 1966, DO 193/79, p. 362. Cited in Ashton and Louis, *British Documents on the End of Empire*, part II, p. 447.

103 See Michael Lipton and John Firn, *The Erosion of a Relationship: India and Britain since 1960* (London: Oxford University Press, 1975).

104 Diplomatic Oral History Programme, interview transcript, Sir Peter Hall, 8 November 2002, p. 13 – pdf available at https://www.chu.cam.ac.uk/archives/collections/bdohp/. See also Colin Jackson, ed., *Labour in Asia: A New Chapter?* (London: Fabian Society, 1973), p. 6. For Indira Gandhi's foreign policy, see Surjit Mansingh, *India's Search for Power: Indira Gandhi's Foreign Policy, 1966–1982* (New Delhi: Sage, 1984); Priya Chacko, Chapter 5, *Indian Foreign Policy: The Politics of Postcolonial Identity from 1947 to 2004* (Abington: Routledge, 2002).

105 'India Will Quit C'Wealth if Necessary – P. M.', *Times of India*, 29 December 1968.

106 'Visit of the Prime Minister to the United Nations 19–24 October 1970: Meeting with Mrs Gandhi, Prime Minister of India', 13 October 1970, FCO 7/1835, p. 99.

107 Ibid., p. 92

108 'Record of Conversation Between the Foreign and Commonwealth Secretary and the Prime Minister of Singapore at Dorneywood at 2.45pm on Sunday, 4 October 1970, FCO 37/632, p. 179.

109 'Address by Mr Edvard Hambro, President of the Twenty-Fifth Session of the General Assembly', 13 October 1970, FCO 7/1834, p. 89.

110 In the end the declaration was adopted without a vote. '25th Anniversary Declaration', 15 October 1970, FCO 7/1833, p. 103.

111 UN General Assembly, 'Declaration on the Occasion of the Twenty-Fifth Anniversary of the United Nations', twenty-fifth session, 1883rd plenary meeting, 24 October 1970, A/RES/2627(XXV).

112 Ibid., p. 70.

113 'Southern Africa: Brief by the Foreign and Commonwealth Office', 13 October 1970, FCO 7/1833, p. 14.

114 'Indefensible', *Times of India*, 8 January 1971.

115 S. R. Ashton, 'British Government Perspectives on the Commonwealth, 1964–71: An Asset or a Liability?', *Journal of Imperial and Commonwealth History*, 35: 1 (2007), p. 89.

116 'Declaration about the Commonwealth: Minute by Sir A. Douglas-Home to Mr Heath on an African Initiative Ahead of the Singapore Prime Ministers' Conference', 22 December 1970, PREM 15/279. Cited in Ashton and Louis, *British Documents on the End of Empire*, part II, p. 449–50.

117 Ibid., p. 448.

118 S. R. Ashton, 'British Government Perspectives on the Commonwealth, 1964–71: An Asset or a Liability?', pp. 89–90.

119 Britain abstained in the Security Council vote in 1963. 'Speaking Notes for Secretary of State's Call on Mr Rogers', 28 August 1970, FCO 37/632, p. 205.

120 J. D. Singh, 'UK Will Sell Copters to S Africa', *Times of India*, 23 February 1971.

121 See 'Britain and the European Communities', 13 October 1970, FCO 7/1833, pp. 49–54.

122 'Prime Minister Shearer (Jamaica): Brief by Foreign & Commonwealth Office', 12 October 1970, FCO 7/1835, pp. 25–6.

123 Ram P. Anand, *New States in International Law* (Gurgaon: Hope India, 2008), pp. 1–3, 113.

124 'Non-Military Means of Influence in the Persian Gulf, South-East Asia and Australia', 18 March 1968, FCO 37/238, pp. 7–8, 22–4.

6. Race and Immigration in a Decolonising World

1 Arthur Percival, *An Introduction to the Study of Colonial History* (London: Society for Promoting Christian Knowledge, 1919), pp. 5, 7.

2 Hugh Egerton, *A Short History of British Colonial Policy, 1606–1909* (London: Methuen, 1910), p. 525.

3 On race and culture, see Daniel Gorman, 'Lionel Curtis, Imperial Citizenship, and the Quest for Unity', *The Historian*, 66: 1 (2004), p. 82. For a discussion of eugenics in the context of wider trends in racial thought, see Paul Rich, 'The Long Victorian Sunset: Anthropology, Eugenics and Race in Britain, c. 1900–48', *Patterns of Prejudice*, 18: 3 (1984), p. 4.

4 Robert Knox, *The Races of Men: A Philosophical Enquiry Into the Influence of Race Over the Destinies of Nations* (London: Henry Renshaw, 1862), pp. 8, 10, 288, 314.

5 'Dr Knox's Lectures on Races of Men', *Manchester Guardian*, 18 September 1847.

6 'Doubts the Paternity of Queen Elizabeth', *New York Times*, 1 November 1930. See also Greta Jones, *Social Darwinism and English Thought: The Interaction between Biological and Social Theory* (Sussex: Harvester Press, 1980); Michael Harkins, *Social Darwinism in European and American Thought, 1860–1945: Nature as Model and Nature as Threat* (Cambridge: Cambridge University Press, 1997); Chloe Campbell, *Race and Empire: Eugenics in Colonial Kenya* (Manchester: Manchester University Press, 2007).

7 Hobson was here referring to political developments in South Africa. J. A. Hobson, *Crisis of Liberalism: New Issues of Democracy* (London: P. S. King, 1909), p. 244. See also Paul Rich, *Race and Empire in British Politics* (Cambridge: Cambridge University Press, 1990), pp. 53–4. On Hobson's antisemitism, see Peter Cain, *Hobson and Imperialism: Radicalism, New Liberalism, and Finance 1887–1938* (Oxford: Oxford University Press, 2002), pp. 91, 92–3, 109.

8 James Bryce, *Race Sentiment as a Factor in History: A Lecture Delivered Before the University of London on February 22, 1915* (London: University of London Press, 1915), pp. 4, 27, 35; 'Vanity Cause of War: Viscount Bryce Traces Conflict to Feelings of Racial Consciousness', *New York Times*, 23 February 1915. See also Paul Rich, *Race and Empire in British Politics*, pp. 20–4.

9 Philip Kerr, *What the British Empire Really Stands For* (Toronto: Council for the Round Table in Canada, 1917), pp. 15–16, 19. See also Paul Rich, *Race and Empire in British Politics*, pp. 58–9.

10 Cited in Hugh Tinker, *Race, Conflict, and the International Order: From Empire to United Nations* (London: Macmillan, 1977), p. 132.

11 W. E. B. Du Bois, *The Souls of Black Folk* (Oxford: Oxford University Press, 2007), p. 3.

12 W. E. B. Du Bois, 'The Souls of White Folk', *Independent* (New York), 18 August 1910. Cited in Marilyn Lake and Henry Reynolds, *Drawing the Global Colour Line: White Men's Countries and the International Challenge of Racial Equality* (Cambridge: Cambridge University Press, 2008), p. 2.

13 W. E. B. Du Bois, 'Atlanta University', in *From Servitude to Service: Being the Old South Lectures on the History and Work of Southern Institutions for the Education of the Negro* (Boston: American Unitarian Association, 1905), pp. 155–97.

14 See Chapter 1, above.

15 See Frederick R. Dickinson, *World War I and the Triumph of a New Japan, 1919–1930* (Cambridge: Cambridge University Press, 2013), p. 67.

16 E. J. Dillon, *The Inside Story of the Peace Conference* (New York/London: Harper & Brothers, 1920), pp. 4, 6, 288.

17 Jawaharlal Nehru, 'Future Taking Shape', speech in New Delhi, 7 September 1946, in Jawaharlal Nehru, *India's Foreign Policy: Selected Speeches, September 1946–April 1961* (New Delhi: Ministry of Information and Broadcasting, Government of India, 1961), p. 1.

18 HC Deb. 22 August 1945, vol. 413, cols. 663–4.

19 Cited in Johannes Morsink, *The Universal Declaration of Human Rights: Origins, Drafting, and Intent* (Philadelphia: University of Pennsylvania Press, 1999), p. 102. For the discussion on caste in the UDHR, see p. 115 of the same text. For a profile of Masani, see 'Personalities of IRTDA', *Times of India*, 21 November 1953.

20 'Races of Mankind: "None Mentally Superior To The Other"', *Times of India*, 21 July 1950; 'Mental Prowess is Not Racial: Unesco Scientists Say All Start Equal', *Manchester Guardian*, 18 July 1950. There is considerable debate as to the extent to which the first UNESCO 'statement on race' retained racial conceptions despite its professed anti-racism. The lack of transnational scholarly acceptance of UNESCO's first statement, which led to a subsequent statement on race in 1951, reveals the persistence of biologically deterministic definitions of race. See Elazar Barkan, 'The Politics of the Science of Race: Ashley Montagu and UNESCO's Anti-Racist Declarations' in Larry T. Reynolds and Leonard Lieberman, eds., *Race and Other Misadventures: Essays in Honor of Ashley Montagu in His Ninetieth Year* (Dix Hills, NY: General Hall, 1996), pp. 96–105; Michelle Brattain, 'Race, Racism, and Antiracism: UNESCO and the Politics of Presenting Science to the Postwar Public', *The American Historical Review*, 112: 5 (December 2007); Sebastián Gil-Riaño, 'Relocating Anti-Racist Science: the 1950 UNESCO Statement on Race and Economic Development in the Global South', *The British Journal for the History of Science*, 51: 2 (June 2018).

21 E. H. Carr, *The New Society* (London: Macmillan, 1956), pp. 92–3.

22 Harry Hodson, 'Race Relations in the Commonwealth', *International Affairs*, 26: 3 (1950), pp. 305, 307–9, 311–15; Robert Wade-Gery, 'Hodson, Henry Vincent [Harry] (1906–1999)', *Oxford Dictionary of National Biography* (Oxford: Oxford University Press, 2004) – online edition, available at oxforddnb.com. See also David Mills, *Difficult Folk? A Political History of Social Anthropology* (New York: Berghahn, 2008), pp. 129–47.

23 Philip Mason, 'Ten Years of the Institute', *Race*, 10: 2 (1968), p. 193.

24 Ibid. See also Paul Rich, *Race and Empire in British Politics*, p. 200.

25 Philip Mason, 'Ten Years of the Institute', p. 194.

26 Ronald Hyam, *Britain's Declining Empire: The Road to Decolonisation, 1918–1968* (Cambridge: Cambridge University Press, 2007), p. 315.

27 Kenneth Little, 'Racial Mixture in Great Britain: Some Anthropological Characteristics of the Anglo-Negroid Cross: A Preliminary Report', *Eugenics Review*, 33: 4 (1942), p. 113.

28 Michael Banton, *White and Coloured: The Behaviour of British People Towards Coloured Immigrants* (London: Jonathan Cape, 1959), p. 15.

29 Arnold Toynbee, 'The Ultimate Choice', *Race*, 2: 2 (1960), pp. 5–6. See also Arnold Toynbee, 'Is a "Race War" Shaping Up?', *New York Times Magazine*, 29 September 1963.

30 Patrick Gordon Walker, *The Commonwealth* (London: Seker & Warburg, 1962), pp. 353, 382.

31 See Randall Hansen, *Citizenship and Immigration in Post-War Britain: The*

Institutional Origins of a Multicultural Nation (Oxford: Oxford University Press, 2000), p. 132.

32 HC Deb, 16 November 1961, vol. 649, col. 799; HC Deb, 17 November 1964, vol. 702, col. 290.

33 Adlai Stevenson, UN General Assembly, eighteenth session, third committee, 1217th plenary meeting, 1 October 1963, A/C.3/SR.1217, p. 30; Alexandre Verret, UN General Assembly, twentieth session, 1406th plenary meeting, 21 December 1965, A/PV.1406, pp. 9–10. See also 'United Nations Declaration on the Elimination of All Forms of Racial Discrimination', UN General Assembly resolution 1904, 20 November 1963; Steven Jensen, *The Making of International Human Rights: The 1960s, Decolonization, and the Reconstruction of Global Values* (Cambridge: Cambridge University Press, p. 2016), p. 113; Patrick Thornberry, *International Convention on the Elimination of All Forms of Racial Discrimination*, p. 5.

34 Tanganyika National Assembly Debates (Hansard), 17–18 October 1961. Cited in Ronald Aminzade, *Race, Nation, and Citizenship in Postcolonial Africa: The Case of Tanzania* (Cambridge: Cambridge University Press, 2013), p. 117.

35 See Erik Bleich, *Race Politics in Britain and France: Ideas and Policymaking since the 1960s* (Cambridge: Cambridge University Press, 2003), p. 61.

36 Ibid., p. 75.

37 Jenny Bourne, 'The Race Relations Act 1965 – Blessing or Curse?', Institute of Race Relations, available at https://irr.org.uk/.

38 Michael Dawson, 'Breaking Away from the "Big Boys"? Jamaican and "White Commonwealth" Expectations at the 1966 British Empire & Commonwealth Games', *Sport in History* 34: 3 (2014), p. 439. See 'Rhodesia Pulls Out of Commonwealth Games', *Daily Gleaner* (Kingston), 14 April 1966.

39 'Zambia Quits Games over Rhodesia', *Daily Gleaner* (Kingston), 16 July 1966. Cited in Dawson 'Breaking Away from the "Big Boys"?', p. 439. The 1986 Commonwealth Games would be largely boycotted by African and Caribbean states in protest at British relations with apartheid South Africa.

40 Mike Agostini, 'Kenya's Hope Keino Should Win', *Daily Gleaner* (Kingston), 29 May 1966. Cited in Dawson 'Breaking Away from the "Big Boys"?', p. 440.

41 'Clarke's Fine Finish Still Fails to Keep Keino at Bay', *Manchester Guardian*, 10 August 1966. Cited in Dawson, 'Breaking Away from the "Big Boys"?', p. 441.

42 'Clarke Beaten by Unknown', *Courier-Mail* (Brisbane), 8 August 1966. Cited in Dawson, 'Breaking Away from the "Big Boys"?', p. 441.

43 'Death Knell of Games', *New Zealand Herald*, 11 August 1966. Cited in Dawson, 'Breaking Away from the "Big Boys"?', pp. 441–2.

44 'The Value of the Commonwealth to Britain', 24 April 1967, CAB 129/129. Cited in S. R. Ashton and Wm Roger Louis, eds, *British Documents on the End of Empire: East of Suez and the Commonwealth 1964–1971* (London: Stationary Office, 2004), part II, p. 422.

45 Cited in Erik Bleich, *Race Politics in Britain and France*, p. 75.

46 See Ronald Hyam, *Britain's Declining Empire*, p. 246.

47 HC Deb, 8 November 1966, vol. 735, col. 1189. Cited in Peter Brooke, *Duncan*

Sandys and the Informal Politics of Britain's Late Decolonisation (London: Palgrave, 2018), p. 150.

48 'Mr Sandys Calls for End of Immigration', *The Guardian*, 25 July 1967; ITN *News at Ten*, 25 July 1967. See also Brooke, *Duncan Sandys and the Informal Politics of Britain's Late Decolonisation*, p. 152.

49 'Leroy, Rap and Balthazar', *Economist*, 29 July 1967.

50 See Peter Brooke, *Duncan Sandys and the Informal Politics of Britain's Late Decolonisation*, p. 161.

51 'Race Protest on Sandys Speech Demand for Prosecution', *The Times*, 11 August 1967.

52 'By Fostering Racism to Halt Coloured Immigration, a Tory MP Stirs Up … ', *New York Times*, 15 December 1968. See Camilla Schofield, *Enoch Powell and the Making of Postcolonial Britain* (Cambridge: Cambridge University Press, 2013), pp. 199, 218.

53 HC Deb, 8 April 1968, vol. 762, col. 902.

54 Sandra Fredman, *Discrimination Law* (Oxford: Oxford University Press, 2011), p. 61.

55 'Black Man in Search of Power', *The Times*, 4 March 1968; 'Black Man in Search of Power', *The Times*, 6 March 1968.

56 Stephen Clarke, Peter Evans, Michael Knipe, Garry Lloyd, Dan van der Vat, Colin Webb and William Norris, *The Black Man in Search of Power: A Survey of the Black Revolution Across the World* (London: Thomas Nelson, 1968), p. 171.

57 'The Man From Peking', *The Times*, 15 March 1968.

58 Stephen Clarke et al., *Black Man in Search of Power*, pp. 13, 166.

59 'Black Alliance Threatens to Take Militant Action', *The Times*, 29 April 1968.

60 Cited in John Narayan, 'British Black Power: The Anti-Imperialism of Political Blackness and the Problem of Nativist Socialism', *Sociological Review*, 67: 5 (2019), p. 949.

61 Harold R. Isaacs, 'Colour in World Affairs', *Foreign Affairs*, 47: 2 (1969), pp. 236, 238–9.

62 Roy Preiswerk, review of 'Race in International Politics: A Dialogue in Five Parts', *Race & Class*, 13: 1 (1971), pp. 100–3. For further discussion of the overestimation of the role of race in 1960s world politics, see Robert Vitalis, *White World Order, Black Power Politics: The Birth of American International Relations* (Ithaca, NY: Cornell University Press, 2015), pp. 126–8.

63 Philip Mason, 'Ten Years of the Institute', *Race*, 10: 2 (1968), p. 196.

64 James Rosenau, *Race in International Politics: A Dialogue in Five Parts* (Denver: University of Colorado, 1970), pp. 1–3.

65 Gloria Emerson, 'Kaunda, Addressing UN Unit, Weeps over White Oppression', *The New York Times*, 17 September 1968.

66 James Rosenau, *Race in International Politics*, pp. 2, 9, 11, 15, 17.

67 Joe Rogaly, 'Keeping a Cool Head about Race', *Financial Times*, 21 March 1972.

68 See Paul Rich, *Race and Empire in British Politics*, p. 203.

69 Avery Gordon, 'On "Lived Theory": An Interview with A. Sivanandan', *Race & Class*, 55: 4 (2004), p. 2.

70 Edward Said acknowledged Kiernan's work as the forebear of his *Orientalism* (New York: Pantheon, 1978). See Victor Kiernan, *Lords of Human Kind: Black Man, Yellow Man, White Man* (Boston: Little, Brown, 1969).

71 C. L. Mowat, 'The White Man's Burden', *New Statesman*, 21 March 1969, p. 411.

72 See Chapter 2, above.

73 'The Value of the Commonwealth to Britain', 24 April 1967, CAB 129/129. Cited in Ashton and Louis, *British Documents on the End of Empire*, part II, p. 422.

74 'Indian Immigration into Britain', 18 September 1967, FCO 37/19, p. 117.

75 'Asian United Kingdom Citizens', 15 September 1967, FCO 37/18, p. 3.

76 Freeman to Commonwealth Office, 27 September 1967, FCO 37/19, p. 54.

77 'Indian Immigration into Britain', 18 September 1967, FCO 37/19, p. 117.

78 Freeman to Commonwealth Office, 9 October 1967, FCO 37/19, p. 25.

79 'Possible Extension of Commonwealth Immigrant Act, 1962, to UK Citizens with Connections in the UK', 24 October 1967, FCO 37/20, p. 84.

80 Ibid., p. 86.

81 Holmer to Commonwealth Office, 9 October 1967, FCO 37/19, p. 28. See also Twist to Commonwealth Office, 10 October 1967, FCO 37/19, p. 27.

82 Walker to Commonwealth Office, 10 October 1967, FCO 37/19, p. 11.

83 Hampshire to Commonwealth Office, 10 October 1967, FCO 37/19, p. 6.

84 Britten to Commonwealth Office, 10 October 1967, FCO 37/19, p. 5.

85 Gandee to Commonwealth Office, 10 October 1967, FCO 37/19, p. 22.

86 Peck to Commonwealth Office, 10 October 1967, FCO 37/19, p. 18.

87 Twist to Commonwealth Office, 19 December 1967, FCO 37/20, p. 51.

88 MacLennan to Commonwealth Office, 10 October 1967, FCO 37/19, p. 26.

89 Johnson to Commonwealth Office, 10 October 1967, FCO 37/19, p. 23.

90 Lintott to Commonwealth Office, 10 October 1967, FCO 37/19, p. 21.

91 Lok Sabha, question no. 1267, 19 December 1968, reproduced in FCO 37/390, p. 31.

92 'Asians in Kenya Petition C'wealth', *Daily Nation* (Nairobi), 6 January 1969.

93 *Daily News* (Dar es Salaam), 19 August 1972. Cited in Aminzade, *Race, Nation, and Citizenship in Postcolonial Africa*, p. 236.

94 'Immigration Bill: Notification of Commonwealth Governments', 7 January 1971, FCO 37/763, p. 180.

95 'Immigration Act: Notes on Sections', 2 November 1971, FCO 50/404, p. 175.

96 'Speech Made by the Rt. Hon Reginald Maudling on the 2 February 1971 at the Indian Journalists' Association Republic Day Dinner at the Connaught Rooms, London', FCO 37/763, pp. 171–4.

97 Philippa Drew to FCO, 18 March 1971, FCO 37/763, pp. 123–4.

98 'India: Brief by the Foreign and Commonwealth Office', 22 December 1970, FCO 37/544, p. 107.

99 'Objectionable Features of British Immigration Bill', Indiagram Information Service Press Release, 7 April 1971, FCO 37/763, p. 84. A handwritten note on the press release by an FCO official reads: 'Quite mild but an ominous

mention of reciprocal action!' See also 'Indian Reactions to the Immigration Bill', 3 March 1971, FCO 37/763, p. 133.

100 'Objectionable Features of British Immigration Bill', Indiagram Information Service Press Release, 7 April 1971, FCO 37/763, p. 85.

101 'Note of a Meeting with the High Commissioner for India at 3 p.m. on Wednesday, 24 March', FCO 37/763, pp. 105–10.

102 Ibid., p. 107. See also Sana Aiyar, *Indians in Kenya: The Politics of Diaspora* (Harvard: Harvard University Press, 2015), p. 155.

103 'Note of a Meeting', 3 June 1971, FCO 37/763, p. 36.

104 Lord Bridges, 19 December 1972, FCO 37/1117, p. 20.

105 Garvey, 18 December 1972, FCO 37/1117, p. 37. For Garvey's preoccupation with cricket, see William Gould, 'South Asian Immigration to the United Kingdom and "Foreign Office Files for India, Pakistan and Afghanistan"' (2014), scoping document for Adam Matthew Digital, p. 5, pdf available at http://www. amdigital.co.uk/.

106 'The New Immigration Rules', 21 March 1973, FCO 37/1204, p. 183.

107 Cited in S. R. Ashton, 'Introduction', in Ashton and Louis, *British Documents on the End of Empire*, part I, p. xxx.

7. Inflating the Threat

1 Richard Bourne, 'Eight Pakistanis Will Not Be Allowed to Stay', *The Guardian*, 23 August 1967; Arun Gandhi, 'Slave Trade 1967; In England Now', *Times of India*, 8 October 1967. It should be noted that Bourne and Gandhi give conflicting accounts.

2 HC Deb. 15 November 1967, vol. 754, col. 469.

3 See David Steel, *No Entry* (London: C. Huret, 1968), p. 135; 'Background Brief: United Kingdom Immigration Policy', 8 September 1972, FCO 50/404, p. 157. See also, 'Special Arrangements with India and Pakistan', 14 October 1968, FCO 37/260, p. 9.

4 Wm Roger Louis, 'The British Withdrawal from the Gulf, 1961–1971', *The Journal of Imperial and Commonwealth History*, 31: 1 (2003), p. 84.

5 HC Deb. 15 November 1967, vol. 754, cols. 448, 519, 558.

6 Ibid., cols. 514–15, 520.

7 Ibid., cols. 448, 467.

8 Ibid., cols. 467–9, 506, 530–1.

9 See Peter Brooke, *Duncan Sandys and the Informal Politics of Britain's Late Decolonisation* (London: Palgrave, 2018), pp. 222–3.

10 'Emergency Planning: Asian UK Citizens', 15 August 1967, FCO 37/18, p. 34.

11 Ibid., p. 33.

12 Ibid., p. 34.

13 Ibid., p. 41.

14 Ibid., p. 47.

15 Ibid.

16 'Emergency Planning: Asian UK Citizens', 31 August 1967, FCO 37/18, p. 6.

17 'Asian-United Kingdom Citizens in East Africa', 13 September 1967, FCO 37/19, p. 94.

18 'Emergency Planning: Asian UK Citizens', 21 August 1967, FCO 37/18, p. 13.

19 'Emergency Planning: Asian UK Citizens' 15 August 1967, FCO 37/18, p. 44.

20 Commonwealth Office to British high commissions, 6 October 1967, FCO 37/19, p. 32.

21 'Emergency Planning: Asian UK Citizens', 15 August 1967, FCO 37/18, p. 43.

22 Ibid., p. 49

23 Ibid.

24 On 14 March 1968, the Commonwealth affairs secretary admitted in the House of Commons that there 'were about 2,000 Tamils in Ceylon who were UK citizens'. Officials estimated, however, that only twenty to thirty of these 'actually possessed UK passports'. See 'The Sirima-Shastri Agreement', 4 May 1973, FCO 37/1204, p. 87.

25 On the succession to postcolonial citizenship regimes in East Africa, see Bronwen Manby, *Citizenship in Africa: The Law of Belonging* (Oxford: Hart, 2018), pp. 176–98.

26 'Application of Immigration Control to Citizens of the United Kingdom and Colonies Who Do Not Belong to the United Kingdom', Official Committee on Commonwealth Immigration, Home Office, 4 October 1967, FCO 37/19, p. 46; 'Admission to the United Kingdom of Certain non-Europeans without UK Connexions', 13 September 1967, FCO 37/19, p. 99.

27 'Emergency Planning: Asian UK Citizens', 15 August 1967, FCO 37/18, p. 32.

28 Ibid., p. 33. See also 'Commonwealth Office Paragraphs for Use in Draft Home Office Paper Amplifying CI (0) (67)15', 1967, FCO 37/19, p. 35.

29 'Emergency Planning: Asian UK Citizens', 15 August 1967, FCO 37/18, p. 33.

30 'Emergency Planning: Asian UK Citizens', 15 August 1967, FCO 37/18, p. 51.

31 Ibid., p. 50.

32 Ibid., p. 29.

33 'Emergency Planning: Asian UK Citizens', 16 August 1967, FCO 37/18, p. 17.

34 'Emergency Planning: Asian UK Citizens', 21 August 1967, FCO 37/18, p. 14.

35 'Admission to the United Kingdom of Certain Non-Europeans without UK Connexions', 13 September 1967, FCO 37/19, p. 96.

36 'Application of Immigration Control to Citizens of the United Kingdom and Colonies Who Do Not Belong to the United Kingdom', Official Committee on Commonwealth Immigration, Home Office, 4 October 1967, FCO 37/19, p. 46.

37 The 1948 British Nationality Act had created the status of 'British subjects without citizenship' as a transitional category before such people gained citizenship of a Commonwealth state. BSWCs were to be found in Australia, Newfoundland, South Africa, Southern Rhodesia, India and Pakistan, since these countries had not passed their own citizenship laws by 1 January 1949, when the 1948 Act came into force. 'Admission to the United Kingdom of Certain Non-Europeans without UK Connexions', 13 September 1967, FCO 37/19, p. 99.

38 Ibid.

39 'Control of Immigration of Asian United Kingdom Citizens', 25 September 1967, FCO 37/19, pp. 69–70.

40 'Emergency Planning: Asian UK Citizens', 16 August 1967, FCO 37/18, p. 17.

41 Ibid.

42 Ibid.

43 See Ritchie to Commonwealth Office, 10 October 1967, FCO 37/19, p. 7.

44 'Asian-United Kingdom Citizens in East Africa', 13 September 1967, FCO 37/19, p. 95.

45 Commonwealth Office to Port of Spain, 25 September 1967, FCO 37/19, p. 83.

46 Commonwealth Office to Kuala Lumpur, 25 September 1967, FCO 37/19, p. 65.

47 Further registrations for CUKC status were unlikely, thought Holmer, following 'recent legislation' in Singapore 'moving towards the abolition of dual citizenship'.

48 Holmer to Commonwealth Office, 27 September 1967, FCO 37/19, p. 62.

49 Holmer to Commonwealth Office, 9 October 1967, FCO 37/19, p. 28.

50 Commonwealth Office to New Delhi, 16 February 1968, FCO 37/20, p. 44; 'Commonwealth Office Paragraphs for Use in Draft Home Office Paper Amplifying CI (0) (67)15', 1967, FCO 37/19, p. 34.

51 Commonwealth Office to British High Commissions, 6 October 1967, FCO 37/19, pp. 30–1.

52 Ibid., p. 31. See also Commonwealth Office to Nairobi, 16 October 1967, FCO 37/19, p. 2.

53 Gandee to Commonwealth Office, 10 October 1967, FCO 37/19, p. 22.

54 Crombie to Commonwealth Office, 10 October 1967, FCO 37/19, p. 20.

55 Smedley to Commonwealth Office, 10 October 1967, FCO 37/19, p. 13.

56 Fingland to Commonwealth Office, 10 October 1967, FCO 37/19, p. 9.

57 Tull to Commonwealth Office, 11 October 1967, FCO 37/19, p. 3.

58 Tory to Commonwealth Office, 10 October 1967, FCO 37/19, p. 8.

59 Costar to Commonwealth Office, 10 October 1967, FCO 37/19, p. 10.

60 Ritchie to Commonwealth Office, 10 October 1967, FCO 37/19, p. 7.

61 Hampshire to Commonwealth Office, 10 October 1967, FCO 37/19, p. 7.

62 Britten to Commonwealth Office, 10 October 1967, FCO 37/19, p. 4; Bennett to Commonwealth Office, 9 October 1967, FCO 37/19, p. 29.

63 Freeman to Commonwealth Office, 9 October 1967, FCO 37/19, p. 25; James to Commonwealth Office, 16 June 1969, FCO 37/391, pp. 28–9.

64 'Passport To Britain', *The Times* editorial, 19 October 1967.

65 'Note of an Interview', 21 February 1968, FCO 37/20, p. 36.

66 See 'Mass Expulsions on the Uganda Model: Note by the [Cabinet] Secretaries', 1 December 1972, FCO 37/1117, p. 12.

8. The Kenyan South Asian Crisis

1 'Kenya Exodus Exaggerated, Asians Say', *The Times*, 17 February 1968.

2 Cited in Donald Rothchild, 'Kenya's Minorities and the African Crisis over

Citizenship', *Race*, 6: 4 (1968), p. 424. For the 1968 Kenya Citizenship Act, see Bronwen Manby, *Citizenship in Africa: The Law of Belonging* (Oxford: Hart, 2018), p. 178.

3 Two of the eight were Kenyan citizens. See 'Kenya Asians Get Notice', *Economic and Political Weekly*, 1: 3 (3 September 1966), p. 105.

4 E. Norris, 18 November 1968, FCO 37/390, p. 79. See also 'Admission to the United Kingdom of Certain Non-Europeans without UK Connexions', 13 September 1967, FCO 37/19, p. 99; 'Asian Emigration to the UK', 5 September 1967, FCO 37/19, p. 112.

5 See Peter Brooke, *Duncan Sandys and the Informal Politics of Britain's Late Decolonisation* (London: Palgrave, 2018), p. 184.

6 'Commonwealth Office Paragraphs for Use in Draft Home Office Paper Amplifying CI (0) (67)15', 1967, FCO 37/19, p. 37.

7 'Asian-United Kingdom Citizens in East Africa', 13 September 1967, FCO 37/19, p. 93; 'Commonwealth Office Paragraphs for Use in Draft Home Office Paper Amplifying CI (0) (67)15', 1967, FCO 37/19, p. 35; Peck to Commonwealth Office, 27 September 1967, FCO 37/19, p. 56. See also Prem Bhatia, *Indian Ordeal in Africa* (Delhi: Vikas, 1973), p. 45.

8 'Kenya Exodus Exaggerated, Asians Say', *The Times*, 17 February 1968.

9 'Asian Emigration to the UK', 5 September 1967, FCO 37/19, p. 112. See also Peck to Commonwealth Office, 7 September 1967, FCO 37/19, p. 106; 'Admission to the United Kingdom of Certain non-Europeans without UK Connexions', 13 September 1967, FCO 37/19, p. 99.

10 This was according to Home Office figures made public in February 1968. See HC Deb. 15 February 1968, vol. 758, cols. 392–3.

11 Eric Silver, 'Asian Immigrants from East Africa Rise to 400 a Week', *The Guardian*, 25 September 1967.

12 'New Appeal to Reunite Kenyan Asian Family', *The Guardian*, 1 July 1969.

13 Cited in Amrit Wilson, *Finding A Voice: Asian Women in Britain* (London: Virago, 1978), p. 121.

14 'Why Integration is Easier for the Kenya Asians', *The Times*, 17 January 1969.

15 Cited in Randall Hansen, *Citizenship and Immigration in Post-War Britain: The Institutional Origins of a Multicultural Nation* (Oxford: Oxford University Press, 2000), p. 154.

16 'Application of Immigration Control to Citizens of the United Kingdom and Colonies Who Do Not Belong to the United Kingdom', Official Committee on Commonwealth Immigration, Home Office, 4 October 1967, FCO 37/19, pp. 44–6.

17 According a statement made by Kenyan vice-president Daniel arap Moi in February 1968, only 40,000 South Asians automatically became Kenyan citizens at independence. See 'Asian Immigration from East Africa', 15 March 1968, FCO 37/391, p. 85. However, Bronwen Manby and Yash Tandon suggest that a much higher number of South Asians automatically became Kenyan citizens. See Bronwen Manby, *Citizenship in Africa*, p. 178; Yash Tandon, 'The Asians in East Africa in 1972', in Colin Legum, ed., *African*

Contemporary Record: Survey and Documents 1972–1973 (London: Lex Collins, 1973).

18 'Asian UK Citizens: Evacuation', 18 August 1967, FCO 37/18, p. 15.

19 1964 British Nationality Act §1(1–3). See Bronwen Manby, *Citizenship in Africa*, pp. 61–5.

20 'Application of Immigration Control to Citizens of the United Kingdom and Colonies Who Do Not Belong to the United Kingdom', Official Committee on Commonwealth Immigration, Home Office, 4 October 1967, FCO 37/19, p. 45.

21 E. Norris to FCO, 28 January 1969, FCO 37/391, p. 96. The British High Commission in Lusaka estimated that 1,529 Zambian South Asians had applied for Zambian citizenship between 1 January 1966 and 30 November 1968. Pumphrey to FCO, 30 January 1969, FCO 37/391, p. 89.

22 See Sana Aiyar, *Indians in Kenya: The Politics of Diaspora* (Cambridge: Harvard University Press, 2015), p. 279.

23 Jessica Kuper, '"Goan" and "Asian" in Uganda: An Analysis of Racial Identity and Cultural Categories', in William Shack and Elliot Skinner, eds, *Strangers in African Societies* (Berkeley, CA: University of California Press, 1979), p. 255.

24 'Application of Immigration Control to Citizens of the United Kingdom and Colonies Who Do Not Belong to the United Kingdom', Official Committee on Commonwealth Immigration, Home Office, 4 October 1967, FCO 37/19, pp. 44–6. The issue of consular protection is pointed out by the British high commissioner in Freetown. See Fingland to Commonwealth Office, 10 October 1967, FCO 37/19, p. 9.

25 See Niraja Gopal Jayal, 'Citizenship', in Sujit Choudhry, Madhav Khosla, and Pratap Bhanu Mehta, eds, *The Oxford Handbook of the Indian Constitution* (Oxford: Oxford University Press, 2016). See also A. N. Sinha, *Law of Citizenship and Aliens in India* (Bombay: Asia Publishing House, 1962), p. 3.

26 Prem Bhatia, *Indian Ordeal in Africa*, p. 34.

27 Peck to Commonwealth Office, 10 October 1967, FCO 37/19, p. 18.

28 Scott to Commonwealth Office, 10 October 1967, FCO 37/19, p. 14.

29 Tom Mboya to Duncan Sandys, 24 November 1967. Cited in Peter Brooke, *Duncan Sandys and the Informal Politics of Britain's Late Decolonisation* (London: Palgrave, 2018), p. 197.

30 Jeanne Hromnik, review of Sana Aiyar, *Indians in Kenya: The Politics of Diaspora*, 2016, *Awaaz*, 13: 2 (30 November 2016), available at awaazmagazine.com.

31 Sana Aiyar, *Indians in Kenya*, p. 266.

32 Paul Theroux, 'Hating the Asians', *Transition*, 75/76 (1967), p. 60.

33 Jatinder Verma, 'Transformations in Culture: The Asian in Britain', *RSA Journal*, 137: 5,400 (1989), p. 768.

34 Bernard Weinraub, 'Kenya's Asians, in Growing Anxiety, Watch Uganda Developments', *New York Times*, 29 August 1972.

35 See Sana Aiyar, *Indians in Kenya*, p. 194.

36 Greatbatch to Commonwealth Office, 7 February 1968, FCO 37/20, p. 60.

37 Peck to Commonwealth Office, 27 September 1967, FCO 37/19, p. 57.

38 Ibid., p. 58.

39 Greatbatch to Commonwealth Office, 7 February 1968, FCO 37/20, p. 59.

40 See Anaïs Angelo, *Power and the Presidency in Kenya: The Jomo Kenyatta Years* (Cambridge: Cambridge University Press, 2019), p. 220.

41 Peck to Commonwealth Office, 30 October 1967, FCO 31/250/55. Cited in Poppy Cullen, *Kenya and Britain after Independence: Beyond Neo-Colonialism* (Basingstoke: Macmillan, 2017), pp. 163–4.

42 'S of S [George Thomson] visit to Kenyatta', Peck to Commonwealth Office, 30 October 1967, FCO 31/250. Cited in Brooke, *Duncan Sandys and the Informal Politics of Britain's Late Decolonisation*, pp. 190–1.

43 See Peter Brooke, *Duncan Sandys and the Informal Politics of Britain's Late Decolonisation*, p. 189.

44 This was according to Home Office figures made public in February 1968. See HC Deb. 15 February 1968, vol. 758, cols. 392–3.

45 'Asian Emigration to the UK', 5 September 1967, FCO 37/19, p. 112. See also Peck to Commonwealth Office, 7 September 1967, FCO 37/19, p. 106; 'Admission to the United Kingdom of Certain non-Europeans without UK Connexions', 13 September 1967, FCO 37/19, p. 99.

46 *East African Standard*, 5 September 1967, reproduced in E. Peck to Commonwealth Office, 5 September 1967, FCO 37/19, p. 111.

47 Commonwealth Office to Nairobi, 6 September 1967, FCO 37/19, p. 110.

48 Peck to Commonwealth Office, 7 September 1967, FCO 37/19, pp. 107, 109.

49 Keith Renshaw, 'Britain Faces New "Invasion"', *Sunday Express*, 10 September 1967.

50 'Application of Immigration Control to Citizens of the United Kingdom and Colonies Who Do Not Belong to the United Kingdom', Home Office memorandum, 20 September 1967, FCO 37/19, p. 74.

51 'Admission to the United Kingdom of Certain non-Europeans without UK Connexions', 13 September 1967, FCO 37/19, p. 99. See also, Peck to Commonwealth Office, 8 September 1967, FCO 37/19, p. 104.

52 'Admission to the United Kingdom of Certain non-Europeans without UK Connexions', 13 September 1967, FCO 37/19, p. 99.

53 'Possible Extension of Commonwealth Immigrants Act, 1962 to UK Citizens with Connections in the UK', 24 October 1967, FCO 37/20, p. 85.

54 Ibid., p. 94.

55 'Application of Immigration Control to Citizens of the United Kingdom and Colonies Who Do Not Belong to the United Kingdom', Official Committee on Commonwealth Immigration, Home Office, 4 October 1967, FCO 37/19, pp. 39, 40.

56 'Indian Youth Can Stay', *The Guardian*, 14 September 1967.

57 'Application of Immigration Control to Citizens of the United Kingdom and Colonies Who Do Not Belong to the United Kingdom', Official Committee on Commonwealth Immigration, Home Office, 4 October 1967, FCO 37/19, p. 40.

58 'Control of Immigration of Asian United Kingdom Citizens', 25 September 1967, FCO 37/19, p. 70.

59 'UK Citizens of Asian Origin', 4 October 1967, FCO 37/19, p. 52. See also Greatbatch to Commonwealth Office, 7 February 1968, FCO 37/20, p. 61.

60 'Asian United Kingdom Citizens', 15 September 1967, FCO 37/18, p. 3. See also 'Indian Immigration into Britain', 18 September 1967, FCO 37/19, p. 117.

61 'Commonwealth Office Paragraphs for Use in Draft Home Office Paper Amplifying CI (0) (67)15', 1967, FCO 37/19, p. 34.

62 'India Gives Warning of Rift with Britain', *The Times*, 26 February 1968.

63 Twist to Commonwealth Office, 19 December 1967, FCO 37/20, p. 51.

64 Pickard to Commonwealth Office, 20 February 1968, FCO 37/20, pp. 37–8.

65 'UK Asians in East Africa', 18 December 1967, FCO 37/20, p. 64.

66 Cited in Anirudha Gupta, 'India and the Asians in East Africa', in Michael Twaddle, ed., *Expulsion of a Minority: Essays on Ugandan Asians* (London: University of London/Athlone, 1975), p. 129.

67 'UK Asians in East Africa', 18 December 1967, FCO 37/20, p. 64.

68 Ibid.

69 Ibid.

70 Commonwealth Office to British high commissions, 6 October 1967, FCO 37/19, p. 32.

71 'Emergency Planning: Asian UK Citizens', 31 August 1967, FCO 37/18, p. 5.

72 'Asian-United Kingdom Citizens in East Africa', 13 September 1967, FCO 37/19, p. 94.

73 Ibid.

74 'Application of Immigration Control to Citizens of the United Kingdom and Colonies Who Do Not Belong to the United Kingdom', Home Office memorandum, 20 September 1967, FCO 37/19, p. 77.

75 R. M. Purcell, 'Control of Immigration of Asian United Kingdom Citizens', 25 September 1967, FCO 37/19, p. 69.

76 Ibid., p. 68.

77 Ibid., p. 69.

78 'Application of Immigration Control to Citizens of the United Kingdom and Colonies Who Do Not Belong to the United Kingdom', Home Office memorandum, 20 September 1967, FCO 37/19, p. 76.

79 'Commonwealth Office Paragraphs for Use in Draft Home Office Paper Amplifying CI (0) (67)15', 1967, FCO 37/19, p. 34.

80 'Control of Immigration of Asian United Kingdom Citizens', 25 September 1967, FCO 37/19, p. 69.

81 Crossley to Commonwealth Office, 10 October 1967, FCO 37/19, p. 16.

82 Scott to Commonwealth Office, 10 October 1967, FCO 37/19, p. 14.

83 For a discussion of the potential outcomes of the 1968 Commonwealth Immigrants Act, see 'Practical Problems', 1967, FCO 37/19, p. 33.

84 'Asian Immigration from East Africa', CO, 15 March 1968, FCO 37/391, p. 86.

85 Ibid.

86 'The Cost of Whiteness', *Economist*, 2 March 1968.

87 Greatbatch to Commonwealth Office, 8 February 1968, FCO 37/20, p. 53.
88 See David Steel, *No Entry* (London: Hurst, 1969), pp. 138–42.
89 'Asian Immigrants from East Africa', FCO 37/20, pp. 47–8. See also Commonwealth Office to New Delhi, 16 February 1968, FCO 37/20, p. 44. Details of Thomson's visit to Nairobi are given in Prem Bhatia, *Indian Ordeal in Africa*, p. 131. Macdonald's comments are cited in Brooke, *Duncan Sandys and the Informal Politics of Britain's Late Decolonisation*, p. 241.
90 Greatbatch to Commonwealth Office, 9 February 1968, FCO 37/20, p. 57; 'Mr Kenyatta Reassures Foreigners', *Daily Nation* (Nairobi), 9 February 1968.
91 Greatbatch to Commonwealth Office, 9 February 1968, FCO 37/20, p. 58.
92 'Kenya's Asians', *Times of India*, 19 February 1968.
93 Indira Gandhi, speech in Kathmandu, Nepal, 4 October 1966, in *The Years of Challenge: Selected Speeches of Indira Gandhi, January 1966-August 1969* (New Delhi: Ministry of Information and Broadcasting, 1971), p. 404.
94 'Visit of the Prime Minister to the United Nations 19–24 October 1970: Meeting with Mrs Gandhi, Prime Minister of India', 13 October 1970, FCO 7/1835, p. 97.
95 'India: Brief by the Foreign and Commonwealth Office', 22 December 1970, FCO 37/544, p. 106.
96 Delhi to FCO, 5 January 1973, FCO 37/1204, p. 190.
97 Freeman to Commonwealth Office, 19 February 1968, FCO 37/20, pp. 40–3.
98 Prem Bhatia, *Indian Ordeal in Africa*, pp. 130–5.
99 Thomson gives Dhawan a conservative estimate of 167,000 Kenyan South Asian British citizens. 'Note of an Interview', 21 February 1968, FCO 37/20, p. 34.
100 Ibid., p. 36.
101 Allinson, 29 February 1968, FCO 37/20, p. 14.
102 'Note of an Interview', 21 February 1968, FCO 37/20, p. 36.
103 'Police Fight Thousands at Airport', *The Times*, 28 February 1968.
104 See David Steel, *No Entry*, p. 143.
105 'Demonstrator Tears up Her British Passport', *The Times*, 26 February 1968. See also 'Asians Condemn "Panic, Hysteria"', *The Times*, 24 February 1968.
106 Dom Moraes, '"Shall I Paint Myself White?" The Kenyan Asians Find That Some People with British Passports Are More Equal than Others', *New York Times*, 5 May 1968.
107 'Asians in East Africa', 26 February 1968, FCO 27/20, p. 22.
108 'Asian Immigrants from East Africa', FCO 37/20, p. 47.
109 Dom Moraes, '"Shall I Paint Myself White?" The Kenyan Asians Find That Some People with British Passports Are More Equal than Others', *New York Times*, 5 May 1968.
110 'Some Asians Rebuffed in Kenya When They Try to Fly to Britain', *New York Times*, 1 March 1968.
111 'Panic and Prejudice', *The Times* editorial, 27 February 1968.
112 Peregrine Worsthorne, 'Race: Who Should be Ashamed', *Sunday Telegraph*, 3 March 1968.

113 Author interview with Jatinder Verma, 5 August 2020. See also Jatinder Verma, 'The Shape of a Heart', *Studies in Theatre and Performance*, 26: 1 (2006), p. 91.

114 Dom Moraes, '"Shall I Paint Myself White?" The Kenyan Asians Find That Some People with British Passports Are More Equal than Others', *New York Times*, 5 May 1968.

115 'Kenya Exodus Exaggerated, Asians Say', *The Times*, 17 February 1968.

116 S. E. Croft, 29 January 1969, FCO 37/391, p. 83; 'Asian Immigration from East Africa', 15 March 1968, FCO 37/391, p. 85.

117 'Police Fight Thousands at Airport', *The Times*, 28 February 1968.

118 HC Deb. 28 February 1968, vol. 759, col. 1581. See also Paul Weis, *Nationality and Statelessness in International Law* (Alphen aan den Rijn: Sijthoff & Noordhoff, 1979), p. 50.

119 R. H. Mason to Heddy, 12 February 1969, FCO 50/265/27. Cited in Cullen, *Kenya and Britain after Independence*, p. 166.

120 B3 Division to Cubbon, 31 January 1969, FCO 50/265/28. Cited in Cullen, *Kenya and Britain after Independence*, p. 166; Migration and Visa Department, 17 April 1969, FCO 37/391, p. 56.

121 'Asian Britons Who Don't "Belong"', *Sunday Telegraph*, 15 February 1970. See also, 'Shuttlecocks and Migronauts', *The Guardian*, 4 August 1972.

122 Mehta was interviewed on the BBC documentary, *Playing the Race Card* (1999), available at youtube.com/watch?v=bU61w2c9EXs.

123 'United Kingdom Passport Holders in India', 9 January 1973, FCO 37/1300, p. 66.

124 'Endorsements in Passports to Enable Holders Who Are Subject to Immigration Control to enter Zambia and India', 20 June 1969, FCO 37/391, p. 22.

125 'Anglo-Indian Understanding on Kenyan Asians', FCO 37/390, p. 122. For legal aspects of the arrangement under Indian law, see Richard Plender, 'The Expulsion of Asians from Uganda: Legal Aspects', *Journal of Ethnic and Migration Studies*, 1: 5 (1972), p. 424–5.

126 David Steel, *No Entry*, p. 222.

127 Prem Bhatia, *Indian Ordeal in Africa*, p. 126.

128 'The "Indian" Endorsement', 20 June 1969, FCO 37/391, p. 24. See 'Possible Extension of Commonwealth Immigrants Act, 1962 to UK Citizens with Connections in the UK', 24 October 1967, FCO 37/20, p. 84. In Pakistan the required period of residence before registration for citizenship was one year. See 'Asian Immigration from East Africa: Consultation with Indian & Pakistan Governments', 21 February 1968, FCO 37/20, p. 32.

129 E. Norris, 18 November 1968, FCO 37/390, p. 79. See also 'Admission to the United Kingdom of Certain non-Europeans without UK Connexions', 13 September 1967, FCO 37/19, p. 99; 'Asian Emigration to the UK', 5 September 1967, FCO 37/19, p. 112.

130 'Nairobi Remains Much the Same Despite Asian Exodus to Britain', *New York Times*, 24 March 1968.

131 'Racial Conflict: Prospects for a Balanced Society', *The Times*, 12 December 1969.

132 Cited in Ann Dummett and Andrew Nicol, *Subjects, Citizens, Aliens and Others: Nationality and Immigration Law* (London: Weidenfeld & Nicolson, 1990), pp. 203–4.

133 HC Deb. 10 February 1970, vol. 795, col. 1077.

134 Edward Mortimore, 'Asians Stage Paris Sit-in', *The Times*, 6 March 1970. See also, 'Home Office Lets Detained Asians Stay for Three Months', *The Guardian*, 23 August 1969.

135 James Read, 'Some Legal Aspects of the Expulsion', in Twaddle, ed., *Expulsion of a Minority*, p. 230, n. 17.

136 'Jet Sit-In Asians to be Charged', *The Guardian*, 26 June 1976.

137 Nairobi to FCO, 11 November 1976, FCO 37/1800, p. 39. See also 'The Quota Voucher Scheme in India', 9 December 1974, FCO 37/1414, p. 12.

138 'Britain is Target of Kenyan Asians', *New York Times*, 11 April 1971.

139 Brennan to Hawley, 2 November 1976, FCO 37/1800, p. 53.

140 This fact is not currently acknowledged in the scholarly and historical literature. See, for example, Itty Abraham, *How India Became Territorial: Foreign Policy, Diaspora, Geopolitics* (Stanford: Stanford University Press, 2014), p. 70.

141 Indira Gandhi, replies to questions posed by *Asia Magazine*, 19 July 1968, in Gandhi, *Years of Challenge*, p. 49.

142 Narain Singh, 'India's Offer: Why Does Britain Hesitate?', *National Herald* (New Delhi), 11 May 1969.

143 'The Troubles of Mr Shah', *Economist*, 14 March 1970; 'Immigration: UKPH in East Africa and India', 26 March 1973, FCO 37/1204, pp. 171–2.

144 Prem Bhatia, *Indian Ordeal in Africa*, p. 141.

9. The Ugandan South Asian Crisis

1 UN General Assembly, twenty-fifth session, International Development Strategy for the Second United Nations Development Decade, report of the second committee, 16 October 1970, A/8124.

2 'Development Decade: Brief by the Foreign and Commonwealth Office', 16 October 1970, FCO 7/1833, p. 127.

3 'The Strategy for the Second Development Decade', 15 October 1970, FCO 7/1833, p. 75.

4 David Gowland, Arthur Turner, Alex Wright, *Britain and European Integration since 1945: On the Sidelines* (Abingdon: Routledge, 2010), pp. 73–4.

5 Catherine Schenk, *The Decline of Sterling: Managing the Retreat of an International Currency, 1945–1992* (Cambridge: Cambridge University Press, 2010), pp. 315–93.

6 Henry Wallich, C. J. Morse and I. G. Patel, *The Monetary Crisis of 1971: The Lessons to be Learned* (Washington: Per Jacobsson Foundation, 1972), p. 71.

7 See Poppy Cullen, *Kenya and Britain after Independence: Beyond Neo-Colonialism* (Basingstoke: Macmillan, 2017), pp. 181–212.

8   See Mahmood Mamdani, *Politics and Class Formation in Uganda* (New York/ London: Monthly Review, 1976), pp. 40–227.

9   See Richard J. Reid, *A History of Modern Uganda* (Cambridge: Cambridge University Press, 2017), p. 63.

10 'Extract from letter by Colonel Senior', 5 February 1966, DO 213/210. Cited in Chibuike Uche, 'The British Government, Idi Amin and the Expulsion of British Asians from Uganda', *Interventions*, 19: 6 (2017), p. 819.

11 'Brief for Mr Rippon', 14 August 1972, FCO 31/1376, p. 78.

12 Horace Campbell, *Four Essays on Neocolonialism in Uganda: The Military Dictatorship of Idi Amin* (Toronto: Afro-Carib, 1975), p. 23.

13 Vishnu Sharma and F. Wooldridge, 'Some Legal Questions Arising from the Expulsion of the Ugandan Asians', *International and Comparative Law Quarterly*, 23: 2 (1974), p. 400.

14 Derek Humphry and Michael Ward, *Passports and Politics* (Harmondsworth: Penguin, 1974), p 21.

15 Cited in Jean-Marie Henckaerts, *Mass Expulsion in Modern International Law and Practice* (The Hague: Martinus Nijhoff, 1995), pp. 210–15.

16 'Brief for Mr Rippon', 14 August 1972, FCO 31/1376, p. 77.

17 'Asians Milked the Cow: They Did Not Feed It', *Uganda Argus*, 7 August 1972.

18 'Paper for IC Committee Meeting – 12 noon, 11 August', FCO 31/1376, p. 2.

19 'Brief for Mr Rippon', 14 August 1972, FCO 31/1376, p. 78.

20 'The Asian Problem in East and Central Africa', 9 January 1973, FCO 37/1300, p. 89.

21 Diplomatic Oral History Programme, Interview transcript, Sir James Hennessey, 2018, p. 10. Available at https://www.chu.cam.ac.uk/archives/collections/bdohp/.

22 Mahmood Mamdani, *From Citizen to Refugee: Uganda Asians Come to Britain* (Oxford: Pambazuka, 2011), pp. 12–17.

23 Cited in Anonymous, 'A Uganda Diary', *Transition*, 42 (1973), p. 16.

24 'Asians Milked the Cow: They Did Not Feed It', *Uganda Argus*, 7 August 1972.

25 'Conclusions of a Meeting of the Cabinet Held at 10 Downing Street on Tuesday, 8 August 1972, at 11am', CM (72), CAB 128/50/41.

26 Strictly speaking, British Protected Persons were not British nationals, although the status was treated as a form of British nationality. See Laurie Fransman, Adrian Berry and Alison Harvey, *Fransman's British Nationality Law* (London: Bloomsbury Professional, 2011), pp. 173–4.

27 See 'Background to the Uganda Situation', 11 September 1972, FCO 50/404, p. 109. See also J. G. Wallace, East African Department, 14 August 1972, FCO 31/1376, p. 16.

28 Alvin Shuster, 'Miners' Chiefs in Britain Accept Strike Settlement', *New York Times*, 19 February 1972.

29 'The United Kingdom Passport Holders from Uganda Now in Britain', 9 January 1973, FCO 37/1300, p. 65; 'Immigration: UKPH in East Africa and India', 26 March 1973, FCO 37/1204, p. 173; 'Speaking Notes: Queue-Jumpers and Others', 10 May 1973, FCO 37/1204, p. 64.

30 'Background to the Uganda Situation', 11 September 1972, FCO 50/404, p. 110.

31 'Racism in Uganda', *New York Times*, 11 August 1972.

32 HC Deb. 7 August 1972, vol. 842, cols. 1261, 1264.

33 See David Kohler, 'Public Opinion and the Ugandan Asians', *Journal of Ethnic and Migration Studies*, 2: 2 (1973), p. 194.

34 For the figure of South Asian Ugandan citizens in August 1972, see James Read, 'Some Legal Aspects of the Expulsion', in Michael Twaddle, ed., *Expulsion of A Minority: Essays on Ugandan Asians* (London: Athlone, 1975), p. 193.

35 Edward Heath, *The Course of My Life: My Autobiography* (London: Hodder & Stoughton, 1998), p. 457.

36 See Gil Loescher, *The UNHCR and World Politics: A Perilous Path* (Oxford: Oxford University Press, 2001), p. 151.

37 Margery Perham, 'Reflections on the Nigerian Civil War', *International Affairs*, 46: 2 (1970), p. 231.

38 'Expulsion of Holders of British Passports of Asian Origin from Uganda', 17 August 1972, FCO 31/1380. Cited in Yumiko Hamai, '"Imperial Burden" or "Jews of Africa"? An Analysis of Political and Media Discourse in the Ugandan Asian Crisis (1972)', *Twentieth Century British History*, 22: 3 (2011), p. 424.

39 See 1951 Convention Relating to the Status of Refugees, Article 1(2), 28 July 1951. See also Richard Plender, *International Migration Law* (Dordrecht: Martinus Nijhoff, 1988), pp. 393–458.

40 'Asian Britons Who Don't "Belong"', *Sunday Telegraph*, 15 February 1970.

41 Cited in Yumiko Hamai, '"Imperial Burden" or "Jews of Africa"? An Analysis of Political and Media Discourse in the Ugandan Asian Crisis (1972)', p. 427.

42 'Conclusions of a Meeting of the Cabinet Held at 10 Downing Street on Tuesday, 8 August 1972, at 11am', CM (72), CAB 128/50/41. See also 'The United Kingdom Passport Holders in East Africa', 10 August 1972, FCO 31/1376, p. 111.

43 'Statement by Lady Tweedsmuir', 10 August 1972, FCO 31/1376, p. 110.

44 'Asian Community', New Delhi to FCO, 11 August 1972, FCO 31/1376, p. 67.

45 Mahmood Mamdani, *From Citizen to Refugee*, pp. 20–1.

46 For the FCO's figures, see 'Background to the Uganda Situation', 11 September 1972, FCO 50/404, pp. 107–110. For Slater's comments, see Kampala to FCO, 15 September 1972, FCO 50/404, p. 54.

47 'UK Passport Holders in Uganda', 17 October 1968, HO 344/327. Cited in Sara Cosemans, 'The Politics of Dispersal: Turning Ugandan Colonial Subjects into Postcolonial Refugees (1967–76)', *Migration Studies*, 6: 1 (2018), p. 104.

48 See Tony Kushner and Katherine Knox, *Refugees in an Age of Genocide: Global, National and Local Perspectives during the Twentieth Century* (London: Frank Cass, 1999), p. 267.

49 'Racism in Uganda', *New York Times* editorial, 11 August 1972.

50 D. A. Scott, 'Uganda', 11 August 1972, FCO 31/1376, p. 81.

51 'Paper for IC Committee Meeting – 12 noon, 11 August', FCO 31/1376, p. 4; 'Notes for Supplementaries', 10 August 1972, FCO 31/1376, p. 113.

52 'Note of Conversation with Mr Lauterpract [sic]', 14 August 1972, FCO

31/1376, p. 18. Lauterpacht himself had met personally with Amin in Kampala for an hour on 12 August.

53 'Brief for Mr Rippon', 14 August 1972, FCO 37/1204, p. 79.

54 Blantyre to FCO, 14 August 1972, FCO 37/1204, p. 65.

55 Lagos to FCO, 13 August 1972, FCO 31/1376, p. 25; Yaounde to FCO, 29 September 1972, FCO 31/1391, p. 146.

56 'Record of Conversation Between the Foreign and Commonwealth Secretary and Dr Q. K. J. Masire Vice-President of Botswana at the Foreign and Commonwealth Office: Tuesday 19 September at 3.45p.m', FCO 31/1391, p. 140.

57 Monrovia to FCO, 26 September 1972, FCO 31/1392, p. 71.

58 'Record of Conversation Between the Foreign and Commonwealth Secretary and Dr Abbas Ali Khalatari, Iranian Foreign Minister, at the Waldorf Towers Hotel, New York, at 5 p.m. on Wednesday, 27 September 1972', FCO 31/1392, p. 183.

59 Freetown to FCO, 2 September 1972, FCO 50/404, p. 17.

60 'Monday Club Message', 12 August 1972, FCO 31/1376, p. 9; 'Monday Club Message', 14 August 1972, FCO 31/1376, p. 7. See also H. Shaw, Political Office, 11 August 1972, FCO 31/1376, p. 104.

61 Frederick Mason to T. W. Keeble, 26 September 1972, FCO 31/1392, p. 72.

62 'Draft Message from Prime Minister to Emperor', 12 August 1972, FCO 37/1300, p. 42.

63 'Message from the Prime Minister to the President of Pakistan and the Prime Ministers of India and Bangla Desh', 12 August 1972, FCO 31/1376, p. 33. See also 'Uganda Asians', British High Commission, New Delhi, 29 August 1972, FCO 37/1300, p. 49.

64 'Record of Conversation Between the Foreign and Commonwealth Secretary and the Secretary General of the United Nations at the United Nations Headquarters on Monday, 25 September', 25 September 1972, FCO 31/1392, p. 139.

65 Cited in Humphry and Ward, *Passports and Politics*, p. 31.

66 Pretoria to FCO, 12 August 1972, FCO 31/1376, p. 35.

67 'Asians Not South Africa's Problem', *Die Burger* (Cape Town), 4 September 1972.

68 Kampala to FCO, 14 August 1972, FCO 31/1376, p. 13.

69 Mahmood Mamdani, *From Citizen to Refugee*, p. 20.

70 'Treatment to be Accorded to Asians in Uganda Who Are or Who Must Be Regarded as Stateless', 2 October 1972, FCO 31/1392, p. 111.

71 See Antara Datta, *Refugees and Borders in South Asia: The Great Exodus of 1971* (Abingdon: Routledge, 2013).

72 'Uganda Asians', British High Commission, New Delhi, 29 August 1972, FCO 37/1300, p. 49.

73 Ibid., p. 48; Garvey to FCO, 18 December; 1972, FCO 37/1117, p. 37.

74 'Uganda Asians', British High Commission, New Delhi, 29 August 1972, FCO 37/1300, p. 49.

75 FCO to New Delhi, 13 September 1972, FCO 50/404, p. 201. See also 'Draft Confidential Agreement with the Government of India and Draft Public

Statement for Use in India and the United Kingdom', 15 September 1972, FCO 31/1406, p. 186.

76 'Agreement with Indian Home Office on Admission of Uganda-Asian UKPH', 20 September 1972, FCO 31/1406, p. 42. India used the secret arrangement to ensure that the dependants of Ugandan South Asian British passport holders exempt from Amin's expulsion order should be able to travel immediately to Britain for settlement, if they so wished.

77 See 'Uganda Asians', British High Commission, New Delhi, 29 August 1972, FCO 37/1300, pp. 49–50. See also, Watson to Critchley, 23 March 1973, FCO 37/1204, p. 179.

78 'East African Asians: The Indian Attitude', 7 September 1972, FCO 31/1406, p. 64.

79 See Islamabad to FCO, 23 September 1972, FCO 31/1406, pp. 178–9.

80 'Uganda Asians', British High Commission, New Delhi, 29 August 1972, FCO 37/1300, p. 50; 'Ugandan Asians May Get UN Aid', Times of India, 21 August 1972.

81 Kampala to FCO, 14 September 1972, FCO 50/404, pp. 191–4.

82 'Stateless Persons in Uganda – Legal Position', 28 September 1972, FCO 31/1391, p. 121.

83 Kampala to FCO, 15 September 1972, FCO 50/404, p. 54; 'Background to the Uganda Situation', 11 September 1972, FCO 50/404, p. 109.

84 'Uganda Asians', British High Commission, New Delhi, 29 August 1972, FCO 37/1300, p. 50.

85 'UKPH from Uganda in India', 13 February 1973, FCO 50/470, p. 60.

86 'Visit of the Prime Minister to the United Nations 19–24 October 1970: Meeting with Mrs Gandhi, Prime Minister of India, October 1970', FCO 7/1835, p. 93. The scholarly literature (as with the Kenyan crisis in 1968) has tended to underplay India's engagement with Ugandan South Asians in 1972. See, for example, Itty Abraham, How India Became Territorial: Foreign Policy, Diaspora, Geopolitics (Stanford: Stanford University Press, 2014), pp. 75–6; Marie Carine-Lall, 'Mother India's Forgotten Children', in Eva Ostergaard-Nielsen, ed., International Migration and Sending Countries: Perceptions, Policies and Transnational Relations (Basingstoke: Palgrave Macmillan, 2003), p. 122.

87 'Statement by the Minister of External Affairs in the Lok/Rajya Sabha on September 4, 1972 Regarding Asians in Uganda', FCO 50/404, pp. 77–103.

88 Alvin Shuster, 'British Resentment Rises over Coming Asian Influx', New York Times, 31 August 1972.

89 'Statement by the Minister of External Affairs in the Lok/Rajya Sabha on September 4, 1972 Regarding Asians in Uganda', FCO 50/404, pp. 77–103.

90 Delhi to FCO, 13 September 1972, FCO 50/404, pp. 9–10.

91 See Anirudha Gupta, 'India and the Asians in East Africa', in Twaddle, Expulsion of a Minority, p. 137.

92 'Resettlement of Ugandan Asian United Kingdom Passport Holders Outside the United Kingdom', 13 September 1972, FCO 31/1406, p. 197.

93 Kampala to FCO, 26 September 1972, FCO 31/1406, p. 181.

94 'UKPH', 14 September 1972, FCO 50/404, p. 61.

95 Kampala to FCO, 14 September 1972, FCO 50/404, p. 190.

96 Mahmood Mamdani, *From Citizen to Refugee*, p. 22.

97 'Main Points from Mr C. p. Scott's Report on his Visit to Kampala from 23–25 September Inclusive', 28 September 1972, FCO 31/1391, pp. 116–20.

98 'Record of Meeting Held in Mr Scott's Room in the FCO at 2 p.m. on Tuesday, 26 September', 27 September 1972, FCO 31/1392, p. 74.

99 FCO to UK Mission, Geneva, 4 October 1972, FCO 31/1406, p. 100. See also 'Draft Confidential Agreement with the Government of India and Draft Public Statement for Use in India and the United Kingdom', 15 September 1972, FCO 31/1406, p. 186.

100 FCO to Bern and Vienna, 12 September 1972, FCO 50/404, pp. 258–9. See also 'Resettlement of Ugandan Asian United Kingdom Passport Holders Outside the United Kingdom', 13 September 1972, FCO 31/1406, p. 196.

101 'Resettlement of Ugandan Asian United Kingdom Passport Holders Outside the United Kingdom', 13 September 1972, FCO 31/1406, p. 197.

102 FCO to Abu Dhabi, 6 October 1972, FCO 31/1406, p. 26.

103 'Resettlement of Ugandan Asian United Kingdom Passport Holders Outside the United Kingdom', 13 September 1972, FCO 31/1406, pp. 192, 196.

104 'Malawi to Take Some Asians from Uganda', Malawian Ministry of Information and Broadcasting, 20 September 1972, FCO 31/1406, pp. 171–3; Blantyre to FCO, 13 September 1972, FCO 50/404, p. 253.

105 Port of Spain to FCO, 3 October 1972, FCO 31/1392, p. 123.

106 Governor of British Honduras to FCO, 14 September 1972 FCO 50/404, p. 4.

107 'Resettlement of Ugandan Asian United Kingdom Passport Holders Outside the United Kingdom', 13 September 1972, FCO 31/1406, pp. 190, 196–7. See also FCO to Kampala, 3 October 1972, FCO 31/1406, p. 116.

108 Washington to FCO, 12 September 1972, FCO 50/404, p. 269.

109 Annenberg to Douglas-Home, 2 October 1972, FCO 31/1406, p. 83.

110 Stockholm to FCO, 13 September 1972, FCO 50/404, p. 212.

111 FCO to Abu Dhabi, 6 October 1972, FCO 31/1406, p. 26.

112 FCO to Bern and Vienna, 12 September 1972, FCO 50/404, pp. 258–9.

113 FCO to Wellington, 13 September 1972, FCO 50/404, p. 199.

114 'Resettlement of Ugandan Asian United Kingdom Passport Holders Outside the United Kingdom', 13 September 1972, FCO 31/1406, p. 198.

115 FCO to Abu Dhabi, 6 October 1972, FCO 31/1406, p. 26; Singapore to FCO, 29 September 1972, FCO 31/1406, p. 12.

116 'Meeting with Third Country Representatives and Uganda Resettlement Board at 10.30 a.m. on Friday, 29 September 1972 in Conference Room E102', FCO 31/1406, pp. 158–64.

117 See 'The Resettlement Process', HO 289/95, p. 66.

118 FCO to Kampala, 4 October 1972, FCO 31/1406, p. 104. See also 'Uganda Asians: Falkland Islands', 4 October 1972, FCO 31/1406, p. 110.

119 'Uganda Asians', 14 September 1972, FCO 31/1406, p. 18.

120 UK Mission, Geneva, to FCO, 13 September 1972, FCO 50/404, pp. 245–6. See also 'Resettlement of Ugandan Asian United Kingdom Passport Holders Outside the United Kingdom', 13 September 1972, FCO 31/1406, p. 196; UK Mission, Geneva, to FCO, 21 September 1972, FCO 31/1406, p. 97.

121 Brussels to FCO, 4 October 1972, FCO 31/1406, pp. 107–8. See also Brussels to FCO, 3 October 1972, FCO 31/1406, p. 127.

122 Brussels to FCO, 4 October 1972, FCO 31/1406, pp. 107–8.

123 P. A. Grier, UK Permanent Delegation to the Council of Europe, to George Lee, FCO, 8 September 1972, FCO 31/1391, p. 135.

124 Ibid., p. 134.

125 'UKPH', 14 September 1972, FCO 50/404, p. 61.

126 'Resettlement of Ugandan Asian United Kingdom Passport Holders Outside the United Kingdom', 13 September 1972, FCO 31/1406, p. 191.

127 'Issue of Entry Certification to Ugandan United Kingdom Passport Holders Over and Above the First 3,000 Families', Ministerial Committee on Immigration and Community Relations, 13 September 1972, FCO 31/1392, pp. 174–5; 'Minutes of a Meeting Held in Conference Room E, Cabinet Office on Thursday, 14 September 1972 at 10.30 a.m.', Ministerial Committee on Immigration and Community Relations, 13 September 1972, FCO 31/1392, p. 170.

128 'Ugandan Asians: Dispersal From Congested Areas', Ministerial Committee on Immigration and Community Relations, 15 September 1972, FCO 31/1392, pp. 167–8. See also Yumiko Hamai, '"Imperial Burden" or 'Jews of Africa'?: An Analysis of Political and Media Discourse in the Ugandan Asian Crisis (1972)', p. 426.

129 Mahmood Mamdani, *From Citizen to Refugee*, p. 55.

130 FCO to Bern and Vienna, 12 September 1972, FCO 50/404, pp. 258–9.

131 See Bern to FCO, 13 September 1972, FCO 50/404, p. 257.

132 'Stateless Asians: Possible Transport to Other Countries', 29 September 1972, FCO 31/1406, pp. 183–4.

133 Brussels to FCO, 3 October 1972, FCO 31/1406, p. 127; Brussels to FCO, 9 October 1972, FCO 31/1406, p. 4.

134 'Meeting with Third Country Representatives and Uganda Resettlement Board at 10.30 a.m. on Friday, 29 September 1972 in Conference Room E102', FCO 31/1406, pp. 158–64.

135 Copenhagen to FCO, 6 October 1972, FCO 31/1406, p.33; 'Diplomatic Offensive', 28 September 1972, FCO 31/1391, pp. 93, 89.

136 Cited in Sara Cosemans, 'The Politics of Dispersal: Turning Ugandan Colonial Subjects into Postcolonial Refugees (1967–76)', p. 109.

137 'Sir Alec's Address to General Assembly', 27 September 1972, FCO 31/1391, p. 107.

138 UN General Assembly, twenty-seventh session, 2043rd plenary meeting, 27 September 1972, A/PV.2043, p. 20.

139 UK Mission, New York, to FCO, 29 September 1972, FCO 31/1391, p. 81; 'British Asians in Uganda: Background Information to the Issue', Uganda Mission to the United Nations, 28 September 1972, FCO 31/1392, p. 132.

140 UN General Assembly, twenty-seventh session, 2049th plenary meeting, 2 October 1972, A/PV.2049, p. 15.

141 UK Mission, New York, to FCO, 29 September 1972, FCO 31/1391, p. 80.

142 UK Mission, New York, to FCO, 3 October 1972, FCO 31/1392, p. 146.

143 See Moses Moskowitz, *International Concern with Human Rights* (Leiden: A. W. Sijthoff, 1974), p. 103.

144 UK Mission, Geneva, to FCO, 29 September 1972, FCO 31/1391, p. 147. See also 'Record of Call by UNHCR Representative on the Minister of State on 28 September', 28 September 1972, FCO 31/1392, p. 185.

145 UK Mission, New York, to FCO, 30 September 1972, FCO 31/1391, p. 55.

146 Kampala to FCO, 29 September 1972, FCO 31/1391, p. 73.

147 'Uganda: Documentation of Stateless Asians', 4 October 1972, FCO 31/1392, p. 103.

148 Kampala to FCO, 5 October 1972, FCO 31/1406, p. 84.

149 'Stateless Asians: Possible Transport to Other Countries', 29 September 1972, FCO 31/1406, pp. 183–4.

150 'Main Points from Mr C. p. Scott's Report on his Visit to Kampala from 23–25 September Inclusive', 28 September 1972, FCO 31/1391, p. 119.

151 'Discussion with UNHRC', 29 September 1972, FCO 31/1392, p. 101.

152 'Record of a Meeting Held at 3 p.m. on Monday 2 October 1972 in Room E303, Foreign and Commonwealth Office, to Consider the Problem of Stateless Persons of Asian Origin in Uganda', 3 October 1972, FCO 31/1392, pp. 45–6.

153 'Uganda: Documentation of Stateless Asians', 4 October 1972, FCO 31/1392, pp. 103–5.

154 See Anonymous, 'Asians from Uganda in European Transit Camps', *Journal of Ethnic and Migration Studies*, 2: 3 (1973), p. 276.

155 'The ICRC in Action: Information Notes', International Committee of the Red Cross, 16 February 1973, FCO 50/470, p. 23. See also UNHCR, 'How They Did It: Resettlement of Asians from Uganda in Europe and North America. Special Report May 1973', in Zane Lalani, ed., *Ugandan Asian Expulsion: 90 Days and Beyond through the Eyes of the International Press* (Bloomington: Expulsion Publications/Indiana University Press, 1997), p. 164.

156 'Resettlement Plans for Asian Refugees', *Times of Malta*, 22 March 1973; Anonymous, 'Asians from Uganda in European Transit Camps', p. 276.

157 Gil Loescher, *The UNHCR and World Politics*, p. 168. See Yumiko Hamai, '"Imperial Burden" or "Jews of Africa"? An Analysis of Political and Media Discourse in the Ugandan Asian Crisis (1972)', p. 431.

158 N. S. Rose to H. J. Downing, 15 January 1973, FCO 50/470, p. 87.

159 See Mary Dines, 'Cool Reception', *Journal of Ethnic and Migration Studies*, 2: 4 (1973), pp. 380–3.

160 FCO to UK Mission, New York, 3 October 1972, FCO 31/1406, p. 80.

161 '"Repatriation" from Third Countries of UKPH Asians Expelled from Uganda', 30 March 1973, FCO 50/470, p. 19; W. A. R. Gorman to p. T. Gardner, 21 March 1972, FCO 50/470, pp. 101–18.

162 Yash Tandon and Arnold Raphael, *The New Position of East Africa's Asians: Problems of a Displaced Minority*, Report no. 16 (London: Minority Rights Group, 1978), p. 15.

163 Figure taken from Uganda Resettlement Board, *Uganda Resettlement Board Final Report* (London, Stationery Office, 1974), p. 7.

164 'Diplomatic Offensive', 28 September 1972, FCO 31/1391, p. 97.

165 'Main Points from Mr C. p. Scott's Report on his Visit to Kampala from 23–25 September Inclusive', 28 September 1972, FCO 31/1391, p. 120; 'Visit to Kampala and Nairobi, 23–25 September', 28 September 1972, FCO 31/1391, p. 113.

166 'Diplomatic Offensive', 28 September 1972, FCO 31/1391, p. 97.

167 Yumiko Hamai, "'Imperial Burden" or "Jews of Africa"? An Analysis of Political and Media Discourse in the Ugandan Asian Crisis (1972)', p. 424.

168 'Mr Heath takes up Mr Powell's Challenge', *The Times*, 11 October 1972.

169 See Charles Cunningham, 'The Work of the Uganda Resettlement Board', *Journal of Ethnic and Migration Studies*, 2:3 (1973), p. 261.

170 There were sixteen reception and resettlement camps: Stradishall, Suffolk; Hemswell and Faldingworth, Lincolnshire; West Malling, Kent; Greenham Common, Berkshire; Heathfield and Plasterdown, Devon; Houndstone and Doniford, Somerset; Piddlehinton, Dorset; Raleigh Hall, Staffordshire; Tonfanau, Gwynedd; Gaydon, Warwickshire; Hobbs Barracks, Surrey; Kensington Barracks, London; and Maresfield, Sussex.

171 Cited in Kushner and Knox, *Refugees in an Age of Genocide*, p. 285.

172 Mahmood Mamdani, *From Citizen to Refugee*, p. 64.

173 'Evacuation and Settlement of Ugandan Asians: Report by Mr D. R. Dewick', 1974, HO 289/95. See Derek Humphry and Michael Ward, *Passports and Politics*, p. 63.

174 Cited in S. R. Ashton, 'Keeping Change within Bounds: A Whitehall Reassessment', in Martin Lynn, ed., *The British Empire in the 1950s: Retreat or Revival?* (Basingstoke: Palgrave, 2006), p. 47.

175 'Evacuation and Settlement of Ugandan Asians: Report by Mr D. R. Dewick', 1974, HO 289/95. See Becky Taylor, 'Good Citizens? Ugandan Asians, Volunteers and "Race" Relations in 1970s Britain', *History Workshop Journal*, 85 (2018), p. 126. Britain needed American permission to use Greenham Common Air Force Base as a transit centre. See John A. Reed to Brian Watkins, 11 September 1972, FCO 31/1406, p. 62.

176 Cited in Humphry and Ward, *Passports and Politics*, p. 64.

177 'Preparing for the Uganda Asians', *Observer*, 20 August 1972.

178 'Maresfield', 7 December 1972, HO 289/50, pp. 7–11.

179 Jayantbhai M. Patel et al. to the Administrator, Maresfield Camp, HO 289/50, p. 5.

180 'Evacuation and Settlement of Ugandan Asians: Report by Mr D. R. Dewick', 1974, HO 289/95.

181 W. A. R. Gorman to p. T. Gardner, 21 March 1972, FCO 50/470, pp. 101–18.

182 'The Resettlement Process', HO 289/95, p. 67.

183 Uganda Resettlement Board, *Uganda Resettlement Board Final Report*, pp. 7–8.
184 Mike McCart, 'Wandsworth: Unsettled Ugandan Refugees', *Journal of Ethnic and Migration Studies*, 2: 4 (1973), p. 384.
185 'Mass Expulsions on the Uganda Model: Note by the [Cabinet] Secretaries', 1 December 1972, FCO 37/1117, p. 13.
186 Heath to Kenyatta, 29 November 1972, FCO 37/1117, p. 60; 'Draft Message to Mrs Indira Gandhi from the Prime Minister', 1 December 1972, FCO 37/1117, p. 13.
187 'Possible Expulsion of United Kingdom Passport Holders', 9 January 1973, FCO 37/1300, p. 88.
188 'The Asian Problem in East and Central Africa', 9 January 1973, FCO 37/1300, pp. 89–98; 'Immigration: UKPH in East Africa and India', 26 March 1973, FCO 37/1204, pp. 171–2.
189 Tom Bridges to Anthony Acland, 8 January 1973, FCO 37/1300, p. 69.
190 Sutherland to C. P. Scott, 22 January 1973, FCO 37/1301, p. 20.
191 Garvey to Sutherland, 9 February 1973, FCO 37/1301, p. 7. See also 'Uganda Asians: Resettlement Finance', 16 February 1973, FCO 27/1204, p. 198.
192 Garvey to FCO, 10 January 1973, FCO 37/1300, p. 36.
193 'Record of Conversation Held in Sir Denis Greenhill's Room on Monday 8 January', FCO 37/1300, p. 103.
194 Garvey to FCO, 13 January 1973, FCO 37/1300, p. 25.
195 Gandhi to Heath, 22 January 1973, FCO 37/1301, p. 14.
196 'Draft Framework for Operational Plan', 5 July 1973, FCO 37/1204, pp. 28–32.
197 'United Kingdom Passport Holders (UKPH) in East Africa: European Commission on Human Rights', 25 April 1974, 50/503, p. 215.
198 'The Asian Problem in East and Central Africa', 9 January 1973, FCO 37/1300, pp. 95–6.

Epilogue

1 Richard Drayton, 'The Archives of Britain's Colonial Rulers', *The Times*, 19 April 2012. For a discussion of outstanding issues relating to these additional FCO files, see Mandy Banton, 'Destroy? "Migrate"? Conceal? British Strategies for the Disposal of Sensitive Records of Colonial Administrations at Independence', *Journal of Imperial and Commonwealth History*, 40: 2 (2012), p. 323.
2 Amelia Gentleman, '"Lambs to the Slaughter": 50 Lives Ruined by the Windrush Scandal', *The Guardian*, 19 March 2020.

Index